Catholic Church History: Pre-Christian to Modern Times

Fr. Peter Samuel Kucer, MSA

⊕*ENROUTE*
Make the time

En Route Books and Media, LLC
5705 Rhodes Avenue
St. Louis, MO 63109

Cover credit: TJ Burdick

Library of Congress Control Number: 2017956386

ISBN-10: 0-9994704-1-8
ISBN-13: 978-0-9994704-1-1

DEDICATION

In memory of my mother, Roberta Kucer, who instilled in me a love of study and a love of her people, the chosen people.

In addition, I dedicate this book to the members of my community, the Missionaries of the Holy Apostles.

ACKNOWLEDGEMENTS

I would particularly like to acknowledge Fr. Isaac Martinez, MSA, former General of the Missionaries of the Holy Apostles, who gave me permission to publish, and Bishop Christian Rodembourg, MSA, who as the first MSA to be ordained a bishop brought our MSA charism into a deeper ecclesial dimension by assuming the office of bishop the year this book was prepared for publication.

Special thanks to Dr. Sebastian Mahfood, OP, of En Route Books and Media, for publishing this work.

CONTENTS

Chapter 1

A Catholic View and Non-Catholic Views of History

Introduction

In this introductory chapter, we will see how the Stoic, the Enlightenment, and the Post-Modern understanding of history profoundly differs from a Catholic understanding. We will also see how ancient myths from around the world encouraged a historical view that is markedly different from a Catholic one. Finally, the uniquely the Catholic view of history, especially of Church History, will be presented.

The Stoic View of History: Is History a Circle?

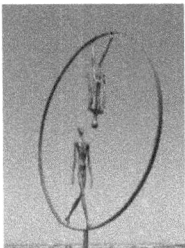

---

[1] Dimitry Gerrman, "Circle of Time," sculpture, http://commons.wikimedia.org/wiki/File%3AGerrman_circle_of_time.jpg (accessed March 9, 2015).

Stoicism was a popular Greek philosophical school active before, at, and during the time of the early Church. In accordance with their deterministic view of the cosmos, the stoics thought history is cyclical. A historical cycle, explained the stoics, begins out of a fiery chaos, develops in an intelligibly discernible manner until it finally once again returns to its fiery state to begin a new cycle. As explained by the Stanford Encyclopedia of Philosophy:

> God is identified with an eternal reason (*logos*, Diog. Laert. 44B) or intelligent designing fire (Aetius, 46A) which structures matter in accordance with Its plan. This plan is enacted time and time again, beginning from a state in which all is fire, through the generation of the elements, to the creation of the world we are familiar with, and eventually back to fire in a cycle of endless recurrence. The designing fire of the conflagration is likened to a sperm which contains the principles or stories of all the things which will subsequently develop (Aristocles in Eusebius, 46G). Under this guise, God is also called 'fate.' It is important to realize that the Stoic God does not craft its world in accordance with its plan from the outside, as the demiurge in Plato's *Timaeus* is described as doing. Rather, the history of the universe is determined by God's activity internal to it, shaping it with its differentiated characteristics. The biological conception of God as a kind of living heat or seed from which things grow seems to be fully intended. The further identification of God with *pneuma* or breath may have its origins in medical theories of the Hellenistic period.[3]

---

[2] "Djungarian Hamster Pearl White run wheel," photograph, http://commons.wikimedia.org/wiki/File:Djungarian_Hamster_Pearl_White_run_wheel.jpg#filehistory (accessed March 9, 2015).
[3] "Stoicism," Stanford Encyclopedia of Philosophy, http://plato.stanford.edu/entries/stoicism/ (accessed June 6, 2015); Dirk Baltzly, "Stoicism",

The German, modern historian, Oswald Spengler similarly held that the pattern of history resembles a circle. In explaining his view, Spengler likens history to a biological organism, like an amoeba whose growth, decline and death follows a pre-determined set of biological laws.

Helmut Werner's Summary of Spengler's Thought

> The transitory is the symbol of a becoming which follows a form, an organism. Cultures are organisms. If we disentangle their shapes we may find the primitive Culture-form that underlies all individual cultures and is reflected in their various manifestations.[4]

The Enlightenment View of History

A   B   C   [5]

As we will eventually study, the age of the Enlightenment (1600s - early 1800s) coincided with the so-called scientific revolution. Some Enlightenment philosophers and scientists had a tendency not to see history as cyclical but rather as one of continual progress. According to this almost naïve approach to history, the world is getting better and better as man invents new forms of technology, understands the laws of the world, and develops his mind. If the German political philosopher Karl Marx (1818-1883) is considered as part of the tail end of the Enlightenment movement, in him we see an Enlightenment philosopher proposing that human history will eventually end in a near-perfect civilization where the state withers away, is replaced by

---

The Stanford Encyclopedia of Philosophy (Spring 2014 Edition), Edward N. Zalta (ed.), URL = <http://plato.stanford.edu/archives/ spr2014/entries/stoicism/>.

[4] Oswald Spengler, *The Decline of the West*, An Abridged Edition, trans. Charles Francis Atkinson (Oxford: Oxford University Press, 1991), 71-72.

[5] Mazino7, "Ray (A, B, C)," diagram, http://commons.wikimedia.org/wiki/ File:Ray_(A,_B,_C).svg (accessed March 9, 2015).

advances in technology, and is absent from class conflict.

The Post-Modern View of History

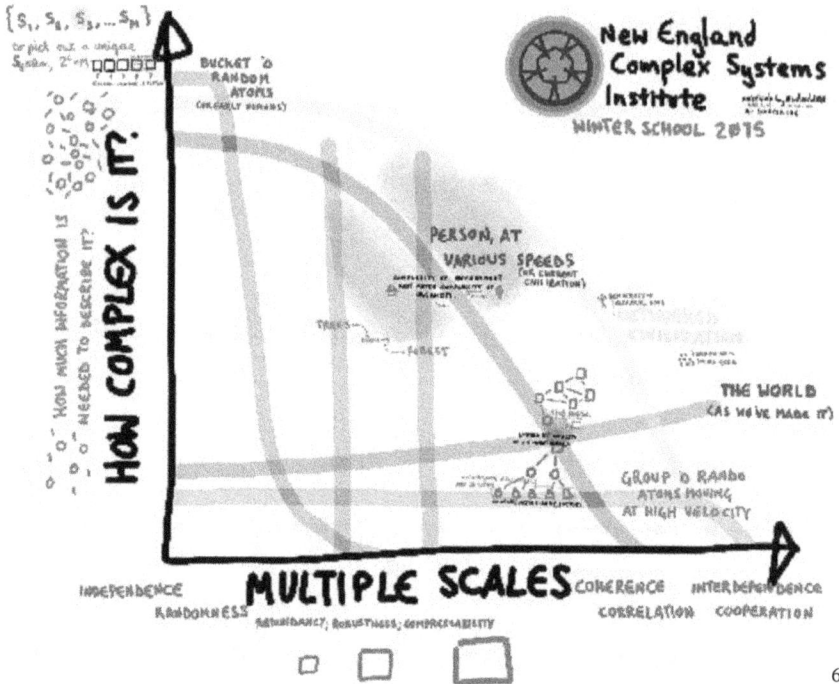

When attempting to explain phases in history, which often occur as a reaction to preceding phases, historians ordinarily describe a Romantic Era, which exalted the emotions, as coming after the Age of the Enlightenment. This Romantic Era was in turn replaced by the Modern Era, in which once again the mind's ability to grasp and understand inherent laws within the universe was stressed over myths, stories, and feelings. Once again, though, this era was replaced by the current time in which we live called the Post-Modern era. According to postmodern thought, at least as represented by Jean-François Lyotard in his book *The Post-modern*

---

6 Willowbloo, "Highly complex things (a bucket of atoms all moving at random) aren't differentiated at a large scale. Large-scale things (a traditional army) can be seen from a further zoom, but lack internal complexity," diagram, http://commons.wikimedia.org/wiki/File%3AComplexity_and_Scale.jpg (accessed March 9, 2015).

Condition, the world is irrational with no over-arching explanatory myths. He asserts:

> Simplifying to the extreme, I define postmodern as incredulity toward metanarratives. This incredulity is undoubtedly a product of progress in the sciences: but that progress in turn presupposes it. To the obsolescence of the metanarrative apparatus of legitimation corresponds, most notably, the crisis of metaphysical philosophy and of the university institution which in the past relied on it. The narrative function is losing its functors, its great hero, its great dangers, its great voyages, its great goal. It is being dispersed in clouds of narrative language elements—narrative, but also denotative, prescriptive, descriptive, and so on. Conveyed within each cloud are pragmatic valencies specific to its kind. Each of us lives at the intersection of many of these. However, we do not necessarily establish stable language combinations, and the properties of the ones we do establish are not necessarily communicable.[7]

Ancient Myths and History

The deconstruction encouraged by postmodern thinkers is not a brand new approach to understanding the world. The postmodern belief that our rationality and sense of logic is not fundamental but only springs forth from an attempt to order the irrational, chaotic universe resonates with virtually all ancient myths. According to these myths, the world was not created by a reasonable God but rather was formed out of a primordial chaos. From disorder came forth gods who then created men, woman and the world as we know it.

---

[7] Jean-François Lyotard, *The Post Modern Condition: A Report on Knowledge*, trans. Geoff Bennington and Brian Massumi (Minneapolis: University of Minnesota Press, 1984), xxiv.

According to a Catholic interpretation of Genesis, in light of
the first chapter of John's gospel, God the Father created the world
through his Word, the Son, in the love of the Holy Spirit. What is
most fundamental to the universe, consequently, is not chaos and
irrationality but reason, as Christ the Word, informed by love, the
Holy Spirit, in eternal relationship with the Father. Even though
creation contains differences, which at times can seem to be
fundamentally in disorder as they clash about, this aspect is not
what gives ultimate definition to the universe. Rather, they are to
be understood in light of Trinitarian difference, which preceded
and upholds created difference. In Trinitarian difference, the
Father, Son, and Holy Spirit are not constantly smashing and
clashing into one another because they are different, but through
their differences the greatest unity possible exists.[8] This means
that creation, in its deepest sense, bears the imprint of an orderly,
peaceful, harmonious, Triune Creator. As the noted theologian
Bishop Robert Barron convincingly and rightly argues, the most
basic pulse of the universe is one of peace, order, and harmony not
violence, chaos, and disorder. He writes:

> [I]t is certainly clear that, from very early in the
> theological tradition, Christian thinkers speak of
> God's creation as taking place *ex nihilo* (from
> nothing). And we find this teaching confirmed in all
> of the great theologians.... Jesus, in speaking peace
> to those who had betrayed and killed him, opened
> up a new conception of God, one who brings order,
> not through violence, but through compassion.
> Accordingly, when Christians began to reflect on
> the nature of creation, they speculated that this true
> God of Jesus Christ brings the world into being, not
> through an orgy of violence, as in so many of the
> ancient myths, but precisely through a sheerly non-
> violent act of generous love. To make the universe
> *ex nihilo* is to bring forth without competition,

---

[8] John Milbank, *Theology and Social Theory* (Oxford: Blackwell Publishing,
1993), 423-430.

antagonism, or violence – fighting nothing, wrest-
ing nothing into shape, pressing nothing to the
ground. And more to the point, as Thomas Aquinas
and others point out, this nonviolence act of God is
not a once and for all event at the beginning of
time; rather, it is the ongoing, continual act by
which the world, at every moment, is sustained in
existence. Hence divine nonviolence is the actualiz-
ing and unifying energy of all of creation.

And therefore when we walk in the path of
nonviolence we are ... claiming and unleashing a
"truth force" ... participating in an energy that runs
through the cosmos in all its dimensions. This is
why, of course, nonviolence, when effectively practiced is remarkably powerful. In the century just
concluded, the bloodiest on record, nonviolent
methods liberated the subcontinent of India,
effected a massive social change in the United
States, and, most stunningly, brought down a
Communist Empire defended by an enormous
military establishment. ... Paul said that the
proclamation of the Gospel of Jesus crucified and
risen from the dead is the *dynamis* (power) to a
cosmos in need of transformation, and this Gospel
is nothing but the good news of God's nonviolent
love. When we Christians announce it and, more to
the point, live it, we tap into the divine *dynamis*
which overmatches any of the powers of the world.[9]

Once peace and harmony is seen more and more as the
fundamental building blocks of the universe, then we will be more
likely to found our civilizations, above all civilizations fostered by
Christian belief and practice, upon a foundation of peace and not
upon the sand of violence. If, though, people assume that what is

---

[9] Robert Barron, *The Strangest Way: Walking the Christian Path*
(Maryknoll: Orbis Books, 2002), 154-155.

most basic to the universe is chaotic violence, then civilizations, and the history of civilizations, will be understood as merely a reflection of the destructive chaos from which it emerged. Incidences of love, peace, harmony, and order that one may find in history, especially as evident in the lives of the saints, are then dismissed as merely incidental to a universe that is ultimately ruled by chance and violence. As evident below, some of the most ancient civilizations thought precisely in this manner, for they assumed that violence is what is most basic to the universe. This is evident in their mythology.

Japanese Creation Myth

> Before the heavens and the earth came into existence, all was a chaos, unimaginably limitless and without definite shape or form. Eon flowed eon: then, lo! Out of this boundless, shapeless mass something light and transparent rose up and formed the heaven. This was the Plain of High Heaven, in which materialized a deity called Ame-no-Minaka-Nushi-no-Mikoto (the Deity-of-the-August-Center-of-Heaven). Next the heavens gave birth to a deity named Takami-Musubi-no-Mikoto (the High-August-Producing-Wondrous-Deity), followed by a third called Kammi-Musubi-no-Mikoto (the Divine-Producing-Wondrous-Deity. These three divine beings are called the Three creating Deities.[10]

Norse Creation Myths

> Originally there was a chasm, Ginnungagap, bounded on either side by fire (from the world known as Muspelheim) and ice (from the world known as Niflheim). When fire and ice met, they

---

[10] Henry M. Sayre, *The Humanities: Culture, Continuity and Change,* Book 1 (Upper Saddle River: Prentice Hall, 2012), 29.

combined to form a giant, named Ymir, and a cow, named Audhumbla (Auðhumla), who nourished Ymir. She survived by licking the salty ice blocks. From her licking emerged Bur (Búri), the grandfather of the Aesir. Ymir, father of the frost giants, employed equally unusual procreative techniques. He sweated a male and a female from under his left arm.

Odin, the son of Bur's son Borr, killed Ymir. The blood pouring out of the giant's body killed all the frost giants Ymir had created, except Bergelmir. From Ymir's dead body, Odin created the world. Ymir's blood was the sea; his flesh, the earth; his skull, the sky; his bones, the mountains; his hair, the trees. The new Ymir-based world was Midgard. Ymir's eyebrow was used to fence in the area where mankind would live. Around Midgard was an ocean where a serpent named Jormungand lived. He was big enough to form a ring around Midgard by putting his tail in his mouth.[11]

Greek Creation Myths

In the beginning there was only chaos. Then out of the void appeared Erebus, the unknowable place where death dwells, and Night. All else was empty, silent, endless, darkness. Then somehow Love was born bringing a start of order. From Love came Light and Day. Once there was Light and Day, Gaea, the earth appeared.

Then Erebus slept with Night, who gave birth to Ether, the heavenly light, and to Day the earthly

[11] N.S. Gill "Creation of the World - Norse Mythology on the Creation of the World," About Education, http://ancienthistory.about.com/od/creationmyths/a/11083199Norse.htm (accessed March 10, 2015).

light. Then Night alone produced Doom, Fate, Death, Sleep, Dreams, Nemesis, and others that come to man out of darkness.

Meanwhile Gaea alone gave birth to Uranus, the heavens. Uranus became Gaea's mate covering her on all sides. Together they produced the three Cyclopes, the three Hecatoncheires, and twelve Titans.

However, Uranus was a bad father and husband. He hated the Hecatoncheires. He imprisoned them by pushing them into the hidden places of the earth, Gaea's womb. This angered Gaea and she plotted against Uranus. She made a flint sickle and tried to get her children to attack Uranus. All were too afraid except, the youngest Titan, Cronus.

Gaea and Cronus set up an ambush of Uranus as he lay with Gaea at night. Cronus grabbed his father and castrated him, with the stone sickle, throwing the severed genitals into the ocean. The fate of Uranus is not clear. He either died, withdrew from the earth, or exiled himself to Italy. As he departed he promised that Cronus and the Titans would be punished. From his spilt blood came the Giants, the Ash Tree Nymphs, and the Erinnyes. From the sea foam where his genitals fell came Aphrodite.[12]

Babylonian Creation Myth

Enuma Elish – The Seven Tablets of Creation

Excerpts

---

[12] "The Creation," Greek Mythology, http://www.greekmythology.com/ Myths/The_Myths/The_Creation/the_creation.html (accessed March 10, 2015).

FIRST TABLET

1. When the heavens above were yet unnamed, 2. And the name of the earth beneath had not been recorded, 3. Apsu, the oldest of beings, their progenitor, 4. "Mummu" Tiâmat, who bare each and all of them-- 5. Their waters were merged into a single mass. 6. A field had not been measured, a marsh had not been searched out, 7. When of the gods none was shining, 8. A name had not been recorded, a fate had not been fixed, 9. The gods came into being in the midst of them. 10. The god Lakhmu and the goddess Lakhamu were made to shine, they were named. 11. [Together] they increased in stature, they grew tall. 12. Anshar and Kishar came into being, and others besides them. 13. Long were the days, the years increased. 14. The god Anu, their son, the equal of his fathers, [was created]. 15. The god Anshar made his eldest son Anu in his own image. 16. And the god Anu begat Nudimmud (Ea) the image of himself. 17. The god Nudimmud was the first among his fathers, 18. Endowed with understanding, he who thinketh deeply, the orator 19. Exceedingly mighty in strength above his father Anshar who begat him. 20. Unrivalled amongst the gods his brothers ... 21. The confraternity of the gods was established. 22. Tiâmat was troubled and she ... their guardian. 23. Her belly was stirred up to its uttermost depths. 24. ....25. Apsu (the watery abyss) could not diminish their brawl ...

SECOND TABLET.

1. Tiâmat made solid that which she had moulded. 2. She bound the gods her children with [evil bonds]. 3. Tiâmat wrought wickedness to avenge

Apsu. 11. Mother Tiâmat who gave us birth hath sown these things. 12. She hath set in order her assembly, she rageth furiously.

FOURTH TABLET

13. "O god Marduk, thou art our avenger....27. When the gods his fathers saw the issue of the utterance of his mouth. 28. They rejoiced and adored [him, saying], "Marduk is King." 29. They conferred upon him the sceptre, the throne, and the symbol of royalty (?) 30. They gave him the unrivalled weapon, the destroyer of the enemy [saying]: 31. "Go, cut off the life of Tiâmat. 32. "Let the wind carry her blood into the depth [under the earth]."... 101. Marduk grasped the spear, he split up her belly, 137. He slit Tiâmat open like a flat (?) fish [cut into] two pieces, 138. The one half he raised up and shaded the heavens therewith

SIXTH TABLET

1. On hearing the words of the gods, the heart of Marduk moved him to carry out the works of a craftsman. 2. He opened his mouth, he spake to Ea that which he had planned in his heart, he gave counsel [saying]: 3. "I will solidify blood, I will form bone. 4. "I will set up man, 'Man' [shall be] his name. 5. "I will create the man 'Man.'...23. "[It was] Kingu who created the strife, 24. "Who made Tiâmat to revolt, to join battle [with thee]." 25. They bound him in fetters [they brought] him before Ea, they inflicted punishment on him, they let his blood, 26. From his blood he (i.e., Ea) fashioned mankind for the service of the gods, and

he set the gods free.[13]

The Catholic Understanding of History

14

A Catholic conception of history can be represented by a spiral, which includes both a linear and cyclical dimension. The rise and fall of the spiral represents both sinful patterns in history and natural cycles such as seasonal changes from spring, summer, fall, winter. The linear movement of the spiral is ultimately due to Christ being the Alpha and Omega of history, the beginning and end of history. In addition, Christ's birth in time is cyclically repeated and tapped into by means of the celebration of the Eucharist as we spiral to the end of time as we know and experience time.[15] In the beginning of time, God the Father created

---

[13] British Museum, "The Babylonian Legends of the Creation," Project Gutenberg, http://www.gutenberg.org/files/9914/9914-h/9914-h.htm (accessed March 10, 2015).

[14] Pearson Scott Foresman "Line Art Drawing of a Coil," drawing, http://commons.wikimedia.org/wiki/File%3AСoil_(PSF).jpg (March 13, 2015).

[15] In distinguishing ancient, medieval, and modern understandings of time Eugene Vodolazkin writes, "Antiquity usually conceived of time in cyclical terms, while time in the modern age is thought to progress in a linear fashion toward a determinate end. In the Middle Ages, time also had direction, but in a very special way: Old events are repeated on a new level. The Middle Ages compromised between antiquity and modernity, conceiving of time as a spiral. The modern age impatiently waits for the future, which it sees as the apex toward which to strive. The Middle Ages accepted the future, but related to it calmly. For the man of the Middle Ages, the highest moment of history is the incarnation of Jesus Christ, a point in time that has already passed, but which gets repeated again and again in the liturgy of the Church. This accounts for one of the fundamental differences between the Middle Ages and the modern age: The Middle Ages did not know the idea of progress, while the modern age regards it as fundamental. That is why the Middle Ages did not give rise to utopias. At the very essence of a utopia is the idea of progressive movement toward a not-yet-

the world through his Son. At the end of time, as we experience it now, God the Father will send his Son to judge the living and the dead. This means that history has a beginning from Christ and a direction towards Christ. The human experience of history is not, therefore, like what a hamster experiences when it is exercising in his miniature tread mill. Even though the hamster might feel it is going from one point to another he actually is only going in circles. Despite the world's natural cycles and cycles due to sin, the history of man has a specific direction given to it, to Christ by God the Father in the love of the Holy Spirit.

In addition, saints, borrowing terminology from the British historian Arnold Toynbee, can be seen as "creative minorities" who alter the course of history by their holy lives.[16] We are not, according to the Catholic faith, at the mercy of cycles in history but can, when we cooperate with grace, change the course of history. Can you think of anyone who exemplifies this currently? The Church officially canonizes these saints in order to set before us examples of holy men and women who used their God given freedom to build up the Kingdom of God in our present here and not yet experience of heavenly realities. In order to understand Church history properly as distinct from other histories, it is necessary to remember the saints who give Church history its specific Christian contours. Although the quote from below from the then Cardinal Ratzinger was written in relationship to theologians, I think the term theologian can be replaced by the term historian and still be valid. For historians to rightly understand and present the uniqueness of Catholic Church history, the role of the saints must not be overlooked.

> [T]he work of the theologian [historian] is "secondary" with regard to the real experience of the saints. Without this reference point, without the deep anchoring in such an experience, his work

achieved perfection." Eugene Vodolazkin, "The Age of Concentration," The Institute on Religion and Public Life, https://www.firstthings.com/article/2017/06/the-age-of-concentration (accessed June 15, 2017).

[16] Joseph Ratzinger, *Europe, Today and Tomorrow*, trans. Michael J. Miller (San Francisco: Ignatius Press, 2007), 24-25.

becomes detached from reality. This is the humility demanded from reality. This is the humility demanded for the theologian [historian]...without the realism of the saints, without their contact with the reality of which theology [Catholic Church history] speaks, it degenerates into an empty intellectual game and also loses its scientific character.[17]

We will end this chapter by viewing Church history in one final way, as a circular pool of water into which Christ dives gracefully into its center, representing the fullness of time. The waves caused by this perfect dive affects all of history, present, past, and future. The shores of the pool represent eternity, and, in a certain sense, our heavenly destination. The various circles represent different stages of Christian history.

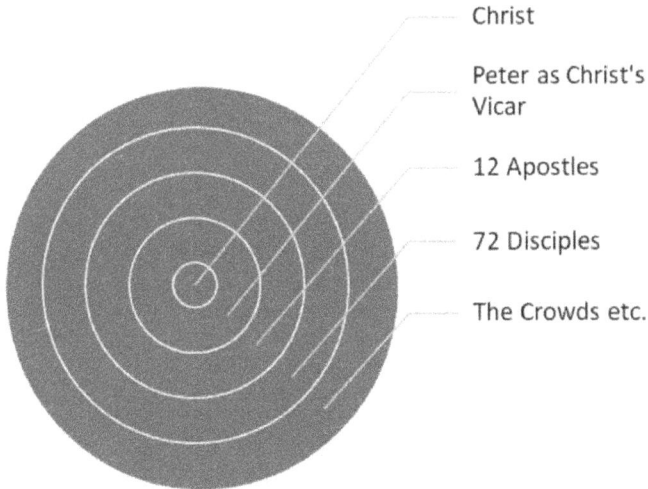

Christ

Peter as Christ's Vicar

12 Apostles

72 Disciples

The Crowds etc.

[18]

---

[17] Joseph Ratzinger, *Christianity and the Crisis of Cultures*, trans. Brian McNeil (San Francisco: Ignatius Press, 2006), 109.
[18] The idea of concentric circles in relationship to Jesus comes from John P. Meier, *A Marginal Jew*, Volume III (New York: Double Day, 2001), 21.

Quiz 1

1. First describe and then diagram, the following philosophical approaches to history: Stoic, Oswald Spengler's, Enlightenment and Modern, Postmodern, and Christological.

2. How can saints be considered creative minorities? When answering this question please use Arnold Toynbee's term "creative minorities" in a Catholic manner. In addition, refer to a specific saint and describe how the saint was a creative minority. In your answer include the term freedom. (Write a minimum of four sentences.)

3. Explain how Greek, Roman, Norse and similar myths on the origins and history of the world differ from the Catholic belief of creation and history. In responding focus on one myth. In your reply include the following terms, the Trinity, truth, love, order, harmony, chaos, violence, and disorder. (Write a minimum of nine sentences.)

Chapter 2

Historical Context of the Early Church

Introduction

We will begin this chapter with a wide historical gaze by understanding and appreciating the historical context in which Christianity was born. Providentially, three cultures influenced Christianity: Jewish, Greek, and Roman. Then, we will narrow our historical gaze by focusing on a few of the earliest non-biblical references to Christianity.

The Historical Context of Christianity

St. Paul's description of Christ as being sent by the Father in the "fullness of time" (Galatians 4:4) has been interpreted as meaning that the Father chose the most fitting time to send his son into the world. In the land in which Jesus was born, three cultures providentially intersected with one another in a way that would allow Christianity to flourish. The Jewish element, above all the Jewish scriptures, provided the soul of Christianity whose fulfillment is Christ as the living Scripture. The Greek element provided key universal, philosophical ideas that Christianity later used to translate the many particular aspects of the Old Testament in a more of a universal sense. This enabled Christians to bring forth the message of Christ, as prophesied in the Old Testament, to all people. Roman law, roads, and organizational structure were also used and appropriated by Christians in their effort to spread the Good News to as many people as possible in a time saving, orderly, and peaceful manner.

Jewish

As stated previously, the "soul" dimension that Judaism offered to Christianity is most evident in the scriptures. Since neither the Old Testament nor the New Testament has an inspired table of contents, when and how did the Catholic Church know which books, and for our purposes here Hebrew books, are canonical?[19] At the time when Jesus lived in Palestine, there were two versions of what we understand as the Old Testament and what Christians, before the New Testament was written, simply considered Sacred Scripture. One is known as the Palestinian Canon. The other is called the Alexandrian canon, which formed a Greek translation of the Old Testament known as the Septuagint.

The Septuagint was translated around 250 BC by Alexandrian Jews living in Egypt. The Alexandrian Canon contained more books than the Palestinian Canon, books that the Catholic Church accepts as inspired. The Alexandrian Canon was the canon that the New Testament cites repeatedly, including from books that the Palestinian Canon lacks. For example, Matthew 4:4 cites Wisdom 16:26. The Book of Wisdom was not included in the Palestinian Canon. It was, though, included in the Alexandrian Canon. Similarly, Matthew 4:15 cites from 1 Maccabees 5:15, another non-Palestinian Canon book. Other non-Palestinian Canon books that are in the Alexandrian Canon from which the New Testament cites from are Baruch, Sirach, Tobit, Judith, and Daniel.[20]

The process by which the Holy Spirit inspired the Catholic Church to officially sanction the Alexandrian Canon over the

---

[19] Patrick Madrid, *Envoy for Christ* (Cincinnati: Franciscan Media, 2012), 47.
[20] Dave Armstrong, *100 Biblical Arguments Against Sola Scriptura* (San Diego: Answers Press, 2012), loc. 509-609.

Palestinian Canon included the following steps. First, in 390 AD
St. Jerome translated Palestinian canon books written in Hebrew
into Latin. Eventually, with some objection, he also translated
from the Greek Septuagint books that were not present in the
Palestinian Canon. In 393 A.D., the Synod of Hippo recognized the
Septuagint, based on the Alexandrian Canon, as the Old
Testament canon of the Catholic Church. St. Jerome's translation
of the Old Testament into Latin became known as the Vulgate. In
1442 AD, the Council of Florence, and in 1546 the Council of Trent
confirmed the Alexandrian Canon, i.e. the Septuagint, as the
inspired Catholic canon. As Catholics, therefore, we recognize 46
Old Testament books and 27 New Testament books as inspired.[21]

Another aspect that Christianity incorporated and, according
to our faith, elevated, is the Jewish notion of oral tradition, a
concept with which many Protestants have difficulties. An
example of the New Testament honoring Jewish oral tradition is
found in Paul's second letter to Timothy where he writes, "As
Jannes and Jambres opposed Moses, so these people, of corrupt
mind and counterfeit faith, also oppose the truth."[22] These two
men are never named in the Old Testament. They are, though,
referred to in Jewish oral tradition that has since been written
down.[23]

Greek

The Northern Macedonian ruler, Alexander the Great (356-
323 BC), created an empire out of Greek states that were
previously united by his father King Philip II. Alexander aimed at
replacing the Persian Empire with his Greek empire.[24] In the 330s

---

[21] George Reid, "Canon of the Old Testament," The Catholic Encyclopedia, Vol. 3 (New York: Robert Appleton Company, 1908), http://www.newadvent.org/cathen/03267a.htm (accessed March 13, 2015).

[22] NRSVCE 2 Timothy 3:8.

[23] "Jannes and Jambres (more correctly Mambres; also, Yoḥanai and Mamre)," Jewish Encyclopedia 1906, http://www.jewishencyclopedia.com/articles/8513-jannes-and-jambres (accessed March 13, 2015); Cf. Dave Armstrong, *100 Biblical Arguments Against Sola Scriptura* (San Diego: Answers Press, 2012), loc 535, 2431.

[24] Robin Osborne, Greek History (Routledge: London, 2004), 125-132.

BC, while only in his twenties, Alexander the Great defeated the Persian Empire. As stated by Philip Freeman, without Alexander the Great, "and his conquests, the philosophy, art, and literature of ancient Greece that have so influenced our lives for more than two thousand years would instead have been only one of many voices in a chorus of ancient civilizations."[25] Alexander's ambition to extend the Greek empire led him even to India. A few years after his invasion of India, Alexander the Great died in 323 at the young age of 32. Since Alexander lacked a clear heir to his throne, his empire eventually became divided four ways between four men: Cassander, Lysimachus, Ptolemy, and Seleucus I Nicator. The two great empires that developed out of the four regions were the Seleucid Empire, based in formerly Persian lands, and the Ptolemaic Empire based in Egypt.[26]

With the land of Israel, (also known as Judea) caught in the middle, the Seleucid and the Ptolemaic empires repeatedly fought each other. Since the Jewish people tended to be treated better in the Ptolemaic empire, many Jews migrated to Egyptian land especially to the Greek, Egyptian city of Alexandria, named after Alexander the Great. Many of these Hellenized (this term means Greek influenced) Jews forgot their native tongue of Hebrew. Therefore, around 250 BC Jewish scholars translated their Sacred Scriptures into Greek.[27] According to legend, this occurred when a Ptolemaic emperor asked 72 scholars to separately translate the Jewish Bible. By a miracle, all their translations matched.

> It happened to Ptolemy the king that he took seventy-two elders from Jerusalem, and placed them in seventy-two separate chambers, and did not inform them to what purpose he had brought them. And afterward he entered to each of them, and said to them: Translate me the Torah of Moses from memory. And the Holy One, blessed be He,

---

[25] Philip Freeman, *Alexander the Great* (New York: Simon & Schuster, 2011), 323.

[26] Freeman, 321-323, 340.

[27] H.H Ben-Sasson, *A History of the Jewish People*, trans. George Weidenfeld (Cambridge: Harvard University Press, 19756), 185-200, 279.

sent into the heart of each of them a counsel, and
they all agreed to have one mind....[28]

The above referred to Greek translation of the Jewish Sacred
Scriptures included a number of books that from around 200 AD
Jewish people have not considered to be part of their official bible.
These books include Tobias, Judith, Maccabees, and Sirach. At the
time of Jesus, these books were accepted by many Jews, including
Christian ones, as is evident in the repeated reference to these
books in the New Testament.

A possible factor for explaining why Jewish people distanced
themselves from the Greek Septuagint is their horrific experience
under the Greek, Seleucid emperor Antiochus IV, who in 176 BC
conquered Judea. He insisted that the Jewish people either accept
Greek ways, including worshiping the Greek gods, or die. This
rigid policy caused a rebellion led by the Jewish priest Mattathias
and his son. When Mattathias died in 165 BC, his son Judas
Maccabee continued rebelling against the Greeks. Since Rome, in
conquering Macedonia in 168 BC, had replaced the Greek Empire
with a Roman Empire, Judas Maccabeus allied the newly formed
Jewish state with the Romans in 161 BC. Finally, in great part to
Roman rule, Jewish people were able to restore Jerusalem to
Jewish leadership. The Temple was then rededicated, an event
that the yearly Jewish feast Hanukkah celebrates. In 37 BC, the
Romans brought an end to the Jewish state and installed the
Roman appointed ruler, Herod the Great, as King of Judea
(reigned 37-4 BC).[29]

Even though the Romans ruled Palestine during the early days
of Christianity, the Romans looked up to the Greeks as their
teachers while considering themselves sort of like Mediterranean

---

[28] "Tractate Megillah," Chap. 1, Jewish Virtual Library,
http://www.jewishvirtuallibrary.org/jsource/Talmud/megillah1.html (accessed
March 15, 2015).

[29] H.H Ben-Sasson, *A History of the Jewish People*, trans. George
Weidenfeld (Cambridge: Harvard University Press, 19756), 185-200; David
Flusser, and R. Steven Notley, *The Sage from Galilee: Rediscovering Jesus'
Genius* (Grand Rapids: Wm. B. Eerdmans Publishing Co., 2007), 166-167.

policemen.[30] The Roman poet Virgil (70-19 BC) represented this Roman view:

> Others (I can well believe) will hammer out bronze that breathes with more delicacy than us, draw out living features from marble: plead their causes better, trace with instruments the movement of the skies, and tell the rising of the constellations. Remember, Roman, it is for you to rule the nations with your power, (that will be your skill) to crown peace with law, to spare the conquered, and subdue the proud.'[31]

Along with the Romans, the early Christians providentially looked up to the Greeks as their philosophical, intellectual guides. Many thought that the Greeks could provide Christianity with philosophical terms that would help make the message of salvation readily accessible and understandable to all. Consequently, since the earliest ecumenical councils, the Catholic Church has used Greek terminology to explain delicate doctrine most notably Trinitarian and Christological.

Roman

Thousands of years ago, the land we call Italy was divided among various Indo-European groups. Three of these groups were the Etruscans, Latiums, and Romans. Our word Latin originates from the name of the Latiums. The Latium people were situated in central Italy, a region that Italians still called Lazio. Traditionally, the city of Rome was founded in the Lazio in 753 BC. Eventually, the Roman people, who claimed to be related to the ancient Greek

---

[30] Remi Brauge, "Athens – Jerusalem – Rome," *Communio* 40.1 (Spring 2013): 27.

[31] Virgil, *Aeneid*, Book VI, 808-853, trans. A.S. Kline, Poetry in Translation, http://www.poetryintranslation.com/PITBR/Latin/VirgilAeneidVI.htm#_Toc22 42942 (accessed March 13, 2015) Virgil's *Aeneid* was modeled after Homer's *Illiad* and *Odyssey*. It tells the story of the Trojan Aeneas who landed on the shore of Italian lands. Aeneas was considered by the Romans as the primordial founder of Rome and the ancestor of Romulus and Remus.

hero Aeneas,[32] united Italian lands under their leadership. First, though, according to ancient tradition, the Romans freed themselves from being ruled by kings. The first king was Romulus. According to one version of an ancient tradition, Romulus and his brother Remus were abandoned in the wilderness by their mother. A compassionate she-wolf adopted the two brothers and raised them. As the two brothers grew older, a desire grew in them to found a city. After the two brothers founded the city, Romulus in a fit of rage murdered his brother Remus and the city, Rome, was called after his own name, Romulus.[33]

"The Capitoline She-Wolf with the Boys Romulus and Remus"

[34]

---

[32] According to tradition, Aeneas is the father of the Romulus and Remus and, consequently, of the Romans. The Roman poet Virgil (70-19 BC) in his *Aeneid* describes the life of the Trojan Aeneas who lands on the banks of Italian lands. "Titus Livius (Livy), *The History of Rome*, Book 1, trans. Benjamin Oliver Foster, Perseus, http://www.perseus.tufts.edu/hopper/text?doc=Perseus%3A text%3A1999.02.0151%3Abook%3D1%3Achapter%3D1 (accessed March 16, 2015).

[33] "Titus Livius (Livy), *The History of Rome*, Books 4-7, trans. Benjamin Oliver Foster, Persues, http://www.perseus.tufts.edu/hopper/text?doc= Perseus%3Atext%3A1999.02.0151%3Abook%3D1%3Achapter%3D4 (accessed March 16, 2015); Thomas F.X. Noble, *The Foundations of Western Civilization*, Lectures 1-24 (Chantilly: The Great Courses, 2002), 242-282.

[34] Benutzer:Wolpertinger on WP de, "The Capitoline she-wolf with the boys Romulus and Remus. Museo Nuovo in the Palazzo dei Conservatori, Rome... figures of Romulus and Remus added in the 15th century," sculpture, http://commons.wikimedia.org/wiki/File%3AShe- wolf_suckles_Romulus_and_Remus.jpg (accessed March 15, 2015). According to

As explained by St. Augustine in his *City of God*, the ancient city of Rome and the new city of the Catholic Church founded by Christ are different right in their origins. The Rome of old was founded by and named after a man who murdered his brother. In contrast, Christ, the founder of the new city represented by Peter and his successors, did not commit violence but rather allowed violence to be done unto him. The Catholic Church's origin in Christ is one of peace. Ancient Rome's origin, at least according to legend, is one of violence.

In 509 BC, the Romans ended their monarchical political system that, according to tradition, Romulus had begun. This took place when the Roman's seventh king was banished. The Romans then established a republic, complete with democratic, aristocratic, and monarchical elements. By the second century BC, the Romans had established themselves as the successor empire to the Greek Empire founded by Alexander the Great (356-323 BC). As leaders of an empire, the Romans skillfully integrated diverse people into their empire. They did this by requiring the vanquished to sign a moderate treaty and by offering Roman citizenship to those they had conquered. The Romans prided themselves on their political shrewdness, backed by their strong military, while looking up to the Greeks for intellectual guidance.[35]

As the first century BC ended, the Roman Republic began to weaken. Around 60 BC, two Roman military leaders, Julius Caesar and Pompey, along with one of Rome's wealthiest and most influential men, Crassus, banded together to lead Rome. Their union is referred to as the first Triumvirate (in Latin means three men). This union ended when the following occurred. In 53 BC, Crassus was murdered by the Parthians. In 52 BC, Pompey was appointed by the Roman senate as the sole consul (chief Roman ruler). In 49 BC, the senate, encouraged by Pompey, outlawed Julius Caesar. That same year Julius Caesar made his famous cross over the Rubicon River (crossing the Rubicon) towards

---

H.W. Janson, the wolf from this statue dates to 5 BC. H.W. Janson, and Anthony F. Janson, *History of Art* (New York: Harry N. Abrams, 2001), 155-156.

[35] Thomas F.X. Noble, *The Foundations of Western Civilization*, Lectures 1-24 (Chantilly: The Great Courses, 2002), 242-282.

Rome in order to fight Pompey and the senate. In 45 BC, Julius Caesar emerged victorious and assumed absolute control over Rome.[36] As leader of Rome, Julius Caesar instituted several reforms including establishing the Julian calendar. The Julian calendar was replaced in the West in 1582 by Pope Gregory XIII to compensate for the Julian calendar's slightly inaccurate measurement of a year that over time caused the celebration of Easter and other essential Christian days to drift away from their original seasonal context. The Gregorian calendar, consequently, is 365.2425 days long.[37]

In 44 BC, a group of senators began to deeply resent Julius Caesar for not heeding their request to step down. Led by Marcus Junius Brutus, they collectively murdered their leader.[38] The following year, in 43 BC, Octavian Caesar (the adopted son and grandnephew of Caesar),[39] Marcus Antonius, and Marcus Lepidus, reacted to the political chaos by forming themselves into a second Triumvirate.[40] Upon achieving their goal, the three divided up the Roman Republic and ruled as military autocrats. In 33 BC, the second Triumvirate collapsed as these three men began fighting each other. Octavian forcefully exiled Lepidus. Finally, in 31 BC, Octavian, after defeating Marcus Antonius at the Battle of Actium, emerged as the victor. Humiliated, Mark Antony committed suicide.[41]

From 27 BC to 14 AD, Octavian, also known as Caesar Augustus, ruled Rome as its first emperor. His sense of absolute

---

[36] Marshall Cavendish, *Ancient Rome: An Illustrated History* (Tarrytown: Marshall Cavendish Corporation, 2011), 61-66.

[37] The prior Roman calendar only consisted of 355 days. An extra month would be added every year to this calendar. In Julius Caesar's calendar a year consisted of 365 days with one day to be added on every four years since it was calculated that a year really consisted of 365.25 days. The Gregorian calendar replaced the Julian calendar since it was determined that the Julian calendar, although fairly accurate, was off by eleven minutes, 14 seconds per year. Marshall Cavendish Reference, Ancient Rome: An Illustrated History (Tarrytown: Marshall Cavendish Corporation, 2011), 70; David Braverman, *The Mathematics of the Gregorian Calendar* (Bloomington: Xlibris, 2010), 13.

[38] Paul A. Zoch, *Ancient Rome: An Introductory History* (Norman: University of Oklahoma Press, 1998), 207.

[39] Zoch, 214.

[40] Cavendish, 69-71.

[41] Cavendish, 71.

power is evident in two of the titles he eventually assumed. The first was *Pontifex Maximus*, which signifies the high priest of Rome's religions. The other was *Imperator Caesar Divi Filius*.[42] The last two words of this title translates into Son of God. Caesar Augustus used his power to bring about order in his empire that is referred to as the *Pax Romana*. This peace of Rome was held together by Roman law, political structures, and by a vast network of well-kept roads. Many of these Roman elements would either be used or assimilated by the early Christians as they grew in numbers and spread the Good News.

As Catholics, we believe that despite Caesar Augustus' great earthly power the only true high priest and Son of God is Jesus Christ. Christ has promised that if we pledge our allegiance to him and follow his example we will then experience not a *Pax Romana*, which ends in this world, but a *Pax Christi*, whose fulfillment will be in the world to come.

Non-Biblical References to Early Christianity

We will now turn our attention to some of the earliest Roman, non-biblical references to Christianity. The first two are from the early Christian era Roman historians, Tacitus and Suetonius. The last reference comes from the writings of a Roman attorney, bureaucrat, and Governor of Bithynia, Pliny the Younger.[43]

Tacitus on Christianity

Publius Cornelius Tacitus (c. 58-c. 116 AD) was a senator and a historian of the Roman Empire. One of his most frequently cited works is the *Annals*. In his *Annals,* he describes the reign of early Roman emperors.[44] Below is an excerpt from the *Annals* which refers to Christ and Christians in the context of the Emperor Nero.

---

[42] Michael Koortbojian, *The Divinization of Caesar and Augustus* (New York: Cambridge University Press, 2013), 11-12, 145, 165.

[43] Rex Winsbury, *Pliny the Younger: A Life in Roman Letters* (New York: Bloomsbury Publishing, 2014), 188, 203.

[44] Tacitus, *Annals and Histories*, trans. Alfred John Church (New York: Alfred A. Knopf, 2009), ix-xiii.

Consequently, to get rid of the report, Nero fastened the guilt and inflicted the most exquisite tortures on a class hated for their abominations, called Christians by the populace. *Christus*, from whom the name had its origin, suffered the extreme penalty during the reign of Tiberius at the hands of one of our procurators, Pontius Pilatus, and a most mischievous superstition, thus checked for the moment, again broke out not only in *Judæa*, the first source of the evil, but even in Rome, where all things hideous and shameful from every part of the world find their center and become popular. Accordingly, an arrest was first made of all who pleaded guilty; then, upon their information, an immense multitude was convicted, not so much of the crime of firing the city, as of hatred against mankind. Mockery of every sort was added to their deaths. Covered with the skins of beasts, they were torn by dogs and perished, or were nailed to crosses, or were doomed to the flames and burnt, to serve as a nightly illumination, when daylight had expired. Nero offered his gardens for the spectacle....[45]

Suetonius on Christianity

In his *Lives of the Caesars* (*De Vita Caesarum*), the Roman government official and historian Gaius Suetonius Tranquillus (c.70 - c. 122 AD) explicitly refers to Christ.[46] (It is debated among scholars whether Suetonius was referring to the Christ of the Gospels.) In doing so, Suetonius wrote:

He allowed the people of Ilium perpetual exemp-

---

[45] Tacitus, *Annals and Histories*, trans. Alfred John Church (New York: Alfred A. Knopf, 2009), 353-354.
[46] Suetonius, *Lives of the Caesars* trans. Catherine Edwards (Oxford: Oxford University Press, 2008), viii-xxx.

tion from tribute, on the ground that they were the founders of the Roman race, reading an ancient letter of the senate and people of Rome written in Greek to king Seleucus, in which they promised him their friendship and alliance only on condition that he should keep their kinsfolk of Ilium free from every burden. Since the Jews constantly made disturbances at the instigation of *Chrestus*, he expelled them from Rome.[47]

Pliny the Younger on Christianity

As mentioned previously, Pliny the Younger (c. 61 - c. 113 AD) served Rome as an attorney and a bureaucrat and as Governor of Bithynia. When he was the Governor of Bithynia, he referred to Christians in his correspondence with Emperor Trajan. In one of his letters to the emperor, Pliny describes Christians by stating:

...They asserted, however, that the sum and substance of their fault or error had been that they were accustomed to meet on a fixed day before dawn and sing responsively a hymn to Christ as to a god, and to bind themselves by oath, not to some crime, but not to commit fraud, theft, or adultery, not falsify their trust, nor to refuse to return a trust when called upon to do so. When this was over, it was their custom to depart and to assemble again to partake of food--but ordinary and innocent food. Even this, they affirmed, they had ceased to do after my edict by which, in accordance with your instructions, I had forbidden political associations. Accordingly, I judged it all the more necessary to find out what the truth was by torturing two female slaves who were called deaconesses. But I

---

[47] Gaius Suetonius, *"The Lives of the Twelve Caesars,"* trans. J.C. Rolfe, *Claudius*, 25, University of Chicago edu, http://penelope.uchicago.edu/ Thayer/E/Roman/Texts/Suetonius/12Caesars/Claudius*.html (March 20, 2015).

discovered nothing else but depraved, excessive superstition....[48]

Trajan responded with:

> You observed proper procedure, my dear Pliny, in sifting the cases of those who had been denounced to you as Christians. For it is not possible to lay down any general rule to serve as a kind of fixed standard. They are not to be sought out; if they are denounced and proved guilty, they are to be punished, with this reservation, that whoever denies that he is a Christian and really proves it-- that is, by worshiping our gods--even though he was under suspicion in the past, shall obtain pardon through repentance. But anonymously posted accusations ought to have no place in any prosecution. For this is both a dangerous kind of precedent and out of keeping with the spirit of our age.[49]

Quiz 2

1-2. In reference to Judaism, Greek culture, and Roman culture, interpret St. Paul's description of Christ being sent by the Father in the "fullness of time" (Galatians 4:4). Answer this question in a broad way.

3. What specifically did Judaism offer to Christianity and was fulfilled in Christianity?

---

[48] Pliny the Younger, "*Pliny to the Emperor Trajan Letters 10.96-97*," Georgetown, http://faculty.georgetown.edu/jod/texts/pliny.html (accessed March 20, 2015).
[49] Pliny the Younger, Ibid.

4. What did Christians learn and take from Greek culture?

5. What did the early Christians learn and take from Roman culture and Roman rule?

6-10. In a paragraph, describe the legend of Romulus and Remus and contrast the founding of Rome, as described in this legend, with the Catholic Church founded by Jesus Christ.

11-14. Cite and explain how one of the following authors referred to Christianity: Tacitus, Suetonius, and Pliny the Younger.

Chapter 3

Catholic Church History

Introduction

You have been introduced to both the historical context of the early Christians and to the Christians' distinct view of history. In this chapter, we will focus on what distinguishes history from Catholic Church history.

First, we will begin with how the Catholic Church was prefigured before Christ's incarnation. In a certain sense, the Catholic Church has existed since Adam and Eve, our first parents. The foreshadowing of the Catholic Church was fulfilled in Christ who, as the New Adam with Mary as the New Eve, visibly established his Church with Peter as his vicar (Matthew 16:18). Peter, the other eleven apostles, and the successors of the apostles were intended by Christ, according to Catholic faith, to act as the Church's visible foundation (Revelation 21:14).

Second, we will reflect on both the questions who are the Church and who is the Church. Then, we will narrow our historical vision by studying, from a historical standpoint, Jesus and Mary and the various Jewish groups that at times were in tension with one another and with Jesus and his followers. These groups will include the Essenes, Pharisees, Sadducees, Herodians, Zealots, and the Samaritans.

The Catholic Church Prefigured

According to early Christian documents, such as *The Shepherd of Hermas* (c.100s AD), the Catholic Church was "foreshadowed from the world's beginning."[50] Not only was the Catholic Church foreshadowed from the beginning, but the world, believed early Christians, was even created for her.

The Shepherd of Hermas on the Church

> Now, brethren, a revelation was made unto me in my sleep by a youth of exceeding fair form, who said to me, "Whom thinkest thou the aged woman, from whom thou received the book, to be?" I say, "The Sibyl" "Thou art wrong," saith he, "she is not." "Who then is she?" I say. "The Church," saith he. I said unto him, "Wherefore then is she aged?" "Because," saith he, "she was created before all things; therefore is she aged; and for her sake the world was framed."[51]

A term that is like foreshadowing but bears within it a greater sense of form is prefigured. One definite way, according to Catholic faith, that the Church was visibly prefigured in a people was when the Israelites, led by Moses, gathered around Sinai to receive the Ten Commandments. In a way that does not totally remove all meaning from the Old Testament type of Church, every time Catholics gather to celebrate the Eucharist the Catholic Church is fulfilling what once happened at Sinai. As Catholics fulfill the Israel of old when they receive the Body and Blood of the risen Christ during the celebration of the Eucharist, they are collectively being knit together ever more deeply into Christ's mystical body who is the Church. Similarly, the Twelve Apostles

---

[50] Catechism of the Catholic Church (Liguori: Liguori Publications, 1994), no. 760, p. 200.

[51] "The Shepherd of Hermes," 4[8}:1 trans. J.B. Lightfoot, Early Christian Writings, http://www.earlychristianwritings.com/text/shepherd-lightfoot.html (accessed March 22, 2015).

and their episcopal successors, as the foundation stones of the new Church as the Catholic Church or New Jerusalem,[52] fulfill the 12 foundational people of Israel, the sons of Israel's patriarch Jacob.[53]

Below is a chart that shows how the Catholic Church was gradually prepared for during Old Testament times.

Family Form	Mediator	Covenant Sign
One Holy Couple	Adam (Gen 1-3)	Sabbath
One Holy Family	Noah (Gen 9)	Rainbow
One Holy Tribe	Abraham (Gen 15, 17,22)	Circumcision
One Holy Nation	Moses (Ex 24/ Deut 29)	Tablets
One Holy Kingdom	David/Solomon (II Sam. 7)	Ark and Tent/Temple
One Holy Catholic Church	Jesus (Mk 14)	Eucharist

[54]

Who Are the Church?

When commenting on the Apostle's Creed, St. Thomas Aquinas makes a distinction between the Catholic Church as "one body" and the Catholic Church as comprising many "different members." Aquinas then asserts that:

> It must be known that "church" is the same as assembly. So, the Holy Church is the same as the assembly of the faithful, and every Christian is a member of this Church, of which it is written: "Draw near to Me, you unlearned; and gather

---

[52] Revelation 21: 12-14; Matthew 19:28; Luke 22:30; Cf Catechism of the Catholic Church (Liguori: Liguori Publications, 1994), no. 765, p. 201.

[53] Catechism of the Catholic Church (Liguori: Liguori Publications, 1994), no. 765, p. 201.

[54] Sarah Christmyer, *A Quick Journey Through the Bible: An 8-Part Introduction to the Bible Timeline Student Workbook* (West Chester: Ascension Press, 2008), 12.

yourselves together into the house of discipline"
[Sir 51:31].[55]

In his *book Who are the Church?* the notable Catholic
ecclesiologist, Joseph A. Komonchak, refers to the above excerpt
from Aquinas.[56] In accordance with his title, Komonchak describes
the Church from the perspective of the many "different members"
who make up the one Church.

Politically Many

One way of appreciating the "many" dimension of the Catholic
Church is by studying her politically. In her political makeup as a
heavenly *polis* (*polis* in Greek means city) the Catholic Church on
earth participates in the Kingdom of God in a present but not yet
fully realized state. In this "painful between state,"[57] God has
ordained that the Catholic Church be politically constituted by a
mixture of all three basic political regimes: rule by one, rule by
few, and rule by many.[58] The rule by one is Christ represented by
his vicar the Pope. The bishops, priests, and deacons refer to the
few who also participate in Christ's governance of His Church. The
many can be understood as the faithful, who Christ:

> willed to confer on her a share in his own
> infallibility. By a 'supernatural sense of faith' the
> People of God, under the guidance of the Church's
> living Magisterium, 'unfailingly adheres to this
> faith.[59]

---

[55] Thomas Aquinas, "Expositio in Symbolum Apostolorum, The Apostles
Creed,   trans.   Joseph   B.   Collins,"   Dominican   House   Priory,
http://dhspriory.org/thomas/Creed.htm#9 (accessed March 23, 2015).

[56] Joseph A. Komonchak, *Who are the Church?* (Milwaukee: Marquette
University Press, 2008), 59-60.

[57] Joseph Ratzinger, *Das Neue Volk Gottes* (Düsseldorf: Patmos, 1969), 167. "
...das bedeutet das schmerzliche „Zwischen", in dem die Kirche einstweilen noch
steht."

[58] Aquinas favors the mixed constitution form of government. See his
Summa Theologica, I-II, q. 105, art. 1)

[59] Catechism of the Catholic Church (Liguori: Liguori Publications, 1994), no.
889, p. 235.

The Many as a Hierarchy

As indicated above, the many are hierarchically ordered in the Catholic Church. The term hierarchy can be defined in a variety of ways. The way it could be defined, according to the just described political aspect of the Church, is as a sacred rule shared by the Catholic faithful in different degrees and kinds. This is because the term hierarchy can be translated as a sacred rule since the first part of the word comes from the Greek *hieros,* meaning sacred, and the second part of the word comes from the Greek word *arche*, meaning rule.

Cardinal Joseph Ratzinger provides a deeper definition of the term hierarchy, by which the many are knit together as one in Christ. Ratzinger argues:

> The correct translation of this term is probably not 'sacred rule' but 'sacred origin'. The word *arche* can mean both things, origin and rule. But the likelier meaning is 'sacred origin'. In other words, it communicates itself in virtue of an origin, and the power of this origin, which is sacred, as it were the ever-new beginning of every generation in the Church. It doesn't live by the mere continuum of generations but by the presence of the ever-new source itself, which communicates itself unceasingly through the sacraments. That, I think, is an important, different way of looking at things: the category that corresponds to the priesthood is not that of rule. On the contrary, the priesthood has to be a conduit and a making present of a beginning and has to make itself available for this task. When priesthood, episcopacy, and papacy are understood essentially in terms of rule, then things are truly wrong and distorted.[60]

---

[60] Ratzinger, *Salt of the Earth*, trans. Adrian Walker (San Francisco: Ignatius Press, 1997), 190-191.

Who is the Church?

Christ, as the one sacred origin of the Catholic Church, wills that the many people who constitute the Church are one in faith, hope, and charity.[61] As one, Catholic, and Apostolic Church that is holy, because of Christ, the Church, is not "a subject who sins"[62] but rather one who "assum[es] the weight of her children's faults in maternal solidarity."[63] The common term "Holy Mother the Church" upholds this teaching that the Church is one subject and holy.[64] As we study the history of the Catholic Church, which includes both saints and sinners, please bear in mind this important distinction. Keeping in play the various models and profiles of the Church as we study the various people of the Church may help us to remember that the Church is one, holy, Catholic and Apostolic.

Models of the Church

Cardinal Avery Dulles describes the unity of the Catholic Church through six different models, each of which sheds light on the others. The first model is the Church as an institution.[65] We covered this model when we were describing the various levels of the Church that constitute her state on earth. The second model is the Church as mystical communion.[66] Pope Pius XII's 1943 encyclical *Mystici Corporis Christi* describes this model. Through

---

[61] Thomas Aquinas, "Expositio in Symbolum Apostolorum, The Apostles Creed, trans. Joseph B. Collins," Dominican House Priory, http://dhspriory.org/thomas/Creed.htm#9 (accessed March 23, 2015).

[62] International Theological Commission, *Memory and Reconciliation: The Church and the Faults of the Past December 1999*, 3.4, The Vatican, http://www.vatican.va/roman_curia/congregations/cfaith/cti_documents/rc_co n_cfaith_doc_20000307_memory-reconc-itc_en.html (accessed March 23, 2015).

[63] International Theological Commission, *Memory and Reconciliation: The Church and the Faults of the Past December 1999*, 3.4, Ibid.

[64] For this reason Hans Urs von Balthasar prefers to ask the question, "Who is the Church?" and not "Who are the Church?" Hans Urs von Balthasar, "Who is the Church?" in *Explorations in Theology*, vol. 2, *Spouse of the Word*, 143-92.

[65] Avery Dulles, *Models of the Church* (New York: Image Books, 2002), 26-39.

[66] Dulles, 39-55.

Christ we are united mystically as one body. The third model is the Church as sacrament.[67] As a sacrament the Church acts as a visible sign of God's grace. The fourth model is the Church as herald.[68] In this role the Church, in her fidelity to truth, proclaims the Good News. The fifth model is the Church as servant.[69] As a servant the Church cares for the physically and spiritually poor. The sixth model is the Church as school of discipleship.[70] In this model, which can be understood as the overarching model, all within the Church are to learn from Christ the one teacher. In a certain sense, the biblical and conciliar reference to the Church as a people of God, as disciples of Jesus, can be interpreted as expressing this last model.

Jesus, Mary and Jewish Groups

In this final section, beginning with Jesus, we will shift our attention from the big picture to key people and groups of people of early Christianity.

Jesus

The English name Jesus originally, via Latin and Greek, comes from the Hebrew name *Yehoshua*, meaning God saves. *Yehoshua* is the Hebrew name for Joshua who leads the Israelites across the Jordan River into the Promised Land.[71] The two English names of Joshua and Jesus, therefore, are simply two different ways of rendering the same Hebrew name Yehoshua into English. Realizing that the name of Jesus is interchangeable with the name of Joshua is important since, as the new Joshua, Jesus Christ, according to our Catholic faith, fulfills the very meaning of his name by offering salvation to all. All are invited to follow Jesus as

---

[67] Dulles, 55-68.
[68] Dulles, 68-81.
[69] Dulles, 81-95.
[70] Dulles, 195-219.
[71] "Jesus," Online Etymology Dictionary, http://etymonline.com/index.php?allowed_in_frame=0&search=jesus&searchmode=none (accessed March 25, 2015); Interlinear NIV Hebrew-English Old Testament (Numbers 14:30).

he crosses over the waters of death into the promised land of heaven.

Although we identify Jesus being born in 1 AD (*Anno Domini* means in Latin in the year of the Lord), he was actually born around 4 BC. This has been repeatedly pointed out by many, including by Benedict XVI in his book *Jesus of Nazareth*. Benedict XVI explains that since the census referred to by Luke (Luke 2:1) was ordered by Caesar Augustus during the time King Herod was alive and ruling (Matthew 2:1), Jesus had to have been born in or prior to 4 BC. This is because, according to historical record, King Herod the Great died in 4 BC. The reason for this error in dating Jesus' birth is traceable to the monk Dionysius Exiguus (death c. 550 AD), who dated Jesus' birth a few years too late.[72]

The place that Jesus was born was a town about five miles south of Jerusalem called Bethlehem, which in Hebrew literally means house (*beth*) of bread (*lehem*). At the time of Jesus, the shepherds of Bethlehem would send their lambs to Jerusalem to be sacrificed in the Temple and to be eaten during the annual Passover meal. As the Lamb of God (John 1:29), Jesus, as taught by our Catholic faith, fulfills the meaning of these multiple sacrifices.[73]

For the first thirty years or so of his life, Jesus learned from his foster father Joseph the trade of building with hard material (in Greek *tekton*). His position as a *tekton* meant that his social class was not that of the poorest of the poor, made up by day laborers, beggars and slaves. Rather, he could be understood, a bit anachronistically, as part of the working middle class of his times.[74]

During his three years of public ministry, Jesus was recognized as a rabbi even though his status as a "rabbi" was unusual since there is no indication he was formally trained in Judaism. In

---

[72] Benedict XVI, *Jesus of Nazareth: The Infancy Narratives*, trans. Philip J. Whitmore (New York: Image, 2012), 61-62.

[73] "Babylonian Talmud, Book 2, Chapter VII: Tracts Erubin, Shekalim, Rosh Hashana, trans. Michael L. Rodkinson (1918)," Sacred Texts, http://www.sacred-texts.com/jud/t02/shk11.htm (accessed March 25, 2015).

[74] John P. Meier, *Jesus the Marginal Jew*, Volume 3 (New York: Random House, 2001), 620.

addition, his practice of celibacy was also unusual for his times. Another way that Jesus distinguished himself was by refusing to promote any political, economic, or social platform. Instead, he chose to teach in parables and with "allusive, riddle-like speech."[75]

Mary

Like her son, Jesus, Mary has a biblical Hebrew name. Her name in Hebrew is Miriam. She shares the same name as Moses's sister Miriam. The Old Testament Miriam saved her baby brother's life by helping Moses' mother in hiding him from Pharaoh's guards, who had been ordered to make sure all the new born male babies of the Hebrew people were killed (Exodus 2:1-10). After the Israelites departed from Pharaoh's lands, Miriam helped her two brothers, Moses and Aaron, in leading the Israelites across the desert to the Promised Land. "For I brought you up from the land of Egypt, and redeemed you from the house of slavery; and I sent before you Moses, Aaron, and Miriam." (NRSVCE Micah 6:4)[76] The Mary of the New Testament, in continuity and fulfillment of the Miriam of the Old, assists Jesus and his priests in leading the Catholic Church, as the New Israel, to the promised land of heaven. Similar to the Miriam of the Old Testament, Mary of the New Testament saves the savior of her people by, along with her husband, Joseph, fleeing Egypt from King Herod the Great who had ordered all the male babies in Bethlehem to be killed.[77]

---

[75] Meier, 621-624.

[76] Micah 6:4 NASB.

[77] Meier, 616. The Cappadocian Father St. Gregory of Nyssa (c. 330-c. 395) explicitly makes this typological connection. "But besides other things the action of Miriam the prophetess also gives rise to these surmisings of ours. Directly the sea was crossed she took in her hand a dry and sounding timbrel and conducted the women's dance. By this timbrel the story may mean to imply virginity, as first perfected by Miriam; whom indeed I would believe to be a type of Mary the mother of God. Just as the timbrel emits a loud sound because it is devoid of all moisture and reduced to the highest degree of dryness, so has virginity a clear and ringing report amongst men because it repels from itself the vital sap of merely physical life. Thus, Miriam's timbrel being a dead thing, and virginity being a deadening of the bodily passions, it is perhaps not very far removed from the bounds of probability that Miriam was a virgin. However, we can but guess

Essenes

The origins of the Essenes is debated among historians. Some maintain that the Essenes originated from the Hasideans, a group that successfully revolted against the Greek Seleucid Empire during the middle of the second century (1 Macc. 2:42; 7:13; 2 Macc. 14:6).[78] At the time of Jesus, there were Essene communities. Similar to our understanding of monasteries, some of these communities lived a celibate way of life.[79] Very different

---

and surmise, we cannot clearly prove, that this was so, and that Miriam the prophetess led a dance of virgins, even though many of the learned have affirmed distinctly that she was unmarried, from the fact that the history makes no mention either of her marriage or of her being a mother; and surely she would have been named and known, not as "the sister of Aaron," but from her husband, if she had had one; since the head of the woman is not the brother but the husband. But if, amongst a people with whom motherhood was sought after and classed as a blessing and regarded as a public duty, the grace of virginity, nevertheless, came to be regarded as a precious thing, how does it behoove us to feel towards it, who do not "judge" of the Divine blessings "according to the flesh"? Gregory of Nyssa, "NPNF2-05. Gregory of Nyssa: Dogmatic Treatises, etc." Ascetic and Moral, chap xix, ccel.org, http://www.ccel.org/ccel/schaff/npnf205html (accessed June 5, 2016).

[78] Joan E. Taylor, *The Essenes, The Scrolls, and the Dead Sea* (Oxford: Oxford University Press, 2012), 3-21.

[79] Josephus, "The Wars Of The Jews, Book II, Book 2, Chapter 8, section 2," Early Jewish Writings, http://www.earlyjewishwritings.com/text/josephus/war2.html (accessed March 26, 2015). "For there are three philosophical sects among the Jews. The followers of the first of which are the Pharisees; of the second, the Sadducees; and the third sect, which pretends to a severer discipline, are called Essenes. These last are Jews by birth, and seem to have a greater affection for one another than the other sects have. These Essenes reject pleasures as an evil, but esteem continence, and the conquest over our passions, to be virtue. They neglect wedlock, but choose out other person's children, while they are pliable, and fit for learning, and esteem them to be of their kindred, and form them according to their own manners. They do not absolutely deny the fitness of marriage, and the succession of mankind thereby continued; but they guard against the lascivious behavior of women, and are persuaded that none of them preserve their fidelity to one man."

Josephus, "The Wars Of The Jews, Book II, Book 2, Chapter 8, section 13," Early Jewish Writings, http://www.earlyjewishwritings.com/text/josephus/war2.html (accessed March 26, 2015). "Moreover, there is another order of Essenes, who agree with the rest as to their way of living, and customs, and laws, but differ from them in the point of marriage, as thinking that by not marrying they cut off the principal part of human life, which is the prospect of succession; nay, rather, that if all men should be of the same opinion, the whole race of mankind would fail. However, they try their spouses for three years; and if they find that they have their natural purgations thrice, as trials that they are likely to

from the faith that Catholic monks hold to, the Essenes, as recorded by the Jewish historian Flavius Josephus (37-100 AD), held that God's fate determines all events.[80]

Pharisees

According to Josephus, the Pharisees believed in a dual Torah. In other words, they held that God gave Moses both an oral law and a written law. Other beliefs the Pharisees held were the immortality of the soul, reward or punishment after death, the resurrection of the dead, the existence of angels, human freedom, and divine providence.[81] Due to the Pharisees' support of these

---

be fruitful, they then actually marry them. But they do not use to accompany with their wives when they are with child, as a demonstration that they do not many out of regard to pleasure, but for the sake of posterity. Now the women go into the baths with some of their garments on, as the men do with somewhat girded about them. And these are the customs of this order of Essenes."

[80] Josephus, "Antiquities, Book 13, Chapter 5, Section 9," Sacred-texts Judaism, http://www.sacred-texts.com/jud/josephus/ant-13.htm (accessed March 26, 2015). "At this time there were three sects among the Jews, who had different opinions concerning human actions; the one was called the sect of the Pharisees, another the sect of the Sadducees, and the other the sect of the Essenes. Now for the Pharisees, they say that some actions, but not all, are the work of fate, and some of them are in our own power, and that they are liable to fate, but are not caused by fate. But the sect of the Essenes affirm, that fate governs all things, and that nothing befalls men but what is according to its determination. And for the Sadducees, they take away fate, and say there is no such thing, and that the events of human affairs are not at its disposal; but they suppose that all our actions are in our own power, so that we are ourselves the causes of what is good, and receive what is evil from our own folly. However, I have given a more exact account of these opinions in the second book of the Jewish War."

[81] Josephus, "The Wars Of The Jews, Book II, Book 2, Chapter 8, section 14," Early Jewish Writings, http://www.earlyjewishwritings.com/text/josephus/war2.html (accessed March 26, 2015 "But then as to the two other orders at first mentioned, the Pharisees are those who are esteemed most skillful in the exact explication of their laws, and introduce the first sect. These ascribe all to fate [or providence], and to God, and yet allow, that to act what is right, or the contrary, is principally in the power of men, although fate does co-operate in every action. They say that all souls are incorruptible, but that the souls of good men only are removed into other bodies, - but that the souls of bad men are subject to eternal punishment. But the Sadducees are those that compose the second order, and take away fate entirely, and suppose that God is not concerned in our doing or not doing what is evil; and they say, that to act what is good, or what is evil, is at men's own choice, and that the one or the other belongs so to everyone, that they may act as they please. They also take away the belief of the immortal duration of

popular beliefs, they were well liked by many Jews.[82]

Sadducees

Unlike the Pharisees, the Sadducees rejected the immortality of the soul, did not believe that a person would be rewarded or punished after death and did not believe in the angels.[83] They also rejected the Pharisees' belief that God providentially arranges history. In contrast, the Sadducees maintained that God does not intervene in the world, that fate does not exist, and that man determines his own outcome.[84] In addition, as described by Josephus, the Sadducees were privileged Jews, were disliked by many common people, and were supported by the wealthy and influential. In ruling the Temple, they also collaborated with the Romans.[85] Not surprisingly, the Sadducees were not well-liked by

the soul, and the punishments and rewards in Hades. Moreover, the Pharisees are friendly to one another, and are for the exercise of concord, and regard for the public; but the behavior of the Sadducees one towards another is in some degree wild, and their conversation with those that are of their own party is as barbarous as if they were strangers to them. And this is what I had to say concerning the philosophic sects among the Jews.";

NASB Acts 23: 6-8. "But perceiving that one group were Sadducees and the other Pharisees, Paul [began] crying out in the Council, "Brethren, I am a Pharisee, a son of Pharisees; I am on trial for the hope and resurrection of the dead!" As he said this, there occurred a dissension between the Pharisees and Sadducees, and the assembly was divided. 8For the Sadducees say that there is no resurrection, nor an angel, nor a spirit, but the Pharisees acknowledge them all."

[82] Meier, 289-388, especially 330-331.

[83] See previous footnotes on the Pharisees. Also see NIV Mark 12:18, "Then the Sadducees, who say there is no resurrection, came to him with a question."

[84] Josephus, "Antiquities, Book 13, Chapter 5, Section 9," Sacred-texts Judaism, http://www.sacred-texts.com/jud/josephus/ant-13.htm (accessed March 26, 2015).

[85] Josephus, "Antiquities, Book 13, Chapter 10, Section 6," Sacred-texts Judaism, http://www.sacred-texts.com/jud/josephus/ant-13.htm (accessed March 26, 2015). "...And concerning these things it is that great disputes and differences have arisen among them, while the Sadducees are able to persuade none but the rich, and have not the populace obsequious to them, but the Pharisees have the multitude on their side. But about these two sects, and that of the Essenes, I have treated accurately in the second book of Jewish affairs." Josephus, "Antiquities, Book 18, Chapter 1, Section 4," Sacred-texts Judaism, http://www.sacred-texts.com/jud/josephus/ant-13.htm (accessed March 26, 2015). "But the doctrine of the Sadducees is this: That souls die with the bodies; nor do they regard the observation of anything besides what the law enjoins them; for they think it an instance of virtue to dispute with those teachers of

the common people.[86]

Herodians

The Herodians were those who served in King Herod Antipas' court. Some of the Herodians may have been used by King Herod Antipas, speculates the biblical scholar J.P. Meier to, "spy on, oppose, and discredit Jesus in public."[87] Meier draws this conclusion since the Roman Empire at the time of Jesus utilized a network of spies.[88]

Zealots

The term zealot during Jesus' lifetime referred to Jewish people who practiced Jewish law with great zeal. Not until after 66-70 AD, when the Jewish people violently revolted against Roman rule, did this term refer to a revolutionary group intent on killing Romans and those who collaborated with them.[89]

Samaritans

According to Jesus' Jewish contemporaries, the Samaritans were descendants of the Israelite, Northern tribes of Ephraim and Manasseh who had intermarried with Assyrians and Greeks. They lived in the region of Samaria whose capital was Samaria before being renamed Sebaste by Herod the Great. Their religion was like Judaism in the sense that they worshiped only one God and accepted the first five books of the bible. They differed from the Jews by insisting that God's temple was not situated in Jerusalem but rather in Samaria on Mount Gerizim. J.P. Meier rightly points

---

philosophy whom they frequent: but this doctrine is received but by a few, yet by those still of the greatest dignity. But they are able to do almost nothing of themselves; for when they become magistrates, as they are unwillingly and by force sometimes obliged to be, they addict themselves to the notions of the Pharisees, because the multitude would not otherwise bear them."

[86] Meier, 392-396.
[87] Meier, 564-565.
[88] Meier, 564-565.
[89] Meier, 205-207.

out that these three ways of defining Samaritans (geographically, ethnically, and religiously) while overlapping do not, according to history, completely equal each other.[90]

Quiz 3

1. Fill in the spaces below. (Scriptural references are not required.)

Progressive Growth of God's family from One Couple to One Catholic Church[91]

Family Form	Mediator	Covenant Sign
1.	7.	13
2.	8.	14.
3.	9.	15.
4.	10.	16.
5.	11.	17.
6.	12.	18.

19-20. According to Catholic teaching, is the Catholic Church a subject who sins? (There is only one correct answer to this) Why or why not?

19.

20.

21-22. Can the Catholic Church be adequately defined in political, economic or social terms? Why or why not?

21.

---

[90] Meier, 534.
[91] *The Bible Timeline* by Jeff Cavins, Tim Gray and Sarah Christmyer.

22.

23-25. Explain three of the Cardinal Avery Dulles six models of the Church.

23.

24.

25.

26. What biblical Old Testament figure, who takes the place of Moses, does Jesus share the same name with? Why is this important?

27-31. Briefly distinguish the Essenes, the Pharisees, the Sadducees, the Samaritans, and the Herodians from each another.

27. Essenes:

28. Pharisees:

29. Sadducees:

30. Samaritans:

31. Herodians:

Chapter 4

Early Christian Life

Introduction

In this chapter, the various expressions of early Christian life will be discussed. We will begin with what Christians believed before moving on to how these beliefs were expressed liturgically, artistically, and structurally. In the following chapter, we will see how the practices of the Christians that flowed out of their beliefs distinguished them from non-Christians.

The apologist Jimmy Akin observes that the geographic spread of early Christianity is truly amazing. Within a short amount of time, the hubs of Christianity were Jerusalem, Rome, and cities in Asia Minor (modern day Turkey). Since it could take months to travel from one of these cities to the next, the wide spread, highly historically verifiable practice of Christianity indicates that Christianity had a well-organized evangelization campaign. This means that there were organizers, whom we call Apostles, which in Greek means messengers, delegates, or the ones sent. The person who did the sending was Jesus Christ. Messengers, of course, need a sender.[92]

---

[92] Jimmy Akin, "Catholic Answers Lecture," July, 2015.

Early Christian Belief

Resurrection

1 Corinthians 15: 12-19 (RSVCE)

> Now if Christ is proclaimed as raised from the dead, how can some of you say there is no resurrection of the dead? If there is no resurrection of the dead, then Christ has not been raised; and if Christ has not been raised, then our proclamation has been in vain and your faith has been in vain. We are even found to be misrepresenting God, because we testified of God that he raised Christ—whom he did not raise if it is true that the dead are not raised. For if the dead are not raised, then Christ has not been raised. If Christ has not been raised, your faith is futile and you are still in your sins. Then those also who have died in Christ have perished. If for this life only we have hoped in Christ, we are of all people most to be pitied.

For the early Christians, as St. Paul testifies, faith in the resurrection of Jesus was of utmost importance. They also held that it was reasonable to believe in the resurrection of Jesus since he appeared to many as St. Paul states:

1 Corinthians 15: 3-8 (RSVCE)

> For I handed on to you as of first importance what I in turn had received: that Christ died for our sins in accordance with the scriptures, and that he was buried, and that he was raised on the third day in accordance with the scriptures, and that he appeared to Cephas, then to the twelve. Then he appeared to more than five hundred brothers and sisters at one time, most of whom are still alive,

though some have died. Then he appeared to James, then to all the apostles. Last of all, as to one untimely born, he appeared also to me.

In explaining that it is reasonable to believe that the resurrection of Jesus actually took place in history, the philosopher Peter J. Kreeft rejects a number of counter explanations. One counter explanation is that Jesus did not die on the cross but rather swooned. Afterward, he regained his strength, walked around, and appeared to various people who only thought he had risen from the dead. This explanation, argues Kreeft, is not likely since the Romans took such great care to ensure those who were condemned to death died that they even condemned Roman soldiers to death who had allowed a condemned person to escape. That the Roman soldiers, accountable to this law, did not break the legs of Jesus indicates that they were certain he was dead. The blood and water that flowed from the pierced side of Jesus also indicates that he had died (Jn. 19:34-35). Other aspects which further weaken this counter explanation include the following. The gospels record that a huge boulder at the entrance of Jesus' tomb was removed. It is unreasonable to hold that Jesus in a highly weakened state moved this boulder and then overpowered the Roman guards. It is also unreasonable to maintain that the disciples stole Jesus, in his swooned state, from the tomb, since the guards would have been awakened by the moving of the entrance stone and, in order not to be executed, would have prevented this from occurring.[93]

The second counter explanation the Kreeft rejects is that the disciples lied about the Resurrection. This is unreasonable, since there is no historical evidence that any early Christian confessed that the Resurrection was a lie and in the two thousand years of Christianity no such lie has ever been exposed. Furthermore, since up until 313 AD Christians were persecuted by the Romans, what motive did the early Christians have for lying? Their faith in Jesus

---

[93] Peter J. Kreeft and Ronald K. Tacelli *Handbook of Catholic Apologetics* (San Francisco: Ignatius Press, 2009), 193-194.

was answered by exile, torture, and death.[94]

In rejecting the third counter explanation that the disciples hallucinated, Kreeft points out that hallucinations are private and not public phenomena in which hundreds of people participate. Christ, though, appeared to hundreds of people all at the same time as the above passage from Paul's first letter to Corinthians indicates. In addition, the New Testament post-Resurrection appearance accounts describe Christ as carrying on long, thought-provoking conversations, and at one point with eleven people at the same time (Acts 1:3). Hallucinations, though, rarely are extended this long except in cases when an individual, unlike those who witnessed Jesus' resurrection, isolates himself from reality.[95]

Another counter explanation Kreeft rejects is that the disciples invented a resurrection myth that was believed as a historical fact. This is unreasonable from a historical standpoint since there is evidence that Christians living at the time of the disciples believed that Jesus' Resurrection was a historical event and not a myth. This early belief in the Resurrection is testified to by St. Paul whose first letter to the Thessalonians is commonly dated to the early 50s AD. Similarly, Peter, in his second letter, explicitly rejects defining the Resurrection as a myth. He states, "For we did not follow cleverly devised myths when we made known to you the power and coming of our Lord Jesus Christ, but we were eyewitnesses of his majesty" (2 Peter 1:16 RSVCE). If the Resurrection was an invented myth then the Christians who were eyewitnesses of Jesus would have quickly dismissed the account of Jesus' resurrection as being fictional. This means, asserts Kreeft, there was not enough time for such a myth to be created and widely accepted. In the case of other religious founders, such as Buddha and Muhammad, argues Kreeft, a number of generations were needed to have passed before myths concerning the founder developed. Referring to Julius Muller's book *The Theory of Myths in Its Application to the Gospel History Examined and Confuted*, Kreeft points out that no historian has demonstrated that a great myth or legend of a historical figure has arisen and "generally

---

[94] Kreeft and Tacelli 195-197.
[95] Kreeft and Tacelli, 197-199.

believed within thirty years after the figure's death."[96]

In rejecting the Resurrection as a myth, Kreeft shifts his attention to the New Testament writings. He convincingly demonstrates there is no historical evidence that a mythological layer was later added upon a supposedly original form of the New Testament writings. Extra biblical writings that date to the first century support the New Testament's description of the Resurrection as actually taking place. These include writings of the following first century Christians: St. Barnabas, Pope St. Clement, St. Polycarp, and St. Ignatius of Antioch.[97]

That the New Testament is the most reliable ancient text we have also substantially weakens the argument that a mythological layer was added to the New Testament. According to Kreeft, "We have five hundred different copies [of the New Testament] earlier than A.D. 500. The next most reliable ancient text we have is the *Iliad* for which we have only fifty copies that date from five hundred years or less after its origins."[98]

The style in which the New Testament was written even more weakens the argument for a mythological New Testament layer. If the myth was invented, the inventors would have described men and not women as testifying to the resurrection. This is because at the time of Jesus the witness of a woman was of little value. Such inventors also would have naturally harmonized the gospels, by systematically rejecting New Testament sections that appear to contradict one another.[99]

Trinity

Belief in the Trinity, even though not yet formulated in the earliest days of the Church, was also essential to early Christian identity. Bishop Theophilus of Antioch in his *Apologia ad Autolycum* (181 AD) was the first to use the Greek word for Trinity when referring to God the Father, God the Son, as Logos, and God

---

[96] Kreeft and Tacelli, 203.
[97] Kreeft and Tacelli, 203-204.
[98] Kreeft and Tacelli, 171.
[99] Kreeft and Tacelli, 202-205.

the Holy Spirit, as Sophia.¹⁰⁰ He was followed by the Latin early Church writer Tertullian (160-225 AD), who used the Latin word *trinitas* in reference to the three divine persons.¹⁰¹

Early Christian Art

After the death and resurrection of Jesus Christ, early Christians began to be persecuted in varying ways by Roman officials and emperors. The persecution officially ended in 313 when the Christian friendly Emperor Constantine with his Edict of Milan allowed Christians to publicly practice their faith. Since prior to the 313 Edict of Milan, it was difficult for Christians to publicly express their faith, the Christian art from these times is fairly simplistic. Below are examples early Christian symbolic art.

Alpha and Omega

The first and last letters of the Greek alphabet (α or A) and omega (ω or Ω) were interpreted by early Christians as referring to Christ, the Word of the Father spoken eternally in the love of the Holy Spirit. The Book of Revelation even explicitly identifies Christ as "the Alpha and the Omega, the first and the last, the beginning and the end" (RSV Revelation 22:13).

---

¹⁰⁰ Theophilus of Antioch, "Apologia ad Autolycum Book 2, Chapter 15," http://www.earlychristianwritings.com/text/theophilus-book2.html, Early Christian Writings (accessed March 30, 2015).
¹⁰¹ Tertullian, Adversus Praxean," Chapter 3, http://www.tertullian.org/works/adversus_praxean.htm, Tertullian.org (accessed March 31, 2015).

Alpha and Omega Symbols from a Roman Commodilla catacomb (c. 300s BC)

IH

The initials of the name of Jesus in Greek consists of the letter iota (I) and eta (H). In the following ancient Christian, monogram symbol, these two letters were superimposed over one another.[103]

---

[102] "This image (or other media file) is in the public domain because its copyright has expired. This applies to Australia, the European Union and those countries with a copyright term of life of the author plus 70 years." "The Greek letters alpha and omega surround the halo of Jesus in the catacombs of Rome from the 4th century," mural painting, http://en.wikipedia.org/wiki/Alpha_and_Omega#/media/File:Christ_with_beard.jpg (accessed March 22, 2015).

[103] Larry W. Hurtado, *The Earliest Christian Artifacts: Manuscripts and Christian Origins* (Grand Rapids: Wm. B. Eerdmans Publishing Co., 2006), 137-139.

104

IX

Yet another ancient Christian symbol consisted of the first Greek letter of the name Jesus (iota or I) and the first letter of the name Christ (chi or X).[105]

106

---

[104] Antv, "IH Monogram with iota (I) and eta (H) superimposed one on the other," symbol, http://commons.wikimedia.org/wiki/File%3AIH_Monogram_with_iota_and_eta_superimposed.jpg (accessed March, 23, 2015).

[105] Hurtado, 139.

[106] Wolfgang Menzel, "Symbol aus: Wolfgang Menzel: Christliche Symbolik. G. Joseph Manz, Regensburg 1854, S. 193" symbol, http://commons.wikimedia.org/wiki/File%3AChristliche_Symbolik_(Menzel)_I_193_4.jpg (accessed March 23, 2015).

Staurogram

The Staurogram consists of the Greek letter rho (P) placed upon the Greek letter tau (T). In early Christianity the Staurogram, also called the tau-rho, served as an abbreviation of the two main consonants of the Greek word σταυρός (pronounced stauros) which in English means the cross.[107]

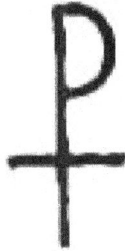

108

109

Chi Rho

The Chi Rho consists of the Greek letter chi (X) placed upon the Greek letter rho (P). This two letter combination served as an

---

[107] Hurtado, 135-136.

[108] Menzel, Ibid.

[109] Nick Thompson, "21.4.2011: burial instruction of Victoria, a virgo dei or consecrated Virgin who died at the age of 28. The chi-rho monogram is united with a tau, representing the cross. Kircherian Museum collection, late 4th cent. AD. Terme di Diocleziano, Museo Nazionale Romano, Rome," funerary art, https://www.flickr.com/photos/pelegrino/6409816167/in/photolist-fJnu5P-oeYSN6-aLpWgB-aLpZ2R-bx5in1-ovPwoT-ouNGUe-eLoC2T-9NerzJ-7ZdCsx-pETCPh (accessed March, 23, 2015).

abbreviation for the first two consonants of the Greek word Χριστός, which in English means Christ.

Cross

One of the earliest symbols was a simple cross. The early Christian Tertullian (c. 160- c. 225 AD) describes Christians as "devotees of the cross." He writes:

> He who calls us devotees of the cross shall be our fellow devotee. In its essence the cross is a wooden symbol. You also worship an image of wood, but for you that wood represents the human form, while for us the wood speaks for itself. Forget about the actual shape as long as the essence is wood; same for the form as long as the wood represents the form of a god. But if a distinction is to be made, what is the difference between a wooden cross on the one hand and a shapeless wooden strip representing Pallas Athena or Pharian Ceres on the other hand? Any piece of wood planted upright in

---

[110] Holly Hayes, "Early Christian symbols - bird and Christogram - excavated from the ancient church and burial ground of St. Lawrence. Basilica di San Lorenzo fuori le Mura (Saint Lawrence outside the Walls), Rome, Italy," early Christian symbol, https://www.flickr.com/photos/sacred_destinations/3381812974/in/photolist-69QFbf-7YcDty-53MvGH-fBhFB6-8CD12B-eaTS69-eaNdAt-eaNeEz-5W4pis-eaTPTE-eaNbMD-34Ydj3-oEu8Fx-7maAqX-4VcDiD-6DWSF9-cb8LYQ-8ZUEPA-nakNUY-or3TWL-2vVkpu-nakMbs-ncoh1K-eaNdXk-4VsEnC-syoDM-ooeKpQ-5GQeYU-aq1pja-9B7sxu-XXKFK-nakW81-53RH6G-aUpF2i-48srZG-569wMG-7viGhS-ncovKM-2t5Sgo-KGZcR-7i6L4j-ooh6uz-bC3bQx-5kETh8-ncovGk-DPaCc-74jqAs-8RiqFh-7i6FPd-bq2fDy (accessed March 23, 2015).

the ground is part of a cross and indeed the larger part of a cross. But we Christians are credited with an entire cross complete with a transverse beam and a projecting seat. You are all the more to be condemned because you present a deformed and roughhewn chunk of wood while others consecrate a full and finished offering.

The fact of the matter is that in the end the fullness of your religion derives from the fullness of a cross, as I shall now show. You are not even aware of the fact that the very origins of your gods derive from the cross, this instrument of torment. Every image, whether it has been shaped from wood or stone, forged from brass or finished from some opulent substance -- its shape was imparted by manual craftsmanship. Those formative hands first shaped the wood in the figure of a cross. This is because the very structure of our body suggests the essential and primal outline of a cross. The head ascends to the peak, the spine stands upright, the shoulders traverse the spine. If you position a man with his arms outstretched, you shall have created the image of a cross.

With this cross as a starting point, the craftsman gradually fills out the limbs by laying on clay. By adding further layers of clay, he fills out the cross within to assume the body and posture of his original intention. Then through the further refinement of precise drawing instruments and body parts cast from lead, the artisan transforms the cross into the likeness of a god fashioned of marble or clay or bronze or silver or whatever material suits his purpose. From the cross to the clay; from the clay to the god. In a manner of speaking, the cross becomes a god through the medium of the clay. You therefore consecrate the cross from which your consecrated god derives its origin. Indeed from the pit of an olive, from the stone of a peach, from the grain of a pepper plant – once placed beneath the soil there emerges a full tree with branches and foliage true in every particular to its species. Now if you transplant it or start a new tree from a cutting, what would be the true origin of this transfer if not the selfsame pit, stone, or grain? The third stage derives from the second and the second derives from the first and so the third stage takes its origin from the first through the intermediary of the second.

There is no further need to deliberate on this matter since the law of nature ordains that every species derives its type from its source. To the extent that the type derives from its origin, to that extent the origin is in accord with the type. If then you worship the cross as the origin of your gods, this will be the primal seed and source from which your wooden images are engendered.

Now for some examples. You revere your victories as gods, and the more grand the occasion, the more joyous the festivities. To heighten the sanctity of the occasion, crosses are the very guts and innards on which to display the trophies you have won in combat. In this way the religion of warfare worships the cross in the ritual of victory. It adores these symbols, it swears vows by these symbols, it holds these symbols in higher regard than Jupiter himself. But this heap of images and this fetish for gold are no more than trinkets on your crosses. The same is true of the banners and flags that your soldiers guard with no less veneration. These are simply petticoats for the crosses. I suppose you are ashamed to worship a plain and unadorned cross.[111]

Fish

Early Christians understood the fish as symbolizing Christianity. According to St. Cyprian (c. 200-258 AD), "It is in the water that we are reborn, in the likeness of Christ our Master, the Fish."[113] Similarly, Tertullian (c. 160-220 AD) stated, "We small fish, like our Fish, Jesus Christ, swim in the [baptismal] water, and we can be saved only by remaining in it."[114] One reason why the

---

[111] Tertullian, "Ad Nationes I Chapter 12," Tertullian.org, http://www.tertullian.org/articles/howe_adnationes1.htm (accessed March 31, 2015).

[112] Holly Hayes, "Lamb of God with cross on the so-called Sarcophagus of Valentinian III in the west (right) niche of the Mausoleum of Galla Placidia. The mausoleum dates from around 430 AD, making it one of the oldest monuments in Ravenna. The tomb in the right arm, traditionally associated with Valentinian III (d.455) but now dated to the beginning of the 6th century, has a front panel carved into three niches. The side niches have fluted columns and an arch enclosing a shell and a cross; the central one has a pointed roof instead of an arch. Inside it are two doves perching on the arms of a tall cross, which stands on a rock from which four rivers flow and on which the Lamb of God stands. The back has a similar design, but was done much more quickly and simply. The lid is carved with a pattern like overlapping fish scales over the top and Greek crosses within medallions on the end., funerary art, https://www.flickr.com/photos/sacred_destinations/3086661855/in/photolist-873vx5-86ZiKx-873vdh-86Zj3k-873wSS-86ZkHP-86Zkra-9dzC5f-9dwyDZ-9dzAWJ-9dzBrb-9dwwv8-9dwxWe-9dzAEG-cui1u-7j4XVm-7YvEQP-6xg177-bBb1gs-5GQeYU-8397bx-qGiLYB-5GKX2R-5YjjKq-9dRyYJ-dyPnXR-5GKXhD-8XZofD-5GKXkx-6jxKHM-5cCfqs-6jNcw4-6jBU3C-6jxPYR-6jC62s-5GKXmP-6LzAt-8XLGet-8XPKzs-8XPKCj-8XPKsJ-8XPKxh-8XLFY4-8XPKN3-5BgyGr-nHkT1p-bQ5CZp-keqjcY-keoHyk-8XLG3D (accessed March 23, 2015).

[113] Quoted by Alva William Steffler in *Symbols of the Christian Faith* (Grand Rapids: Wm. B. Eerdmans Publishing Co., 2002), 9.

[114] Quoted by Alva William Steffler, Ibid.

fish was easily identifiable with Jesus Christ is because each letter of the Greek word for fish (Ichthus) can stand for the phrase, Jesus Christ, of God, the Son Savior. In Greek, this reads *Iesuous Christos Theou Uiou Soter* (Ἰησοῦς Χριστός, Θεοῦ Υἱός, Σωτήρ).[115] The Church Father St. Augustine (354-430 AD) in explaining the meaning of ICTHS writes:

> But if you join the initial letters of these five Greek words, Ἰησοῦς Χριστος Θεοῦ υἱὸς σωτήρ, which mean, "Jesus Christ the Son of God, the Saviour," they will make the word ἰχθὺς, that is, "fish," in which word Christ is mystically understood, because He was able to live, that is, to exist, without sin in the abyss of this mortality as in the depth of waters.[116]

[115] Quoted by Alva William Steffler, Ibid.

[116] Augustine, "The City of God, Chapter 23.—Of the Erythræan Sibyl, Who is Known to Have Sung Many Things About Christ More Plainly Than the Other Sibyls," Christian Classics Ethereal Library, http://www.ccel.org/ccel/schaff/npnf102.iv.XVIII.23.html (accessed March 31, 2015).

[117] David Bjorgen, "An early Christian ichthys symbol carved into some marble in the ruins of Ephesus, Turkey," marble ichthys symbol, http://commons.wikimedia.org/wiki/File%3AEphesus_Ichthys.jpg (accessed March 23, 2015).

Anchor

At times, the symbol of the fish was depicted along with an anchor, understood as representing the security that Christian faith offers to its believers. The New Testament even explicitly associates faith and hope with the image of an anchor. Using images from the sea in explaining realities of faith came naturally to the early Christians who were living close to the Mediterranean Sea.

~ Hebrews 6:19-20[118] ~

We have this hope, a sure and steadfast anchor of the soul, a hope that enters the inner shrine behind the curtain, where Jesus, a forerunner on our behalf, has entered, having become a high priest forever according to the order of Melchizedek.

---

[118] NRSVCE.

[119] Mary Harrsch, "Funerary stele of early Christian woman depicting fish symbols discovered near Vatican necropolis early 3rd century CE. This stele is one of the earliest examples of Christian funerary art discovered in Rome.," stele, https://www.flickr.com/photos/mharrsch/3710305719/in/photolist-nGfMuE-cq4tvo-6rdDVu-pvrmtB-pbFWSo-pegMnH-oEWguL-dxkMvM-6r9umc-

Good Shepherd

The image of Christ as Shepherd also comes directly from the bible. (John 10:1-18, Hebrews 13:20-21; 1 Peter 5:4)

Hebrews 13:20-21 (RSVCE)

> Now may the God of peace, who brought back from the dead our Lord Jesus, the great shepherd of the sheep, by the blood of the eternal covenant, make you complete in everything good so that you may do his will, working among us that which is pleasing in his sight, through Jesus Christ, to whom be the glory forever and ever. Amen

120

6DWSBh-q9y58v-fiu9Xr-d9Exdt-kXU52M-8Juqrt-6DSHRX-pgYtaM-5DEBXF-5DEBP6-9G1bsw-oXpzsz-6FAzdq-7CxKze-6DShCg-714wnT-gcZiJG-nity9z-5KHdyw-4NtfMd-7S8kiu-pvtzss-7nUn2e-i2YGJr-7GNKTM-e3Gwgw-k4UTSr-4c4tbD-atBfMP-dTAY57-pSfymB-6WyQgK-7BBTCT-ebYYuS-cbjDLb-fPTkRe-5ZBtb1-gtGR0y-9830XZ-5Dxobg-6PBtJV (accessed March 23, 2015).

120 Harrsch, Ibid.

Dove

The dove as a symbol for the Holy Spirit also comes directly from Scripture. The Old Testament reference to the dove that flies with an olive branch in its beak to Noah (Gen. 8:11) is fulfilled, Catholics believe, by the New Testament dove, representing the Holy Spirit that hovers over waters of the Jordan River as Jesus is baptized by John the Baptist (Mat. 3:16). The artwork below is from a Roman catacombs (c. 200s-400s AD). Christ is in the center with the dove to his right and a Chi-Rho symbol to his left.

121

Peacock and Phoenix

Another early Christian animal symbol is the peacock. As far back as the Greek philosopher Aristotle, it was believed that peacock flesh does not rot. Since early Christians, including St. Augustine, thought this was the case, they naturally associated peacocks with the Resurrection of Christ in which we have been

---

121 Harrsch, Ibid.

offered to participate.[122] The mythical bird, the phoenix, which according to legend is reborn after death, was also understood by Christians as representing Christ who truly rose from the dead.[123]

124

Pelican

Another bird that was associated with Christ, who saved us with his blood (Romans 5:9), is the pelican. It was thought, as the stain glass below illustrates, that pelicans willingly offer their blood to their hungry offspring.[125]

---

[122] Alva William Steffler, *Symbols of the Christian Faith* (Grand Rapids: Wm. B. Eerdmans Publishing Co., 2002), 60; Cf. Augustine, "City of God, Book 21, Chapter 4," Christian Classics Ethereal Library, h. http://www.newadvent.org/fathers/120121.htm.

[123] Erwin Fahlbusch, *The Encyclopedia of Christianity* (Grand Rapids: Wm. B. Eerdmans Publishing Co., 2008), 263.

[124] Sharon Mollerus, "Peacock Sarcophagus, Basilica of San Vitale, Ravenna," funerary art, https://www.flickr.com/photos/38315261@N00/6094775009/ (accessed March 23, 2015).

[125] Steffler, 30-31.

Early Christian Liturgical Practice

~ St. John Chrysostom ~

There flowed from his side water and blood. Beloved, do not pass over this mystery without thought; it has yet another hidden meaning, which I will explain to you. I said that water and blood symbolized baptism and the holy Eucharist. From these two sacraments the Church is born...[127]

Baptism

As clearly stated in the New Testament, and repeated by the Church Fathers, baptism was and is an essential Christian rite. (Matthew 3:1-11; Acts 2:41; Acts 10:44-48; Romans 6:4-5; Col. 2:12). Early Christians believed baptism to be so essential that even infants, as members of a household, were baptized. (Acts 16:15, Acts 16:33, 1 Cor. 1:16) According to Origin (182-254 AD),

---

[126] mira66, "East window, St Michael, Peasenhall, Suffolk," stain glass https://www.flickr.com/photos/21804434@N02/6154917945/in/photolist-anTyEV-anTyLM-9NvceG-9rAApN-9rxBMt-9rxBWD-9rAAzb-9rxCeV-9Nvdh1-6vmNCh-9Nvc3C-9FEb4M-cLJM45-9Nspdz-9oLSSk-9NvbUh-9NspzD-9rxCaa-9rxC5Z-9yQqQS-9CYZ3X-62p3Pq-73XJY9-0C95t9-73XFJS-73XM1f-73TLvc-73XJqA-73XKrw-73TRb8-73TQzn-9oLSQi-9oM1jk-9EPWDT-anWmxj-9yQqMA-9oMcAk-guC7qG-efDPX3-cjSbBo-9wE2ez-maSZa1-cZHbn0-9NvbBh-9Nx6rB-9UTi6j-9FE6wx-9ESTsq-9NvcwG-9Nsqbx (accessed March 23, 2015).

[127] John Chrysostom "Catechesis 3, 3-19: SC 50, 174-177," in The Liturgy of the Hours, vol II (New York: Catholic Book Publishing Co.,1976), 474.

"To these things can be added the reason why it is required, since the baptism of the Church is given for the forgiveness of sins, that, according to the observance of the Church, that baptism also be given to infants; since, certainly, if there were nothing in infants that ought to pertain to forgiveness and indulgence, then the grace of baptism would appear superfluous."[128]

As Christianity developed in time, the instruction required before baptism, which we call the catechumenate from the Greek *katekhoumenos* meaning one being instructed,[129] was formalized. The length of the catechumenate was not, though, fixed during its earliest forms of development. According to the Council of Elvira (305), catechumens were allowed to be baptized after they had demonstrated "good behavior" for two years."[130] The fourth century Syrian *Apostolic Constitutions*, however, required not two years but three years before someone could receive baptism.[131] Although some, most notably Emperor Constantine, delayed baptism well beyond two years without being required to, this practice was denounced by Church leaders as notable as St. John Chrysostom who, in reference to this practice, said "Is it not, then, utter senselessness to defer accepting the gift: Let the cate-chumens listen to this – those who are putting off to their last breath their own salvation."[132] During medieval times, the catechumenate vanished only to be revived by Vatican II in 1965.

Eucharist

The celebration of the Eucharist as the second sacrament from which "the Church is born"[133] and belief that Jesus is present in

---

[128] Origin, *Homilies on Leviticus*, trans. Gary Wayne Barkley (Washington, D.C.: Catholic University of America Press, 1990), 158.

[129] "Catechesis," Etymology Online, http://etymonline.com/index.php?allowed_in_frame=0&search=catechesis&searchmode=none (accessed April 1, 2015).

[130] William Harmless, *Augustine and the Catechumenate* (Collegeville: Liturgical Press, 2014), 62.

[131] Harmless, Ibid.

[132] Harmless, 68. Harmless cites John Chrysostom, *In s. Johannis evangelium*, Homily 18.1 (PG 59:115); trans. Goggin, FOTC 33:175.

[133] John Chrysostom "Catechesis 3, 3-19: SC 50, 174-177)," in The Liturgy of the Hours, vol II (New York: Catholic Book Publishing Co.,1976), 474.

the Eucharist is traceable to the earliest days of Christianity. In the following Scripture passage, Paul asserts that if someone receives the Eucharist unworthily then they will be answerable for having sinned against the very body and blood of the Lord. This indicates that St. Paul believed that the Eucharist is not simply a symbol of Jesus' presence but rather contains the body and blood of Jesus.

1 Corinthians 11:23-27 (RSVCE)

> For I received from the Lord what I also handed on to you, that the Lord Jesus on the night when he was betrayed took a loaf of bread, and when he had given thanks, he broke it and said, "This is my body that is for you. Do this in remembrance of me." In the same way he took the cup also, after supper, saying, "This cup is the new covenant in my blood. Do this, as often as you drink it, in remembrance of me." For as often as you eat this bread and drink the cup, you proclaim the Lord's death until he comes. Whoever, therefore, eats the bread or drinks the cup of the Lord in an unworthy manner will be answerable for the body and blood of the Lord.

In the chapter that precedes the above quotation, Paul describes Christians as partaking in the body and blood of Christ when they receive the Eucharist.

1 Corinthians 10:14-17 (RSVCE)

> Therefore, my dear friends, flee from the worship of idols. I speak as to sensible people; judge for yourselves what I say. The cup of blessing that we bless, is it not a sharing in the blood of Christ? The bread that we break, is it not a sharing in the body of Christ? Because there is one bread, we who are many are one body, for we all partake of the one bread.

Jesus, as recorded by John, also affirms his Eucharistic presence.

John 6:52-58 (RSVCE)

> Then the Jews began to argue sharply among themselves, "How can this man give us his flesh to eat?" Jesus said to them, "Very truly I tell you, unless you eat the flesh of the Son of Man and drink his blood, you have no life in you. Whoever eats my flesh and drinks my blood has eternal life, and I will raise them up at the last day. For my flesh is real food and my blood is real drink. Whoever eats my flesh and drinks my blood remains in me, and I in them. Just as the living Father sent me and I live because of the Father, so the one who feeds on me will live because of me. This is the bread that came down from heaven. Your ancestors ate manna and died, but whoever feeds on this bread will live forever."

In conformity with the above scripture passages, Christ's presence in the Eucharist throughout early Christian writing is repeatedly affirmed.

St. Ignatius of Antioch
Letter to the Smyrnaeans (c. 110 AD)

> Take note of those who hold heterodox opinions on the grace of Jesus Christ which has come to us, and see how contrary their opinions are to the mind of God ... They abstain from the Eucharist and from prayer because they do not confess that the Eucharist is the flesh of our Savior Jesus Christ, flesh which suffered for our sins and which that Father, in his goodness, raised up again. They who deny the gift of God are perishing in their

disputes.[134]

St. Ignatius of Antioch
Letter to the Romans (AD 110)

> The prince of this world would fain carry me away,
> and corrupt my disposition towards God. Let none
> of you, therefore, who are [in Rome] help him;
> rather be on my side, that is, on the side of God. Do
> not speak of Jesus Christ, and yet set your desires
> on the world. Let not envy find a dwelling-place
> among you; nor even should I, when present with
> you, exhort you to it, be persuaded to listen to me,
> but rather give credit to those things which I now
> write to you. For though I am alive while I write to
> you, yet I am eager to die. My love has been
> crucified, and there is no fire in me desiring to be
> fed; but there is within me a water that lives and
> speaks, saying to me inwardly, Come to the Father.
> I have no delight in corruptible food, nor in the
> pleasures of this life. I desire the bread of God, the
> heavenly bread, the bread of life, which is the flesh
> of Jesus Christ, the Son of God, who became
> afterwards of the seed of David and Abraham; and I
> desire the drink of God, namely His blood, which is
> incorruptible love and eternal life.[135]

Catholics not only believe that the risen Christ is present
(body, blood, soul, and divinity) in the Eucharistic body, but we

---

[134] Ignatius of Antioch, *Letter to the Letter to the Smyrnaeans* 6:2–7:1. Alexander Roberts, James Donaldson, and A. Cleveland Coxe, *Ante-Nicene Fathers*, vol. 1, ed. Alexander Roberts, James Donaldson, and A. Cleveland Coxe (Buffalo, NY: Christian Literature Publishing Co., 1885) Revised and edited for New Advent by Kevin Knight. http://www.newadvent.org/fathers/0109.htm.

[135] Ignatius of Antioch, *Letter to the Romans*, Chapter 7. Alexander Roberts, James Donaldson, and A. Cleveland Coxe, *Ante-Nicene Fathers*, vol. 1, ed. Alexander Roberts, James Donaldson, and A. Cleveland Coxe (Buffalo, NY: Christian Literature Publishing Co., 1885) Revised and edited for New Advent by Kevin Knight. http://www.newadvent.org/fathers/0107.htm.

also maintain that during each mass the sacrifice of Christ on the cross is mysteriously re-presented in the mass. In explaining this mystery, the Second Vatican Council states, "He did this in order to perpetuate the sacrifice of the Cross throughout the centuries until He should come again, and so to entrust to His beloved spouse, the Church, a memorial of His death and resurrection: a sacrament of love, a sign of unity, a bond of charity, a paschal banquet in which Christ is eaten, the mind is filled with grace, and a pledge of future glory is given to us."[136]

This belief is also a further development and fulfillment, according to the Catholic faith, of the Jewish concept of time when the Passover meal is annually celebrated. At the time of Jesus, the celebrating of the Passover was understood not simply as a sacrificial meal in which the Jewish people remember the important event of the Exodus, but it was also understood as re-living the Exodus events by making present the liberation that their ancestors had experienced after they were freed from Egyptian captivity. According to the Mishnah:

> In each generation a man is obligated to regard himself as if he came forth out of Egypt, as it is written 'And you shall tell your son on that day, saying, 'It is because of that which the Lord did for me when I came forth out of Egypt' (Exodus 13:8). Therefore we are obligated to thank, to praise, to laud, to glorify, to exalt, to adorn, to bless, to elevate, and to honor Him. Who did all these miracles for our fathers and for us; He brought us forth from slavery to freedom, from grief to joy, from mourning to Festival, from darkness to a great light, and from servitude to redemption.[137]

---

[136] Vatican Council II, *Sacrosantum Concilium*, December 4, 1963, art. 47, The Vatican, http://www.vatican.va/archive/hist_councils/ii_vatican_council/documents/vat-ii_const_19631204_sacrosanctum-concilium_en.html (accessed January 2, 2015).

[137] Mishnah, Pesahim 10:5 http://www.emishnah.com/PDFs/Pesahim%2010.pdf; cf Brant Pitre, *Jesus and the Jewish Roots of the Eucharist* (New York: Doubleday, 2011), 64-65. According to traditional Jewish belief,

A modern day Hagadah, the liturgy for the Passover meal also known as the Seder, similarly states:

> In every generation, each person should feel as though she or he were redeemed from Egypt, as it is said: "You shall tell your children on that day saying, "It is because of what the Lord did for me when I went free out of Egypt.' For the Holy One redeemed not only our ancestors; He redeemed us with them.[138]

Early Christian Ecclesial Structure and Understanding

In the early Church, with few exceptions, Christians were baptized into the Catholic Church. Not until after the 1054 schism between Eastern Christianity and Western Christianity and after the Protestant Reformation of the 1500s were people baptized into a wide variety of churches and ecclesial communities. Before these divisions, being Catholic was understood as the reality that intrinsically identifies a Christian. To appreciate the meaning of being Catholic, we will first briefly define the term. Then, we will see how this term is reflected in the hierarchical nature of the Catholic Church.

Catholic

The Apostolic Father, St. Ignatius of Antioch (c. 35-117 AD), was the first to use this term. In his *Letter to the Smyrnaeans* he writes:

> See that ye all follow the bishop, even as Jesus Christ does the Father, and the presbytery as ye

---

Moses was given both a written law on Mt. Sinai and an oral law. The oral law was later written down in the Mishnah (220 AD). Eventually, two important commentaries were written on the Mishnah, the Jerusalem/Palestinian Talmud (c. 400 AD) and Babylonian Talmud (c. 500s AD). The section in the Talmuds that contains commentary on the Mishnah is called the Gemara.

[138] Michael Strassfeld, *Jewish Holidays* (Harper Collins Publishers), loc. 154.

would the apostles; and reverence the deacons, as being the institution of God. Let no man do anything connected with the Church without the bishop. Let that be deemed a proper Eucharist, which is [administered] either by the bishop, or by one to whom he has entrusted it. Wherever the bishop shall appear, there let the multitude [of the people] also be; even as, wherever Jesus Christ is, there is the Catholic Church. It is not lawful without the bishop either to baptize or to celebrate a love-feast; but whatsoever he shall approve of, that is also pleasing to God, so that everything that is done may be secure and valid.[139]

St. Ignatius of Antioch's use of Catholicism, as repeatedly affirmed by the best of Catholic theologians, indicates, explains Ratzinger, that "to be a Christian means to be a Catholic, means to be on one's way to an all-embracing unity."[140] The first region where Christianity rapidly embraced others into the one fold of the

---

[139] Ignatius of Antioch, "Ignatius to the Smyrnaeans," Robert-Donaldson English Translation, Chapter 8, Early Christian Writings, http://www.earlychristianwritings.com/text/ignatius-smyrnaeans-roberts.html (accessed April 2, 2015).

[140] Joseph Ratzinger, *Principles of Catholic Theology*, trans. Sister Mary Frances McCarthy (San Francisco: Ignatius Press, 1987), 49. The context of the quotation is as follows, "What is being expressed here is, first of all, a collective view of Christianity to replace the individual or purely institutional manner of thinking. It was in this framework that Henri de Lubac's designation of the church as a sacrament made its appearance in the 1930s... The concept of a Christianity concerned only with *my* soul, in which I seek only *my* justification before God, *my* saving grace, *my* entrance into heaven, is for de Lubac that caricature of Christianity that, in the nineteenth and twentieth centuries, made possible the rise of atheism. The concept of sacraments as a means of the grace that I received like a supernatural medicine in order, as it were, to ensure only my private eternal health is *the* supreme misunderstanding of what the sacrament truly is. De Lubac, for his part, is convinced that Christianity is, by its very nature, a mystery of union. The essence of original sin is the split into individuality, which knows only itself. The essence of redemption is the mending of the shattered image of God, the union of the human race through and in the One who stands for all and in whom, as Paul says (Gal 3:28), all are one: Jesus Christ. On this premise, the word *Catholic* became for de Lubac the main theme of all his theological speculation: to be a Christian means to be a Catholic, means to be on one's way to an all-embracing unity."

Church was in Asia Minor, mainly in the country we now call Turkey. This explains why the seven major Churches referred to by John in the book of Revelation are all in the Roman province of Asia.[141]

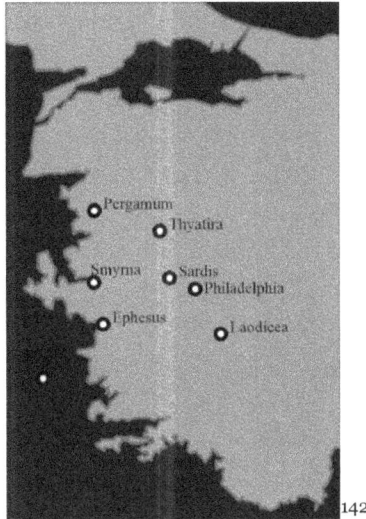

142

Apostolic

When St. Ignatius of Antioch uses the term Catholicism, meaning in Greek pertaining to the whole, he was writing on the role of bishops. As successors of the Apostles, bishops have been entrusted with the sacred mission of guarding the universal nature of the Church. As the Apostolic Father, Pope St. Clement of Rome (reigned 90-100 AD) states, "Christ therefore was sent forth by God, and the apostles by Christ. Both these appointments, then, were made in an orderly way, according to the will of God."[143] For

---

[141] Peter V. Armenio, *The History of the Church: A Complete Course* (Woodridge: Midwest Theological Forum, 2011), 69; Revelation 1:11.

[142] en:User:Jonadab, "Map of *Western Anatolia* showing the "Seven Churches of Asia" and the Greek island of Patmos," map, http://commons.wikimedia.org/wiki/File%3ASeven_churches_of_asia.svg (accessed April 2, 2015).

[143] Clement of Rome, "Letter of Clement to the Corinthians," Robert-Donaldson English Translation, Chapter 42, Early Christian Writings,

this reason, St. Ignatius insists,

> Moreover, it is in accordance with reason that we
> should return to soberness [of conduct], and, while
> yet we have opportunity, exercise repentance
> towards God. It is well to reverence both God and
> the bishop. He who honors the bishop has been
> honored by God; he who does anything without the
> knowledge of the bishop, does [in reality] serve the
> devil. Let all things, then, abound to you through
> grace, for ye are worthy. Ye have refreshed me in all
> things, and Jesus Christ [shall refresh] you. Ye have
> loved me when absent as well as when present. May
> God recompense you, for whose sake, while ye
> endure all things, ye shall attain unto Him.[144]

Papacy

One bishop that St. Ignatius of Antioch and other early
Christian Fathers, in accordance with Matthew 16:13-20, affirm as
having primacy is the bishop of Rome. In his *Epistle to the
Romans,* St. Ignatius of Antioch clearly affirms the primacy of the
bishop of Rome:

> Ignatius, who is also called Theophorus, to the
> Church which has obtained mercy, through the
> majesty of the Most High Father, and Jesus Christ,
> His only-begotten Son; the Church which is beloved
> and enlightened by the will of Him that willeth all
> things which are according to the love of Jesus
> Christ our God, which also presides in the place of
> the report of the Romans, worthy of God, worthy of

---

http://www.earlychristianwritings.com/text/1clement-roberts.html   (accessed
April 4, 2015).

[144] Ignatius of Antioch, "Ignatius to the Smyrnaeans," Robert-Donaldson
English Translation, Chapter 9, Early Christian Writings, http://www.
earlychristianwritings.com/text/ignatius-smyrnaeans-roberts.html   (accessed
April 2, 2015).

honor, worthy of the highest happiness, worthy of praise, worthy of obtaining her every desire, worthy of being deemed holy, and which presides over love, is named from Christ, and from the Father, which I also salute in the name of Jesus Christ, the Son of the Father: to those who are united, both according to the flesh and spirit, to every one of His commandments; who are filled inseparably with the grace of God, and are purified from every strange taint, [I wish] abundance of happiness unblameably, in Jesus Christ our God.[145]

By intervening in the affairs of the non-Roman diocese of Corinth Pope St. Clement (reigned c. 90-100 AD) in his letter to the Corinthians indicates that his primacy is not to be understood simply as one of honor but also one that entails a special, God-given authority that allows the Bishop of Rome to settle disputes in other dioceses to maintain the Catholic nature of the Church.[146] Benedict XVI reminds us that primacy of jurisdiction, which St. Clement and all popes have by virtue of their office, is based on the deeper primacy of the Eucharist. The Pope's primacy of jurisdiction, therefore, is an expression of Eucharist, intended by Christ to unite Christians and not divide Christians.[147]

Quiz 4

1. Complete the following verse of St. Paul (1 Corinthians 15:14) "if Christ has not been raised..."

---

[145] Ignatius of Antioch, "Ignatius to the Romans," Robert-Donaldson English Translation, Prologue, Early Christian Writings, http://www.earlychristianwritings.com/text/ignatius-romans-roberts.html (accessed April 2, 2015).

[146] Clement of Rome, "Letter of Clement to the Corinthians," Robert-Donaldson English Translation, Early Christian Writings, http://www.earlychristianwritings.com/text/1clement-roberts.html (accessed April 4, 2015); cf. Patrick Madrid, *Pope Fiction* (Dallas: Basilica Press, 1999), 120.

[147] This is a theme within in Benedict XVI thought. Armin Schwibach, "Keeping Alive the 'Magnificent Theology' of Benedict XVI," *Inside the Vatican*, August-September (2016): 39.

2. In a paragraph, defend the resurrection of Christ as reasonable to believe from an historical standpoint. In doing so, respond to one of the following objections. A. Jesus did not die on the cross he only swooned. B. The disciples of Jesus lied about the Resurrection. C. The disciples hallucinated about the resurrection. D. The disciples invented a resurrection myth that was believed as an historical fact.

3. Name the Greek theologian who was first to use the Greek word for Trinity when referring to the three divine persons.

4. Name the Latin theologian who was first to use the Latin word for Trinity when referring to the three divine persons.

5-7. Based on Chapter 4 draw and explain three ancient Christian symbols.

5.

6.

7.

8. Explain the early Church's catechumenate.

9-11. In a paragraph with reference to Scripture, an early Church Father, and the Jewish Passover explain the early Church belief in the Eucharist.

12. Name the early Church Father who first used the term Catholic when referring to Christians.

Chapter 5

Early Christian Persecution

Introduction

In this chapter, we will study how the early Christians distinguished themselves from non-Christians. Then, we will examine the various ways Christians were persecuted during the first three centuries before the 313 AD Edict of Milan was issued by the pro-Christian emperor, Constantine. Finally, we will speculate on why Christians were persecuted.

Christian Difference

Christians distinguished themselves from non-Christians religiously, by their sense of Christian dignity, and by their respect for the sacredness of life.

Religious Difference

In his doctoral dissertation, *Volk und Haus Gottes in Augustins Lehre von der Kirche*, Ratzinger, relying on St. Augustine, distinguishes between the early Christian view on religion from the Roman. He explains that according to the Roman scholar Marcus Terentius Varro (116-27 BC), who lived shortly before the birth of Christ, the Roman city gives birth to its gods for the practical reason of effecting unity in the city of Rome and, through Rome, the entire empire whose people have been offered Roman citizenship. In a certain sense, therefore, the city of Rome was the Church through which Roman citizens throughout the Roman Empire were offered an earthly type unity, peace, and salvation.

In contrast, as explained by St. Augustine, true salvation is not offered through any earthly city but rather through the Kingdom of God in its present but not yet state on earth as the Catholic Church. God relates to the motherhood of the Church and to all types of earthly motherhoods of cities and nations as a father who precedes their existences. Faith in God, therefore, and not simply patriotic sentiments for one's city or nation, ought to be the ultimate standard that determine the love, unity, peace and order within in a city.[148]

Varro further associates the Roman city as the Church of its religion by dividing theology into three types: mythical, civil, and natural. For him, Roman mythical theology, with its personal Gods, is created by poets who are at the service of the city. Civil religion consists of the worship of these Gods by the people of Rome. Natural theology is the theology proper to philosophers. Only the god of philosophy, the god of nature, argues Varro, actually exists. This god, according to Varro, is not personal but rather an internal driving force of the world in the form of something as elementary as fire, numbers, or atoms.[149]

Augustine, as interpreted by Ratzinger, profoundly differs from Varro's Roman theology. He does so by asserting that the God of the Catholic people, which correlates with Varro's civic religion, is the same God of natural theology and truly exists. This personal, triune God is not, consequently, a creation of poets who are working at the service of a city.[150]

---

[148] Joseph Ratzinger, *Volk und Haus Gottes in Augustins Lehre von der Kirche* (Sankt Ottilien: Eos Verlag, 1992), 266. „....die Kirche ihrer Religion, und ihr populus ist ein cultor populus." Cf. *De civ Dei* II 25, 2 Sp 74; III 1 Sp 79; II 29 Sp 77 f.

[149] Ratzinger, *Volk und Haus Gottes*, 267-271; Cf *De civ Dei* VI 5 Sp 180-182.

[150] Ratzinger, *Volk und Haus Gottes,* 272. Cf. *De civ Dei* VI 5, 2 Sp 181; 4, 2 Sp 180.

Varro's Theological Categories	Christian Theology	Varro's Roman Theology
Mythical Theology (created by Poets)	Fictional	Fictional
Civil Theology (religion of the common people)	Personal Triune God Who is Existence	Fictional
Natural Theology (religion of the philosopher)	Personal Triune God who is known through the effects of His creation.	Actual but in an impersonal manner.

Christian Dignity

The Christmas Day, Catholic Church's Roman Office of Readings comes from the early Church Father Pope St. Leo the Great (reigned 440-461 AD). In this reading, St. Leo reminds Christians of their dignity given to them by baptism:

> Christian, remember your dignity, and now that you share in God's own nature, do not return by sin to your former base condition. Bear in mind who is your head and of whose body you are a member. Do not forget that you have been rescued from the power of darkness and brought into the light of God's kingdom.

> Through the sacrament of baptism you have become a temple of the Holy Spirit. Do not drive away so great a guest by evil conduct and become again a slave to the devil, for your liberty was bought by the blood of Christ.[151]

---

[151] Pope St. Leo the Great, "Sermo 1 in Nativitate Domini, 1-3: PL 54, 190-193" in The Liturgy of the Hours, Vol. I (New York: Catholic Book Publishing Co., 1975), 405.

The Christian Understanding of Life as Sacred

The *Didache* (in Greek Διδαχή means teaching) is referred to in English as *The Teaching of the Twelve Apostles* after its heading, "The Lord's Teaching through the Twelve Apostles to the Nations."[152] It is dated to the late first or early 2nd century AD. It could even be dated as early as 40 to 60 AD, for as John A.T. Robinson argues, "there is little or nothing of the signs of persecution or 'falling away', so characteristic of the 60s."[153] The treatise contrasts the Christian way of life with paganism that is referred to as a "way of death." According to Christianity from its earliest days, all life, including the life of enemies, is sacred and merits respect:

> Chapter 1. The Two Ways[154] and the First Commandment. There are two ways, one of life and one of death, but a great difference between the two ways. The way of life, then, is this: First, you shall love God who made you; second, love your neighbor as yourself, and do not do to another what you would not want done to you. And of these sayings the teaching is this: Bless those who curse you, and pray for your enemies, and fast for those who persecute you. For what reward is there for loving those who love you? Do not the Gentiles do the same? But love those who hate you, and you

---

[152] "Didache," Roberts-Donaldson English Translation, Early Christian Writings, http://www.earlychristianwritings.com/text/didache-roberts.html (accessed April 7, 2015).

[153] John A.T. Robinson, *Redating the New Testament* (Eugene: Wipf and Stock Publishers, 1976), 327.

[154] See the following scripture passages. Genesis 2:16-17 "The Lord God gave man this order: 'You are free to eat from any of the trees of the garden except the tree of knowledge of good and bad. From that tree you shall not eat: the moment you eat from it you are surely doomed to die.'" (NAB) Deuteronomy 30:15, 19-20 "Here, then, I have today set before you life and prosperity, death and doom. ... I call heaven and earth today to witness against you: I have set before you life and death, the blessing and the curse. Choose life, then, that you and your descendants may live, by loving the Lord, your God, heeding his voice, and holding fast to him. ..."

shall not have an enemy. Abstain from fleshly and worldly lusts. If someone strikes your right cheek, turn to him the other also, and you shall be perfect. If someone impresses you for one mile, go with him two. If someone takes your cloak, give him also your coat. If someone takes from you what is yours, ask it not back, for indeed you are not able. Give to everyone who asks you, and ask it not back; for the Father wills that to all should be given of our own blessings (free gifts). Happy is he who gives according to the commandment, for he is guiltless. Woe to him who receives; for if one receives who has need, he is guiltless; but he who receives not having need shall pay the penalty, why he received and for what. And coming into confinement, he shall be examined concerning the things which he has done, and he shall not escape from there until he pays back the last penny. And also concerning this, it has been said, Let your alms sweat in your hands, until you know to whom you should give.

Chapter 5. The Way of Death. And the way of death is this: First of all it is evil and accursed: murders, adultery, lust, fornication, thefts, idolatries, magic arts, witchcrafts, rape, false witness, hypocrisy, double-heartedness, deceit, haughtiness, depravity, self-will, greediness, filthy talking, jealousy, over-confidence, loftiness, boastfulness; persecutors of the good, hating truth, loving a lie, not knowing a reward for righteousness, not cleaving to good nor to righteous judgment, watching not for that which is good, but for that which is evil; from whom meekness and endurance are far, loving vanities, pursuing revenge, not pitying a poor man, not laboring for the afflicted, not knowing Him Who made them, murderers of children, destroyers of the handiwork of God, turning away from him who

81

is in want, afflicting him who is distressed, advocates of the rich, lawless judges of the poor, utter sinners. Be delivered, children, from all these.[155]

The Christian assertion that human life is sacred contrasts with the Roman pagan view. This is even more clearly delineated in the second century *Epistle of Mathetes to Diognetus* (c. AD 130). As you read the text below, reflect on the following questions. Is there similar hatred directed towards Catholics today? If so, does the epistle shed light on the reason for this animosity? How did the early Christians, as described by Mathetes, react to this persecution? Did they react by assimilating the culture, by rejecting the culture, by attempting to transform the culture, or, perhaps, in all three ways?

CHAPTER V -- THE MANNERS OF THE CHRISTIANS.

For the Christians are distinguished from other men neither by country, nor language, nor the customs which they observe. For they neither inhabit cities of their own, nor employ a peculiar form of speech, nor lead a life which is marked out by any singularity. The course of conduct which they follow has not been devised by any speculation or deliberation of inquisitive men; nor do they, like some, proclaim themselves the advocates of any merely human doctrines. But, inhabiting Greek as well as barbarian cities, according as the lot of each of them has determined, and following the customs of the natives in respect to clothing, food, and the rest of their ordinary conduct, they display to us their wonderful and confessedly striking method of life. They dwell in their own countries, but simply as sojourners. As citizens, they share in all things with others, and yet endure all things as if foreigners. Every foreign land is to them as their

---

[155] "Didache," Roberts-Donaldson English Translation, Early Christian Writings, http://www.earlychristianwritings.com/text/didache-roberts.html (accessed April 7, 2015).

native country, and every land of their birth as a land of strangers. They marry, as do all [others]; they beget children; but they do not destroy their offspring. They have a common table, but not a common bed. They are in the flesh, but they do not live after the flesh. They pass their days on earth, but they are citizens of heaven. They obey the prescribed laws, and at the same time surpass the laws by their lives. They love all men, and are persecuted by all. They are unknown and condemned; they are put to death, and restored to life. They are poor, yet make many rich; they are in lack of all things, and yet abound in all; they are dishonoured, and yet in their very dishonour are glorified. They are evil spoken of, and yet are justified; they are reviled, and bless; they are insulted, and repay the insult with honour; they do good, yet are punished as evil-doers. When punished, they rejoice as if quickened into life; they are assailed by the Jews as foreigners, and are persecuted by the Greeks; yet those who hate them are unable to assign any reason for their hatred.

CHAPTER VI -- THE RELATION OF CHRISTIANS TO THE WORLD.

To sum up all in one word--what the soul is in the body, that are Christians in the world. The soul is dispersed through all the members of the body, and Christians are scattered through all the cities of the world. The soul dwells in the body, yet is not of the body; and Christians dwell in the world, yet are not of the world. The invisible soul is guarded by the visible body, and Christians are known indeed to be in the world, but their godliness remains invisible. The flesh hates the soul, and wars against it, though itself suffering no injury, because it is prevented from enjoying pleasures; the world also hates the Christians, though in nowise injured, because they abjure pleasures. The soul loves the flesh that hates it, and [loves also] the members; Christians like- wise love those that hate them. The soul is imprisoned in the body, yet preserves that very body; and Christians are confined in the world as in a prison, and yet they are the preservers of the world. The immortal soul dwells in a mortal tabernacle; and Christians dwell as sojourners in corruptible [bodies], looking for an incorruptible dwelling in the heavens. The soul, when but ill-provided with food and drink, becomes better; in like manner, the Christians, though subjected day by day to punishment, increase the more in number. God has assigned them this illustrious position, which it were unlawful for them to forsake.[156]

The early Church Father St. Basil the Great (330-379 AD) in his *First Canonical Letter* carefully explains the Christian teaching on the sacredness of human life. In the letter, he touches upon a number of issues including killing in self-defense, killing during war, and abortion. Below are a few excerpts:

VIII. The man who in a rage has taken up a hatchet against his own wife is a murderer. ... A case of an act purely unintentional, and widely removed from the purpose of the agent, is that of a man who throws a stone at a dog or a tree, and hits a man. The object was to drive off the beast or to shake down the fruit. The chance comer falls fortuitously in the way of the blow, and the act is unintentional. Unintentional too is the act of any one who strikes another with a strap or a flexible stick, for the purpose of chastising him, and the man who is being beaten dies. In this case it must be taken into consideration that the object was not to kill, but to improve, the offender. Further, among unintentional acts must be reckoned the case of a man in a fight who when warding off an enemy's attack with cudgel or hand, hits him without mercy in some vital part, so as to injure him, though not quite to

---

[156] "The Epistle of Mathetes to Diognetus," Roberts-Donaldson English Translation, Early Christian Writings, http://www.earlychristianwritings.com/text/diognetus-roberts.html (accessed April 7, 2015).

kill him. This, however, comes very near to the intentional; for the man who employs such a weapon in self-defense, or who strikes without mercy, evidently does not spare his opponent, because he is mastered by passion....

....Women also who administer drugs to cause abortion, as well as those who take poisons to destroy unborn children, are murderesses.

XIII. Homicide in war is not reckoned by our Fathers as homicide; I presume from their wish to make concession to men fighting on behalf of chastity and true religion. Perhaps, however, it is well to counsel that those whose hands are not clean only abstain from communion for three years.[157]

Christian Persecutions

In fulfillment of Christ's prophecy that "they will deliver you up to tribulation, and put you to death; and you will be hated by all nations for my name's sake" (Matthew 24: 9 RSVCE), followers of Christ were persecuted from the beginning of Christianity. The first to persecute the early Christians were some Jewish people. This very light form of persecution was followed a succession of Roman persecutions.

Jewish

Prior to his conversion, the zealous, Jewish Pharisee, St. Paul sought out Christians to imprison and even to kill them. One notable example is Paul's public approval of Stephen's stoning (Acts 7-8). Shortly after Stephen was martyred, the first apostles were martyred, and James, the son of Zebedee, was murdered by Herod

[157] Basil the Great, "Letter 188, Canonica Prima," New Advent, http://www.newadvent.org/fathers/3202188.htm (accessed April 7, 2015).

Agrippa I.[158] (Acts 12: 1-2) When Herod died, he was replaced by Roman procurators. These procurators did not actively persecute Christians. After the death of the Roman procurator Festus, though, Christians were once again persecuted by their Jewish brethren. According to the Jewish historian Flavius Josephus (37-100 AD), the High Priest and Sadducee, Ananus, led this brief period of anti-Christian hostility. Ananus had James the Just stoned to death along with a number of other Christians on the charges of having broken Jewish law.[159]

Roman

The toleration of Christians ended during the reign of Emperor Nero (reigned 54-68 AD). Under his reign, as stated by Tertullian, Peter and Paul were both martyred in Rome:

~ Tertullian (160-220 AD)
On the Prescription of Heretics ~

[If] thou art near to Italy, thou hast Rome, where we too have an authority close at hand. What a happy Church is that whereon the Apostles poured out their whole doctrine together with their blood; where Peter suffers a passion like his Lord's, where Paul is crowned with the death of John, whence John the Apostle, after being immersed in boiling oil and taking no hurt, is banished to an island.[160]

---

[158] John Williams Charles Wand, *A History of the Early Church to AD 500* (London: Routledge, 1996), 8. Also known as Herod the Great, or Herod I. He had three sons: Archelaus, who inherited Judea, Herod Antipas, who inherited Galilee and Peraea, and Philip, who inherited additional territory.

[159] Flavius Josephus, "Antiquities of the Jews," Book XX, Chapter 9, trans. William Whiston, Christian Classics Ethereal Library, http://www.ccel.org/j/josephus/works/ant-20.htm (accessed April 8, 2015).

[160] Tertullian, "De Praescriptione Haereticorum," Chapter 36, trans. Bindley, 1914, Tertullian Project, http://www.tertullian.org/articles/bindley_test/bindley_test_07prae.htm (accessed April 9, 2015).

~ Tertullian *Scorpiace* ~

And yet, that the apostles endured such sufferings, we know: the teaching is clear. This only I perceive in running through the Acts. I am not at all on the search. The prisons there, and the bonds, and the scourges, and the big stones, and the swords, and the onsets by the Jews, and the assemblies of the heathen, and the indictments by tribunes, and the hearing of causes by kings, and the judgment-seats of proconsuls and the name of Caesar, do not need an interpreter. That Peter is struck, that Stephen is overwhelmed by stones, that James is slain as a victim at the altar, that Paul is beheaded has been written in their own blood. And if a heretic wishes his confidence to rest upon a public record, the archives of the empire will speak, as would the stones of Jerusalem. We read the lives of the Caesars: At Rome Nero was the first who stained with blood the rising faith. Then is Peter girt by another, when he is made fast to the cross. Then does Paul obtain a birth suited to Roman citizenship, when in Rome he springs to life again ennobled by martyrdom.[161]

According to the early Roman historian Suetonius (c. 70-130 AD), Nero was responsible for setting the city of Rome on fire. Another early Roman historian and contemporary of Suetonius, Tacitus (c. 56-117 AD), asserts that after Nero blamed the 64 AD Great Fire of Rome on the Christians he then tortured and killed them with a vengeance. Nero was also reputed to have murdered his mother and falsely accused his wife Octavia of adultery. He then beheaded Octavia and gave her head to his mistress

---

[161] Tertullian, "Scorpiace," Chapter XV, Trans. Thelwall, 1870, Tertullian Project, http://www.tertullian.org/anf/anf03/anf03-45.htm (accessed April 9, 2015).

Poppaea.[162] Finally, Nero killed himself.[163]

~ Suetonius on Nero ~

But he showed no greater mercy to the people or the walls of his capital. When someone in a general conversation said: "When I am dead, be earth consumed by fire," he rejoined "Nay, rather while I live," and his action was wholly in accord. For under cover of displeasure at the ugliness of the old buildings and the narrow, crooked streets, he set fire to the city so openly that several ex-consuls did not venture to lay hands on his chamberlains although they caught them on their estates with tow and fire-brands, while some granaries near the Golden House, whose room he particularly desired, were demolished by engines of war and then set on fire, because their walls were of stone. For six days and seven nights destruction raged, while the people were driven for shelter to monuments and tombs. At that time, besides an immense number of dwellings, the houses of leaders of old were burned, still adorned with trophies of victory, and the temples of the gods vowed and dedicated by the kings and later in the Punic and Gallic wars, and whatever else interesting and noteworthy had survived from antiquity. Viewing the conflagration from the tower of Maecenas and exulting, as he said, in "the beauty of the flames," he sang the whole of the "Sack of Ilium," in his regular stage costume. Furthermore, to gain from this calamity too all the spoil and booty possible, while promising the removal of the debris and dead bodies free of

[162]Julian Morgan, *Nero: Destroyer of Rome* (New York: Rosen Publishing Group, 2003), 25, 40.

[163] Seutonius, "Lives of the 12 Caesars: Nero," 49, Loeb Classical Library, 1914, University of Chicago.edu, http://penelope.uchicago.edu/Thayer/E/Roman/Texts/Suetonius/12Caesars/Nero*.html#38 (accessed April 9, 2015).

cost he allowed no one to approach the ruins of his own property; and from the contributions which he not only received, but even demanded, he nearly bankrupted the provinces and exhausted the resources of individuals.[164]

~ Tacitus on Nero ~

But all human efforts, all the lavish gifts of the emperor, and the propitiations of the gods, did not banish the sinister belief that the conflagration was the result of an order. Consequently, to get rid of the report, Nero fastened the guilt and inflicted the most exquisite tortures on a class hated for their abominations, called Christians by the populace. *Christus*, from whom the name had its origin, suffered the extreme penalty during the reign of Tiberius at the hands of one of our procurators, Pontius Pilatus, and a most mischievous superstition, thus checked for the moment, again broke out not only in Judaea, the first source of the evil, but even in Rome, where all things hideous and shameful from every part of the world find their center and become popular. Accordingly, an arrest was first made of all who pleaded guilty; then, upon their information, an immense multitude was convicted, not so much of the crime of firing the city, as of hatred against mankind. Mockery of every sort was added to their deaths. Covered with the skins of beasts, they were torn by dogs and perished, or were nailed to crosses, or were doomed to the flames and burnt, to serve as a nightly illumination, when daylight had expired. Nero offered his gardens for the spectacle, and was

---

[164] Suetonius, "Lives of the 12 Caesars: Nero," 38, Loeb Classical Library, 1914, University of Chicago.edu, http://penelope.uchicago.edu/Thayer/E/Roman/Texts/Suetonius/12Caesars/Nero*.html#38 (accessed April 9, 2015).

exhibiting a show in the circus, while he mingled with the people in the dress of a charioteer or stood aloft on a car. Hence, even for criminals who deserved extreme and exemplary punishment, there arose a feeling of compassion; for it was not, as it seemed, for the public good, but to glut one man's cruelty, that they were being destroyed.[165]

Another Roman Emperor who persecuted Christians was Trajan (reigned 98-117 AD). Unlike Nero, Trajan did not kill Christians out of mere pleasure or anger. Rather, he did so for reasons of Roman security. In response to a letter sent to him by Pliny the Younger, Trajan decreed that those who admitted to professing Christianity, and in so doing refused to worship the Roman Emperor who was held to be divine, were to be executed. However, those who denied they had ever believed in Christianity were not to be punished nor were those who were anonymously accused of being Christians. In addition, Christians who chose to deny their faith were to be pardoned and released.[166]

Emperor Decius (reigned 249-251 AD) also believed that the Christian refusal to sacrifice to the Roman Gods and give homage to the Roman Emperor threatened the unity of the empire. In his mind, Christians were gravely disloyal. For this reason, in 250 AD, he issued an edict that required every inhabitant of the Roman Empire to demonstrate loyalty to the emperor and to the Roman gods. Upon compliance, the inhabitants were issued an official certificate. When this edict was implemented, Christianity began to be persecuted in a different way than in the recent past. Previously, Christians were persecuted only in a sporadic and unsystematic manner. During this first empire-wide persecution, some Christians remained steadfast in the faith while others

---

[165] Tacitus, "*Annals,*" 15:44, trans. Alfred John Church and William Jackson Brodribb, Sacred Texts, http://www.sacred-texts.com/cla/tac/a15040.htm (accessed April 9, 2015).

[166] Julian Bennett, *Trajan: Optimus Princeps* (London: Routledge, 1997), 126.

lapsed.[167]

An emperor who shortly followed Decius also continued to harass Christians. In 258 AD, Emperor Valerian (reign 253-259 AD), in a letter to the Roman Senate, ordered all Christian clergy to be punished. Non-clergy, including Roman nobles, were to lose their titles and their property. If even after being punished Christians refused to renounce their faith, they were then to be executed.[168]

In agreement with Valerian, Emperor Diocletian (reigned 284-305) also held that Christianity and the Roman Empire were so incompatible that, in the words of the scholar W.H.C Frend, they "could not survive together."[169] Under Diocletian rule, Christians once again were subject to an empire wide persecution. Soon, as we will cover in the following chapter, Christian persecution ended under the Christian-friendly emperor, Constantine (reigned 306-337 AD).

Below is an excerpt from the famous account of the early Christian martyrs Perpetua and Felicity. At the time of their martyrdom, Perpetua was a 22-year-old married noble woman who was nursing a child, and Felicity, Perpetua's slave, was pregnant.

~ Martyrdom of Perpetua and Felicity ~

Perpetua and Felicitas were exposed to a mad heifer. Perpetua was tossed first and fell on her back, but raised herself and gathered her torn tunic modestly about her; then, after fastening up her hair, lest she look as if she were in mourning, she rose and went to help Felicitas, who had been badly

---

[167] J. Patout Burns, "Cyprian's Eschatology: Explaining Divine Purpose," in *The Early Church in Its Context: Essays in Honor of Everett Ferguson*, ed. Everett Ferguson, Abraham Johannes Malherbe, Frederick W. Norris, and James W. Thompson (Leiden: Brill, 1998), 60-65; David S. Potter, *The Roman Empire at Bay, AD 180–395* (New York: Routledge, 2014), 237.

[168] W.H.C Frend, *The Rise of Christianity* (Philadelphia: Fortress Press, 1984), 326.

[169] Frend, 327.

hurt by the animal. Side by side they stood, expecting another assault, but the sated audience cried out that it was enough. They were therefore led to the gate Sanevivaria, where victims who had not been killed in the arena were dispatched by gladiators. Here Perpetua seemed to arouse herself from an ecstasy and could not believe that she had already been exposed to a mad heifer until she saw the marks of her injuries. She then called out to her brother and to the catechumen: "Stand fast in the faith, and love one another. Do not let our sufferings be a stumbling block to you." By this time the fickle populace was clamoring for the women to come back into the open. This they did willingly, and after giving each other the kiss of peace, they were killed by the gladiators. Perpetua had to guide the sword of the nervous executioner to her throat.[170]

Christians as the Scapegoat

Sometimes persecution of Christians did not originate from the Roman emperors but rather from the people themselves. Why? One explanation, both in the Old Testament and New Testament, is that holy people, even just by the witness of their lives, prick the conscience of many. This leads some to respond by trying to eliminate the bothersome witness to love shaped by truth.[171] When

---

[170] "The Passion of St. Perpetua, St. Felicitas, and their Companions," EWTN, http://www.ewtn.com/library/MARY/PERPETUA.htm (accessed June, 4, 2014).

[171] Wisdom 2:12, "Let us lie in wait for the righteous man, because he is inconvenient to us and opposes our actions; he reproaches us for sins against the law, and accuses us of sins against our training. [13] He professes to have knowledge of God, and calls himself a child of the Lord. [14] He became to us a reproof of our thoughts; [15] the very sight of him is a burden to us, because his manner of life is unlike that of others, and his ways are strange. [16] We are considered by him as something base, and he avoids our ways as unclean; he calls the last end of the righteous happy, and boasts that God is his father. [17] Let us see if his words are true, and let us test what will happen at the end of his life; [18] for if the righteous man is God's child, he will help him, and will deliver him from the hand of his adversaries. [19] Let us test him with insult and torture, so that we may

we remember that the Church is Christ's body extended through time, we will realize that the reason Christ suffered persecutions and temptations is also, in part, the reason why his Mystical Body the Church faces persecutions and temptations.

As explained by Abbot Vonier, sometimes the Holy Spirit sends the Church as the Mystical Body of Christ into a desert, representing times of persecution, to purify Her. He writes,

> It is indeed a positive relief to one's mind to be able to have this faith in the divinely appointed mission of temptation. It sets one free from the incubus of a false historical presentment of the long life of the Catholic Church. The countless difficulties that have beset her course are not of necessity the result of her shortcomings; a most perfect Church may be carried hither and thither by evil agencies, as the spotless body of Christ was taken through the air, His soul, of course, remaining untouched by the hands of the tempter. No true reading of Christianity is possible except in the light of the theology of temptation. But once that light is thrown on the apparently checkered career of Catholicism, as a beam from a lighthouse, what a difference of meaning and outline appears![172]

A more psychological, and also biblically-based explanation, is found in the practice called scapegoating. Romans scapegoated Christians by accusing them of being atheists, of sexual immorality, and of sacrificing babies and drinking their blood.[173] The renowned French scholar Rene Girard has an interesting take on

---

find out how gentle he is, and make trial of his forbearance. [20] Let us condemn him to a shameful death, for, according to what he says, he will be protected." (NRSV)

[172] Abbot Vonier, *Christianus: The Christian Life* (Bethesda: Zaccheus Press, 1933), loc. 1033.

[173] Andrew McGowan, "Eating People: Accusations of Cannibalism Against the Christians of the Second Century," *Journal of Early Christian Studies* 2:3 (1994): 413-442.

the reason why scapegoating like this occurs. According to Girard, because of *mimesis* (desiring what another has), rivalry occurs within societies. If rivalry causes a society to fragment scapegoating is often triggered. The scapegoating helps to re-unite the society and restore peace. Bishop Robert Barron incisively captures Girard's thought by explaining:

> The cultural anthropologist and philosopher Rene Girard helps us to understand the pervasiveness of this practice in the ancient world as well as the presence of it, in mitigated forms, today. When tensions arise within a society, Girard argues, a scapegoating mechanism is triggered. Following this largely unconscious impulse, we find someone or some group to blame and then, together, we discharge our anxiety onto him or them. In doing so, we feel, however fleetingly, a rush of relief and a sense of common purpose. This is why we tend to feel that the gods are pleased with the scapegoating move. Human sacrifice is the extreme expression of this mechanism, and that is why it was so widely practiced, especially in societies that felt most acutely threatened by enemies or by capricious elements of nature. The great pyramids of Teotihuacan outside of Mexico City are archi-tectural masterpieces, but they were also the setting for thousands upon thousands of human sacrifices offered to the bloodthirsty gods of the Aztecs. As I have suggested, Girard feels that to one degree or another all human groups – from the coffee klatch, to the faculty lounge, to the nation state – tend to organize themselves around scapegoating, blaming, and recrimination.[174]

For short excerpts from Girard on his scapegoat theory see

---

[174] Robert Barron, *Catholicism*, 112.

below. In the excerpts, Girard identifies the term scapegoat in Leviticus and then demonstrates how scapegoating was practiced, is practiced, and why.

> The biblical and Christian power of understanding phenomena of victimization comes to light in the modern meaning of certain expressions such as "scapegoat." A "scapegoat" is initially the victim in the Israelite ritual that was celebrated during a great ceremony of atonement (Lev. 16:21)[175]. This ritual must be very ancient, for it is visibly quite alien to the specifically biblical inspiration as defined in chapters 9 and 10.

> The ritual consisted of driving into the wilderness a goat on which all the sins of Israel had been laid. The high priest placed his hands on the head of the goat, and this act was supposed to transfer onto the animal everything likely to poison relations between members of the community. The effectiveness of the ritual was the idea that the sins were expelled with the goat and then the community was rid of them.

---

[175] In Judaism the holiest day of their year is the Day of Atonement, Yom Kippur. The scapegoat ritual was performed during this celebration. During this ritual one goat was sacrificed on the altar and the other was sent out to die. "15 "Then he shall kill the goat of the sin offering which is for the people, and bring its blood within the veil, and do with its blood as he did with the blood of the bull, sprinkling it upon the mercy seat and before the mercy seat; 16 thus he shall make atonement for the holy place, because of the uncleannesses of the people of Israel, and because of their transgressions, all their sins; and so he shall do for the tent of meeting, which abides with them in the midst of their uncleannesses. ... 20 "And when he has made an end of atoning for the holy place and the tent of meeting and the altar, he shall present the live goat; 21 and Aaron shall lay both his hands upon the head of the live goat, and confess over him all the iniquities of the people of Israel, and all their transgressions, all their sins; and he shall put them upon the head of the goat, and send him away into the wilderness by the hand of a man who is in readiness. 22 The goat shall bear all their iniquities upon him to a solitary land; and he shall let the goat go in the wilderness." (Leviticus 16: 15-16, 20-22 NRSV)

This ritual of expulsion is similar to that of the *pharmakos* in Greece, but it is much less sinister because the victim is never a human being. When an animal is chosen, the injustice seems less, or even nonexistent.

...

"But never," you will tell me, "does the New Testament resort to the term 'scapegoat' to designate Jesus as the innocent victim of an escalation of mimetic contagion." You are right, no doubt, but it does use an expression equal and even superior to "scapegoat," and this is *lamb of God*. It eliminates the negative attributes and unsympathetic connotations of the goat. Thereby it better corresponds to the idea of an innocent victim sacrificed unjustly.

Jesus applies another expression to himself that is extremely revealing. It is drawn from Psalm 118: "The stone the builders rejected has become the cornerstone." This verse tells not only of the expulsion of the single victim but of the later reversal that turns the expelled victim into the keystone of the entire community.

In a world where violence is no longer subject to ritual and is the object of strict prohibitions, anger and resentment cannot or dare not, as a rule, satisfy their appetites on whatever object directly arouses them. The kick the employee doesn't dare give his boss, he will give his dog when he returns home in the evening. Or maybe he will mistreat his wife and his children, without fully realizing that he is treating them as "scapegoats." Victims substituted for the real target are the equivalent of sacrificial victims in distant times. In talking about this kind of phenomenon, we spontaneously utilize the expression "scapegoat."

The real source of victim substitutions is the appetite for violence that awakens in people when anger seizes them and when the true object of their anger is untouchable. The range of objects capable of satisfying the appetite for violence enlarges proportionally to the intensity of the anger.

The effectiveness of sacrificial substitutions is increased when many individual scandals come together against one and the same victim. Scapegoat phenomena, therefore, continue to play a definite role in our world at the level of individuals and communities....

Because of Jewish and Christian influence scapegoat phenomena no longer occur in our time except in a shameful, furtive, and clandestine manner. We haven't given up having scapegoats, but our belief in them is 90 percent spoiled. The phenomenon appears so morally base to us, so reprehensible, that when we catch ourselves "letting off steam" against someone innocent, we are ashamed of ourselves.

It is easier than in the past to observe collective transferences upon a scapegoat because they are no longer sanctioned and concealed by religion. And yet it is still difficult because the individuals addicted to them do everything they can to conceal their scapegoating from themselves, and as a general rule they succeed. Today as in the past, to have a scapegoat is to believe one doesn't have any. The phenomenon in question doesn't usually lead any longer to acts of physical violence, but it does lead to a "psychological" violence that is easy to camouflage. Those who are accused of participating in hostile transference never fail to protest their good faith, in all sincerity.

When human groups divide and become fragmented, during a period of malaise and conflicts, they may come to a point where they are reconciled again at the expense of a victim. Observers nowadays realize without difficulty, unless they belong to the persecuting group, that this victim is not really responsible for what he or she is accused of doing. The accusing group, however, views the victim as guilty, by virtue of a contagion similar to what we find in scapegoat rituals. The members of this group accuse their "scapegoat" with great fervor and sincerity. More often than not some incident, whether fantastic or trivial, has triggered a wave of opinion against this victim, a mild version of mimetic snowballing and the victim mechanism.

...

The spectacle of secret substitutions, and slipping from one victim to another in a world without ritual permits us to see, in pure form we could say, the functioning of the relational (*interdividual*) mechanisms that underlie the ritual organization of the primitive human world. These mechanisms continue in our world usually as only a trace, but occasionally they can also reappear in forms more virulent than ever and on an enormous scale. An example is Hitler's systematic destruction of European Jews, and we see this also in all the other genocides and near genocides that occurred in the twentieth century. I will say more about this later [ch. 14].

...

Scapegoating phenomena cannot survive in many

instances except by becoming more subtle, by resorting to more and more complex casuistry in order to elude the self-criticism that follows scapegoaters like their shadow. Otherwise, we could no longer resort to some wretched goat to rid ourselves of our resentments. We now have need of procedures less comically evident.

...

Thus the expression "scapegoat" designates (1) the victim of the ritual described in Leviticus, (2) all the victims of similar rituals that exist in archaic societies and that are called rituals of expulsion, and finally (3) all the phenomena of nonritualized collective transference that we observe or believe we observe around us. ... My own view is that the modern uses of the term are a sign that the Jewish and Christian revelation is becoming continually more effective and so is far from being a dead letter in our society.[176]

Quiz 5

1. What is another name for the ancient Christian document (40-60 AD) named the *Didache*?

2. 3. What two ways does the *Didache* describe?

 2.

 3.

4.-6. Name and describe three distinct ways by which Christians

---

[176] René Girard, *I See Satan Fall Like Lightning,* trans. James G. Williams (Maryknoll: Orbis Press, 2001), 154-160.

distinguished themselves from pagan Romans. Include in your answer a section where you compare and contrast Varro's early Roman theology with St. Augustine's early Christian theology.

4.

5.

6.

7. Who was the Roman emperor who in 64 AD blamed Christians for setting Rome on fire?

9-10. According to ancient Roman historian Seutonius in his *Lives of the 12 Caesars* who actually set Rome on fire and why?

9.

10.

11. In a paragraph, describe the martyrdom of Perpetua and Felicity.

12. In a paragraph, discuss Rene Girard's scapegoat theory as a possible explanation for Roman persecutions directed against early Christians.

Chapter 6

Catholic Orthodoxy and Heresy

Introduction

With his 313 AD Edict of Milan, Emperor Constantine brought an end to Christian persecution. This edict, though, did not bring an end to the struggle and suffering that Christianity faced and will continue to face. Jesus warned his followers of this suffering they would undergo. "[Y]ou will be hated by all because of my name. But the one who endures to the end will be saved" (Matthew 10:22 NRSVCE). The form the suffering took was in heresies that threatened the purity of the Catholic faith. This was even evident in the life of Emperor Constantine who chose to be baptized by an Arian bishop. In this chapter, consequently, we will study the tail end of the Roman persecution of Christianity before moving on to examine the various early heresies that the Church fought against.

The End of Roman Persecution

In agreement with Emperor Valerian, Emperor Diocletian (reigned 284-305) also held that Christianity and the Roman Empire were so incompatible that, in the words of the scholar W.H.C. Frend, as stated in the previous chapter, they "could not survive together."[177] In an effort to eradicate Christianity, Diocletian directed an empire wide persecution of Christianity. Although his gift as an efficient administrator posed a great threat to Christianity as it was systematically persecuted, a key person of the administrative system he established would bring an end to Christian persecution. This person was Constantine, who will be discussed later on in this chapter.

In 293 AD, after he had already divided his empire into a *Dyarchy* (rule by two), Diocletian divided the Roman Empire four ways in a system called the *Tetrarchy* (rule by four).[178] Each of the four administrative districts and its provinces were further divided into dioceses, which is where the Roman Catholic term diocese originated. The eastern district was ruled both by a major emperor called the *Augustus* and a minor emperor called the *Caesar*. Similarly, the western district was governed by a major emperor and a minor emperor. Diocletian was the first Eastern Augustus with Galerius as the first Eastern Caesar. In the western district, Maximian was the Western Augustus with Constantius as the western Caesar.[179] Besides the adoption of the term diocese by the west when distinguishing the territory of one bishop from another, the Catholic Church was also influenced by the division of the Roman Empire into two distinct regions. In time, two quite distinct forms of Christianity developed, one centralized around the Eastern portion of the empire and the other centralized around the western.

We return to Diocletian. On May 1, 305 AD, both Diocletian and Maximian abdicated. This meant that Constantius and Galerius effectively became the major emperors (*Augusti*), or at least according to a certain way of interpreting historical documents of this confusing time.[180] As explained by the historian Roger Rees, the coins from 310 AD indicate that all four of the

---

[177] W.H.C Frend, *The Rise of Christianity* (Philadelphia: Fortress Press, 1984), 327.

[178] Many historians maintain that Diocletian promoted Maximian the second Augustus of a *Dyarchy* in 287 AD. 6.

[179] Roger Rees, *Diocletian and the Tetrarchy* (Edinburgh: Edinburgh University Press, 2004), 3-7.

[180] Rees, 8.

leaders (Constantius, Galerius, Severus – died and were replaced by Licinius, and Maxentius) considered themselves major *Augusti* and not minor Caesars. In 307, Constantius died. His son Constantine eventually succeeded him as emperor, but before solidifying his rule he had to contend with Maxentius, the son of Maximian. In the East, Galerius (reigned 305-311 AD) continued Diocletian's empire wide persecution of Christians until 311 AD when he issued an edict of toleration that allowed Christians to freely practice their religion as long they obeyed Roman law and prayed for the empire:[181]

~ Edict of Toleration by Galerius (311 AD) ~

(Ch. 34.) Among other arrangements which we are always accustomed to make for the prosperity and welfare of the republic, we had desired formerly to bring all things into harmony with the ancient laws and public order of the Romans, and to provide that even the Christians who had left the religion of their fathers should come back to reason ; since, indeed, the Christians themselves, for some reason, had followed such a caprice and had fallen into such a folly that they would not obey the institutes of antiquity, which perchance their own ancestors had first established; but at their own will and pleasure, they would thus make laws unto themselves which they should observe and would collect various peoples in diverse places in congregations. Finally when our law had been promulgated to the effect that they should conform to the institutes of antiquity, many were subdued by the fear of danger, many even suffered death. And yet since most of them persevered in their determination, and we saw that they neither paid the reverence and awe due to the gods nor

---

worshipped the God of the Christians, in view of our most mild clemency and the constant habit by which we are accustomed to grant indulgence to all, we thought that we ought to grant our most prompt indulgence also to these, so that they may again be Christians and may hold their conventicles, provided they do nothing contrary to good order. But we shall tell the magistrates in another letter what they ought to do. Wherefore, for this our indulgence, they ought to pray to their God for our safety, for that of the republic, and for their own, that the republic may continue uninjured on every side, and that they may be able to live securely in their homes. (c.35)This edict is published at Nicomedia on the day before the Kalends of May, in our eighth consulship and the second of Maximinus.[182]

Eastern Augustus	Eastern Caesar	Western Augustus	Western Caesar
Diocletian (293-305)	Galerius (293-305)	Maximian (286-305)	Constantius (293-305)
Galerius (305-d.311)	Maximinus II (305-308)	Constantius (305-d.306) Maximian's son Maxentius is passed over.	
Maximinus II (311-312)			Constantine (306-312)
Licinius (313-324)			

[182] "Galerius and Constantine: Edicts of Toleration 311/313," from Lactantius, *De Mort. Pers.* ch. 34, 35. Opera, ed. O. F. Fritzsche, II, P. 273. (Bibl. Patt. Ecc. Lat. XI, Leipzig, 1844), Fordham University Sourcebook, http://www.fordham.edu/halsall/source/edict-milan.asp (accessed April 13, 2015).

According to the above chart, who was in control of the Roman Empire in 311? This question is a bit complicated to answer since Maxentius, although son of Maximus, had been passed over when his father died. In his place, Constantius was named the Western Augustus. This caused Maxentius to foster resentment towards Constantius and Constantius's son, Constantine. Maxentius was, consequently naturally drawn to ally himself with Licinius, and the two of them fought against Constantine. In 312, Constantine defeated Maxentius, and in 324 Constantine finally defeated Licinius. By defeating Licinius in 324, Constantine was able to become the sole emperor of both the Eastern and Western halves of the Roman Empire.[183]

Since Constantine's 312 victory over Maxentius is frequently referred to in Christian circles, its details merit further attention. On October 28th, 312, Constantine fought Maxentius in a conflict called the Battle at the Milvian Bridge. The Milvian Bridge crosses over the Tiber River of Northern Rome. According to the early church historian Eusebius of Caesarea (c. 260 – 340 AD), prior to the battle and near the Milvian bridge Constantine had a vision in which God promised Constantine victory if his soldiers wore the Chi-Rho symbol on their shields.[184]

~ Eusebius on Constantine's Vision ~

Chapter XXVIII.—How, while he was praying, God sent him a Vision of a Cross of Light in the Heavens at Mid-day, with an Inscription admonishing him to conquer by that.

Accordingly he called on him with earnest prayer

---

[183] Rees, 11, 83-85; Julian Morgan, *Constantine: Ruler of Christian Rome* (New York: Rosen Publishing Group, 2003), 43-44.

[184] Eusebius of Caesarea, *Church History: On the Life of Constantine*, Philip Schaff, *Nicene and Post-Nicene Fathers: Volume I, Eusibius Pamphilius, Church History, Life of Constantine, Oration in Praise of Constantine* (Grand Rapids: Eerdmans Publishing Company, 1890), Chapter 28, Christian Classics Ethereal Library, http://www.ccel.org/ccel/schaff/ npnf201.iv.vi.i.xxviii.html (accessed April 13, 2015); Roger Rees, *Diocletian and the Tetrarchy* (Edinburgh: Edinburgh University Press, 2004), 11.

and supplications that he would reveal to him who he was, and stretch forth his right hand to help him in his present difficulties. And while he was thus praying with fervent entreaty, a most marvelous sign appeared to him from heaven, the account of which it might have been hard to believe had it been related by any other person. But since the victorious emperor himself long afterwards declared it to the writer of this history, when he was honored with his acquaintance and society, and confirmed his statement by an oath, who could hesitate to accredit the relation, especially since the testimony of after-time has established its truth? He said that about noon, when the day was already beginning to decline, he saw with his own eyes the trophy of a cross of light in the heavens, above the sun, and bearing the inscription, Conquer by this. At this sight he himself was struck with amazement, and his whole army also, which followed him on this expedition, and witnessed the miracle.[185]

Within a relatively short time after Constantine emerged victorious in his battle with Maxentius he, along with Emperor Licinius, issued the 313 AD Edict of Milan by which Christians were granted permission to freely practice their religion and which mandated that property of Christians be restored to them.[186] Even though on this issue Constantine and Licinius were in agreement, they still fought each other. In 324 AD, as previously stated, Constantine emerged victorious and then consolidated the entire Roman Empire under his single rule as emperor. A little over a decade later, Constantine, near death, requested in 337 AD to be baptized. As recorded by Eusebius, Constantine chose the Arian

---

[185] Eusebius of Caesarea, *Church History: On the Life of Constantine*, Philip Schaff, *Nicene and Post-Nicene Fathers: Volume I, Eusibius Pamphilius, Church History, Life of Constantine, Oration in Praise of Constantine*, Ibid.

[186] "Galerius and Constantine: Edicts of Toleration 311/313," from Lactantius, *De Mort. Pers.*, Ibid.

Bishop Eusebius of Nicomedia to baptize him.[187]

Shortly after Emperor Constantine died, his son Constantius II murdered the families of Emperor Constantine's half-brothers in order to remove rivals to the imperial throne to which he ascended and remained as emperor to 361 AD. Constantius II spared, though, a five-year-old or so boy named Flavius Claudius Julianus, or Julian for short.[188] This boy who had experienced his family murdered would himself, upon Constantius II's death in 361 AD, become the Roman Emperor (reigned 361-363 AD). As emperor, Julian attempted to reverse the pro-Christian policy established by Constantine that, very likely, he associated with his family's murderers. To achieve this end, he re-opened pagan temples and reclaimed land and money that were awarded to the Church in accordance with the Edict of Milan. Believing that "no wild beasts are as dangerous to man as the Christians are to each other,"[189] he permitted Arians to resume their teaching. In a further attempt to reduce Christian influence, he also did not allow teachers of rhetoric and grammar to be Christian. Finally, he attempted to surpass the Christian reputation of charity for the poor and needy. Out of competition, he established hostels for travelers and for the poor and provided food for the needy. Fortunately, his efforts were not successful and he was the last emperor of Rome who was a non-Christian. It is reputed he died by crying out, "Thou has conquered, O Galilean."[190]

Early Heresies

Before covering the Arian heresy that Emperor Constantine on his death bed had joined, we will examine several earlier heresies

---

[187] John Chapman, "Eusebius of Nicomedia," *The Catholic Encyclopedia*, Vol. 5 (New York: Robert Appleton Company, 1909), New Advent, http://www.newadvent.org/cathen/05623b.htm (accessed April 13, 2015); R. Joseph Hoffmann, *Julian's Against the Galileans* (Amherst: Prometheus Books, 2004), 12-35.

[188] Hoffmann, 12-17.

[189] Hoffmann, 31-32.

[190] Karl Hoeber, "Julian the Apostate," The Catholic Encyclopedia. Vol. 8. New York: Robert Appleton Company, 1910, http://www.newadvent.org/cathen/08558b.htm (accessed April 14, 2015); 31-35.

with which Christianity contended. We will begin with Gnosticism.

Gnosticism

Even though there were many different expressions of Gnosticism, there were a few common traits of the various Gnostic schools that early Christian writers identified.[191] The first one was that the physical world is a by-product of quasi divine beings that emanated from God. In other words, matter is a degradation of God who is spirit, the one source out of which all else emanates.

For human beings to be saved, therefore, they need to become less material and more spiritual. This process of spiritualization and salvation occurs by rejecting the material world. In contrast with Catholicism, which holds that we are saved through the material world, Gnostics held that human beings can only be saved from the material world by rejecting it. Another key difference between Catholicism and Gnosticism is on the role of the savior. According to Catholicism, the Savior is God who took on human nature in the person of Jesus. In contrast, maintained the Gnostics, human beings are saved not directly by God but rather through an imperfect intermediary being who stands somewhere between God and the degradation of spirit which is matter.

In some forms of Gnosticism, Jesus is considered the savior. He is defined, however, not as equal to God but as a semi-divine intermediary being. His role is to save human beings by giving secret knowledge which the Greek term *gnosis* indicates. Gnostics, consequently, identified their salvation with knowing. In contrast, Catholicism identifies salvation with knowing and loving. Catholicism believes that human beings are not saved by secret knowledge but rather by God's grace and his truth that we are to cooperate with in faith, hope, and charity. Another similar differ-

---

[191] Karen L. King lists these as "Justin Martyr, Irenaeus of Lyons, Clement of Alexandria, Origen of Alexandria, Tertullian of Carthage, Hippolytus of Rome, and Epiphanius of Salamis, all of whom lived in the Roman Empire during the first four centuries C.E. [A.D.] and wrote polemical treatises against other Christians." Karen L. King, *What is Gnosticism?* (Cambridge: Harvard University Press, 2003), 20.

ence between Catholicism and Gnosticism is as follows.[192] Gnostics believed one is condemned for not knowing secret knowledge, often contained in magical formulas.[193]

Catholicism, in contrast, believes that sin and not simply ignorance condemns a person as James reminds us, "You believe that God is one; you do well. Even the demons believe—and shudder" (James 2:19 NRSVCE). It is possible that St. Paul in his first letter to Timothy warned Christians of Gnostic errors by writing, "Timothy, guard what has been entrusted to you. Avoid the profane chatter and contradictions of what is falsely called knowledge (*gneoseos* - γνώσεως in Greek); by professing it some have missed the mark as regards the faith." (1 Timothy 6:20-21) As explained by the scripture scholar William Most, "We cannot be sure what kind of false teachers he may have in mind. They are more likely Jewish speculators than Gnostics."[194]

In 1945, knowledge of Gnostic doctrine greatly increased when 12 complete codices and one incomplete codex of Gnostic texts were found buried near the Egyptian town, Nag Hammadi. These texts are currently located in the Egyptian Cairo, Coptic Museum. The documents belonged to an ancient Gnostic community that lived during the 5th century AD.[195]

Docetism

According to Docetism, from the Greek word *dokeîn* meaning to seem, Jesus only appeared to be human but actually was not. Possibly, the verse "the Word became flesh and lived among us,"[196] of the Gospel of John was directed against this heresy. Later, St. Ignatius of Antioch explicitly rejected Docetism.[197] Along with

---

[192] King, 23-40..

[193] Carl Schmidt, and Violet MacDermot, *The Books of Jeu and the Untitled Text in the Bruce Codex*, Volume 13 (Leiden: E.J. Brill, 1978), 33-38.

[194] William Most, *The Thought of St. Paul: A Commentary on the Pauline Epistles* (Front Royal: Christendom Press, 1994), 274.

[195] James McConkey Robinson, and Richard Smith, *The Nag Hammadi Library in English* (Leiden: E.J. Brill, 1996), 1-26.

[196] John 1:14 (NRSVCE)

[197] Joseph Francis Kelly, *History and Heresy: How Historical Forces Can Create Doctrinal Conflicts* (Collegeville: Liturgical Press, 2012), 23-24.

Arianism, Docetism was condemned at the Council of Nicaea in 325 AD.

Marcionism

Marcion of Sinope (c. 85–160 AD) is the founder of Marcionism. According to St. Irenaeus of Lyons (c. 130-202 AD) in his *Adversus Haereses,* Marcion erred by completely rejecting the Old Testament. He did so because he mistakenly believed that the God described in the Old Testament is a condemning, angry God who is lower than and was superseded by the New Testament's all merciful Good God.[198] In *Adversus Haereses,* Irenaeus also strongly rejects Gnosticism.

Montanism

Montanism is named after its founder Montanus (c. 135 - ?), who was aided by two women "prophets," Priscilla and Maximilla. Montanus rejected Church authority and in its place proposed that the inspiration of the Holy Spirit through prophets like Priscilla and Maximilla is all that is needed for Church order and harmony.[199]

Manichaeism

Manichaeism was founded by the Persian Mani (c. 216-274 AD). Manicheans held that all of reality is dyadic that is comprised of two principles, a light, spiritual, good principle and a dark, material, evil principle. For the world to be redeemed, the good spiritual principle that is intertwined with evil matter needs to be released from its imprisonment.[200]

---

[198] Translated by Alexander Roberts and William Rambaut from Ante-Nicene Fathers, Vol. 1. Edited by Alexander Roberts, James Donaldson, and A. Cleveland Coxe. (Buffalo, NY: Christian Literature Publishing Co., 1885.) Revised and edited for New Advent by Kevin Knight. http://www.newadvent.org/fathers/0103127.htm (accessed April 17, 2015).

[199] Kelly, *History and Heresy,* 29-32.

[200] Nicholas J. Baker-Brian *Manichaeism: An Ancient Faith Rediscovered* (New York: T&T Clark International, 2011), 2, 110-111.

Arianism

Arianism was founded by Arius (c. 250-336 AD), a priest from Alexandria, Egypt. Arius believed that although Christ is divine he is not fully equal to God the Father. He argued that his position is supported by John chapter fourteen, verse twenty-eight where Jesus states, "You heard me say, 'I am going away and I am coming back to you.' If you loved me, you would be glad that I am going to the Father, for the Father is greater than I." (NRSVCE) Catholics believe that in this phrase, Jesus was referring specifically to his human nature united to his divine nature in the one divine person. One effective way by which Arius spread his teaching was through hymns for which he wrote the texts.[201]

Arius and his anti-Trinitarian teaching was condemned at the Council of Nicaea (325 AD). The council consisted of around 250 bishops who gathered with the purpose of carefully defining Catholic doctrine. Emperor Constantine, who believed that Christian unity was important to the security of his empire, not only called the council together but was also present for at least its opening. Documentation of the council indicates that not once did those present debate on whether Jesus was divine. Instead, they discussed to what extent Jesus was divine in relationship to the Father. The decision reached by the council was that Jesus Christ is "the Son of God, the only-begotten from the Father that is from the substance of the Father."[202]

The Council of Nicaea in which Arianism was condemned was the first ecumenical council. To understand the importance of this council it is necessary to know what the term ecumenical means. The term ecumenical comes from the Greek *oikoumenikos* meaning from the whole world.[203] Since a diocesan council does not pertain to the whole Catholic world, but only to a region overseen by a bishop, it is not called an ecumenical council. In

---

[201] Kelly, *History and Heresy,* 54-56.

[202] Norman P. Tanner, *Decrees of the Ecumenical Councils*, Volume I (District of Columbia: Georgetown University Press, 1990), 5.

[203] "Ecumenical," Online Etymology Dictionary, http://etymonline.com/index.php?allowed_in_frame=0&search=ecumenical&searchmode=none (accessed April 17, 2015).

contrasting how the first ecumenical councils were called with how modern-day ecumenical councils come about, Joseph Kelly writes, "Today only a pope can call an ecumenical council. However, no pope called the first 8 councils. Roman or Byzantine emperors called seven of them. The Byzantine empress, Irene, called the Second Council of Nicaea in 787 AD. The second ecumenical council, Constantinople I, was called together in 381 AD, met, decided the issues, and adjourned without informing Pope Damascus I (366-84) that a council had being held."[204]

Donatism

The Donatist heresy developed during the 300s AD. It was a rigorist response to Christians who failed to keep the faith during the Diocletian persecutions. At the time of St. Augustine (354-430 AD), the Donatists held that the holiness of the Church requires that its members be holy, above all its ministers. The Donatists then concluded that since this is the case if a sacrament, such as baptism, is administered by a former traitor to the Catholic faith the sacrament is invalid and must be performed by a minister who had not betrayed the Catholic faith during times of persecution. The Church Father St. Augustine (354-430 AD) countered the Donatists by arguing that sacraments are valid from the sacramental action having been performed not because of the holiness of the minister.[205]

Pelagianism

Pelagianism is named after its founder Pelagius (c. 300s- c 400s). As presented by St. Augustine, Pelagius held that a human

---

[204] Joseph Francis Kelly *The Ecumenical Councils of the Catholic Church a History* (Collegeville: Liturgical Press, 2009), 5.

[205] Maureen A. Tilley, *The Bible in Christian North Africa: The Donatist World* (Minneapolis: Augsburg Fortress, 1997), 11, 29, 98, 103, 157, 161. Maureen A. Tilley in investigating Donatism used five criteria in order to discern which sources are more reliable than others: Multiple attestation, congruency, extrapolation (not a first-hand account), dissimilarity (Donatist sources that are dissimilar to the presentation of their views in polemicists writing), strength (length and intensity in rejecting a Donatist teaching). 4-6.

being can successfully and sufficiently imitate Christ's virtue without needing to rely on grace. The Catholic position is that to imitate Christ, as St. Paul encourages us with "Be imitators of me, as I am of Christ,"[206] we need to rely on grace.[207] We cannot rely upon our efforts alone to experience salvation, which entails participation in the life of Christ (2 Peter 1:4).

Apollinarism

Apollinarism is also named after a heretic, Apollinaris of Laodicea (d. 390 AD). Apollinaris believed that after the incarnation the second person of the Trinity did take on a human body but only had one mind, a divine mind, and not a human mind.[208] This heresy was officially condemned in 381 AD at the First Council of Constantinople. As the council states, "we preserve undistorted the accounts of the Lord's taking of humanity, accepting as we do that the economy of his flesh was not soulless nor mindless nor imperfect. To sum up, we know that he was before the ages fully God the word, and that in the last days he became fully man for the sake of our salvation."[209]

Nestorianism

Nestorius, the Patriarch of Constantinople (386-450 AD), is considered the founder of Nestorianism. Nestorius erred by distinguishing Jesus' human nature from his divine nature while not uniting them sufficiently in one person. St. Cyril of Alexandria opposed Nestorian teaching by emphasizing the unity of Jesus' human and divine nature in the one divine person (*hypostasis*).[210] Nestorianism was condemned at the Council of Ephesus in 431 AD and in the Council of Chalcedon in 451 AD which asserted that

---

[206] 1 Corinthians 11:1 NRSVCE
[207] Brinley Roderick Rees, *Pelagius: Life and Letters* (Woodbridge: The Boydell Press, 1991), 15-25. Rees demonstrates that when Pelagius views are examined it becomes less evident to what extent he held heretical views.
[208] Kelly, *History and Heresy*, 58.
[209] Kelly, *History and Heresy*, 28.
[210] Kelly, *History and Heresy*, 61-65;

"the property of both natures is preserved and comes together into a single person and a single subsistent being; he is not parted or divided into two persons, but is one and the same only-begotten Son, God, Word, Lord Jesus Christ."[211]

Monophysitism

The meaning of the Monophysite heresy is contained in its Greek name. In Greek, *monos* means one and *physis* means nature. Consequently, according to this heresy, after the incarnation, the human nature of the human man with whom the second person of the Trinity was united was totally absorbed into the divine nature. Jesus Christ, therefore, only had one nature that was a combination of the divine and human natures. This heresy was likewise condemned at the Council of Chalcedon.

Monothelitism

The meaning of the Monothelite heresy is also contained in its Greek name. In Greek, *monos* means one and *thelis* means will. As the name indicates, the Monothelites believed that Jesus had only one will, the divine will. In 681 AD, the Third Council of Constantinople condemned this heresy. Oddly, this heresy sprang up within the Catholic Church by those who were hoping to find a way to bring the Monophysites into the Catholic Church. Sadly, the compromises these well-intentioned Catholics made, however, were heretical.[212]

The Third Council of Constantinople (680-681 AD) not only condemned Monothelitism but also condemned Pope Honorius I as one who associated with Monothelitism.[213] As explained by

---

[211] Norman P. Tanner, *Decrees of the Ecumenical Councils*, Volume I (District of Columbia: Georgetown University Press, 1990), 86.
[212] "Monothelitism and Monothelites," newadvent.org, http://www.newadvent.org/cathen/10502a.htm (accessed February 3, 2017).
[213] "This pious and orthodox creed of the divine favor was enough for a complete knowledge of the orthodox faith and a complete assurance therein. But since, from the first, the contriver of evil did not rest, finding an accomplice in the death, so too now he has found instruments suited to his own purpose – namely Theodore, who was bishop of Pharan, Sergius, Pyrrhus, Paul and Peter, who were

Patrick Madrid, the condemnation of Pope Honorius, who died in 638 AD prior to the council, occurred without the approval of the reigning Pope St. Agatho (reigned 678-681 AD). Pope St. Agatho neither approved this condemnation nor confirmed the council's decrees because he died before the council documents were delivered to Rome. The succeeding Pope, Leo II, confirmed the decrees of the council while clarifying that although Pope Honorius had not approved of Monothelitism he ought to have also condemned it. Pope Honorius' condemnation, therefore, was not for heresy but for inaction.[214]

Quiz 6

1. Describe two ways by which administrative decisions of Emperor Diocletian affected how the Church administers territory.

2. Write a short paragraph on the Edict of Milan. Include in your paragraph the following: a similar edict that preceded it, who mandated the Edict of Milan and why, as explained by the church historian Eusebius, and two ways by which Christians benefited from the Edict of Milan.

3. In a few sentences, describe Emperor Julian's reaction to Christianity. Include his competition with the Christian reputation for charity.

4. Identify the following. The terms are as follows: Gnosticism, Docetism, Marcionism, Montanism, Manichaeism, Arianism, Donatism, Pelagianism, Apollinarism, Nestorianism, Monophysitism, and Monothelitism.

---

bishops of this imperial city, and further Honorius, who was pope of elder Rome, Cyrus, who held the see of Alexandria, and Macarius, who was recently bishop of Antioch, and his disciple Stephen – and has not been idle in raising through them obstacles of error against the full body of the church, sowing with novel speech among the orthodox people the heresy of a single will and a single principle of action in the two natures of the one member of the holy Trinity, Christ our true God..." Norman P. Tanner, *Decrees of the Ecumenical Councils*, Volume I (District of Columbia: Georgetown University Press, 2009), 125-126.

[214] Patrick Madrid, *Pope Fiction* (Dallas: Basilica Press, 1999), 158-162.

	The physical world is a byproduct of quasi divine beings that emanated from God. In other words matter is a degradation of God who is spirit, the one source out of which all else emanates from. This heresy at times also held that Jesus is a savior, but He is defined not as equal to God but rather as a semi-divine intermediary being. His role is to save human being by giving secret knowledge.
	According to this heresy the God of the Old Testament is a condemning, angry God who is lower than and was superseded by the New Testament all merciful Good God of the New Testament.
	According to this heresy after the incarnation the human nature of the human man that the second person was united with was totally absorbed into the divine nature. Jesus Christ, therefore, only had one nature that was a combination of the divine and human natures. This heresy was likewise condemned at the Council of Chalcedon.
	According to this heresy, Jesus only appeared to be human but actually was not. Possibly, the verse "the Word became flesh and lived among us," of the Gospel of

	John Jesus was directed against this heresy.
	This heresy held that a human being can successfully and sufficiently imitate Christ's virtue without needing to rely on grace.
	According to this heresy although Christ is divine he is not fully equal to God the Father.
	As the name indicates of this heresy, the followers of this heresy believed that Jesus had only one will, the divine will.
	The error of this heresy is that while it distinguished Jesus human nature from his divine nature it did not adequately ex-plain their union in the one divine person of Jesus Christ.
	This early heresy rejected Church authority and in its place proposed that the inspiration of the Holy Spirit through prophets is all that is needed for Church order and harmony.
	This heresy was a rigorist response to Christians who failed to keep the faith during the Diocletian persecutions. These heretics held that the holiness of the Church requires that its members be holy, above all its ministers. Therefore, if a sacrament, such as baptism, is administered by a former traitor to the Catholic faith the sacrament is invalid and must be performed by a minister who had not be-

	trayed the Catholic faith during times of persecution.
	This heresy believed that after the incarnation the second person of the Trinity did take on a human body but only had one mind, a divine mind, and not a human mind.
	This heresy held that all of reality is dyadic that is comprised of two principles, a light, spiritual, good principle and a dark, material, evil principle. In order for the world to be redeemed, the good spiritual principle that is intertwined with evil matter needs to be released from its imprisonment.

Chapter 7

Fall and Rise

Introduction

In this chapter, we will first focus on the fall of the Western Roman Empire that coincided with the rise to prominence of tribal people who were mainly from Germanic lands. Then, we will discuss another development, the growth of the Catholic religious expression of monasticism. In the subsequent chapter, we will study the ascent to power of a non-Western people, the Arab people.

Fall of the Western Roman Empire

The Roman Empire remained united from 324 AD, when Constantine assumed power over both the Eastern and Western sections of the Roman Empire, until the end of the reign and death of Emperor Theodosius I, in 395 AD. Theodosius I was the last Roman Emperor to rule over both the east and the west. After his death, his sons split the empire in two ways. The eastern portion of the empire, with its headquarters in Constantinople, ended in 1453 AD when the Islamic Ottoman Empire conquered the city. The western portion of the empire ended much sooner in 476 AD when Emperor Romulus Augustus (aka Romulus Augustulus) was removed from his throne by the barbarian Odoacer who also had Romulus' father killed. At the time when Odoacer deposed

Romulus, the majority of the western provinces of the Roman Empire were ruled by barbarian warlords.[215] Prior to this political decapitation, the city of Rome suffered a humiliating defeat when it was sacked in 410 AD by a Germanic tribe known as the Visigoths, led by Alaric I. In describing this sack St. Jerome wrote,

> Rome had been besieged and its citizens had been forced to buy their lives with gold. Then thus despoiled they had been besieged again so as to lose not their substance only but their lives. My voice sticks in my throat; and, as I dictate, sobs choke my utterance. The City which had taken the whole world was itself taken; nay more famine was beforehand with the sword and but few citizens were left to be made captives. In their frenzy the starving people had recourse to hideous food; and tore each other limb from limb that they might have flesh to eat. Even the mother did not spare the babe at her breast. In the night was Moab taken, in the night did her wall fall down. "O God, the heathen have come into thine inheritance; thy holy temple have they defiled; they have made Jerusalem an orchard. The dead bodies of thy servants have they given to be meat unto the fowls of the heaven, the flesh of thy saints unto the beasts of the earth. Their blood have they shed like water round about Jerusalem; and there was none to bury them.[216]

St. Augustine was another great Western saint living at the time of the 410 AD sack of Rome. He responded by writing *The*

---

[215] Adrian Keith Goldsworthy, *How Rome Fell: Death of a Superpower* (New Haven: Yale University Press, 2009), 11.

[216] St. Jerome, "Letter CXXVII. To Principia, 12" Philip Schaff, *Nicene and Post-Nicene Fathers of the Christian Church, Second Series, Volume VI, Jerome: Letters and Select Works* (Grand Rapids: Wm. B. Eerdmans Publishing Company, 1893), http://www.ccel.org/ccel/schaff/npnf206.v.CXXVII.html?highlight=letter,lxv,to,principia#highlight, Christian Classics Ethereal Library (accessed April 20, 2015).

City of God. In this book, Augustine compares and contrasts the City of Rome, as representative of all earthly political systems, with the heavenly city of Jerusalem in which we are called by our baptisms to participate as members of the Catholic Church. Rome fell, asserts Augustine, because of its own "splendid" vices not because of Christian influence:

~ St. Augustine on Roman False Virtues ~

[T]hey built in very close proximity the temples of Virtue and Honor, worshipping as gods the gifts of God. Hence we can understand what they who were good thought to be the end of virtue, and to what they ultimately referred it, namely, to honor; for, as to the bad, they had no virtue though they desired honor and strove to possess it by fraud and deceit.[217]

There are historians who reject Augustine's argument. Instead, they favor the pagan Roman view that Christianity so weakened the empire that it collapsed. One example is Edward Gibbon who in *The History of the Decline and Fall of the Roman Empire* explicitly blames Christianity for weakening Rome. We will first take a brief look at Gibbon's argument before seeing other more reasonable explanations for Rome failure, ending with the great Catholic historian Hilaire Belloc's view. Gibbons writes:

As the happiness of a *future* life is the great object of religion, we may hear without surprise or scandal that the introduction, or at least the abuse of Christianity, had some influence on the decline and fall of the Roman Empire. The clergy successfully preached the doctrines of patience and pusillanimity; the active virtues of society were discouraged; and the last remains of military spirit were buried

---

[217] St. Augustine, *The City of God*, Book V, no. 12, trans. Marcus Dods (New York: Random House, 1993), 161.

in the cloister: a large portion of public and private
wealth was consecrated to the specious demands of
charity and devotion; and the soldiers' pay was
lavished on the useless multitudes of both sexes
who could only plead the merits of abstinence and
chastity. Faith, zeal, curiosity, and more earthly
passions of malice and ambition, kindled the flame
of theological discord; the church, and even the
state, were distracted by religious factions, whose
conflicts were sometimes bloody and always im-
placable; the attention of the emperors was di-
verted from camps to synods; the Roman world was
oppressed by a new species of tyranny; and the
persecuted sects became the secret enemies of their
country. Yet party-spirit, however pernicious or
absurd, is a principle of union as well as of
dissension. The bishops, from eighteen hundred
pulpits, inculcated the duty of passive obedience to
a lawful and orthodox sovereign; their frequent
assemblies and perpetual correspondence maintained the communion of distant churches; and the
benevolent temper of the Gospel was strengthened,
though confirmed, by the spiritual alliance of the
Catholics. The sacred indolence of the monks was
devoutly embraced by a servile and effeminate age;
but if superstition had not afforded a decent retreat,
the same vices would have tempted the unworthy
Romans to desert, from baser motives, the standard
of the republic. Religious precepts are easily obeyed
which indulge and sanctify the natural inclinations
of their votaries; but the pure and genuine influence of Christianity may be traced in its beneficial, though imperfect, effects on the barbarian
proselytes of the North. If the decline of the Roman
Empire was hastened by the conversion of
Constantine, his victorious religion broke the
violence of the fall, and mollified the ferocious

temper of the conquerors." (chap. 39).[218]

The historian Adrian Goldsworthy identifies a main reason for the Western Roman Empire's collapse not in Christianity but rather in politics. Goldsworthy blames the demise of Rome on the civil wars between competing Roman factions. These wars "cost the empire" since it required it to focus its energy on internal disputes at the cost of overlooking external threats.[219] Ludwig von Mises's economic reason for the fall of Rome can be considered as complementary of Goldsworthy's political explanation. According to von Mises, a principle factor for Rome's decline was due to the Roman government's suppression of "economic interconnectedness" by centrally determining prices and by debasing the currency. He states,

> What brought about the decline of the empire and the decay of its civilization was the disintegration of this economic interconnectedness, not the barbarian invasions. The alien aggressors merely took advantage of an opportunity which the internal weakness of the empire offered to them. From a military point of view the tribes which invaded the empire in the fourth and fifth centuries were not more formidable than the armies which the legions had easily defeated in earlier times. ...
>
> ...The interference of the authorities upset the adjustment of supply to the rising demand.
>
> The showdown came when in the political troubles of the third and fourth centuries the emperors resorted to currency debasement. With the system of maximum prices the practice of debasement completely paralyzed both the production and the marketing of the vital foodstuffs and disintegrated society's economic organization. The more eagerness the authorities displayed in enforcing the maximum prices, the more desperate became the

---

[218] Edward Gibbon, *The History of the Decline and Fall of the Roman Empire* (London: T. Cadell Strand, 1837), 611-612.
[219] Adrian Keith Goldsworthy, *How Rome Fell: Death of a Superpower* (New Haven: Yale University Press, 2009), 409.

conditions of the urban masses dependent on the purchase of food. Commerce in grain and other necessities vanished altogether. To avoid starving, people deserted the cities, settled on the countryside, and tried to grow grain, oil, wine, and other necessities for themselves. ...

The emperors were alarmed with that outcome which undermined the financial and military power of their government. But their counteraction was futile as it did not affect the root of the evil. The compulsion and coercion to which they resorted could not reverse the trend toward social dis-integration which, on the contrary, was caused precisely by too much compulsion and coercion. No Roman was aware of the fact that the process was induced by the government's interference with prices and by currency debasement.[220]

Non-political and non-economic factors that may have also contributed to the decline and fall of the Roman Empire include plagues,[221] lead poisoning from Roman cooking ware and plumbing,[222] and even environmental ones such as excessive grazing and deforestation.[223] In striving to be objective, with respect to the environmental factor, Jared M. Diamond acknowledges that the barbarians' movement into Roman territory was the decisive reason that brought an end to the Western portion of the Roman Empire. He then asks,

What was the fundamental reason for that shift in fortune? Was it because of changes in the barbarians themselves, such that they became more numerous or better organized, acquired better weapons or more horses, or profited from climate

[220] Ludwig von Mises, *Human Action, The Scholar's Edition*, trans. (Auburn: Ludwig von Mises Institute, 1998), 762-763.
[221] William H. McNeill, *Plagues and Peoples* (New York: Random House, 1976), 131-136.
[222] H.A. Waldron, "Lead and Lead Poisoning in Antiquity," *Medical History* 29.1 (1985): 107-108. This article is a review of the book by Jerome O. Nriagu, *Lead and Lead Poisoning in Antiquity*.
[223] Jared M. Diamond, *Collapse: How Societies Choose to Fail Or Succeed* (New York: Penguin Group, 2005), 14-15.

change in the Central Asian steppes? In that case, we would say that barbarians really could be identified as the fundamental cause of Rome's fall. Or was it instead that the same old unchanged barbarians were always waiting on the Roman Empire's frontiers, and that they couldn't prevail until Rome became weakened by some combination of economic, political, environmental, and other problems. In that case we would blame Rome's fall on its own problems, with the barbarians just providing the coup de grâce. This question continues to be debated.[224]

The prominent twentieth Catholic historian Hilaire Belloc argued that conceiving the barbarians as waiting for the right moment to invade and overtake Rome vastly simplifies history. According to Belloc, there is no evidence in history of such a barbarian invasion into Roman territory. Instead, tribes of people, many from German lands, gradually over time immigrated to the Roman Empire to experience a higher standard of living. These people were accepted by the Romans and even into the Roman military. After they gradually rose to key positions, they took over the Western Roman Empire and conclusively brought it to an end in 476 AD. In stating this, Belloc writes,

> What we are commonly told is that the Western Empire was overrun by savage tribes called "Goths" and "Visigoths" and "Vandals" and "Suevi" and "Franks" who "conquered" the Western Roman Empire that is, Britain and Gaul and the civilized part of Germany on the Rhine and the upper Danube, Italy, North Africa, and Spain.
>
> There was no barbarian conquest, but there was a continuation of what had been going on for centuries, an infiltration of people from outside the Empire into the Empire because within the Empire

---

[224] Diamond, 13-14.

they could get the advantages of civilization. There was also the fact that the army on which everything depended was at last almost entirely recruited from barbarians. As society gradually got old and it was found difficult to administer distant places, to gather the taxes from far away into the central treasury, or to impose an edict over remote regions, the government of those regions tended to be taken over more and more by the leading officers of the barbarian tribes, who were now Roman soldiers; that is, their chieftains and leaders. In this way were formed local governments in France and Spain and even Italy itself which, while they still felt themselves to be a part of the Empire, were practically independent.

For instance, when it became difficult to govern Italy from so far off as Constantinople, the Emperor sent a general to govern in his place and when this general became too strong he sent another general to supersede him. This second general (Theodoric) was also, like all the others, a barbarian chief by birth, though he was the son of one who had been taken into the Roman service and had himself been brought up at the Court of the Emperor. This second general became in his turn practically independent. The same thing happened in southern France and in Spain. The local generals took over power. They were barbarian chiefs who handed over this power, that is, the nominating to official posts and the collecting of taxes, to their descendants.[225]

<hr/>

[225] Hillaire Belloc, *"The Great Heresies,"* Chapter Three: The Arian Heresies, EWTN, http://www.ewtn.com/library/HOMELIBR/HERESY3.TXT (accessed April 22, 2015).

Rise of Barbarians

During the first four centuries, the Catholic Church adopted and transformed Roman governmental structures (dioceses), customs, language and laws. As more and more people from the North, principally of Germanic origin, came into the Church, though, they brought with them their languages, laws, structures, and customs. As they became members of Christ's mystical body, the Holy Spirit transformed these human elements of culture as well. We will briefly look at a number of the tribes that were influenced by Christianity, whether or not many members of these tribes converted. The map below indicates the migration of these people into the Roman Empire.

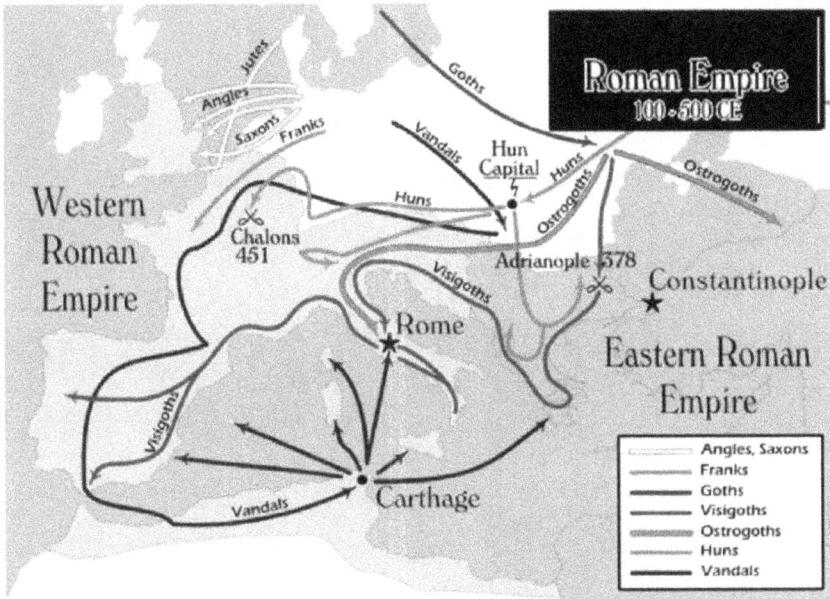

226

---

226 I have slightly modified the map due to its inaccurate use of the term invasions. User:MapMaster, "The Barbarian invasions of the 5th century were triggered by the destruction of the Gothic kingdoms by the Huns in 372-375. The city of Rome was captured and looted by the Visigoths in 410 and by the Vandals in 455," map, http://commons.wikimedia.org/wiki/File%3AInvasions_of_the_Roman_Empire_1.png (accessed April 22, 2015).

Huns

The Huns were likely from modern day Mongolia. Under the leadership of Attila the Hun (died 453 AD), they ruled over a vast empire. In the 440s and 450s, Attila invaded both the Eastern and Western portions of the Roman Empire. The map below depicts the extent of the Hunnic Empire at the time of Attila. In 452 AD, one year before he died, Attila invaded the Western Roman Empire, leaving destroyed cities in his wake. With the hope of negotiating with Attila, the Western Emperor Valentinian III sent three envoys to Attila. One of these envoys was Pope St. Leo the Great (reigned 440-461 AD). After this encounter with Pope Leo and the other two envoys, Attila withdrew.[227]

228

---

[227] Hyun Jin Kim, *Huns, Rome and the Birth of Europe* (New York: Cambridge University Press, 2013) 79, 83; Bronwen Neil, *Leo the Great* (New York: Routledge, 2009), 8-9.

[228] Slovenski Volk, "Extent of Attila's Empire. Based on Map 10 Empires and Barbarians. The Fall of Rome and the Birth of Europe. Peter Heather. Oxford University Press, 2010.," map, http://commons.wikimedia.org/wiki/File%3A Huns450.png (accessed April 22, 2015).

Goths

The term Goths is a general term that can refer to several tribes, both of Germanic origin and non-Germanic origin, who migrated into the Roman Empire. According to one simplified application of the term, the Goths include, but is not solely limited to, the Ostrogoths (eastern Goths) and Visigoths (western goths).[229] In 410 AD, Alaric I led the Visigoths into Roman territory and successfully sacked Rome. St. Augustine wrote his famous work *The City of God* in reaction to this sack of Alaric. That same year Alaric died, but this did not deter the Visigoths in gaining territory. Within a short time they had established themselves as rulers over territory we associate with Spain and Portugal (Hispania), and Southern France.[230]

Vandals

As is evident in one of the above maps, after moving around Southern Western Europe, which included sacking and looting Rome in 455 AD, the Vandals settled down in North Africa, a region they ruled until they were defeated by Justinian I (reigned 527-565 AD) emperor of the Eastern Roman Empire.[231]

Lombards

According to the monk and historian Peter the Deacon (c. 720s-799 AD) in his *History of the Lombards*, the Lombards originally came from Scandinavia before moving to Germany. Under the Lombard King Audoin (reigned 546-565 AD), the Lombards migrated further south to Italian lands. There they set up a Lombard Kingdom which lasted up until 774 when Charlemagne brought the Lombard Kingdom under his rule. The

---

[229] Herwig Wolfram, and Thomas J. Dunlap, *History of the Goths* (Los Angeles: University of California Press, 1988), 19-20, 25-26.

[230] Peter Heather, *The Visigoths from the Migration Period to the Seventh Century: An Ethnographic Perspective* (Woodbridge: The Boydell Press, 1999), 9, 10, 43, 55, 523.

[231] Andrew Merrills, and Richard Miles, *The Vandals* (Oxford: Blackwell Publishing, 2010), 116-117, 235-248.

region of Italy called Lombardy is named after this tribe.[232]

Franks

Another medieval historian, St. Gregory Bishop of Tours (ruled 573-594 AD) wrote a book on the Franks in a similar style as Peter the Deacon's. In Gregory of Tours' *History of the Franks*, he describes both Franks invading the Roman province of Germania and Franks becoming members of the Roman military. One of the Franks who joined the Romans and rose to prominence was the Merovingian King Childeric (c. 440-482 AD). Childeric's son Clovis I (c. 466-511 AD), following the good example of his Catholic Burgundian wife Clotild, converted to Catholicism bringing the Roman province of Gaul under the sway of Catholicism. Clovis also succeeded in uniting the various factions of the Franks under his leadership.[233]

Burgundes

Clovis I's wife Clotild belonged to the Germanic Burgundes tribe. Clotild was the granddaughter of the Burgundes King Gundioc and daughter of Chilperic.[234]

Angles, Saxons, and Jutes

According to Venerable Bede, in his *History of the English People*, in 449 AD this Germanic tribe was invited by the King of England. Bede writes,

> Then the nation of the Angles, or Saxons, being invited by the aforesaid king, arrived in Britain with three long ships, and had a place assigned them to reside in by the same king, in the eastern part of the

---

[232] Paul the Deacon, *History of the Lombards*, trans. William Dudley Foulke (Philadelphia: University of Pennsylvania Press, 2003), ix, 3, 41.

[233] Gregory of Tours, *The History of the Franks*, trans. Lewis Thorpe (New York: Penguin, 1974), intro, 120-132, 141-144, 208, 340.

[234] Gregory of Tours, 140-141.

island, that they might thus appear to be fighting for their country, whilst their real intentions were to enslave it. Accordingly they engaged with the enemy, who were come from the north to give battle, and obtained the victory; which, being known at home in their own country, as also the fertility of the country, and the cowardice of the Britons, a more considerable fleet was quickly sent over, bringing a still greater number of men, which, being added to the former, made up an invincible army. The newcomers received of the Britons a place to inhabit, upon condition that they should wage war against their enemies for the peace and security of the country, whilst the Britons agreed to furnish them with pay. Those who came over were of the three most powerful nations of Germany - Saxons, Angles, and Jutes.[235]

Rise of Monasticism

A very different historical development from the barbarian incursion into the Roman Empire that precipitated the fall of Rome was the rise of monasticism. The rise of monasticism occurred after 313 AD when Constantine permitted Christianity to practice freely. When the time of persecution had ended, some Christians discerned they were called to seek a martyrdom that was not the red martyrdom of Perpetua, Felicity, and St. Ignatius of Antioch, to name but a few. Instead, they sought a white martyrdom that consisted of seeking salvation through poverty, chastity, and obedience.[236]

As monasticism developed, it began to incorporate a more

---

[235] Bede, "*The Ecclesiastical History of the English Nation*," translator not clearly indicated (But it seems to be L.C. Jane's 1903 Temple Classics translation), introduction by Vida D. Scudder (London: J.M. Dent; New York E.P. Dutton, 1910), chap. XV, Fordham University Medieval Sourcebook, http://legacy.fordham.edu/halsall/basis/bede-book1.asp (accessed April 23, 2015).

[236] Paul Burns, *Butler's Lives of the Saints*, New Full Edition, January (Collegeville: The Liturgical Press, 1998), 123.

pronounced aim of evangelization. Under Pope St. Gregory the Great (reigned 590-604 AD and who once was a monk), St. Augustine of Canterbury, a monk of a monastery in Rome, was tasked with the mission of evangelizing England. As more and more monks embraced the mission of evangelization, they retained their common life of prayer (principally the mass and the Liturgy of the Hours), work, and study. Their deep appreciation for reading led the monks to preserve countless precious manuscripts to which we would not today have access if it were not for their monastic libraries that served students and teachers when monasteries became centers of learning.

Another way that monks evangelized was by living a stable life. Their monastic vocation committed them to live on the same plot of land. In order to adhere to this stability, they learned how to cultivate their land for food and other resources without destroying it in the process. If they did, this would mean they would need to leave. Their respectful and civilized stewardship of nature's resources inspired others, including the highly mobile barbarian tribes, to do the same. In the process of inspiring others to cultivate the soil of the earth, the monks also imparted to others the need of cultivating the soil of their souls.

Finally, and most importantly, one purpose of the monasteries was to give to people a foretaste of heaven. This also helped to civilize, ennoble, and sanctify those who came in contact with monasteries. Below, is a very brief introduction to four key people who were at the beginning of the monastic movement that allowed heavenly realities to shine forth with greater clarity on earth: St. Paul the Hermit, St. Antony of Egypt, St. Pachomius, and St. Benedict of Nursia.

St. Paul the Hermit

The main source that we have on the life of St. Paul the Hermit (c. 233-245 AD aka St. Paul of Thebes) is a biography edited by St. Jerome. According to the biography, St. Paul the Hermit lived when Emperor Decius persecuted Christians. St. Paul the Hermit responded by hiding in a desert cave. Once the persecution had ended, he remained in the desert and there dedicated his life to solitary prayer. For this reason he is considered Christianity's first hermit.[237]

St. Antony of Egypt

St. Anthony of Egypt (251-356 AD) was also a prominent Egyptian hermit. When he was a young man, around age twenty, his wealthy parents died, and he inherited their land and wealth. Following Matthew 19:21 literally, he gave some of his inheritance away, sold the rest, and then gave the proceeds to the poor. Afterward, under the direction of a local spiritual master, he devoted himself to a life of prayer. Around age 35, he moved to the desert where he lived a life of prayerful solitude. In 306 AD, he moderated his solitary life by accepting spiritual pupils who lived in a number of relatively closely clustered hermit cells. Even though he sought and encouraged isolation from society, he did not lose sight of the Christian centrality of loving one's neighbor. According to St. Anthony, "Life and death, depend on our neighbor. If we gain our brother, we gain Christ; but it we scandalize our neighbor, we sin against Christ."[238]

St. Pachomius

Whereas St. Paul the Hermit and St. Antony of Egypt are both associated with solitary monasticism, the Egyptian St. Pachomius (c. 292-346) is viewed as the founder of community monasticism. This is because he organized hermits into a recognizable community consisting of a maximum of forty monks with various levels of authority, weekly assignments, and an orderly manner of selling items made by the monks to support the monastery. Pachomius's influence spread to the West after St. Jerome in 404 AD translated Pachomius's rule and letters into Latin.[239]

---

[237] Burns, 104-105.
[238] Burns, 122-126.
[239] David Hugh Farmer, *Butler's Lives of the Saints*, New Full Edition, May (Collegeville: The Liturgical Press, 1996), 47-48.

St. Benedict of Nursia

St. Benedict of Nursia (c. 480–540) further developed the monastic model set forth in St. Pachomius's rule and letters. He did so with his own rule now called the Rule of St. Benedict, and by founding various monasteries in what is now modern day Italy. Twelve of these monasteries, of ten men each, were situated in a town outside of Rome called Subiaco. Around 25 years later he, along with a few monks, moved to south of Rome to Monte Cassino where he founded another monastery. There, he finished writing his rule. The *Rule of St. Benedict* became the most influential religious rule of western Christianity.[240]

St. Benedict Medal

241

---

[240] Peter Doyle, *Butler's Lives of the Saints*, New Full Edition, July (Collegeville: The Liturgical Press, 1999), 77-79.
[241] Unknown Original uploader was Bwag at de.wikipedia, "A Jubilee medal by the monk Desiderius Lenz, of the Beuron Art School, made for the 1400th anniversary of the birth of St. Benedict in 1880," photograph, http://commons.wikimedia.org/wiki/File%3ABenediktusmedaille.jpg (accessed April 24, 2015).

242

The letters that circle around the medal stand for "*Vade retro satana; Nunquam suade mihi vana. Sunt mala quae libas. Ipse venena bibas*, which in English, Begone, Satan! And suggest not to me thy vain things: the cup thou profferest me is evil; drink thou they poison."[243] The four letters in the quadrants of the medal stand for *Crux Santi Patris Benedicti*, which in English translates, "The Cross of Holy Father Benedict."[244] The horizontal letters that are within the cross stand for, *Crux Sacra Sit Mihi Lux* which in English means "May the Holy Cross be my Light." The vertical letters of the cross signify, *Non Draco Sit Mihi Dux*, which in English means "Let not the Dragon be my Guide."[245]

Quiz 7

1. Who sacked Rome in 410 AD?

---

[242] Daniel Tibi, "St. Benedict Medal, back,"diagram, http://commons.wikimedia.org/wiki/File%3ASt_benedict_medal-2006_04_24.png (accessed April 4, 2015).
[243] Prosper Louis P. Guéranger, *The Medal or Cross of St. Benedict* (London: Burns and Oates, 1880), 13.
[244] 11-12.
[245] 12.

Fr. Peter Samuel Kucer, MSA

2. Who sacked Rome in 476 AD and what happened to the Roman Emperor after this sack?

3. Describe factors that helped to cause Rome's collapse.

4. According to the Catholic historian Hilaire Belloc, was the barbarian movement into Western Europe one characterized primarily by conquest or not? Briefly explain your answer.

5. Chose three of the tribes listed and identify them: Huns, Goths, Vandals, Lombards, Franks, Burgundes, and Angles.

6. Briefly identify one of the following saints: St. Paul the Hermit, St. Antony of Egypt, St. Pachomius, and St. Benedict of Nursia.

7. Based on the chapter, provide three important contributions of monasteries to western European civilization.

136

Chapter 8

Rise of Islam

Introduction

About a century after the Western Roman Empire fell, Arab people, united by Islam, grew in power. In this chapter, beginning with Mohammed, we will focus our attention on this rise. Then, we will examine the central tenants of Islam. This will be followed by various Catholic critiques of Islam notably by St. John of Damascus, Hilaire Belloc, and Benedict XVI.

Muhammad

According to multiple sources, the religious leader Muhammad (c. 570–632) was introduced to Christianity when he was a child from Mecca traveling through Syria with his uncle. In the Syrian town of Bosra, Muhammed met a Christian monk called Bahira, in Arabic, and, in the West, Sergius the Monk. This monk indicated that Muhammad would become a prophet. Early Muslim references to Muhammed's encounter with this Christian monk include the Muslims Ibn Ishaq (died c. 770), Ibn Sa'd (784-845), Ibn Hisham (died c. 828) al-Tabari (839-923 AD).[246] As we will see

---

[246] A. Abel "Bahira," *Encyclopedia of Islam, Second Edition*, Brill Online, 2013, http://referenceworks.brillonline.com/search?s.q=bahira&s.f.s2_ parent=s.f.book.encyclopaedia-of-islam-2&search-go=Search (accessed April 28, 2015)..

later, early Christians also referred to this incident. According to the Christian accounts the monk Muhammad met was a heretic, possibly Arian.

~ Ibn Ishaq (died c. 770) on Muhammed's Meeting with Bahira ~

Abu Talib had planned to go in a merchant caravan to Syria, and when all preparations had been made for the journey, the apostle of God, so they allege, attached himself closely to him so that he took pity on him and said that he would take him with him, and that the two of them should never part; or words to that effect. When the caravan reached Busra [Bosra] in Syria, there was a monk there in his cell by the name of Bahira, who was well versed in the knowledge of Christians. A monk had always occupied that cell. There he gained his knowledge from a book that was in the cell, so they allege, handed on from generation to generation. They had often passed by him in the past and he never spoke to them or took any notice of them until this year, and when they stopped near his cell he made a great feast for them. It is alleged that that was because of something he saw while in his cell. They allege that while he was in his cell he saw the apostle of God in the caravan when they approached, with a cloud overshadowing him among the people. Then they came and stopped in the shadow of a tree near the monk. He looked at the cloud when it overshadowed the tree, and its branches were bending and drooping over the apostle of God until he was in the shadow beneath it. When Bahira saw that, he came out of his cell and sent word to them, 'I have prepared food for you, O men of Quraysh, and I should like you all to come both great and small, bond and free.' One of them said to him, 'By God, Bahira! Something extraordinary has happened today, you used not to treat us so, and we have often passed by you. What has befallen you today?' He answered, 'You are right in what you say, but you are guests and I wish to honor you and give you food so that you may eat.'

So they gathered together with him, leaving the apostle of God behind with the baggage under the tree, on account of his extreme youth. When Bahira looked at the people he did not see the mark which he knew and found in his books,' so he said, 'Do not let one of you remain behind and not come to my feast.'[247]

Below is Muslim art from c. 1315 that depicts Muhammed's meeting with Bahira.

[248]

Later in his life, Muhammed claimed he received revelations from God: in his heart, from a voice, and from the angel Gabriel.[249] As will be evident in the subsequent section, these "truths" resemble the Arian heresy. The likeness does not necessarily indicate causality, although some early and modern Christians have argued for this causality. Like the Arians, Muhammed rejected the Trinity in his assertion that God is not three persons in one divine nature and he, Muhammed, is the greatest of all prophets, even greater

---

[247] Ibn Ishaq, *The Life of Muhammad*, trans. A. Guillaume (Oxford: Oxford University Press, 2004), 79-80.

[248] Author unknown, "Young Muhammad meets the monk Bahira. From Jami' al-Tavarikh ("The Universal History" or "Compendium of Chronicles") written by Rashid Al-Din and illustrated in Tabriz, Persia, c. 1315," photograph, http://en.wikipedia.org/wiki/File:Muammad-as-youth-meeting-monk-bahira-compendium-persia-1315-edin-550.jpg#filelinks (accessed April 28, 2015).

[249] These are referred to as "manners of revelation." *Koran*, trans. Marmaduke Pickthall (New York: Alfred A. Knopf, 1992), ix.

than Moses. Muhammed further claimed that Jesus is not divine but only a prophet of lesser importance to the last and greatest of prophets, Muhammed. Another biblical person that Muhammed revered is Abraham. (Muslims claim they are descendants of Abraham through Abraham's son Ishmael.) Muhammad believed his God given mission as the greatest prophet was not to establish a new religion but rather to restore religions to their pure state. The true undistorted religion of Islam, believed Muhammed, is to correct the Jewish excessive stress on law, justice, and the goods of this earthly world, and is to correct the Christian excessive stress on mercy and the heavenly world to come.[250]

In the beginning, Muhammad only attracted a few followers. He also was persecuted by his fellow Arabs who forced him to flee from his home town of Mecca, in modern day Saudi Arabia, to Medina (The Hijrah of 622). In time, Muhammed successfully rallied together various Arabic clans under his leadership.[251] In 630, Muhammad, supported by ten thousand troops, marched back to Mecca and captured the city. The Meccans then converted to Islam. After only a few days had passed a nomadic army assembled against Muhammad's troops.

Once again, Muhammad's army emerged victorious in their battle with the nomads. Around six months later, Muhammad headed north towards Damascus of modern day Syria. He stopped, though, short of Syria in Tabuk. Later, when he had amassed even more allies from the various Arab tribes he pushed forward to Syria. According to some accounts, Muhammad was accompanied this time by thirty thousand men. In 631, after a number of military skirmishes and battles, the majority of Arab tribes struck an alliance with Muhammad. The following year, 632, Muhammad made a pilgrimage to Mecca and then died a few months later in June of 632.[252] Muhammad's ability to conquer and unite people has gained him the reputation of being one of the world's most

---

[250] Gabriel Said Reynolds, "Jesus the Muslim Hippie," *First Things* December (2013), 23; *Koran*, trans. Marmaduke Pickthall (New York: Alfred A. Knopf, 1992), xx-xxi.

[251] *Koran*, trans. Marmaduke Pickthall (New York: Alfred A. Knopf, 1992), xiii.

[252] *Koran*, xiii-xv.

effective military leaders, as the military historian Richard A. Gabriel points out in his book, *Muhammad: Islam's first General*:

> To think of Muhammad as a military man will come as something of a new experience to many. And yet Muhammad was truly a great general. In the space of a single decade he fought eight major battles, led eighteen raids, and planned thirty-eight other military operations where others were in command but operating under his orders and strategic direction. He was wounded twice, suffered defeats, and twice had his positions overrun by superior forces before rallying his troops to victory.[253]

Central Tenants of Islam

Islam's sacred book of revelation that Muhammad received but did not write down is called the Koran. It is possible that some scribes of Muhammad wrote down certain portions of Muhammad's revelations that he passed down orally. However, it was not until circa 650, eighteen years after he died, that the first official text of the Koran was made. In 900, the order of the many chapters of the Koran, called surahs, was officially agreed upon. At this time the text was also standardized. Prior to 900, the text only consisted of consonants without vowels. This made it difficult for later generations to determine what words a group of consonants were intended to form.[254]

Other sacred texts of Islam, which are not placed on the same sacred level of the Koran, include the Sunnah and the Hadith. The Sunnah of Muhammad is an esteemed work in Islam that describes the practices and habits of Muhammad that followers of Islam are to follow. Logically it is considered by Muslims as a main source of their legal code, called Sharia, Allah's will for his people. The Hadith consists of additional teachings attributed to Muham-

---

[253] Richard A. Gabriel, *Muhammad: Islam's First General* (Norman: University of Oklahoma Press, 2007), xviii-xix.

[254] *Koran*, xvii-xviii.

mad that are not found in the Koran. There are various collections of Hadith.[255]

The five essential pillars that Muslims believe are required by Allah through the sacred texts of Islam are as follows:

- 1. The Creed (*shahadah*)
  The Islamic creed is simply, "I bear witness that there is no god (*ilah*) but the God (*al-ilah*/Alah) and Muhammad is the messenger of God."[256]

- 2. Daily Prayers (*salat*)
  Muslims are required to pray a set of ritual prayers accompanied by prescribed postures five times a day, "at sunrise, midday, sunset, evening, and at nighttime."[257]

- 3. Almsgiving (*zakah*)
  In Islam almsgiving is mandatory and not voluntary. The alms are to be directed to the furthering of Islam and to help the poor.

- 4. Fasting (*sawm*)
  According to the Islamic fasting regulations, all Muslims who are physically capable of doing so are, during the ninth Islamic month of Ramadan, to fast from sunrise to sunset. During this time, Muslims are also to pray with greater intensity and reflect on the Koran.[258]

- 5. Pilgrimage to Mecca (*hajj*)
  This pilgrimage is mandatory but only for those who can afford to do so and are physically fit. The *hajj* is ideally to take place at least once in a Muslim's life.[259]

---

[255] Tamara Sonn, *Islam: A Brief History* Second Edition (Oxford: Blackwell Publishing Ltd., 2010), 24, 45-46, 141.
[256] Sonn, 29.
[257] Sonn, 29.
[258] Sonn, 30.
[259] Sonn, 30.

A Few Interesting Facts about Islam

Since details about Islam's beliefs concerning Jesus, Mary, Islam's expansion, and extraordinary growth are relevant for church history, we will begin with a few pertinent passages from the Koran.

The Koran has such high esteem for Mary, the mother of Jesus that an entire chapter, surah 19, is named after her. According to this chapter, and other chapters, Mary miraculously as a virgin gave birth to Jesus. (surah 19 Mary: 17-21; surah 3 The Family of Imran: 47; surah Banning 66:12).

Jesus, further claims the Koran, performed miracles but was not divine, and was a Muslim prophet who prepared the way for Muhammad, the final prophet and greatest prophet. (surah The Cow 2:87; surah The Ranks 61:6; surah 3 The Family of Imran:49)

We already saw how Islam quickly expanded under Muhammad's military leadership. Once the vast majority of Arabic tribes had come under the sway of Islam, it began once again to expand even into Christian territory. In 732, during the Battle of Tours, the Islamic army of the Umayyad Caliphate was defeated by the Franks of modern day France led by the Catholic prince Charles Martel. About a century later, in response to repeated Islamic incursions into Italy and Rome, the nearly two mile long Leonine wall that surrounds Vatican Hill that houses St. Peter's Basilica was constructed on orders of Pope Leo IV (reigned 847-855).[260] In 1565, the Islamic Empire attempted to take the Catholic island of Malta (The Great Siege of Malta). Catholic knights successfully warded off this attack.[261] Shortly after this battle, another larger battle occurred not far away in the Gulf of Corinth, off the coast of Western Greece. This was the 1571 Battle of Lepanto that the Catholic October 7th liturgical feast day annually commemorates. Once again, Catholic forces were able to successfully defend their territory from Islamic incursions.

---

[260] Rosamond McKitterick, John Osborne, Carol M. Richardson, and Joanna Story, *Old Saint Peter's, Rome* (Cambridge : Cambridge University Press, 2013), 5-6.

[261] Ernle Bradford, The Great Siege (New York: Harcourt, Brace & World, Inc., 1961).

The sustained growth of Islam is quite astonishing. Currently, according to the CIA 2010 estimate, 22.74% of the world population professes Islam. This means that almost one out of every four people are Muslims. Catholics, in comparison, comprise only 16.85 % of the world population.[262] The Pew Research Center data from 2009 indicates that between 87-90% of Muslims in the world belong to an Islamic group called the Sunni. The second largest group of Muslims are Shia, coming in at 10-13%. Between 68-80% of the Shia population lives in four countries: Iran, Pakistan, India, and Iraq. The country that has the most number of Muslims is Indonesia, followed by Pakistan, India, and Bangladesh. In total, there are around 1.57 billion Muslims in the world.[263]

Catholic Critique of Islam

St. John of Damascus's Critique of Islam

The Church Father St. John of Damascus (c. 675-749 AD) was born shortly after Muhammed's death (632). John of Damascus claimed that Muhammed was a heretic who patterned his version of Christianity on Arianism.

~ St. John of Damascus's On Islam ~

There is also the superstition of the Ishmaelites which to this day prevails and keeps people in error, being a forerunner of the Antichrist. They are descended from Ishmael, [who] was born to Abraham of Agar, and for this reason they are called both Agarenes and Ishmaelites. They are also called Saracens, which is derived from Sarras kenoi, or destitute of Sara, because of what Agar said to the angel: 'Sara hath sent me away destitute.' These

---

[262] "The World Factbook," CIA, https://www.cia.gov/library/publications/the-world-factbook/geos/xx.html (accessed April 30, 2015).
[263] "Mapping the Global Muslim Population," October 7, 2009, Pew Research Center, http://www.pewforum.org/2009/10/07/mapping-the-global-muslim-population/ (accessed April 30, 2015).

used to be idolaters and worshiped the morning star and Aphrodite, whom in their own language they called Khabár, which means great. And so down to the time of Heraclius they were very great idolaters. From that time to the present a false prophet named Mohammed has appeared in their midst. This man, after having chanced upon the Old and New Testaments and likewise, it seems, having conversed with an Arian monk, devised his own heresy. Then, having insinuated himself into the good graces of the people by a show of seeming piety, he gave out that a certain book had been sent down to him from heaven. He had set down some ridiculous compositions in this book of his and he gave it to them as an object of veneration.[264]

On the next page is a 1508 engraving by the Dutch artist Lucas van Leyden. It depicts Muhammed's meeting with the monk Bahira (aka Sergius).

---

[264] "St. John of Damascus's Critique of Islam," Orthodox Christian Information Center, http://orthodoxinfo.com/general/stjohn_islam.aspx (accessed April 30, 2015). The source is from the "*Writings*, by St John of Damascus, *The Fathers of the Church*, vol. 37 (Washington, DC: Catholic University of America Press, 1958), pp. 153-160. Posted 26 March, 2006."

265

Hilaire Belloc's Critique of Islam

The twentieth century British Catholic historian Hilaire Belloc also considered Muhammad a heretic and Islam a heresy. Below is an excerpt from chapter four, "The Great and Enduring Heresy of Mohammed" of Belloc's book *The Great Heresies*. In this excerpt,

---

265 Original uploader was Cmmmm, "Mohammed," photograph, http://en.wikipedia.org/wiki/File:Mohammed2.jpg#filelinks (accessed April 30, 2015). "This 1508 engraving by Dutch artist Lucas van Leyden illustrates a legend about Mohammed that circulated in Europe during the medieval era; according to a 1908 New York Times article which reprinted this image, "The famous print of the year, 1508, is an illustration of the story of the Prophet Mohammed and the Monk Sergius. Mohammed, when in company with his friend Sergius, drank too much wine and fell asleep. Before he awakened a soldier killed Sergius and placed the sword in Mohammed's hand. When the prophet wakened the soldier and his companions told him that while drunk he had slain the monk. Therefore Mohammed forbade the drinking of wine by his followers." A high-resolution reproduction of this engraving can be viewed here, and a museum catalog listing giving all its specifics is here; this copy is in the Fine Arts Museums of San Francisco.," Wikipedia Commons.

Belloc argues that Islam is a heresy of Christianity. Try identifying why he argues for this classification of Islam. Do you think he is correct? Why or why not? In answering these questions, keep in mind the Catechism of the Catholic Church's definition of a heresy, "Heresy is the obstinate post-baptismal denial of some truth which must be believed with divine and catholic faith, or it is likewise an obstinate doubt concerning the same; apostasy is the total repudiation of the Christian faith."[266]

~ Islam as a Christian Heresy ~

Mohammedanism was a heresy: that is the essential point to grasp before going any further. It began as a heresy, not as a new religion. It was not a pagan contrast with the Church; it was not an alien enemy. It was a perversion of Christian doctrine. Its vitality and endurance soon gave it the appearance of a new religion, but those who were contemporary with its rise saw it for what it was not a denial, but an adaptation and a misuse, of the Christian thing. It differed from most (not from all) heresies in this, that it did not arise within the bounds of the Christian Church. The chief heresiarch, Mohammed himself, was not, like most heresiarchs, a man of Catholic birth and doctrine to begin with. He sprang from pagans. But that which he taught was in the main Catholic doctrine, oversimplified. It was the great Catholic world on the frontiers of which he lived, whose influence was all around him and whose territories he had known by travel which inspired his convictions. He came of, and mixed with, the degraded idolaters of the Arabian wilderness, the conquest of which had never seemed worth the Romans' while.

...

---

[266] "Catechism of the Catholic Church," scborromeo.org, http:// scborromeo.org/ccc/para/2089.htm (accessed February 3, 2017).

Mohammed preached with insistence that prime Catholic doctrine, on the human side the immortality of the soul and its responsibility for actions in this life, coupled with the consequent doctrine of punishment and reward after death.   If anyone sets down those points that orthodox Catholicism has in common with Mohammedan- ism, and those points only, one might imagine if one went no further that there should have been no cause of quarrel. Mohammed would almost seem in this aspect to be a sort of missionary, preaching and spreading by the energy of his character the chief and fundamental doctrines of the Catholic Church among those who had hitherto been degraded pagans of the Desert. He gave to Our Lord the highest reverence, and to Our Lady also, for that matter. On the Day of Judgment (another Catholic idea which he taught) it was Our Lord, according to Mohammed, who would be the judge of mankind, not he, Mohammed. The Mother of Christ, Our Lady, "the Lady Miriam" was ever for him the first of womankind. His followers even got from the early fathers some vague hint of her Immaculate Conception.

But the central point where this new heresy struck home with a mortal blow against Catholic tradition was a full denial of the Incarnation. Mohammed did not merely take the first steps toward that denial, as the Arians and their followers had done; he advanced a clear affirmation, full and complete, against the whole doctrine of an incarnate God. He taught that Our Lord was the greatest of all the prophets, but still only a prophet: a man like other men. He eliminated the Trinity altogether. With that denial of the Incarnation went the whole sacramental structure. He refused to know anything of the Eucharist, with its Real Presence; he stopped the sacrifice of the Mass, and therefore the institution of a special priesthood. In other words, he, like so many other lesser heresiarchs, founded his heresy on simplification.

...

Mohammed's teaching never developed among the mass of his followers, or in his own mind, a detailed theology. He was content to accept all that appealed to him in the Catholic scheme and to reject all that seemed to him, and to so many others of his time, too complicated or mysterious to be true. Simplicity was the note of the whole affair; and since all heresies draw their strength from some true doctrine, Mohammedanism drew its strength from the true Catholic doctrines which it retained: the equality of all men before God "All true believers are brothers." It zealously preached and throve on the paramount claims of justice, social and economic.[267]

The following excerpt is also from chapter four of Belloc's book *The Great Heresies*. Here, Belloc offers several explanations for Islam's rapid growth. Once again, as you read the excerpt try identifying Belloc's reasons that explain Islam's initial expansion. Do you agree with these reasons? Why or why not? Do these reasons help to explain Islam's sustained growth?

~ Belloc on Islam's Success ~

...There was indebtedness everywhere; the power of money and consequent usury. There was slavery everywhere. Society reposed upon it, as ours reposes upon wage slavery today. There was weariness and discontent with theological debate,

---

[267] Hilaire Belloc, "The Great Heresies," EWTN, http://www. ewtn.com/library/doctrine/heresy.htm (accessed May, 1, 2015).

which, for all its intensity, had grown out of touch with the masses. There lay upon the freemen, already tortured with debt, a heavy burden of imperial taxation; and there was the irritant of existing central government interfering with men's lives; there was the tyranny of the lawyers and their charges.

To all this Islam came as a vast relief and a solution of strain. The slave who admitted that Mohammed was the prophet of God and that the new teaching had, therefore, divine authority, ceased to be a slave. The slave who adopted Islam was henceforward free. The debtor who "accepted "was rid of his debts. Usury was forbidden. The small farmer was relieved not only of his debts but of his crushing taxation. Above all, justice could be had without buying it from lawyers. . . . All this in theory. The practice was not nearly so complete. Many a convert remained a debtor, many were still slaves. But wherever Islam conquered there was a new spirit of freedom and relaxation.

It was the combination of all these things, the attractive simplicity of the doctrine, the sweeping away of clerical and imperial discipline, the huge immediate practical advantage of freedom for the slave and riddance of anxiety for the debtor, the crowning advantage of free justice under few and simple new laws easily understood that formed the driving force behind the astonishing Mohammedan social victory. The courts were everywhere accessible to all without payment and giving verdicts which all could understand. The Mohammedan movement was essentially a "Reformation," and we can discover numerous affinities between Islam and the Protestant

Reformers on Images, on the Mass, on Celibacy, etc.

The marvel seems to be, not so much that the new emancipation swept over men much as we might imagine Communism to sweep over our industrial world today, but that there should still have remained, as there remained for generations, a prolonged and stubborn resistance to Mohammedanism. There you have, I think, the nature of Islam and of its first original blaze of victory. We have just seen what was the main cause of Islam's extraordinarily rapid spread: a complicated and fatigued society, and one burdened with the institution of slavery; one, moreover, in which millions of peasants in Egypt, Syria and the entire East, crushed with usury and heavy taxation, were offered immediate relief by the new creed, or rather, the new heresy. Its note was simplicity and therefore it was suited to the popular mind in a society where hitherto a restricted class had pursued its quarrels on theology and government.[268]

Benedict XVI on Islam

On September 12, 2006, Pope Benedict XVI delivered a controversial lecture at the University of Regensburg in Germany. It was titled, "Faith, Reason and the University – Memories and Reflections." Without its being intended, this lecture sparked much debate and even street protests in some Islamic countries. Certain enraged Muslims responded to what they heard about this academic lecture by fire bombing two Churches in Israel's West

---

[268] Belloc, Ibid.

Bank and by murdering a Catholic nun serving in Somalia.[269] The "one point" on which Benedict XVI spoke comes from a 1391 conversation on Christianity and Islam between the Byzantine emperor Manuel II Palaeologus, representing a Christian perspective, and an educated Persian, representing an Islamic view.

> ...I would like to discuss only one point - itself rather marginal to the dialogue as a whole - which, in the context of the issue of "faith and reason", I found interesting and which can serve as the starting-point for my reflections on this issue...[The Christian emperor] addresses [the Persian Muslim] his interlocutor with a startling brusqueness on the central question about the relationship between religion and violence in general, saying: "Show me just what Mohammed brought that was new, and there you will find things only evil and inhuman, such as his command to spread by the sword the faith he preached".
>
> The emperor, after having expressed himself so forcefully, goes on to explain in detail the reasons why spreading the faith through violence is something unreasonable. Violence is incompatible with the nature of God and the nature of the soul. "God", he says, "is not pleased by blood - and not acting reasonably ... is contrary to God's nature. Faith is born of the soul, not the body. Whoever would lead someone to faith needs the ability to speak well and to reason properly, without violence and threats... To convince a reasonable soul, one does not need a strong arm, or weapons of any kind, or any other means of threatening a person with death..."

---

[269] http://www.nbcnews.com/id/14846353/page/2/#.UqyUH8iA3wo accessed 12/14/2013. http://www.cbc.ca/news/world/italian-nun-killed-by-somali-gunmen-1.582128 accessed 12/14/2013.

The decisive statement in this argument against violent conversion is this: not to act in accordance with reason is contrary to God's nature. The editor, Theodore Khoury, observes: For the emperor, as a Byzantine shaped by Greek philosophy, this statement is self-evident. But for Muslim teaching, God is absolutely transcendent. His will is not bound up with any of our categories, even that of rationality. Here Khoury quotes a work of the noted French Islamist R Arnaldez, who points out that Ibn Hazn went so far as to state that God is not bound even by his own word, and that nothing would oblige him to reveal the truth to us. Were it God's will, we would even have to practice idolatry.

At this point, as far as understanding of God and thus the concrete practice of religion is concerned, we are faced with an unavoidable dilemma. Is the conviction that acting unreasonably contradicts God's nature merely a Greek idea, or is it always and intrinsically true? ... A profound encounter of faith and reason is taking place here, an encounter between genuine enlightenment and religion. From the very heart of Christian faith and, at the same time, the heart of Greek thought now joined to faith, Manuel II was able to say: Not to act "with logos" is contrary to God's nature.[270]

---

[270] Benedict XVI, "Faith, Reason, and the University: Memories and Reflections," Catholic Education Resource Center, http://www. catholiceducation.org/en/education/catholic-contributions/faith-reason-and-the-university-memories-and-reflections.html (accessed May 1, 2015).

Quiz 8

1. Explain why Hilaire Belloc claimed that Islam was a heresy. In your answer provide at least four specific reasons. Then, after you present Belloc's view, state your opinion on Belloc's view.

2. Explain why Hilaire Belloc believed Islam was successful. In your answer provide at least four specific reasons. Then, after you present Belloc's view, state your opinion on Belloc's view.

3. Identify the following books

   Koran

   Sunnah

   Hadith

4. What is the Islamic legal code called?

5. What is the Islamic view, according to the Koran, regarding the virginity of Mary and Jesus' birth?

6. Why was the Leonine Wall built and completed in 852?

Chapter 9

Evangelization

Introduction

In chapter seven, we studied the rise of the barbarian tribes. Recall, that according to Belloc in *The Great Heresies*, the Western Roman Empire was neither, in the proper meaning of the words, invaded nor conquered by barbarian tribes. Instead, Belloc argues, a gradual migration of peoples from Northern Europe to Western Europe and places close by, in particular North Africa, took place. The tribes relocated to benefit from the higher standard of living that the Roman Empire offered. As members of these tribes began to take key leadership positions within the Roman Empire, while retaining their loyalty to their tribes, the Western Roman Empire was weakened until it finally crumbled and imploded. It then was taken over by tribal leaders. Providentially, though, many of these tribal leaders embraced the Christian faith causing the members of their tribes to follow suit. In this chapter, we will focus our attention on the conversion of these tribes, and a few kingdoms, to Christianity.

Tribes and Kingdoms Convert to Christianity

Franks

According to St. Gregory Bishop of Tours (c. 538-594), as

stated in chapter seven, the Franks settled in the Roman province of Germania, which roughly corresponds to modern day Germany. The Frank Childeric (c. 440-482 AD), who collaborated with the Romans, rose to power in the Roman province of Gaul whose lands are centered in modern day France. Childeric was the son of King Merovech, leader of the Salian Franks. When King Merovech died, circa 453 AD, his son Childeric replaced him as King and ruled in Gaul. The Frankish Merovingian dynasty of which Childeric was a member is named both after his father and his tribe. Childeric was in turn succeeded by his son Clovis I (c. 466-511 AD). Clovis is credited with uniting the various groups of Franks under his rule. He also was a key person in bringing his people into the Catholic faith. First, though, he was brought into the Catholic faith by his Burgundian wife, Clotild, a devout Catholic. Once Clovis was baptized, his people were expected to follow his example, and they did.[271] The excerpt below is from Gregory of Tours' *History of the Franks* in which he describes more than 3,000 soldiers receiving baptism along with King Clovis. These conversions, and subsequent Frankish conversions to the Catholic faith, helped to stem the tide of tribal conversions to the Christian heresy of Arianism. In 507, Clovis further stemmed this tide by defeating the Arian Visigoths at the Battle of Vouille. Once defeated, the Visigothic, Arian kingdom was re-stricted to Hispania, which roughly corresponds to modern day Spain.

~ St. Gregory Bishop of Tours' *History of the Franks* ~

29. He had a first-born son by queen Clotilda, and as his wife wished to consecrate him in baptism, she tried unceasingly to persuade her husband, saying: "The gods you worship are nothing, and they will be unable to help themselves or anyone

---

[271] Gregory of Tours, *The History of the Franks*, trans. Lewis Thorpe (New York: Penguin, 1974), intro, xiv, xvi (this page visually charts the Merovingian dynasty with Clodio, Merovech's father being the first Merovingian king) 120-132, 141-144, 208, 340, 469, 580, and 587.

else. For they are graven out of stone or wood or some metal. And the names you have given them are names of men and not of gods, as Saturn, who is declared to have fled in fear of being banished from his kingdom by his son; as Jove himself, the foul perpetrator of all shameful crimes, committing incest with men, mocking at his kinswomen, not able to refrain from intercourse with his own sister as she herself says: .... But though the queen said this the spirit of the king was by no means moved to belief, and he said: "It was at the command of our gods that all things were created and came forth, and it is plain that your God has no power and, what is more, he is proven not to belong to the family of the gods." Meantime the faithful queen made her son ready for baptism; she gave command to adorn the church with hangings and curtains, in order that he who could not [be] moved by persuasion might be urged to belief by this mystery. The boy, whom they named Ingomer, died after being baptized, still wearing the white garments in which he became regenerate. At this the king was violently angry, and reproached the queen harshly, saying: "If the boy had been dedicated in the name of my gods he would certainly have lived; but as it is, since he was baptized in the name of your God, he could not live at all." To this the queen said: "I give thanks to the omnipotent God, creator of all, who has judged me not wholly unworthy, that he should deign to take to his kingdom one born from my womb. My soul is not stricken with grief for his sake, because I know that, summoned from this world as he was in his baptismal garments, he will be fed by the vision of God."

30. The queen did not cease to urge him to

recognize the true God and cease worshipping idols. But he could not be influenced in any way to this belief, until at last a war arose with the Alamanni, in which he was driven by necessity to confess what before he had of his free will denied. It came about that as the two armies were fighting fiercely, there was much slaughter, and Clovis's army began to be in danger of destruction. He saw it and raised his eyes to heaven, and with remorse in his heart he burst into tears and cried: "Jesus Christ, whom Clotilda asserts to be the son of the living God, who art said to give aid to those in distress, and to bestow victory on those who hope in thee, I beseech the glory of thy aid, with the vow that if thou wilt grant me victory over these enemies, and I shall know that power which she says that people dedicated in thy name have had from thee, I will believe in thee and be baptized in thy name. For I have invoked my own gods but, as I find, they have withdrawn from aiding me; and therefore I believe that they possess no power, since they do not help those who obey them. I now call upon thee, I desire to believe thee only let me be rescued from my adversaries." And when he said thus, the Alamanni turned their backs, and began to disperse in flight. And when they saw that their king was killed, they submitted to the dominion of Clovis, saying: "Let not the people perish further, we pray; we are yours now." And he stopped the fighting, and after encouraging his men, retired in peace and told the queen how he had had merit to win the victory by calling on the name of Christ. This happened in the fifteenth year of his reign.

31. Then the queen asked saint Remi, bishop of Rheims, to summon Clovis secretly, urging him to introduce the king to the word of salvation. And the

bishop sent for him secretly and began to urge him to believe in the true God, maker of heaven and earth, and to cease worshipping idols, which could help neither themselves nor anyone else. .... And of his army more than 3000 were baptized. His sister also, Albofled, was baptized, who not long after passed to the Lord. And when the king was in mourning for her, the holy Remi sent a letter of consolation which began in this way: "The reason of your mourning pains me, and pains me greatly, that Albofled your sister, of good memory, has passed away. But I can give you this comfort that her departure from the world was such that she ought to be envied rather than be mourned." Another sister also was converted, Lanthechild by name, who had fallen into the heresy of the Arians, and she confessed that the Son and the holy Spirit were equal to the Father, and was anointed. [272]

Eventually, the Merovingian dynasty of which Clovis was a member began losing its power to a functionary of the king called the Mayor of the Palace. One notable Mayor of the Palace was Charles Martel (c. 688-741).[273] In 732, under the leadership of Charles Martel, the Muslims, under the Umayyad Caliphate which had overtaken the Roman Provinces of Hispania and Septimania (southern France), were defeated in the Battle of (Poitiers) Tours.[274] The following map details the extent of the Umayyad Caliphate c. 750.

---

[272] Gregory of Tours, "History of the Franks," Bk. 2, 29-31, Internet History Sourcebooks Project, http://www.fordham.edu/halsall/source/gregory-clovisconv.asp (accessed May 12, 2015). The following source is cited by the Internet History Sourcebooks Project. Gregory of Tours, *History of the Franks*, trans. Ernest Brehaut (extended selections), Records of Civilization 2 (New York: Columbia University Press, 1916).

[273] Gregory of Tours, *The History of the Franks*, 340.

[274] David Nicolle, and Graham Turner, *Poitiers AD 732: Charles Martel Turns the Islamic Tide* (Oxford: Osprey Publishing, 2008), 8.

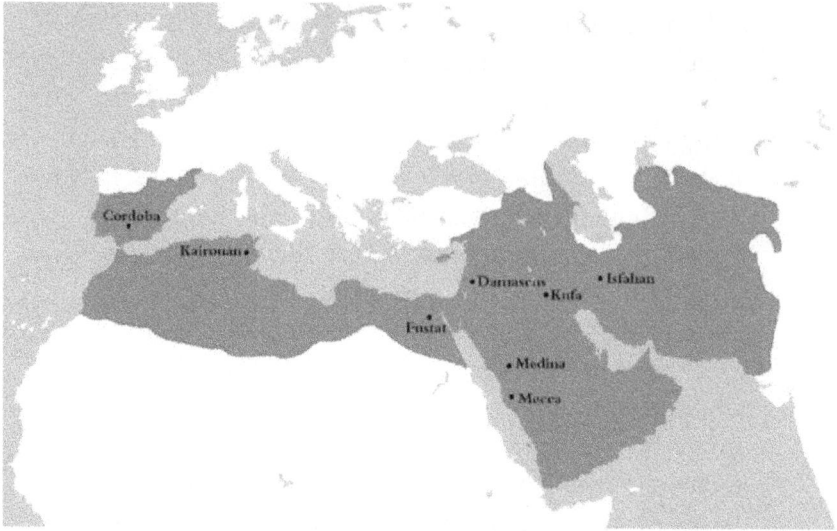

275

Pope Zachary (reigned 741-752) officially acknowledged that the Mayor of the Palace was the actual power behind the Merovingian kingdom by declaring, with reference to Charles Martel's son Pepin the Short (c. 714-768), "It is better to give the a name of king to one who has wisdom and the power rather than to one who has only the name of king without authority."[276] Prior to the papal announcement, Pepin the Short, like his father, was serving the Merovingian king as the Mayor of the Palace. In 754, Pope Stephen II (reigned 752-757) re-affirmed Pepin as king of the Franks by re-consecrating him. These papal interventions signaled the beginning of a new dynasty, the Carolingian dynasty named after Charles Martel. Out of gratitude, King Pepin defended Papal territory from the threat posed by the Lombards.[277]

---

[275] Gabagool, "Locator map for the Umayyad Caliphate at its greatest extent, c. AD 750. (Partially based on Atlas of World History (2007) - World 500-750, map.)," map, http://commons.wikimedia.org/wiki/File%3AUmayyad750ADloc. png (accessed May 12, 2015).

[276] Jim Bradbury, *The Capetians: Kings of France 987-1328* (London: Continuum Books, 2007), 8.

[277] Nicolle and Turner, 14-16; Bradbury, 8.

Visigoths

The Visigoths were the western Goths who, led by Alaric I in 410 AD, sacked Rome. Shortly after sacking Rome, they gained control over land we associate with Spain, Portugal, and Southern France.[278] Since these Visigoths had converted to Arianism[279] their defeat at the 507 Battle of Vouillé by the Catholic military leader Clovis I and Frankish troops is a significant event in Catholic history. If they had not been defeated, it is likely that Arianism would have spread significantly beyond the borders of the Visigothic kingdom that, after the battle, became limited to land of modern day Spain and Portugal. That same century, the Visigothic King Reccared I converted from Arianism to Catholicism and in so doing brought his countrymen with him into the Catholic faith. In 589 AD, a Catholic local council called the Third Council of Toledo was held.[280] This council, led by King Reccared I, officially rejected Arianism and embraced Catholicism as the official religion of the Visigothic kingdom. Below is an excerpt for the church historian Saint Isidore of Seville (c. 560-636):

~ Isidore of Seville's *The History of the Goths, Vandals, and Suevi* ~

52. In the era of 624 (586), the third year of Mauricius' rule, after the death of Leovigild, his son Reccared was crowned with kingship; he was endowed with reverence for religion and was

---

[278] Peter Heather, *The Visigoths from the Migration Period to the Seventh Century: An Ethnographic Perspective* (Woodbridge: The Boydell Press, 1999), 9, 10, 43, 55, 523.

[279] In an article from *Communio*, Ratzinger identifies Arianism as 'the political theology favored by the emperors.' In this connection, a treatise by E. Peterson on ''Monotheism as a Political Problem,' which had been largely forgotten, again became a matter of current interest. In it, Peterson tried to show that Arianism was a political theology favored by the emperors because it ensured a divine analogy to the political monarchy, whereas the triumph of the trinitarian faith exploded political theology and removed the theological justification for political monarchy." Cardinal Joseph Ratzinger, "The Primacy of the Pope and the Unity of the People of God," *Communio* 41 (Spring 2014), 114-115.

[280] Rachel L. Stocking, *Bishops, Councils, and Consensus in the Visigothic Kingdom*, 589-633 (Ann Arbor: University of Michigan Press, 2000), 59-89.

greatly irreligious and very much disposed to war, while he was devout in his faith and renowned for his love of peace; his father by the skills of was expanded the rule of his nation, while he with greater glory elevated the same nation by the victory of faith. For at the very beginning of his reign he embraced the Catholic faith and after removing the sin of their deep-rooted error he brought back the people of the whole Gothic nation to reverence for the true faith.

53. He then called together a synod of bishops from the various provinces of Spain and Gaul for the condemnation of the Arian heresy; this very religious ruler was present at this assembly and supported its proceedings by his presence and signature....[281]

The Catholic status of the Visigothic lands ended in 712 when, at the end of the Battle of Guadalete (711-712), the Visigoths were defeated by the Islamic Umayyad Caliphate. Not until 1492, during the Spanish Reconquista led by Queen Isabella and King Ferdinand, did Spain revert to the Catholic faith.

Angles, Saxons, Jutes and Celts

Christian presence in what we call the United Kingdom[282] dates to the first centuries AD. Historical records indicate that Christians were present there since 177 AD. Three of this land's earliest Christian martyrs were Alban, Aaron, and Julius. Some historians identify their martyrdoms in the Roman Province of Britannia when Emperor Diocletian (reigned 284-305 AD) held an empire wide persecution of Christians. Other historians, though,

---

[281] Isidore of Seville, *The History of the Goths, Vandals, and Suevi*, trans. Guido Donini and Gordon B. Ford (Leiden: E.J. Brill, 1970), 24-25.

[282] The four regions of the UK are England, Wales, Scotland and Northern Ireland.

date their martyrdoms a bit later.[283]

A famous early post-persecution Christian from Britannia was St. Patrick (c. 400s). When he was only sixteen years old, he was kidnapped by Hibernian pirates and forcefully taken to the island we call Ireland. At the time, this island was called Hibernia, a name which originated from the Romans. St. Patrick was held captive in Hibernia for a few years until he successfully escaped to rejoin his family back in Britannia. Back home, he grew in the Catholic faith and opened his heart to God. Following a God given inspiration, Patrick returned to the land of his kidnappers to evangelize. Details about his life come from two letters that St. Patrick wrote in Latin, his *Confessio* and his *Letter to the Soldiers of Coroticus* or *Epistola*, annals and hagiographies. Below is an excerpt from one of St. Patrick's letters:

~ St. Patrick's *Confessio* ~

1. I, Patrick, a sinner, a most simple countryman, the least of all the faithful and most contemptible to many, had for father the deacon Calpurnius, son of the late Potitus, a priest, of the settlement [vicus] of Bannavem Taburniae; he had a small villa nearby where I was taken captive. I was at that time about sixteen years of age. I did not, indeed, know the true God; and I was taken into captivity in Ireland with many thousands of people, according to our deserts, for quite drawn away from God, we did not keep his precepts, nor were we obedient to our priests who used to remind us of our salvation. And the Lord brought down on us the fury of his being and scattered us among many nations, even to the ends of the earth, where I, in my smallness, am now to be found among foreigners.

...

---

[283] Dorothy Jane Watts, *Christians and Pagans in Roman Britain* (New York: Routledge, 1991), 9-10.

23. And after a few years I was again in Britain with my parents [kinsfolk], and they welcomed me as a son, and asked me, in faith, that after the great tribulations I had endured I should not go anywhere else away from them. And, of course, there, in a vision of the night, I saw a man whose name was *Victoricus* coming as if from Ireland with innumerable letters, and he gave me one of them, and I read the beginning of the letter: 'The Voice of the Irish'; and as I was reading the beginning of the letter I seemed at that moment to hear the voice of those who were beside the forest of Foclut which is near the western sea, and they were crying as if with one voice: 'We beg you, holy youth, that you shall come and shall walk again among us.' And I was stung intensely in my heart so that I could read no more, and thus I awoke. Thanks be to God, because after so many years the Lord bestowed on them according to their cry. [284]

The centers around which Irish Catholicism developed were monasteries. Like St. Patrick, one of these monks, Saint Columba (521-597), received an inspiration to evangelize the people of the UK region we call Scotland. During Saint Columba's life, Pope St. Gregory the Great (reigned 590-604) also was inspired to send, in circa 596 AD, a monastic missionary from Rome, St. Augustine of Canterbury, to Britain to spread the gospel.[285]

Tribes within Germany

In the 700s, an English monk named Winfrid (c. 675-754) asked his Abbot if he could evangelize the Germanic tribes. Upon

---

[284] St. Patrick, "Confession of St. Patrick," 1, 23, Christian Classics Ethereal Library, http://www.ccel.org/ccel/patrick/confession.ii.html (accessed May 13, 2015).

[285] Bede (673-735), "Ecclesiastical History of the English Nation, Book I," Chap., XXIII, Internet History Sourcebooks Project, http://legacy.fordham.edu/halsall/basis/bede-book1.asp (accessed May 13, 2015).

receiving permission, Winfrid set out in 716 to the German land of Friesland. There, he began his mission of evangelizing. He was so effective that according to one of the most prominent of modern day Catholic English language historians, Christopher Dawson, he "had a deeper influence on the history of Europe than any Englishman who ever lived."[286] For this reason, he is considered the apostle of Germany. In continental Europe he not only organized, civilized, and evangelized German lands but also helped to restore and to reorganize the Catholic Church in Frankish territory. In recognition of Winfrid's God given gifts, Pope Gregory II (reigned 715-731) granted to Winfrid the official role of evangelizing all Germanic lands as a missionary bishop. This meant that Winfrid was not confined to a specific territory of one diocese. Around this time, Winfrid changed his name to Boniface, which is the name by which he is commonly known.[287] Below is an excerpt written by a contemporary of St. Boniface, Willibald bishop of Eichstatt, Bavaria (c. 700-787). In it, Willibald describes a well-known account of St. Boniface cutting down a tree revered by the pagans.

~ Willibald's *Life of St. Boniface* ~

Now many of the Hessians who at that time had acknowledged the Catholic faith were confirmed by the grace of the Holy Spirit and received the laying-on of hands. But others, not yet strong in the spirit, refused to accept the pure teachings of the church in their entirety. Moreover, some continued secretly, others openly, to offer sacrifices to trees and springs, to inspect the entrails of victims; some practiced divination, legerdemain, and incantations; some turned their attention to auguries, auspices, and other sacrificial rites; while others, of a more reasonable character, forsook all

---

[286] Kathleen Jones, *Butler's Lives of the Saints*, New Full Edition, June (Collegeville: The Liturgical Press, 1997), 43.
[287] Jones, 41-44.

the profane practices of the Gentiles [i.e., pagans] and committed none of these crimes. With the counsel and advice of the latter persons, Boniface in their presence attempted to cut down, at a place called Gaesmere, a certain oak of extraordinary size called in the old tongue of the pagans the Oak of Jupiter. Taking his courage in his hands (for a great crowd of pagans stood by watching and bitterly cursing in their hearts the enemy of the gods), he cut the first notch. But when he had made a superficial cut. Suddenly, the oak's vast bulk, shaken by a mighty blast of wind from above crashed to the ground shivering its topmost branches into fragments in its fall. As if by the express will of God (for the brethren present had done nothing to cause it) the oak burst asunder into four parts, each part having a trunk of equal length. At the sight of this extraordinary spectacle the heathens who had been cursing ceased to revile and began, on the contrary, to believe and bless the Lord. Thereupon the holy bishop took counsel with the brethren, built an oratory from the timber of the oak and dedicated it to Saint Peter the Apostle.[288]

Slavs Convert

About a century later, two men received an invitation by God, similar to St. Boniface's, to evangelize far off lands. The two were brothers, Cyril (827-869) and Methodius (815-884), from Thessaloniki, Greece. Along with St. Benedict of Nursia, Cyril and

---

[288] Willibald "The Life of St. Boniface," Fordham University, Internet History Sourcebooks Project, http://legacy.fordham.edu/halsall/basis/willibald-boniface.asp (accessed May 14, 2015). The following is sited. C. H. Talbot, *The Anglo-Saxon Missionaries in Germany, Being the Lives of SS. Willibrord, Boniface, Leoba and Lebuin together with the Hodoepericon of St. Willibald and a selection from the correspondence of St. Boniface* (London and New York: Sheed and Ward, 1954).

Methodius are considered by the Catholic Church to be patrons of Europe. Cyril and Methodius focused their missionary activity in the Slavic lands, specifically regions we associate with the Czech Republic, Croatia, Slovenia, and Serbia. Their invitation to bring the Good News to the Slavic people was mediated by Ratislav, a leader of the Moravian Tribes.

In 862, Ratislav asked Michael III Emperor of Constantinople to send missionaries to evangelize the Moravian people. Michael III responded by sending a group of missionaries led by Cyril and Methodius. In evangelizing the Slavic people, Cyril and Methodius wanted to translate the Bible and the mass into Slavonic, but they were unable to do so since at that time the Slavonic language lacked an alphabet. To meet this need, the two brothers created the Glagolitic script, which is based on the Greek alphabet. The modern Cyrillic script that Russia and certain Eastern European, Northern, and Central Asian countries use is in turn based on the older Glagolitic script.

Pope Hadrian II (reigned 867-872) supported Cyril's and Methodius's use of the vernacular in the liturgy and even went so far as to allow the celebration of the Slavonic liturgy in Rome. According to some accounts, around the time they were in Rome, the two brothers were consecrated bishops. This, though, is debated. Rome's favorable approach to a Slavonic liturgy changed under Pope John VIII (reigned 872-882). Pope John VIII forbade the use of Slavonic in the liturgy. His decision was affirmed by Pope Stephen VI (885-891) who also prohibited Slavonic from being used for liturgical services. A major factor in the debate was that German missionaries, supported by German bishops, thought they were being unduly challenged by other missionaries who were using Slavonic in their liturgies.[289]

The Rus Convert

During the subsequent century, lands further east converted to Christianity. This occurred in 988 when Vladimir, Prince of the

---

[289] Paul Burns, *Butler's Lives of the Saints*, February, New Full Edition (Collegeville: The Liturgical Press, 1998), 144-147.

Kievan Rus, converted to Catholicism and was baptized into the Byzantine rite. He and his people lived in land we now associate with the Ukraine. After Vladimir embraced Catholicism, his people followed him into the faith. We will conclude this chapter with an excerpt from *The Russian Primary Chronicles* that details Vladimir's decision to become a Catholic of the Byzantine rite.

~ Vladimir Chooses Catholicism ~

Vladimir summoned together his vassals and the city elders, and said to them: "Behold, the [Volga] Bolgars came before me urging me to accept their religion [ID]. Then came the Germans [ID] and praised their own faith [Catholicism]; and after them came the Jews [most likely rabbis from the receding Khazar khaganate (ID)]. Finally the [Eastern Orthodox] Greeks appeared, criticizing all other faiths but commending their own, and they spoke at length, telling the history of the whole world from its beginning. Their words were artful, and it was wondrous to listen and pleasant to hear them. They preach the existence of another world. 'Whoever adopts our religion and then dies shall arise and live forever. But whosoever embraces another faith, shall be consumed with fire in the next world.' What is your opinion on this subject, and what do you answer?" The vassals and the elders replied: "You know, O Prince, that no man condemns his own possessions, but praises them instead. If you desire to make certain, you have servants at your disposal. Send them to inquire about the ritual of each and how he worships God." Their counsel pleased the prince and all the people, so that they chose good and wise men to the number of ten, and directed them to go first among the Bolgars and inspect their faith. The emissaries went their way, and when they arrived at their destination they beheld the disgraceful actions of the Bolgars and their worship in the mosque; then they returned to their own country. Vladimir then instructed them to go likewise among the Germans, and examine their faith, and finally to visit the Greeks. They thus went into Germany, and after viewing the German ceremonial, they proceeded to Constantinople where they appeared before the emperor. He inquired on what mission they had come, and they reported to him all that had occurred. When the emperor heard their words, he rejoiced, and did them great honor on that very day.

On the morrow, the [Byzantine] emperor sent a message to the patriarch to inform him that a Russian delegation had arrived to examine the Greek faith, and directed him to prepare the church [Hagia Sophia (Greek for Holy Wisdom) and the clergy, and to array himself in his sacerdotal robes, so that the Russians might behold the glory of the God of the Greeks. When the patriarch received these commands, he bade the clergy assemble, and they performed the customary rites. They burned incense, and the choirs sang hymns. The emperor accompanied the Russians to the church, and placed them in a wide space, calling their attention to the beauty of the edifice, the chanting, and the offices of the archpriest and the ministry of the deacons, while he explained to them the worship of his God. The Russians were astonished, and in their wonder praised the Greek ceremonial. Then the Emperors Basil and Constantine invited the envoys to their presence, and said, "Go hence to your native country," and thus dismissed them with valuable presents and great honor. Thus they returned to their own country, and the prince called together his vassals and the elders. Vladimir then announced the return of the envoys who had been sent out, and suggested that their report be heard. He thus commanded them to speak out before his vassals. The envoys reported: "When we journeyed among the Bulgars, we beheld how they worship in their temple, called a mosque, while they stand ungirt. The Bulgarian bows, sits down, looks hither and thither like one possessed, and there is no happiness among them, but instead only sorrow and a dreadful stench. Their religion is not good. Then we went among the Germans, and saw them performing many ceremonies in their temples; but we beheld no glory there. Then we went on to Greece, and the Greeks led us to the edifices where they worship their God, and we knew not whether we were in heaven or on earth. For on earth there is no such splendor or such beauty, and we are at a loss how to describe it. We know only that God dwells there among men, and their service is fairer than the ceremonies of other nations. For we cannot forget that beauty. Every man, after tasting something sweet, is afterward unwilling to accept that which is bitter, and therefore we cannot dwell longer here." Then the vassals spoke and said, "If the Greek faith were evil, it would not have been adopted by your grandmother Olga [ID], who was wiser than all other men." Vladimir then inquired where they should all accept baptism, and they replied that the decision rested with him.

...

By divine agency, Vladimir was suffering at that moment from a disease of the eyes, and could see nothing, being in great distress. The princess declared to him that if he desired to be relieved of this disease, he should be baptized with all speed, otherwise it could not be cured. When Vladimir heard her message, he said, "If this proves true, then of a surety is the God of the Christians great," and gave order that he should be baptized. The Bishop of Kherson, together with the princess's priests, after announcing the tidings, baptized Vladimir, and as the bishop laid his hand upon him, he straightway received his sight. Upon experiencing this miraculous cure, Vladimir glorified God, saying, "I have now perceived the one true God." When his followers beheld this miracle, many of them were also baptized.

...

Thereafter Vladimir sent heralds throughout the whole city to proclaim that if any inhabitant, rich or poor, did not betake himself to the river, he would risk the prince's displeasure. When the people heard these words, they wept for joy, and exclaimed in their enthusiasm, "If this were not good, the prince and his boyars would not have accepted it." On the morrow the prince went forth to the Dnepr with the priests of the princess and those from Kherson, and a countless multitude assembled. They all went into the water: some stood up to their necks, others to their breasts, the younger near the bank, some of them holding children in their arms, while the adults waded farther out. The priests stood by and offered prayers. There was joy in heaven and upon earth to behold so many souls saved. ...

When the people were baptized, they returned each to his own abode.[290]

---

[290] "Excerpts from 'Tales of Times Gone By' [*Povest' vremennykh let*] The Russian Primary Chronicles Sources," uoregon, http://pages.uoregon.edu/ kimball/chronicle.htm (accessed May 14, 2015). The following is cited. *Pamiatniki literatury Drevnei Rusi* (Dmitrii Likhachev, etc., eds. MVA:1978) and A. S. Orlov et al., eds., *Khrestomatiia po istorii Rossii s drevneishikh vremen do*

Quiz 9

1. Who was Clovis? What close relative greatly influenced him to convert and be baptized in 496?

2. The Merovingian dynasty (or Merovingian rule) ended around 754. Who began the new dynasty? Who was this new dynasty named after?

3. In 589, Reccared I King of the Visigoths converted from what faith and to what faith? Also, what modern country corresponds to the land he once ruled?

4. In 711-712, during the Battle of Guadalete, what country falls under whose rule? Why was this battle significant for Christianity?

5. Briefly describe two of the following saints in at least two fully written out paragraphs: St. Cyril, St. Methodius, St. Patrick, St. Boniface, St. Vladimir. You are free to refer to both legends and documented history but make sure to distinguish the two when doing so. If you choose St. Cyril and St. Methodius include reference to the Slavonic liturgy.

---

nashikh dnei (MVA:1999), in close consultancy with extended English translations.

Chapter 10

East vs. West

Introduction

We have studied the Western Roman Empire up to and through its fall in 476 AD. We will now direct our attention to the Eastern Roman Empire, which lasted significantly longer than its western half. The Roman Empire was divided in two when Emperor Theodosius I died in 395 AD. His sons then proceeded to divide the empire into two: the Western Roman Empire and the Eastern Roman Empire, also called the Byzantine Empire. The Eastern Roman Empire lasted up until 1453 when the Islamic Ottoman Empire defeated it by capturing the city of Constantinople.

In this chapter, you will be introduced to the Eastern Empire by studying a few key events. We will begin with the reign of the great Eastern Emperor Justinian (reigned 527-565). This will be followed by a section on the east's repeated struggles with iconoclasm, which coincided with Islam's rise during the 600s and 700s.

We will then skip over to the eleventh century to the East-West schism of 1054. This division was exacerbated by the sack of Constantinople in 1204 by western crusaders. Almost right up to the fall of the Eastern Roman Empire to the Ottoman Empire in 1453, repeated attempts were made to heal this division in

Christianity. Unfortunately, none of these efforts had a lasting effect in the sense of healing the schism. We will conclude this chapter by presenting a few reasons for this continued painful division that has not allowed the Catholic Church, to borrow a phrase from Pope St. John Paul II, to fully breathe with both its lungs.[291]

~ John Paul II's *Ut Unum Sint* ~

In this perspective an expression which I have frequently employed finds its deepest meaning: the Church must breathe with her two lungs! In the first millennium of the history of Christianity, this expression refers primarily to the relationship between Byzantium and Rome. From the time of the Baptism of Rus, it comes to have an even wider application: evangelization spread to a much vaster area, so that it now includes the entire Church. If we then consider that the salvific event which took place on the banks of the Dnieper goes back to a time when the Church in the East and the Church in the West were not divided, we understand clearly that the vision of the full communion to be sought is that of unity in legitimate diversity.[292]

Emperor Justinian

As just stated, after Emperor Theodosius I died in 395, his sons, Arcadius and Honorius, divided the Roman Empire in two. Honorius gained the western half while Arcadius ruled the eastern half. The following century, in 476, the western empire disintegrated. The eastern empire, however, remained intact. In the 500's, the Eastern Emperor Justinian I (reigned 527-565) aimed at

---

[291] John Paul II, "Ut Unum Sint," May 25, 1995, no. 54, The Vatican, http://w2.vatican.va/content/john-paul-ii/en/encyclicals/documents/hf_jp-ii_enc_25051995_ut-unum-sint.html (accessed May 18, 2015).
[292] John Paul II, "Ut Unum Sint," Ibid.

reconquering the western half of the Roman Empire that had been divided up among various barbarian tribes. In 534, Justinian's General Belisarios successfully gained back North Africa from the Vandals. Belisarios also brought Italian lands, ruled by Franks and Arian Ostrogoths, under Justinian's Catholic rule.[293]

Besides uniting his empire by relying on his military power, Justinian also established order throughout the empire by rewriting and standardizing law. The code of law that he had promulgated in 529 is called the *Codex Justinianus (Codex Vetus)*.[294] Under his direction, legal opinions were also collected in an orderly manner. In 533, this jurisprudence called the *Pandects*, was published. In Latin, it is called the *Digestum*, which translates in English to *Digest*. The *Digest* significantly shaped the Europeans' understanding of law. The following year, 534, the laws and the jurisprudence were put together and published. This text is currently known as the *Corpus Iuris Civilis*. Below, is an excerpt from the *Digest*:

~ The Digest: Prologue ~

The Emperor Caesar, Flavius, Justinianus, Pious, Fortunate, Renowned, Conqueror, and Triumpher, Ever Augustus, to Tribonianus His Quaestor., Greeting:

With the aid of God governing Our Empire which was delivered to Us by His Celestial Majesty, We carry on war successfully. We adorn peace and maintain the Constitution of the State, and have such confidence in the protection of Almighty God that We do not depend upon Our arms, or upon Our soldiers, or upon those who conduct Our Wars, or upon Our own genius, but We solely, place Our

---

[293] James Allan Stewart Evans, *The Emperor Justinian and the Byzantine Empire* (Westport: Greenwood Press, 2005), 75-76.
[294] "Corpus Iuris Civilis," CUA, http://faculty.cua.edu/pennington/Law508/ Roman%20Law/Justinian.html (accessed May 19, 2015).

reliance upon the providence of the Holy Trinity, from which are derived the elements of the entire world and their disposition throughout the globe.

Therefore, since there is nothing to be found in all things worthy of attention as the authority of the law, which properly regulates all affairs both divine and human, and expels all injustice; We have found the entire arrangement of the law which has come down to us from the foundation of the City of Rome and the times of Romulus, to be so confused that it is extended to an infinite length and is not within the grasp of human capacity; and hence We were first induced to begin by examining what had been enacted former most venerated princes, to correct their constitutions, and make them more easily understood; to the end that being included in a single Code, and having had removed all that is superfluous in resemblance and all iniquitous discord, they may afford to all men the ready assistance of true meaning.[295]

Justinian's empire building was cut short by the deadly Plague of Justinian that wreaked havoc throughout his empire. Capitalizing on the weak state of the Roman Empire, the Lombards took over Italian lands only few years after Justinian's death.[296]

Below are photographs of Turkey's beautiful Hagia Sophia museum. During Justinian's time this museum, situated in modern day Istanbul, was the cathedral of Constantinople. It was

[295] "Medieval Sourcebook: Corpus Iuris Civilis, 6th Century," Internet History Sourcebooks Project, http://legacy.fordham.edu/halsall/source/corpus1.asp (accessed May 19, 2015). The IHSP cites the following. *The Digest of Justinian*, C. H. Monro, ed. (Cambridge, Mass.: Cambridge University Press, 1904).

[296] James Allan Stewart Evans, *The Emperor Justinian and the Byzantine Empire* (Westport: Greenwood Press, 2005), 11, 65, and 78-79. A debated issue among historians is to what extent the Lombards were Arian and when and how Arians converted to Catholicism. Maurice Wiles, *Archetypal Heresy: Arianism Through the Centuries* (Oxford: Clarendon Press, 1996), 52-53.

originally built by Constantine's son, Constantius II (reigned 337-361). Justinian had the church rebuilt after it was destroyed by a fire.[297] According to some historians, since the Hagia Sophia Church was such an admired building, first as a church and then as a mosque, Muslims used it as a model when constructing their mosques. Can you see a resemblance between the Hagia Sophia and mosques? Note well that the four Islamic minarets were added by Muslims after 1453 when Constantinople fell to the Ottoman Empire.

Exterior of the Hagia Sophia

298

---

[297] Evans, xxxiv and 52.

[298] Robert Raderschatt, "Exterior view of the Hagia Sophia, 2004," photograph, http://commons.wikimedia.org/wiki/File:Aya_sofya.jpg (accessed March 31, 2015).

Interior of the Hagia Sophia

299

Iconoclasm

During the time of Islamic expansion under the Umayyad Caliphate (661-750) into Christian lands, including Spain during the 711-712 Battle of Guadalete, an anti-religious image movement, which historians currently call iconoclasm, began to form. Iconoclasm, which means in Greek image breaker,[300] intensified

---

[299] Andreas Wahra, "Interior view of the Hagia Sophia, 1993," photograph, http://commons.wikimedia.org/wiki/File%3AAyasofya-Innenansicht.jpg (accessed March 31, 2015).

[300] "Iconoclast," Online Etymology Dictionary, http://etymonline.com/index.php?term=iconoclast&allowed_in_frame=0 (accessed May 19, 2015).

during the reign of the Eastern Emperor Leo III (reigned 717-741). Some historians, including the Greek chronicler Theophanes (c. 758-817), claim that Leo III was against graven images since he wanted to emulate the Islamic practice of forbidding graven images.[301] According to Theophanes, Leo III's order of removing an image of Christ over an entrance to the Palace of Constantinople sparked a reaction that led to the murder of a few workers. Leo III responded by officially banning the veneration of religious images (icons).[302] Leo III's son Constantine V (reigned 741-775) upheld his father's iconoclastic policies. Constantine V's son, though, Leo IV (reigned 775-780) moderated the iconoclastic policies that he inherited. In part his moderation was due to his wife Empress Irene who loved icons. When he died, she took over as regent for their son, Emperor Constantine VI. In 787, Empress Irene called together the Second Council of Nicaea, which affirmed the goodness of icons. The council issued the following "anathemas concerning holy images"[303]:

> 1 If anyone does not confess that Christ our God can be represented in his humanity, let him be anathema.
> 2 If anyone does not accept representation in art of evangelical scenes, let him be anathema.
> 3 If anyone does not salute such representations as standing for the Lord and his saints, let him be anathema.[304]

This clear ruling from the Second Council of Nicaea did not bring an end to iconoclasm. Under Emperor Leo V (reigned 813-820) icons were once again banned. The following emperor,

---

[301] Coeli Fitzpatrick Ph.D., and Adam Hani Walker, *Muhammad in History, Thought, and Culture: An Encyclopedia of the Prophet of God* (Santa Barbara: ABC-CLIO, LLC, 2014), 83.

[302] Thomas F. X. Noble, *Images, Iconoclasm, and the Carolingians* (Philadelphia: University of Pennsylvania Press, 2009), 53-54.

[303] Norman P. Tanner, *Decrees of the Ecumenical Councils*, Volume I (Washington, D.C: Georgetown University Press, 1990), 137.

[304] Tanner, 137.

Michael II (reigned 820-829), continued supporting Leo V's iconoclasm. The east's major bouts with iconoclasm finally came to an end when the son of Michael II, Theophilos (reigned 829-842,) became emperor, and married Theodora. Empress Theodora, like Empress Irene, loved icons. When her husband died in 842 she followed Empress Irene's example by restoring icon veneration. For this reason, among others, Theodora is considered a saint by Eastern Orthodox Churches.[305]

The East-West Schism of 1054

Although 1054 is the date that is most commonly referred to as the beginning of a schism that split Christianity into an eastern expression of Christianity, called Orthodoxy, and a western expression of Christianity, we call Catholicism, this schism was prepared for by a number of smaller schisms that began in the fifth century. After the 431 Council of Ephesus condemned Nestorianism the Assyrian Church broke from the Catholic Church.[306] Then, in 451 when the Council of Chalcedon condemned Monophysitism, the Armenian, Syrian, Coptic, and Ethiopian Christian Churches also broke from the Catholic Church.

These and similar breaks prepared the way for the East-West Schism of 1054. On July 16th, 1054, papal representatives, led by Cardinal Humbert, entered Constantinople's Hagia Sophia Church to place a papal bull on its altar that excommunicated the head of the Ecumenical Patriarch of Constantinople Michael I Cerularius (reigned 1043-1059). Cerularius was excommunicated since he had refused to recognize the Catholic Church headed by the pope as the head of the churches, and, among other reasons, rejected the Latin practice in Latin Churches in his lands of using unleavened bread during Eucharistic celebrations. In 1052, Cerularius even closed down churches that insisted on using un-

---

[305] Noble, 3, 245, and 366.
[306] Nestorianism holds that Jesus is human and divine but as two distinct persons that are not united in one divine nature. Unlike the monophysites, Nestorianism is dyophysitic.

leavened bread when celebrating the mass.

Cerularius responded to the excommunication directed against him by excommunicating Cardinal Humbert and the other legates. Although these excommunications were directed against the individuals named in the documents and not to the western Latin Church and eastern Greek Church as a whole, the 1054 mutual excommunications at least symbolically represent a schism that had gradually taken place and then was solidified by the tragic Sack of Constantinople of 1204 by western crusaders.[307]

1204 Sack of Constantinople

The Sack of Constantinople occurred during the Fourth Crusade (1202-1204). The original purpose of this crusade was to take control of Jerusalem that was under Islamic control. However, the crusaders were unable to even try to complete their mission because they lacked sufficient funds to pay for ships owned by Venetians.[308] After bargaining, the crusaders agreed, in lieu of payment, to capture the port of Zara for the Venetians. The port of Zara, long desired by the Venetians, was about 165 miles southeast of Venice. It was under the rule of the crusader and Catholic King Emico (Emeric) of Hungary (reigned 1196-1204). As a crusader, King Emico's lands were protected by the papacy from unjust aggression.[309] This contradictory diversion from their original mission was compounded by yet another when Alexios IV Angelos promised the crusaders money, provisions and additional manpower if they would help him become emperor at Constantinople. He also promised to restore the Eastern Empire under papal control.[310] The Crusaders agreed and helped him to gain the throne in 1203, but without much popular support. The following

---

[307] This entire section is based on the following two sources. Frank K. Flinn, *Encyclopedia of Catholicism* (New York: Infobase Publishing, 2007), 330; Aidan Nichols, *Rome and Eastern Churches: A Study in Schism* (San Francisco: Ignatius Press, 2010), 275-280.

[308] Jonathan Phillips, *The Fourth Crusade and the Sack of Constantinople* (New York: Penguin Group, 2004), 109.

[309] Phillips, 110.

[310] Phillips, 127.

year, Alexios IV Angelos was murdered.[311] The crusaders responded by brutally seizing control of Constantinople and by destroying the city in the process. Pope Innocent III, who had called the Fourth Crusader, denounced the crusader's sack of Constantinople:[312]

~ Pope Innocent III on the Sack of Constantinople ~

How, indeed, will the church of the Greeks, no matter how severely she is beset with afflictions and persecutions, return into ecclesiastical union and to a devotion for the Apostolic See, when she has seen in the Latins only an example of perdition and the works of darkness, so that she now, and with reason, detests the Latins more than dogs? As for those who were supposed to be seeking the ends of Jesus Christ, not their own ends, who made their swords, which they were supposed to use against the pagans, drip with Christian blood, they have spared neither religion, nor age, nor sex. They have committed incest, adultery, and fornication before the eyes of men. They have exposed both matrons and virgins, even those dedicated to God, to the sordid lusts of boys. Not satisfied with breaking open the imperial treasury and plundering the goods of princes and lesser men, they also laid their hands on the treasures of the churches and, what is more serious, on their very possessions. They have even ripped silver plates from the altars and have hacked them to pieces among themselves. They violated the holy places and have carried off crosses and relics.

Furthermore, under what guise can we call upon the other Western peoples for aid to the Holy Land

[311] Phillips, 222-226.
[312] Phillips, xv.

and assistance to the Empire of Constantinople? When the Crusaders, having given up the proposed pilgrimage, return absolved to their homes; when those who plundered the aforesaid Empire turn back and come home with their spoils, free of guilt; will not people then suspect that these things have happened, not because of the crime involved, but because of your deed? Let the Lord's word not be stifled in your mouth. Be not like a dumb dog, unable to bark. Rather, let them speak these things publicly, let them protest before everyone, so that the more they rebuke you before God and on God's account, the more they will find you simply negligent.[313]

The Schism and Reconciliation

Despite the 1204 sack of Constantinople greatly reducing the possibility of the East-West Schism being healed two significant attempts were made. The first occurred only about seventy years after the sack at the Second Council of Lyons (1272-1274). By this time, the Eastern Emperor Michael VIII Palaeologus had success- fully, in 1261, gained back Constantinople and associated lands that had been seized in 1204 by crusaders. The reigning pope at the time, Gregory X, sought out Emperor Michael VIII to heal the division in the Church. The three goals of the councils were to restore unity to the Church, to restore the Holy Land to Christian rulers, and to reform the Church.[314] Both Aquinas and Bonaventure were summoned to this council, but only Bonaventure was present since Aquinas died while traveling to the council. This council brought about a union that lasted until

---

[313] Paul Halsall, "Medieval Sourcebook: Pope Innocent III: Reprimand of Papal Legate Pope Innocent III," Internet Medieval History Sourcebooks Project, http://www.fordham.edu/halsall/source/1204innocent.asp (accessed May 20, 2015). The Internet Medieval History Sourcebooks History Sourcebooks Project cites the following. Pope Innocent III, Ep 136, Patrologia Latina 215, 669-702, translated by James Brundage, *The Crusades: A Documentary History* (Milwaukee, WI: Marquette University Press, 1962), 208-09.

[314] Tanner, 303-304.

1289.[315]

During the Council of Basel-Ferrara-Florence-Rome (1431-1445) Eastern Christianity was once again united with Western Christianity. One major incentive that helped to cause Eastern Christianity to want to be united with Western Christianity was the threat the continually expanding Ottoman Empire posed to its lands. When Constantinople fell in 1453 to the Ottoman Empire this incentive vanished, and, soon after, the union, which included unions with Armenians, Copts, Syrians, Chaldeans, and the Maronites, was officially dissolved in 1484 at the Eastern Synod of Constantinople.[316] One Church, the Maronite Church, who the compiler of the acts of this council accused of holding the Monothelite heresy,[317] remained loyal to Rome.[318]

A symbolic, but nonetheless important gesture, was made in 1965 between Pope Blessed Paul VI and the Ecumenical Patriarch of Constantinople Athenagoras I. The two nullified the condemnnations of 1054. This act, though, did not end the East-West schism. See below for an excerpt from this declaration:

~ The Catholic and Orthodox Declaration of 1965 ~

2. Among the obstacles along the road of the development of these fraternal relations of confidence and esteem, there is the memory of the decisions, actions and painful incidents which in 1054 resulted in the sentence of excommunication leveled against the Patriarch Michael Cerularius and two other persons by the legate of the Roman See under the leadership of Cardinal Humbertus, legates who then became the object of a similar sentence pronounced by the patriarch and the Synod of Constantinople.

---

[315] Frank K. Flinn, *Encyclopedia of Catholicism* (New York: Infobase Publishing, 2007), 330-331.
[316] Flinn, 331.
[317] The name of this compiler is Horace Justinian. Matti Moosa, *The Maronites in History* (Piscataway: Gorgias Press, 2005), 231.
[318] Flinn, 331.

3. One cannot pretend that these events were not what they were during this very troubled period of history. Today, however, they have been judged more fairly and serenely. Thus it is important to recognize the excesses which accompanied them and later led to consequences which, insofar as we can judge, went much further than their authors had intended and foreseen. They had directed their censures against the persons concerned and not the Churches. These censures were not intended to break ecclesiastical communion between the Sees of Rome and Constantinople.

4. ... Pope Paul VI and Patriarch Athenagoras I with his synod, in common agreement, declare that:

A. They regret the offensive words, the reproaches without foundation, and the reprehensible gestures which, on both sides, have marked or accompanied the sad events of this period.

B. They likewise regret and remove both from memory and from the midst of the Church the sentences of excommunication which followed these events, the memory of which has influenced actions up to our day and has hindered closer relations in charity; and they commit these excommunications to oblivion.

C. Finally, they deplore the preceding and later vexing events which, under the influence of various factors—among which, lack of understanding and mutual trust—eventually led to the effective rupture of ecclesiastical communion.

5. Pope Paul VI and Patriarch Athenagoras I with his synod realize that this gesture of justice and

mutual pardon is not sufficient to end both old and more recent differences between the Roman Catholic Church and the Orthodox Church....[319]

Causes for the Schism

The reason why the East-West schism persists up until today is multi-faceted. A major factor, and perhaps doctrinally the most significant, is the Catholic Church's claim of papal primacy. The Catholic Church holds that that the pope has primacy of honor and of jurisdiction. This means that the pope is not to be considered the primary bishop in a merely respectful manner, as first among equals. Instead, due to the pope's primacy of jurisdiction (coming from the Latin *ius* meaning law), the pope as universal pastor, may, when warranted, intervene in another bishop's diocese to make a binding decision. Throughout his writings, Benedict XVI, emphasizes that the papal primacy of juridical power is based on the more important papal primacy evident within the context of the Eucharist, since Christ intends the Eucharist to unite us and not divide us.[320]

Two other issues, which vary in importance according to the individual Orthodox Church, include the Catholic Church's use of unleavened bread when celebrating the Eucharist, and the decision by the Catholic Church to insert the *filioque* clause into the Niceno-Constantinopolitan Creed. When this creed received its form at the 381 Council of Constantinople, the clause that the Holy Spirit proceeds from the Father and the Son was not present. The Catechism of the Catholic Church succinctly summarizes the Catholic Church's teaching on the importance of the *filioque* clause as follows:

---

[319] "Joint Catholic-Orthodox Declaration of his Holiness Pope Paul VI and the Ecumenical Patriarch Athenagoras I," The Vatican, http://w2.vatican.va/content/paul-vi/en/speeches/1965/documents/hf_pvi_spe_19651207_common-declaration.html (accessed May 21, 2015).

[320] This is a theme within in Benedict XVI thought. Armin Schwibach, "Keeping Alive the 'Magnificent Theology' of Benedict XVI," *Inside the Vatican*, August-September (2016): 39.

247 The affirmation of the *filioque* does not appear in the Creed confessed in 381 at Constantinople. But Pope St. Leo I, following an ancient Latin and Alexandrian tradition, had already confessed it dogmatically in 447, even before Rome, in 451 at the Council of Chalcedon, came to recognize and receive the Symbol of 381. The use of this formula in the Creed was gradually admitted into the Latin liturgy (between the eighth and eleventh centuries). The introduction of the *filioque* into the Niceno-Constantinopolitan Creed by the Latin liturgy constitutes moreover, even today, a point of disagreement with the Orthodox Churches.

248 At the outset the Eastern tradition expresses the Father's character as first origin of the Spirit. By confessing the Spirit as he "who proceeds from the Father", it affirms that he comes from the Father through the Son. The Western tradition expresses first the consubstantial communion between Father and Son, by saying that the Spirit proceeds from the Father and the Son (*filioque*). It says this, "legitimately and with good reason", for the eternal order of the divine persons in their consubstantial communion implies that the Father, as "the principle without principle", is the first origin of the Spirit, but also that as Father of the only Son, he is, with the Son, the single principle from which the Holy Spirit proceeds. This legitimate complementarity, provided it does not become rigid, does not affect the identity of faith in the reality of the same mystery confessed.[321]

---

[321] "Catechism of the Catholic Church," numbers 247-248, The Vatican, http://www.vatican.va/archive/ENG0015/__P17.HTM (accessed May 21, 2015).

Quiz 10

1. From 379-395 AD Emperor Theodosius ruled over both the eastern and western portions of the Roman Empire. What happened to his empire when he died?

2. _____ (c. 482-565) was the Byzantine Emperor from 527-565AD. Describe at least two of his major accomplishments with respect to his empire.

3. Describe two possible motivations of those who opposed the veneration of icons during the 700s and 800s.

4. Briefly describe the 1054 action at the Hagia Sophia Church that led to the East-West Schism.

5. In 1204 AD, during the Fourth Crusade, what did the crusaders do to Constantinople and what was Pope Innocent III reaction to the crusader's actions? Also, how did this event affect possible reunion of Eastern Christianity with Western Christianity?

6. Describe two factors that helped to cause and to sustain the East-West Schism.

Chapter 11

Rise, Decline and Reform

Introduction

John Vidmar in *The Catholic Church through the Ages* succinctly explains that after the Roman Empire fell in 476 the Eastern Emperors regarded themselves as "emperor[s] of the entire Roman Empire-both east *and* west."[322] This was particularly evident in Emperor Justinian's aim at restoring the western half under his rule. As was mentioned in the previous chapter, a plague (c. 541-542) near the end of Justinian's rule greatly blocked this goal. Then, shortly after his death, the Lombards gained control over the western's Italian lands.[323] Meanwhile, in lands we associate with France and Germany, another tribe was growing in importance, the Franks.

In 754, Pope Stephen II (reigned 752-757) called upon the Franks to defend papal lands in Italy that were being threatened by the Lombards. The pope's naming of Pepin the Short as king was in part due to the pope allying himself with the strong man of

---

[322] John Vidmar, *The Catholic Church through the Ages* (New York: Paulist Press, 2005), 99.

[323] James Allan Stewart Evans, *The Emperor Justinian and the Byzantine Empire* (Westport: Greenwood Press, 2005), 11, 65, and 78-79. As state previously, it is a debated issue among historians is to what extent the Lombards were Arian and when and how Arians converted to Catholicism. Maurice Wiles, *Archetypal Heresy: Arianism Through the Centuries* (Oxford: Clarendon Press, 1996), 52-53.

the Franks who the pope believed was capable of keeping the Lombards at bay. By so doing, the pope effectively brought an end to the Frankish Merovingian dynasty and replaced it with the Carolingian dynasty named after Pepin's father Charles Martel. [324] When Pepin died in 768 his oldest son Charlemagne became King of the Franks. From 768 to 771 he briefly shared this kingly role with his brother Carloman who died in 771.[325] In 774, Charlemagne's power increased when he became King of Italian lands as King of the Lombards.[326]

Then, during a mass on Christmas day, 800, Charlemagne's power was greatly intensified to a point that greatly disturbed the Eastern Empress Irene who was serving as the empress regnant for her young son Emperor Constantine VI. At the mass, Charlemagne was crowned by Pope Leo III as Emperor of the Romans.[327] This crowning was interpreted by Irene as a threat to her rule that she assumed was over both halves of the Roman Empire, east and west. According to the Greek chronicler Theophanes, in an attempt to preserve the union between the East and the West, Pope Leo III arrived in 801/2 in Constantinople along with representatives of Charlemagne. There, he asked Empress Irene to marry Charlemagne. The union of Charlemagne and Empress Irene fell through since a palace revolution that

---

[324] David Nicolle, and Graham Turner, *Poitiers AD 732: Charles Martel Turns the Islamic Tide* (Oxford: Osprey Publishing, 2008), 14-16; Jim Bradbury, *The Capetians: Kings of France 987-1328* (London: Continuum Books, 2007), 8.

[325] Roger Collins, *Charlemagne* (London: MacMillan Press, 1998), 37-38.

[326] Collins, 61-62.

[327] John O'Malley in the chapter titled "Charlemagne: Savior or Master?" of his book A History of the Papacy, questions to what extent Charlemagne helped the Church. His chapter opens with, "The year is 800. Picture Saint Peter's basilica during mass on Christmas Day. At a certain point Pope Leo III takes a crown in his hands and places it on the head of Charlemagne, Pepin's son and the king of the Franks. This crown does not signify mere kingship but the imperial dignity, an interpretation confirmed immediately when the congregation, obviously prepared for what happened, broke into words reserved for the emperor, singing three times, "Charles, most pious, Augustus, crowned by God, great and peace-loving emperor, long-life and victory!" According to accounts from Charlemagne's court, the pope kissed the ground in front of him, a gesture reserved for the emperor. Papal accounts omit that important detail but noted, instead, that Leo anointed Charlemagne and called him his 'excellent son.'" John O'Malley, *A History of the Popes* (Lanham: Sheed & Ward, 2010), loc. 1025.

ousted Empress Irene disrupted the marriage proposal.[328]

In this chapter, we will study the reign of Charlemagne's Carolingian Renaissance, the dissolution of Charlemagne's Empire and the corruption that ensued which was followed by an era of reform.

Carolingian Renaissance

Charlemagne took his role as a Catholic ruler seriously. This explains why he not only, according to the medieval historian Walter Ullmann, wanted to increase the number of clergy serving the people of his realm but also wanted to raise the quality, especially intellectually, of those serving as clerics.[329] Since he lacked the necessary people to raise the level of education in an effective manner, he began recruiting scholars from around his realm and even outside of his realm, including from the Visogothic Spanish kingdom. His efforts to evangelize and unify his people by relying on well-educated clergy sparked an intellectual and cultural movement that is known as the Carolingian Renaissance.[330]

This intellectual and cultural revival included standardizing the Latin language. Under Charlemagne's rule, a standardization of the Latin script, the Carolingian Miniscule script, was created. Interestingly, even though he wanted people to be literate he had difficulty in mastering writing as his biographer states:

> He tried also to learn to write, and for this purpose used to carry with him and keep with him and keep under the pillow of his couch tablets and writing-sheets that he might in his spare moments accustom himself to the formation of letters. But he made little advance in this strange task, which was

---

[328] Adelbert Davids, *The Empress Theophano: Byzantium and the West at the Turn of the First Millennium* (Cambridge: Cambridge University Press, 1995), 104-105.

[329] Walter Ullmann, *The Carolingian Renaissance and the Idea of Kingship: The Birbeck Lectures, 1968-9* (Oxon: Routledge, 2010), 2.

[330] Ullmann, 3.

begun too late in life.[331]

Since the emphasis was on the Latin language, the Greek language and literary tradition of the Greeks were essentially ignored. With few exceptions, only Latin writers were studied including, lists Ullmann, "Tertullian, Cyprian, Jerome, Augustine, Boethius, and Cassiodore."[332] While Charlemagne wanted his clergy and the educated class to know these classical Latin texts he wanted above all that Sacred Scripture be studied, known, and practiced. He asserted that:

> In the Scriptures there will be found the norm, on the basis of which authority is instituted, and according to which the superiors should act towards their subjects and the subjects towards their superiors...how secular counsels are to be taken with prudent deliberation, how the fatherland is to be defended, how the enemy is to be repelled.[333]

The promotion of Sacred Scriptures meant "in relative terms, [that] at no other time in European history was the Bible so

---

[331] Einhard and Notker Balbulus, "Early Lives of Charlemagne by Eginhard and the Monk of St Gall Edited by Prof. A. J. Grant," Part II, Private Life and Character of Charlemagne, no. 25, Gutenberg, http://www.gutenberg.org/files/48870/48870-h/48870-h.html (accessed May 25, 2015).

[332] Ullmann, 11.

[333] Ullmann, 14. Here Scripture is presented as a norm for political activity. Ratzinger cautions the Church from taking the normative aspects of Scripture in relationship to politics to far where the Church becomes a norm for political activity. Since he maintains in an Augustinian manner that the Church as a community belongs to a social order directed to heaven differs from the political order with its focus on earthly peace, the eschatological Kingdom of God proposed by faith is not in itself "a *political* norm of political activity." Joseph Ratzinger, *Eschatology Death and Eternal Life*, trans. Michael Waldstein (San Francisco: Ignatius Press, 1988), 59-60. He explains, "The Kingdom of God which Christ promises does not consist in a modification of our earthly circumstances ... That Kingdom is found in those persons whom the finger of God has touched and who have allowed themselves to be made God's sons and daughters. Clearly, such a transformation can only take place through death. For this reason, the Kingdom of God, salvation in its fullness, cannot be deprived of its connection with dying." Ratzinger, *Eschatology, Death and Eternal Life*, 62.

frequently copied within so short a time."[334] Charlemagne's aim at disseminating biblical truths more widely required more copyists who, logically, were literate. Due to the promotion of the bible, therefore, the rate of literacy increased throughout the Carolingian empire.[335]

To further unite his people, in 802 Charlemagne published a collection of canon law named the *Dionysio-Hariana* that was based on an earlier work from the sixth century by Dionysius Exiguus with additions by Pope Adrian I (reigned 772-795). Charlemagne also brought greater order and harmony into monasteries by issuing a Rule of Benedict that was considered faithful to the original text. Under his son Louis the Pious (reigned 813-840), Charlemagne's vision of a revitalized monastic way of life was furthered when Benedict of Aniane was appointed by Louis as the abbot who oversaw all monasteries of the Carolingian empire. [336]

Although Charlemagne demonstrated great zeal in promoting Catholicism, and, through this promotion, raising the cultural and intellectual level in his empire, he was not a model Catholic and is not considered a saint. His court biographer Einhard (c. 775-840) points out Charlemagne's weakness that was similar to King Solomon's excessive fondness for women:

> [H]aving married at his mother's bidding the daughter of Desiderius, King of the Lombards, he divorced her, for some unknown reason, a year later. He took in marriage Hildigard, of the Subian race, a woman of the highest nobility, and by her he had three sons-viz. Charles and Pippin and Ludovicus [Latin name for Louis], and three daughters-Hrotrud and Bertha and Gisla. He had also three other daughers-Theoderada and Hiltrud and Hruodhaid. Two of these were the children of his wife Fastrada, a woman of the eastern Franks or

---

334 Ullmann, 15.
335 Ullmann, 15.
336 Ullmann, 9.

Germans; the third was the daughter of a concubine, whose name has escaped my memory. On the death of Fastrada he married Liutgard, of the Alemannic race, by whom he had no children. After her death he had four concubines-namely, Madelgarda, who bore him a daughter of the name of Ruothild; Gersuinda, of Saxon origin, by whom he had a daughter of the name of Adolthrud; Regina, who bore him Drogot, and Hugo; and Adallinda, who was the mother of Theoderic.[337]

From Empire to Feudalism

Near the end of his life Charlemagne, states Einhard:

> summoned his own son Lewis [Ludovicus also known as Louis the Pious], King of Aquitania, the only surviving son of Hildigard, and then solemnly called together the Frankish nobles of his whole kingdom; and then, with the consent of all, made Lewis partner in the whole kingdom and heir to the imperial title. After that, putting the diadem on his head, he ordered them to salute him "Imperator" and Augustus. When died his son from his wife Hildigard Louis the Pious replaced him as emperor.[338]

Louis the Pious ruled until his death in 840. Shortly after his death, a three-year civil war flared up between his three sons: Lothar, Louis, and Charles the Bald. The civil war between the brothers ended when they signed the 843 Treaty of Verdun. This treaty divided the Carolingian Empire in three ways. Each brother received one of the three sections to rule. The division of the em-

---

[337] Einhard and Notker Balbulus, "Early Lives of Charlemagne by Eginhard and the Monk of St Gall Edited by Prof. A. J. Grant," Part II, Private Life and Character of Charlemage, no. 18, Gutenberg, http://www.gutenberg.org/files/48870/48870-h/48870-h.html (accessed May 25, 2015).
[338] Balbulus, no. 30, Ibid.

pire solidified a new form of government that greatly differed from the centralized Roman Empire that Charlemagne had modeled his system of governance upon. This new decentralized, political system of governance is known as feudalism.

The seeds of feudalism, as explained in extensive detail by Perry Anderson in *Passages from Antiquity to Feudalism*, lay in an administrative decision of Constantine that in time developed into multiple, relatively small political centers ruled by regional lords and complete with private, fortified castles.[339] Prior to the establishment of feudalism, the Church and Catholic political leaders, like Charles Martel and Charlemagne, had introduced and adapted the well centralized Roman Empire system into lands we now associate with regions by and in Spain, Portugal, France, and Germany.

One clear sign of the "Roman" unity the Church brought to this vast amount of people across a huge amount of territory was the Latinization of languages that Charlemagne promoted. The Latin languages, also known as the Romance languages (especially Spanish, Portuguese, French, Italian and Romanian) are a concrete fruit of the Church's ability to Romanize by centralizing and unifying the barbarian people who had converted to Christianity.[340]

Charlemagne's adoption of the centralized Roman political model served as a governing umbrella for his entire empire. However, beneath this overarching Roman system were elements introduced by Charlemagne that in time developed and replaced the empire model inherited from classical Antiquity.[341] Specifically, this was Charlemagne's appointment of nobles who served as counts of small political units called counties. Within these counties, numbering around 250-350,[342] there developed a practice of exchanging land for service. The exchanged land became known as a benefice and then later as a fief, and the person who was granted this land, eventually under the condition of serving

---

[339] Perry Anderson, *Passages from Antiquity to Feudalism* (New York: Verso, 2013), 142.

[340] Anderson, 135.

[341] Anderson, 136.

[342] Anderson, 138.

his lord militarily and in other ways, was called a vassal. According to Anderson, "By the death of Charlemagne, the central institutions of feudalism were thus already present, beneath the canopy of a pseudo-Roman centralized empire."[343]

Over the two centuries that followed Charlemagne's death, the decentralized, multi-centered political system of feudalism, complete with many regional lords with their own armies and castles, spread across Europe.[344] Feudalism was in turn replaced, in modern times, by the political system of nation states in which a people who share common characteristics, especially ethnicity, are joined together under a centralized system of governance.

Corruption

As Charlemagne's empire split up and became more and more pronounced by feudal practices the papacy underwent a period of decline. The Italian Renaissance historian Bartolomeo Platina (1421-1481) comments on this unfortunate phase in Church history by bemoaning, "I know not how it fell out, that at this same time that the emperors showed so little courage, the Popes too were as greatly wanting in virtue and integrity, which rendered those times very miserable, subjects being very apt (as Plato says) to follow the example of their princes."[345]

In this section, we will focus on two examples of this decline in which the papacy reflected its politically unstable environment. First, we will look at the synod called the Cadaver Synod. Then, we will glance at the papacy of John XII, who was one of the many corrupt papal office holders of the 800s and 900s. During this time, there was a rapid succession of popes from competing Roman factions and families.

At the center of the so called Cadaver Synod was Pope Formosus (reigned 891-896) who had been dead for about a year before the synod. In 872, he was accused of bribing influential

---

[343] Anderson, 141.

[344] Anderson, 135-142.

[345] Bartolomeo Platina, *The Lives of the Popes from the time of our Saviour Jesus Christ to the Accession of Gregory VII* trans. W. Benham (London: Griffith Farran & Co., 188-?), 236-237.

people to gain the papal office. When he finally did become elected to the papacy in 981, he was only Pope for about five years. He was succeeded by Pope Boniface VI who was Pope for just fifteen days. This pope in turn was succeeded by Pope Stephen VI, who reigned one year. During his brief rule, Pope Stephen accused Pope Formosus of having obtained the papacy illicitly. Pope Stephen also held the infamous Cadaver Synod of 897 during which he formally denounced Pope Formosus and even went so far as to invalidate Formosus's papacy. According to Bartolomeo Platina, in 897 Pope Stephen dishonored Pope Formosus's name since when Pope Formosus was alive he had hindered Pope Stephen from becoming a bishop. In describing Pope Stephen's disgraceful actions motivated by unchecked ambition, the Italian Renaissance writer Bartolomeo Platina states:

> Martin the historian says he hated him to that degree, that in a council which he held, he ordered the body of Formosus to be dragged out of the grave, to be stripped of his pontifical habit and put into that of a layman, and then to be buried among secular persons, having first cut off those two fingers of his right hand, which are principally used by priests in consecration, and thrown them into the Tiber, because contrary to his oath, as he said, he had returned to Rome and exercised his sacerdotal function, from which Pope John legally degraded him. This proved a great controversy, and of very ill example; for the succeeding Popes made it almost a constant custom either to break or abrogate the acts of their predecessors, which was certainly far different from the practice of any of those good Popes whose lives we have written.[346]

Pope Stephen died in the same year in which he defamed

---

[346] Platina, 238; Eamon Duffy, *Saints & Sinners: A History of the Popes* (New Haven: Yale University Press, 1997), 83.

Pope Formosus's name. He was succeeded by Pope Romanus who lasted only a few months until he died. Pope Romanus was followed by Pope Theodore II who reigned for little less than a month. During his brief papacy, Pope Theodore II recognized Pope Formosus's decrees as valid. In accordance with his predecessor's policy, the following pope, Pope John IX (reigned 898-900), condemned the actions of Pope Stephen who had ordered men ordained by Pope Formosus to be re-ordained.[347]

Prior to Pope Formosus, and a few of his predecessors, the papacy was ruled by upright men who held their ambitions in check. For example, Pope Nicholas I (reigned 858-867) is recognized as a saint because of his strong, virtuous leadership. He is also called Pope Saint Nicholas the Great. After the death of Pope St. Nicholas though, describes Eamon Duffy, a former member of the Pontifical Historical Commission:

> The papacy became the possession of the great Roman families, a ticket to local dominance for which men were prepared to rape, murder, and steal. A third of the popes elected between 872 and 1012 died in suspicious circumstances – John VIII (872-882) bludgeoned to death by his own entourage, Stephen VI (896-897) strangled, Leo V (903) murdered by his successor Sergius III (904-911), John X (914-928) suffocated, Stephen VIII (939-942) horribly mutilated ... [by] the removal of his eyes, nose, lips, tongue and hands.[348]

The most notorious pope from the following century, the tenth century, was another pope named after the apostle John, Pope John XII (reigned 937-964). As recorded by Bartolomeo Platina, John XII gained the papal office due to his father's powerful political influence. Once in office, he did not tolerate criticism that two of his cardinals had relayed to the Holy Roman Emperor Otto

---

[347] Platina, 239-241.
[348] Duffy, 82-83.

I, crowned by John XII in 962.[349] He reacted in anger by ordering the nose of one cardinal cut off. The other cardinal was punished by having his hand cut off. Since other details of Pope John XII's life, including dying in bed after suffering a stroke while sleeping with a married woman, are less certain, I will end with Bartolomeo Platina's concluding comments on John XII.[350] Platina writes, "This John, who was certainly the most pernicious profligate fellow of any that preceded him in the pontifical chair, died in the eighth year, third month, and fifth day of his popedom."[351]

A false story of papal corruption is often connected to the time of papal corruption of the discussed time period. This is the Pope Joan story. Different accounts of this story place "Pope Joan" in various periods of time. According to the 13th century Metz Dominica chronicler Jean Pierier de Mailly in his *Chronica Universalis Mettensis,* Pope Joan lived in 1099:

> Concerning a certain Pope or rather female Pope, who is not set down in the list of popes or Bishops of Rome, because she was a woman who disguised herself as a man and became, by her character and talents, a curial secretary, then a Cardinal and finally Pope. One day, while mounting a horse, she gave birth to a child. Immediately, by Roman justice, she was bound by the feet to a horse's tail and dragged and stoned by the people for half a league, and, where she died, there she was buried, and at the place is written: 'Petre, Pater Patrum,

---

[349] Duffy, 84. Otto I was crowned in Rome as Emperor of the Romans by Pope John XII on 1962. In exchange Otto promised to restore papal lands to papal control. A medieval theory called the *Translatio Imperii* was used to support the transference of the Roman Empire from Latin lands to Germanic lands, in which Otto lived in. St. Jerome refers to this theory in his *Commentary on Book of Daniel.* In the book of Daniel, the prophet Daniel interprets the dreams of the Babylonian King Nebuchadnezzar. According to Jerome the various kingdoms (Babylonian Empire, Medo-Persian Empire, Greek Empire, and the Roman Empire) are to last until the end of time when the final transferred kingdom will be fully, and definitively replaced by the eternal, heavenly kingdom of God.

[350] Platina, 252-253; Duffy, 83.

[351] Platina, 252-253.

Fr. Peter Samuel Kucer, MSA

Papisse Prodito Partum' [Oh Peter, Father of Fathers, Betray the childbearing of the woman Pope]. At the same time, the four-day fast called the "fast of the female Pope" was first established.[352]

Other accounts claim she lived earlier, around the 850s. Both of these times that are claimed when Pope Joan was in office do not allow for her to ever have been pope. According to well documented history, the following popes held office during the claimed times.

Pope Saint Leo IV (reigned 847-855)
Pope Benedict III (reigned 855-858)
Pope Saint Nicholas I (reigned 858-867)
Pope Blessed Urban II (reigned 1088-1099)
Pascal II (reigned 1099 - 1118)

Furthermore, the earliest accounts of Pope Joan's life were written a few hundred years after she is claimed to having lived. Before these accounts, there is no recorded claim that she ever existed. There is, though, overwhelming concrete evidence that the Popes listed above reigned during the dates given.[353]

Reform

The repeated succession of popes during the ninth and tenth centuries who were overly worldly and did not live up to the de-

---

[352] Terry Breverton, *Breverton's Phantasmagoria: A Compendium of Monsters, Myths, and Legends* (New York: Quercus, 2014), https://books.google.com/books?id=yYoHBAAAQBAJ&pg=PT1&dq=Terry+Brev erton%27s+Phantasmagoria:+A+Compendium+of+Monsters,+Myths+and+Lege nds&hl=en&sa=X&ei=P4UAVf__ObeJsQSz8oFY&ved=0CB4Q6AEwAA#v=onep age&q=copyright&f=false (accessed March 11, 2015).

[353] Patrick Madrid, *Pope Fiction* (Dallas: Basilica Press, 1999), 167-177.

mands of the papal office was followed by a period of reform. We will first focus on the reform that occurred from the top, in other words from the popes, that then affected the Church as a whole. Then we will examine one notable example of reform that began from the bottom up.

Top Down Reform

During the eleventh and twelfth centuries, popes began curtailing the practice of lay investiture in which European monarchs appointed and invested bishops and abbots. Lay investiture was attractive to members in the Church since selling Church offices was profitable and attractive to European monarchs who wanted to control the bishops and abbots who, in addition to their ecclesiastical duties, often had civil responsibilities.

In 1059, Pope Nicholas II (reigned 1059-1061) attempted to end lay investiture with respect to the papal office with his bull *In Nomine Domini*. According to this bull, only a college of cardinals is to elect the pope, and secular rulers are not to have a vote in deciding who will be the next pope.[354] The bull importantly omits any reference to the pope-elect needing to be endorsed by the Holy Roman Emperor. Previously, popes had been nominated and at times appointed by the emperor. The person who it is thought to have basically written *In Nomine Domini* was elected to the papacy in 1073. He assumed the name Gregory VII. His decision not to seek approval for his election from Henry IV (reigned as German King 1054-1084 and Roman Emperor 1084-1105) was one of the many points of contention he had with Henry.[355]

Not only did Pope St. Gregory VII (reigned 1073-1085) continue the papal resistance to lay investiture, but he also brought reform to the Church in number of other key ways including denouncing simony and enforcing celibacy. During a Lenten synod he held in 1074, he decreed that clerics who buy offices and/or

---

[354] "Bull of Pope Nicholas II In nomine Domini on the election of a pope, promulgated in the Lateran Synod, April 13, 1059, CSUN, http://www.csun.edu/~hcfll004/Nicholas2-bull.html (accessed May 28, 2015).

[355] Anura Guruge, *The Next Pope after Pope Benedict XVI* (Alton: WOWNH LLC, 2010), 95-96.

commit grave sexual sins are to be laicized. Several clergy who were in illicit marriages protested this decision which they deemed harsh. The reaction of bishops to the decree was mixed. Some entirely supported the decree and wanted to implement it in a short period of time. Others supported the decree but set about implementing it incrementally. Still others rejected and ignored its demands. One bishop who chose not to ignore the decree but to follow it was almost killed after he promulgated the decree in his diocese.[356]

The following year, in the 1075 Local Synod of Rome, Gregory VII attempted to end lay investiture for good by asserting that only a pope can appoint or depose bishops and abbots. He threatened to excommunicate any secular ruler, including the future Holy Roman Emperor, who had appointed and/or invested bishops or abbots.[357] Henry IV ignored the threat and continued to appoint bishops. Gregory VII responded by excommunicating Henry IV. This action was received with joy by several German priests and aristocrats but not for Godly reasons. They wanted to use Henry IV's excommunication as grounds for rebelling against him so as to take away his power and property, above all his land.[358]

Aware of the precarious nature of his situation, in 1077 Henry IV forced himself to travel from Speyer, Germany to Canossa, Italy where Gregory VII was residing. Upon reaching Canossa, Henry IV, standing barefoot in snow without his royal vestments, begged the pope to lift the excommunication. Gregory VII agreed and lifted the excommunication. This journey of Henry IV is often referred to as the *Walk to Canossa*. Henry IV's lack of sincerity in his request was made evident when in 1080 he invalidly appointed an antipope, Clement III. The following year, Henry IV ordered Rome to be attacked to forcefully remove Gregory VII from office. A few years later, in 1084, Henry IV had his antipope Clement III

---

[356] "Pope St. Gregory VII," New Advent http://www.newadvent.org/cathen/06791c.htm (accessed May 28, 2015). New Advent cites the following. Thomas Oestereich, "Pope St. Gregory VII," The Catholic Encyclopedia, Vol. 6. (New York: Robert Appleton Company, 1909), 28 May 2015 <http://www.newadvent.org/cathen/06791c.htm>.

[357] "Pope St. Gregory VII," New Advent, Ibid.

[358] "Pope St. Gregory VII," New Advent, Ibid.

consecrated in Rome as pope. The antipope in turn crowned Henry IV the Roman Emperor.

The following century a compromise called the *Concordat of Worms*, signed near the city of Worms, was reached between Pope Calixtus II and the Roman Emperor Henry V. According to this concordat, only the pope can invest a bishop or an abbot with sacred authority while a secular ruler may invest a bishop or an abbot with secular authority.

~ The 1122 *Concordat of Worms* ~

Privilege of Pope Calixtus II

I, bishop Calixtus, servant of the servants of God, do grant to thee beloved son, Henry-by the grace of God august emperor of the Romans-that the elections of the bishops and abbots of the German kingdom, who belong to the kingdom, shall take place in thy presence, without simony and without any violence; so that if any discord shall arise between the parties concerned, thou, by the counsel or judgment of the metropolitan and the co-provincials, may'st give consent and aid to the party which has the more right. The one elected, moreover, without any exaction may receive the regalia from thee through the lance, and shall do unto thee for these what he rightfully should. Be he who is consecrated in the other parts of the empire (i.e. Burgundy and Italy) shall, within six months, and without any exaction, receive the regalia from thee through the lance, and shall do unto thee for these what he rightfully should. Excepting all things which are known to belong to the Roman church. Concerning matters, however, in which thou dost make complaint to me, and dost demand aid-1, according to the duty of my office, will furnish aid to thee. I give unto thee true peace, and to all who are or have been on thy side in the time of this discord.

Edict of the Emperor Henry V

In the name of the holy and indivisible Trinity, I, Henry, by the grace of God august emperor of the Romans, for the love of God and of the holy Roman church and of our master pope Calixtus, and for the healing of my soul, do remit to God, and to the holy apostles of God, Peter and Paul, and to the holy catholic church, all investiture through ring and staff; and do grant that in all the churches that are in my kingdom or empire there may be canonical election and free consecration. All the possessions and regalia of St. Peter which, from the beginning of this discord unto this day, whether in the time of my father or also in mine, have been abstracted, and which I hold: I restore to that same holy Roman church. As to those things, moreover, which I do not hold, I will faithfully aid in their restoration. As to the possessions also of all other churches and princes, and of all other lay and clerical persons which have been lost in that war: according to the counsel of the princes, or according to justice, I will restore the things that I hold; and of those things which I do not hold I will faithfully aid in the restoration. And I grant true peace to our master pope Calixtus, and to the holy Roman church, and to all those who are or have been on its side. And in matters where the holy Roman church shall demand aid I will grant it; and in matters concerning which it shall make complaint to me I will duly grant to it justice.[359]

---

[359] "Concordat of Worms 1122," Internet Medieval Sourcebook, http://www.fordham.edu/halsall/source/worms1.html (accessed May 28, 2015). The Internet Medieval Sourcebook cites the following. MG LL folio II, pp. 75 ff,

Reform from the Bottom Up

St. Peter Damian (1007-1072) represents reform that did not issue from the top, by a bishop or by a pope, but rather by a simple monk. In his *Liber Gomorrhianus*, which he addressed to the Pope Leo IX,[360] he brought to the attention of the pope sinful practices that greatly disturbed him and were spreading among the clergy. Below is one gravely sinful practice for which he condemned and recommended punishment:

> A cleric or monk who seduces youths or young boys or is found kissing or in any other impure situations is to be publicly flogged and lose his tonsure. When his hair has been shorn, his face is to be foully besmeared with spit and he is to be bound in iron chains. For six months, he will languish in prison-like confinement and on three days of each week shall fast on barley bread in the evening. After this he will spend another six months under the custodial care of a spiritual elder, remaining in a segregated cell, giving himself to manual work and prayer, subject to vigils and prayers. He may go for walks but always under the custodial care of two spiritual brethren, and he shall never again associate with youths in private conversation nor in counselling them.[361]

Although it may not be prudent to literally apply Peter Damian's punishments for today's clerics who grievously violate the sixth commandment, the principles that underlie his punishments are applicable to our times. For example, clerics found guilty of the crimes/sins Peter Damian mentions ought to be

---

translated in Ernest F. Henderson, *Select Historical Documents of the Middle Ages* (London: George Bell and Sons, 1910), 408-409.

[360] Peter Damian, *Book of Gomorrah: An Eleventh-Century Treatise against Clerical Homosexual Practices*, trans. Pierre J. Payer (Waterloo: Wilfrid Laurier University Press, 1982), 13.

[361] Damian, 61.

punished. These punishments include placing restrictions on the cleric's interactions. Finally, pastoral care by "spiritual brethren" is to be provided to guilty clerics.

In his book addressed to Pope Leo IX, Peter Damian also referred to other grave sins that clerics were committing in the eleventh century, namely priests engaging in sexual relationships with each other and then confessing to one another, active homosexuals seeking ordination, priests having sexual relationships with either male or female penitents, and finally priests "for reasons of fornication approach[ing] his [female] penitent."[362]

Pope Leo IX responded to Peter Damian by first agreeing with him that the Church needs "to combat [the mentioned sinful practices] with appropriate measures of apostolic severity, and moreover to give some evidence of strictness."[363] Pope Leo IX then follows this assertion by distinguishing various sins by their punishments. The worsts sins in his list include clerics who have abused children and clerics who have committed repeated acts of sodomy. These are not to be readmitted to the priesthood.[364]

Matthew Cullinan Hoffman, in his translation of Peter Damian's book *Liber Gomorrhianus,* accurately presents the dynamic between Peter Damian and Pope Leo IX over corruption in the clergy. In an interview with the Catholic World Report, he asserted:

> [I]n the last century English-speaking scholars have begun to circulate the strange claim that the pope somehow "rejected" or even "rebuked" Damian. This notion is not embraced by Damian's principal modern biographer, the French historian Jean Leclercq, but it has been repeated often by English-speaking homosexual scholars who wish to undermine the reputation of the Book of Gomorrah, particularly John Boswell. As I show in my book, this "rejection thesis" is totally false and is based on

---

[362] Damian, 14-15.
[363] Damian, 96.
[364] Damian, 96-97.

a misreading of a short Latin phrase in Leo's letter to Damian, as well as unjustified conjecture about another letter Damian wrote to Leo at a different time. ... [N]only did Leo not reject Damian's recommendations for punishing sodomy, but he went beyond them and imposed a more severe system of punishment than Damian suggested.

...

Western society had fallen into a terrible moral state due to the general breakdown of law and order following the disintegration of Charlemagne's empire in 887 AD, which was accompanied by terrible, predatory invasions by Vikings, Magyars, and Muslims, who ravaged the continent. Italy, France, Spain, and the British Isles were particularly affected. The Catholic Church suffered the consequences of this chaos. The papacy itself came under the influence of secular politics and the personal behavior of the popes was sometimes the cause of serious moral scandal. Historians have generally seen this period as the lowest point in the history of the papacy.

Damian committed his life to struggling against this corruption.... He rebuked emperors, bishops, and even popes in his quest to bring about reform, while always maintaining his unswerving loyalty to the papacy. He was ultimately raised by Pope Alexander II to the second rank in the Roman Church, under only the pope himself, and was sent on numerous reform missions on the pope's behalf.[365]

---

[365] CWR Staff, "Saint Peter Damian, 'Gomorrah', and Today's Moral Crisis," Catholic World Report, November 01, 2015, http://www.catholicworldreport.com/Item/4335/saint_peter_damian_gomorrah_and_todays_moral_crisis.aspx (accessed November 11, 2015).

Quiz 11

1. According to Walter Ullmann, what was the main motivating factor behind Charlemagne's promotion of the so called Carolingian Renaissance? In answering this question include reference to Sacred Scripture, language, and law.

2. According to Perry Anderson, what is one practical way by which the Church helped to Romanize the Europeans who had converted to Christianity? Also, what system of governance replaced the Roman model inherited from Antiquity and why? (Provide at least two reasons why, as explained by Perry Anderson, this occurred.)

3. As detailed by Eamon Duffy, after Pope St. Nicholas (reigned 858-867) died what type of men became popes and why? Include in your answer reference to the Cadaver Synod.

4. Based on the Fr. Peter's chapter and Vidmar's chapter discuss the reasonableness of the belief that a Pope named Joan actually existed.

5. How did Pope Nicholas II (reigned 1059-1061) reform the Church from the top down? In answering this question refer to his bull *In Nomine Domini.*

6. How did Pope St. Gregory VII, (reigned 1073-1085) reform the Church from the top down? In answering this question include reference to his struggle with Henry IV.

7. According to St. Peter Damian (1007-1072) in his *Liber Gomorrhianus*, how should a cleric or monk who gravely sins against the sixth commandment be treated? In your answer refer to the punishments he assigns to such sins and then explain to what extent you agree with his principles and his specific punishments.

Chapter 12

Catholicism and Force

Introduction

In this chapter, we will study medieval Church practices that have been heavily criticized: the Crusades and the Inquisition. In examining the Crusades, we will first discuss factors that caused the Catholic Church to resort to military force. Then, you will be introduced to the steps required to become an official crusader, military orders, a brief history of the crusades, and critiques of these crusades. Finally, we will shift out attention to another similar heavily criticized Church practice, the medieval inquisitions.

Why Did the Crusades Occur?

In 1095, the Byzantine Emperor Alexius I Komnenus (reigned 1081-1118) sent envoys to Pope Urban II (reigned 1088-1099). Through his delegates, Alexius I asked Urban II "and all the faithful of Christ to bring assistance against the heathen for the defense of this holy church, which had now been nearly annihilated in the region by the infidels who had conquered her as far as the walls of

Constantinople."[366] At the time, the Eastern Empire had been invaded by Muslim Seljuk Turks. The Turks had been so successful in expanding their rule that even the great Christian city of Constantinople was at risk of being conquered and falling under Muslim rule.[367] Pope Urban II responded by calling for the first crusade at the 1095 local Council of Clermont, held in France. As recorded by chronicler Fulcher of Chartres (1059 - c. 1128), Urban II requested:

> "Most beloved brethren: Urged by necessity, I, Urban, by the permission of God chief bishop and prelate over the whole world, have come into these parts as an ambassador with a divine admonition to you, the servants of God."

[T]he pope said that in another part of the world Christianity was suffering from a state of affairs that was worse than the one just mentioned. He continued:

> "Although, O sons of God, you have promised more firmly than ever to keep the peace among yourselves and to preserve the rights of the church, there remains still an important work for you to do. Freshly quickened by the divine correction, you must apply the strength of your righteousness to another matter which concerns you as well as God. For your brethren who live in the east are in urgent need of your help, and you must hasten to give them the aid which has often been promised them. For, as the most of you have heard, the Turks and Arabs have attacked them and have conquered the territory of Romania [the Greek Empire] as far west as the shore of the Mediterranean and the

---

[366] Peter Frankopan, *The First Crusade: The Call from the East* (Cambridge, Mass.: Belknap Press of Harvard University Press, 2012), 7.
[367] Frankopan, 1-11.

Hellespont, which is called the Arm of St. George. They have occupied more and more of the lands of those Christians, and have overcome them in seven battles. They have killed and captured many, and have destroyed the churches and devastated the empire. If you permit them to continue thus for a while with impurity, the faithful of God will be much more widely attacked by them. On this account I, or rather the Lord, beseech you as Christ's heralds to publish this everywhere and to persuade all people of whatever rank, foot-soldiers and knights, poor and rich, to carry aid promptly to those Christians and to destroy that vile race from the lands of our friends. I say this to those who are present, it meant also for those who are absent. Moreover, Christ commands it.

"All who die by the way, whether by land or by sea, or in battle against the pagans, shall have immediate remission of sins. This I grant them through the power of God with which I am invested. O what a disgrace if such a despised and base race, which worships demons, should conquer a people which has the faith of omnipotent God and is made glorious with the name of Christ! With what reproaches will the Lord overwhelm us if you do not aid those who, with us, profess the Christian religion! Let those who have been accustomed unjustly to wage private warfare against the faithful now go against the infidels and end with victory this war which should have been begun long ago. Let those who for a long time, have been robbers, now become knights. Let those who have been fighting against their brothers and relatives now fight in a proper way against the barbarians. Let those who have been serving as mercenaries for small pay now obtain the eternal reward. Let those who have been wearing themselves out in both body and soul now work for a double honor. Behold! On this side will be the sorrowful and poor, on that, the rich; on this side, the enemies of the Lord, on that, his friends. Let those who go not put off the journey, but rent their lands and collect money for their expenses; and as soon as winter is over and spring comes, let them eagerly set out on the way with God as their guide."[368]

As is evident from the passage above, a main reason the first crusade (1096-1099) was called by the Pope Urban II in 1095 was to protect the Eastern Empire from being overrun by Muslim forces. Along with this motive another reason was also present, restoring Jerusalem to Christian rule. Due to what Jerusalem represents for Christianity and the increased number of pilgrimages by Christians to the Holy Land during the 11th century this secondary reason became the primary goal.[369]

The Crusader

Pope Urban II's call of the first crusade signaled the beginning of a new way where Catholics fought in religiously motivated wars. Unlike previous religious conflicts, such as the 732 Battle of Tours led by Catholic Frank Mayor of the Palace Charles Martel against the Muslim Umayyad Caliphate army, a crusade is called and led not by a secular ruler but by the pope. Following Urban II's example, subsequent popes presented themselves as leaders of cru-

---

[368] Fulcher of Chartres, "Urban II (1088-1099): Speech at Council of Clermont, 1095," Medieval Sourcebook, http://www.fordham.edu/halsall/source/urban2-5vers.html (accessed June 1, 2015). The Medieval Sourcebook cites the following. Fulcher of Chartres' version of Urban II speech: *Gesta Francorum Jerusalem Expugnantium* Bongars, Gesta Dei per Francos, 1, pp. 382 f., trans in Oliver J. Thatcher, and Edgar Holmes McNeal, eds., A Source Book for Medieval History (New York: Scribners, 1905), 513-17.

[369] Diana Beuster, *The Speech of Pope Urban II 1095 at Clermont in the Versions of the Gesta Francorum and Baldric of Dol* (Norderstedt: Verlag, 2006), 3.

sades. Pope Celestine III (reigned 1191-1198) not only viewed a crusade as a holy war that only could be called forth by the pope but also as a papal duty.[370]

In calling forth the first holy war led by the Pope as the supreme commander, Urban II also issued several papal assurances, called privileges, in which the Church, through the bishops, promised to protect the property and family of the crusader while he was away fighting in the holy war. Pope Blessed Eugenius III (reigned 1145-1153 and beatified in 1872) in the first papal bull dealing with crusades, the 1145 *Quantum Praedecessores*, stated, "We decree that the wives and children [of crusaders] and also their property and possessions are to remain under the protection of holy Church and of us, of archbishops, bishops and other prelates of the Church of God."[371]

Another practice begun by Urban II at the 1095 Council of Clermont and followed by subsequent crusading popes was the requirement of crusaders to a take a vow called the *votum crucis*, vow of the cross. Once this vow was taken, the individual became a crusader, which means someone who has taken the cross.[372] According to the French chronicler Guibert of Nogent (c. 1055-1124) Urban II:

> instituted a sign well suited to so honorable a profession, proposing to those who were about to make war on God's behalf, as a badge of their knighthood, the mark of the Lord's Passion; and he commanded that the shape of the cross, in whatever cloth was available, be sewn on to the tunics, mantles or cloaks of those who were to make the journey.[373]

Once a man took the vow, he was obligated to fulfill his vow to

---

[370] I.S. Robinson, *The Papacy, 1073-1198: Continuity and Innovation* (Cambridge: Cambridge University Press, 1990), 322-323.

[371] Robinson, 338.

[372] James a. Brundage, " 'Cruce Signari': The Rite for Taking the Cross in England," *Traditio*, vol. 22 (1966), 289.

[373] Robinson, 332.

fight in the holy war of the pope. In time, beginning with Urban II in an early form, those who fulfilled this vow in an upright manner were offered an indulgence. According to the indulgence, a crusader, relying on the Church, was offered remission of the temporal punishment he had acquired for his sins.[374] Eugenius 1145 crusading bull, *Quantum Praedecessores*, clearly stated, in reference to Urban II, that by fulfilling a crusade in an upright manner the crusader was assured:

> remission of sins and absolution according to the ordinance of [Urban II], so that whoever begins and completes such a holy journey in a spirit of devotion, or dies during the journey, may obtain absolution from all the sins of which he has made confession with a contrite and humble heart, and may receive the fruit of eternal recompense from him who rewards all goodness.[375]

Military Orders

Some crusaders belonged to Catholic Military Orders. A particularly famous military order was the Knights Templar. Members took promises of poverty, chastity, and obedience.[376] The Knights Templar not only protected pilgrims on route to the Holy Land and the Holy Land itself but also set up a system of banking in which a pilgrim, which also included crusaders in its defintion,[377] could deposit money at one location and then at another location in his route to the Holy Lands could retrieve his money. Upon collecting his money, the pilgrim was charged a transaction fee.

This military order and its banking system was disbanded by

---

[374] Robinson, 341-343.

[375] Robinson, 346.

[376] Malcolm Barber, Victor Mallia-Milanes, and Helen J. Nicholson, *The Military Orders: Volume 3 History and Heritage* (Burlington: Ashgate Publishing, 2008), 125, 150.

[377] Robinson, 330. During the crusading years the Catholic Church understood a crusader as a type of pilgrim, *peregrinus* who was making a pilgrimage to a holy place.

Pope Clement V in 1307 with his papal bull *Pastoralis Praee-minentiae*. The Pope disbanded the Knights Templars after the French King Philip IV (reigned 1285-1314) falsely accused the knights of grievous sins and imprisoned them. Some he tortured and burned at the stake. Philip IV slandered the order since he owed money to them and wanted their money to fight his wars against England.[378] The Grand Master Jacques de Molay, who is pictured below, was one of those whom Philip IV unjustly burned at the stake.[379]

380

Jacques de Molay, the Last Grand Master of the Knights Templars

---

[378] Malcolm Barber, *The Trial of the Templars* (Cambridge: Cambridge University Press, 2006), 44-48, 89-90, 272, 282.

[379] Barber, *The Trial of the Templars* 3-4.

[380] Unknown, "Jacques de Molay, Last (23rd) Grand Master," photograph, http://commons.wikimedia.org/wiki/File%3AJacquesdeMolay.jpg (accessed June 2, 2015).

History of the Crusades

We will begin this section with a summary of those who ruled over the land in which Jesus was born. At the birth of Christ, the Jewish people living in Judea were ruled by a Roman controlled king, Herod the Great. Two years after King Herod died, the Romans founded in 6 AD the Roman Province of Judea (*Iudaea*). When Constantine converted to Christianity in 337, the same year of his death, the Holy Land became ruled for the first time by a Christian emperor. During an Arab conquest from the 630s to 640 the Holy Land fell under Muslim rule which lasted up until around the middle of the first crusade in 1099.[381]

Crusaders ruled over the Holy Land, in varying degrees, until 1291 when once again the Holy Land fell under Islamic rule. Islamic Holy Land rule lasted up until the end of World War I (1914-1918) when the Islamic Ottoman Empire was dissolved. A few years after the war the British Mandate over Palestine began in 1922. It lasted up until 1948, the year when the Jewish State of Israel was founded.

Now we will turn our attention to the various crusades. Since it is not always easy to distinguish between the beginning of one crusade and the beginning of another, scholars offer different ways for distinguishing among them. Here, we will divide the crusades into seven crusades.

The first crusade (1096-1099), promoted and directed by Pope Urban II, resulted in Catholics regaining control over Jerusalem. This victory enabled the crusaders to set up Crusader States.

---

[381] H.H. Ben-Sasson, *A History of the Jewish People* (Cambridge: Harvard University Press, 1976), 239, 242, 245, 246, 363.

Crusader States in 1135 (marked by crosses)

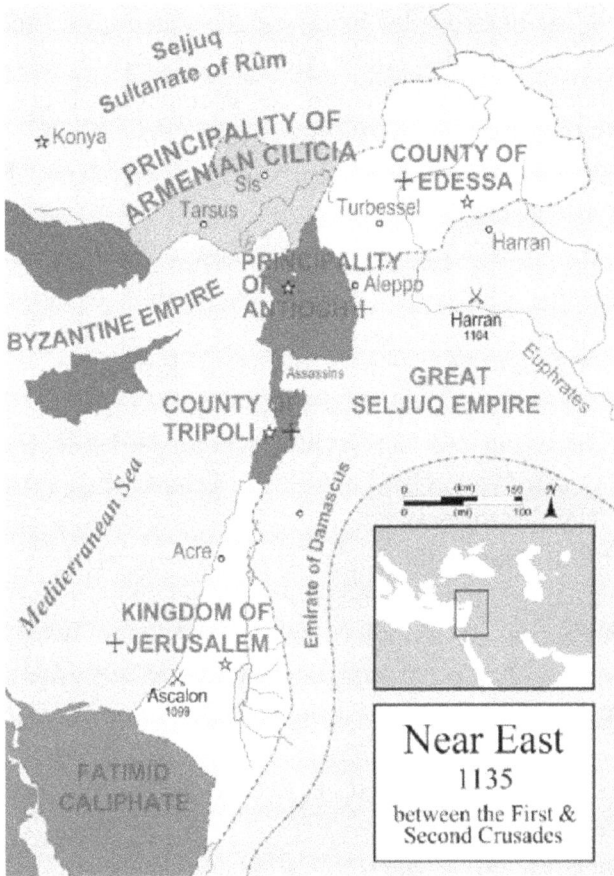

382

The Second Crusade (1147-1149) was called by Pope Bl. Eugenius III who wanted to retake the northern Crusader State of Edessa that had fallen under Muslim rule. St. Bernard of Clairvaux and other Cistercians journeyed throughout Europe to promote this crusade and to recruit crusaders. During this time, Muslims began to unite around a Muslim leader from modern day Iraq known in the West as Saladin. Their banding together under Saladin enabled the Islamic forces to fight against the crusaders

---

382 Mapmaster, "The Near East in 1135, with the Crusader states marked with red crosses," map, http://commons.wikimedia.org/wiki/File%3ANear_East_1135.svg (accessed June 3, 2015).

effectively.

The Third Crusade (1189-1192) was in response to Saladin's successful defeat of Crusader forces in Jerusalem and the Islamic defeat of several Crusader States. Despite the backing of the Holy Roman Emperor Frederick Barbarossa, Richard I of England (aka Richard the Lionheart), and Philip II of France Saladin's forces were not defeated. A peace treaty, though, was signed between Saladin and Richard I.

During the Fourth Crusade (1201-1205), the Greek Christian city of Constantinople was sacked by crusaders in 1204. These crusaders then set up a crusader state called the Latin Empire of Constantinople that lasted until 1261 when the Byzantines retook their land. With the fall of Constantinople in 1453, the Eastern Empire and its lands was lost to the Ottoman Turks. Not until the end of the Greek War of Independence (1821-1829) was Greece freed from Islamic Ottoman rule.

Between the Fourth and Fifth Crusades a non-Holy Land crusade was called by the pope, the Albigensian Crusade (1209-1229) in southern France. The Albigensians (aka Cathars) were dualists who believe only the spirit was good while bodily things are evil. For this reason, they rejected Christ's Incarnation, the sacrament of the Eucharist and Holy Matrimony. Some even advocated suicide in order, they claimed, to free their spirits from being trapped inside their bodies.

St. Francis of Assisi's name is associated with the Fifth Crusade (1218-1221) since during this crusade at the Egyptian Port of Damietta St. Francis crossed into Muslim territory to bring Catholic faith and peace. There he spoke with Egyptian Sultan Al-Damil. The modern role Franciscans have of being custodians of the Holy Land is in part based on this brave, peaceful gesture of St. Francis. In light of St. Francis's offer of peace in 1272, Muslims tolerated Franciscan presence in the Holy Land. In 1333, King Robert d'Angiò of Naples bought the Jerusalem Cenacle from the Sultan of Egypt and donated it to Franciscans. That same century, in 1342, Pope Clement VI with his Papal Bull *Gratiam Agimus* named Franciscans custodians of areas within the Holy Land.[383]

During the Sixth Crusade (1228-1229) a peace treaty was signed between the crusaders and the Islamic forces. Jerusalem was once again restored to Christian rule.

The Seventh Crusade (1248-1254 and 1269-1272) ended with the Muslims gaining more territory until finally in 1291 the Crusader controlled City of Acre in the northern part of the Holy Land was taken by the Muslims. This ended the crusader presence in the Holy Land.[384]

Critique of the Crusades

Steve Weidenkopf in his article *Modern Myths of the Crusades and How to Refute the Various Interpretations of the Crusades* responds to five popular critiques of the crusades. Below, I have presented the five critiques in bold followed by a condensed version of Weidenkopf's refutations.

1. **The Crusades were Wars of Aggression**.

   Weidenkopf argues that according to historical record the Crusades were primarily defensive wars by Catholics against Islam's imperialistic ambitions and aggression.

2. **The Crusades were Motivated Primarily by Greed**.

   Why then, responds Weidenkopf in reference to historical documentation, did first born sons make up the majority of crusaders? The first-born sons' willingness to lose their right of inheritance by going on a crusade indicates that

---

[383] "Franciscan Missionaries Serving the Holy Land," *Custodia Terrea Sanctae*, http://www.custodia.org/default.asp?id=425 (accessed June 3, 2015).

[384] The information on the crusades is based on the following resource. Steve Weidenkopf, and Alan Schreck, *Epic: A Journey through Church History* (West Chester: Ascension Press, 2009), 43-55, 153-154, 209, 210.

greed was not a likely primary motive for them; rather, piety was a more probable cause. [385]

3. The Crusaders were Blood Thirsty Murderers

According to Weidenkopf, the crusaders fought according to the military conventions of their day. At the time of the crusades it was a military custom that if a city surrenders during a siege the inhabitants would be left alone. If the citizens do not surrender, as occurred during the First Crusade, the inhabitants were killed. By killing the inhabitants of Jerusalem when fighting the First Crusade, the Crusaders were acting neither better nor worse than their contemporaries. This argument does not justify the crusaders' actions. It does, though, provide a historical context by which to understand some of their actions that from our perspective, which has benefited from the action of the Holy Spirit enlightening our minds through time, were horrendous.

4. During the Crusades the Church Encouraged the Destruction of the Jewish People

While it is true that there were Catholics who persecuted God's chosen people during the Crusades, it is also true that no Jewish pogrom has ever been encouraged by the Papacy. In addition, many Church leaders and saints, including St. Bernard of Clairvaux (1090-1153) spoke out against the persecution of the Jews. St. Bernard asserted that while, "[w]e have heard with joy that zeal for God burns in you, but wisdom must not be lacking from this

---

[385] Thomas Madden, *New Concise History of the Crusades* (New York, NY: Rowan & Littlefield Publishers, Inc., 2005), 12.

zeal. The Jews are not to be persecuted, nor killed, nor even forced to flee."[386]

5. The Crusades are Responsible for Anti-Christian Sentiment in Muslim Countries

Weidenkopf points out that since the Crusaders only ruled Jerusalem and its surrounding lands briefly from 1096-1291 Islamic countries deemed this time unimportant and, consequently, largely forgot about the Crusader states. Evidence of this forgetfulness is traceable to as late as 1899. In 1899, the German Emperor Kaiser Wilhelm II visited the tomb of the great Muslim leader Saladin and was shocked by the state of disrepair that Saladin's tomb was in. Only in very recent times have the Crusades become a point of contention between Islamic countries and Christian influenced ones.[387]

Inquisitions

Another medieval Church practice that has been frequently misunderstood are the inquisitions. The term inquisition comes from the Latin word *inquisitionem* meaning "a searching into, legal examination."[388] Episcopal inquisitions, led and directed by bishops, were initiated by Pope Lucius III (reigned 1181-1185). He requested in his 1184 Papal Bull *Ad Abolendam* that bishops are to

---

[386] Weidenkopf's cites the following letter of St. Bernard. St. Bernard, *Epistolae*, quoted in *Chronicles of the Crusades*, ed. Elizabeth Hallam (New York, NY: Weidenfeld and Nicolson, 1989), 126.

[387] Steve Weidenkopf, "Crash Course on the Crusades," *Crisis Magazine* July 24 (2004), http://www.crisismagazine.com/2012/crash-course-on-the-crusades (accessed June 4, 2015). Weidenkopf recommends the following resources: Belloc, Hilaire. *The Crusades – The World's Debate*. Rockford, IL: TAN Books and Publishers, Inc., 1992; Karsh, Efraim. *Islamic Imperialism – A History*. New Haven and London CT: Yale University Press, 2006; Madden, Thomas F. *The New Concise History of the Crusades* New York, NY: Rowman & Littlefield Publishers, Inc., 2005; Riley-Smith, Jonathan. *What were the Crusades?* Third Edition. San Francisco, CA: Ignatius Press, 2002.

[388] "Inquisition," Online Etymology Dictionary, http://www.etymonline.com/index.php?term=inquisition (accessed June 5, 2015).

determine in Church courts whether or not someone had fallen into heresy.[389]

Pope Gregory IX (reigned 1227-1241) took a more directive role in inquisitions by requiring church courts, headed by bishops and staffed by Dominican and Franciscan theologians, to determine heresy. Previously, heresy was tried in civil courts, which led to abuse and excess. Pope Innocent IV (1243-1254) also brought moderation to inquisition proceedings by requiring the approval of a bishop for lifelong imprisonment or burning of heretics. Clement V (1305-1314) went one significant step further by asserting that all court decisions dealing with heresy are to be submitted to the bishop for his final approval, otherwise the charges are void.[390] Building upon this precedent, in 1542 Pope Paul III (reigned 1534-1549), with his Apostolic Constitution *Licet ab initio*, established the Congregation of the Inquisition. In 1908, this Congregation was renamed by Pope St. Pius X to the Congregation of the Holy Office. In 1965, the Congregation was once again renamed as the Sacred Congregation for the Doctrine of the Faith. Finally, in 1983 the adjective "sacred" was dropped from the title. Currently, it is called the Congregation for the Doctrine of the Faith, or CDF for short.[391]

A few commonly overlooked aspects that Steven Weidenkopf points out include the following.

1. The Church never killed anyone during the Inquisition since her role, through the inquisitor, was to bring about conversion.

2. Catholic Church Courts during the time of the inquisitions were more humane and moderate than civil courts, as is evident, among other sources, in Bernardo Gui's manual for inquisitors. According to this Medieval Dominican Inquisitor (c. 1261-1331) the

---

[389] Michael C. Thomsett, *The Inquisition: A History* (Jefferson: McFarland & Co., 2010), 13-14.

[390] Thomsett, 29-31.

[391] 207, 246; "Congregation for the Doctrine of the Faith," The Vatican, http://www.vatican.va/roman_curia/congregations/cfaith/documents/rc_con_c faith_pro_14071997_en.html (accessed June 5, 2015).

use of torture, while not prohibited, was discouraged. It was to be used as a last resort. Only if the inquisitor failed was he to hand over the unrepentant heretic to civil authorities.

3. Trials were carefully recorded.
4. When torture was used in terrible ways, it was done by civil authorities, such as by the Spanish during the Spanish Inquisition, led by the Spanish monarchs.[392]

Quiz 12

1. According to chapter 12 what were the two primary factors that caused the Crusades?

2. Why was the initial motivation for the Crusades replaced by another motivation?

3. Explain the privileges that Urban II offered to crusaders.

4. Explain what the *votum crucis* was.

5. Explain the indulgence offered to crusaders. When explaining, include reference to the conditions required.

6. Use the Weidenkopf's analogy of a modern ATM machine to describe how the Knights Templar's banking system worked.

7. Chose two crusades and state their essential details.

---

[392] Steve Weidenkopf, and Alan Schreck, *Epic: A Journey through Church History* (West Chester: Ascension Press, 2009), 154;

8. Respond to the following with specific points. (You are not required to agree with Weidenkopf's views. You are only required to state your view while backing it up in reference to history.)

The Crusades were wars of aggression.

The Crusades were motivated primarily by greed.

The Crusaders were blood thirsty murderers.

During the Crusades the Church encouraged the destruction of the Jewish people.

The Crusades are responsible for anti-Christian sentiment in Muslim countries.

Those in charge of the Medieval Inquisitions trials were blood thirsty and intent on quickly sentencing a person to death.

9. In 1542 Pope Paul III (reigned 1534-1549), with his Apostolic Constitution *Licet ab initio*, established the Congregation of the Inquisition. In 1908, this Congregation was renamed by Pope St. Pius X to the Congregation of the Holy Office. Currently, it is called the _____.

Chapter 13

Medieval Education

Introduction

As with the Crusades, Catholic education during the medieval age has frequently been misrepresented. A common way this occurs is by labeling the medieval time as dark ages when the intellect was fettered by Church control. When examined carefully, this narrative is quickly recognized as false. We will carefully examine medieval education by studying monastic schools, cathedral schools, and universities. Some of the greatest minds came out of these centers of education.

Monastic Education

During the early medieval age, various schools existed. Two primary educational institutes were the monasteries and the non-monastic clerical schools.[393] Some of the most important monastic schools were Tours in France, Jarrow in England, Fulda in Germany, Monte Cassino in Italy, Iona in Scotland, and Clonmacnois in Ireland. Up until the ninth century, only boys interested in becoming monks were allowed into the monastic schools. After the ninth century, monasteries began educating

---

[393] Jean Leclercq, *The Love of Learning and the Desire for God: A Study of Monastic Culture*, trans. Catherine Misrahi (New York: Fordham University press, 1982), 193-194.

those who were not discerning a vocation to their monasteries.[394] In his book *The Love of Learning and the Desire for God*, Jean Leclercq glowingly describes how monastic education undertaken at these monastic schools were not only concerned with growth in knowledge but also growth in sanctification. In contrasting monastic education with the scholastic education in cathedral schools and universities, which replaced the educational leadership role that monasteries provided, Leclercq writes,

> The two theologies draw in common on Christian sources and both enlist the aid of reason. Scholastic theology has recourse more frequently to the philosophers; monastic theology contents itself more generally with the authority of Scripture and the Fathers. But the fundamental sources in both cases are the same. Theology is a method for reflecting on the mysteries revealed in Christian origins. The question now before us is to learn if there are several ways in which this reflection may be practiced and if amongst them there is a mode of reflection more appropriate to the monks. The texts themselves have led us to confirm that what individualizes monastic thought is a certain dependence on experience. Scholastic theology, on the other hand, puts experience aside. It can subsequently hark back to experience, observe that it agrees with its own reasonings, and that it can even receive nourishment from them; but its reflection is not rooted in experience and is not necessarily directed toward it. It is placed, deliberately, on the plane of metaphysics; it is impersonal and universal. In that very fact reside both its difficulty and its grandeur. It seeks in secular learning and philosophy for analogies capable of expressing religious realities. Its purpose

---

[394] Kenneth O Gangel, and Warren S. Benson, *Christian Education: Its History and Philosophy* (Eugene: Wipf and Stock, 1983), 108.

is to organize Christian erudition by means of removing any subjective material so as to make it purely scientific.

As for the monks, they call as if spontaneously upon the testimony of the conscience upon the presence within them of God's mysteries. Their principle purpose is not to reveal the mysteries of God, to explicate them or derive from them any speculative conclusions, but to impregnate their whole lives with them and to order their entire experience to affect their mode of reflecting and for this experience itself to become in large measure the matter of their meditation. These two modes of religious understanding are, in the original meaning of the word, complementary. Monastic theology is, in a way, a spiritual theology which completes speculative theology; it is the latter's completion and fulfillment. It is the added something, the *sursum* in which speculative theology tends to transcend itself and become what St. Bernard calls an integral knowledge of God: *integer congoscere.*[395]

Cathedral Schools

Cathedral schools, overseen by bishops, were also gradually established during the medieval age. At first, the teachers at the Cathedral schools were the bishops themselves. As Church membership grew during the 300s-400s, bishops delegated to a class of clerics called *scholasticus* the role of teaching. Since a good number of these clerics had been formerly trained in classical literature, they began to broaden the curriculum of medieval education, as we will see in the following section on universities.[396] In

---

[395] Leclercq, 213.
[396] Kenneth O. Gangel, and Warren S. Benson, *Christian Education: Its History and Philosophy* (Eugene: Wipf and Stock, 1983), 108.

time, the cathedral schools surpassed the monastic schools in educational leadership. During the eleventh and twelfth centuries, the leading cathedral schools were in Paris, Orleans, Chartres, Liege, Toledo, and Utrecht.[397]

The *scholasticus* are known for their educational approach that is called scholasticism. In contrast with the monastic approach to education, where growth in the spiritual life is central, in the scholastic educational model this often was not as central. Since in its origins monastic education was undergone by monks or those discerning to be monks, naturally monastic schools integrated prayer and study more than the scholastics did.[398] According to the Swiss theologian Hans Urs von Balthasar (1905-1988), the scholastic more abstract, logical, and systematic approach may be the explanation why during the scholastic times there were relatively few saintly theologians. Of course, there were some such as St Albert the Great, St. Thomas Aquinas, and St. Bonaventure. In describing this phenomena Balthasar observes,

> In the whole history of Catholic theology there is hardly anything that is less noticed, yet more deserving of notice, than the fact that, since the great period of Scholasticism, there have been few theologians who were saints. We mean here by "theologian" one whose office and vocation is to expound revelation in its fullness, and therefore whose work centers on dogmatic theology. If we consider the history of theology up to the time of the great Scholastics, we are struck by the fact that the great saints, those who not only achieved an exemplary purity of life, but who also had received from God a definite mission in the Church, were, mostly, great theologians. They were "pillars of the Church", by vocation channels of her life: their own lives reproduced the fullness of the Church's teaching, and their teaching the fullness of the

---

[397] Gangel and Benson, 109.
[398] Leclercq, 20, 22, 53.

Church's life.[399]

Medieval Universities

As cathedral schools, what Gangel and Benson call "professional schools," continued to expand, bishops once again delegated part of their role as overseers. They did this by appointing chancellors who were to supervise the faculty. At the same time, teachers and students began to form themselves into educational guilds based on the apprentice and master model of trade guilds. The combination of these factors led to the term *universitas* to be used when referring to schools of higher education.[400]

The twelfth century mendicant orders (in Latin meaning begging or property less orders) of the Franciscans and Dominicans helped, along with secular teachers, to staff the universities with highly educated teachers. St. Thomas Aquinas O.P. (1225-1274) and St. Bonaventure O.F.M. (1221-1274) are but two examples. They studied together as students at the University of Paris. Along with Paris, major universities of the 1300s were located at Montpellier, Oxford, Cambridge, Salerno, Bologna, and Lisbon.[401] In 1231, the University of Paris was given even greater autonomy from the local bishop when Pope Gregory IX in his papal bull *Parens Scientiarum* permitted it to be relatively self-governing. According to the bull, the University of Paris had the privileges of creating statutes, and punishing according to these statutes.[402]

The Holy Roman Emperor Frederick I Barbarossa also greatly aided the developing educational scene when in 1155 he issued the constitution *Authentica Habita*. Laws instituted by the promulgation of the constitution protected students and scholars when

---

[399] Hans Urs von Balthasar, *Explorations in Theology: I The Word Made Flesh: Unity and Division,* trans. A.V. Littledale (San Francisco: Ignatius Press, 1989), 181.

[400] Gangel and Benson, 109.

[401] Gangel and Benson, 110.

[402] Hunt Janin, *University in Medieval Life, 1179-1499* (Jefferson: McFarland & Company, 2008), 80.

they were traveling to and from foreign lands for academic reasons. If they acquired debt the constitution had a set of laws to ensure they were treated in a just manner. As a further way of protecting students, *Authentica Habita* gave students the option to be tried by teachers or courts overseen by the local bishop.[403]

Teachers taught and students learned according to a basic curriculum template that the universities inherited from antiquity. The program of study was divided into seven ways. The first three ways, or roads according to the literal meaning of the Latin title *trivium*, dealt with language: grammar, rhetoric, and logic. The second four ways, called the *quadrivium*, were comprised of subjects that had a pronounced mathematical component to them: arithmetic, geometry, astronomy, and music. In the 1200s, these seven educational roads were increased to include philosophical studies specifically the study of nature, metaphysics, and moral philosophy. Universities often specialized in a few of these disciplines without totally neglecting the others. The University of Paris, at which both Aquinas and Bonaventure were educated, was famous for its logic and metaphysics classes.[404]

Philosophy	Trivium	Quadrivium
Philosophy of Nature	Grammar	Arithmetic
Metaphysics	Logic	Geometry
Moral Philosophy	Rhetoric	Astronomy
		Music

The rise of the universities meant that there was significantly less emphasis on studying for personal spiritual growth, so characteristic of monastic education. Instead, scholars aimed at grasping concepts rationally and ordering their acquired knowledge in a highly systematic, logical manner. An inherent danger with this approach was identified by Pope Francis who warned

---

[403] Hilde de Ridder-Symoens, *A History of the University in Europe: Volume 1, Universities in the Middle Ages* (Cambridge: Cambridge University Press, 1992), 78.

[404] Ridder-Symoens, 308-309.

about studying God to obtain "answers to all questions." On this point the Holy Father stated:

> If a person says that he met God with total certainty and is not touched by a margin of uncertainty, then this is not good. For me, this is an important key. If one has the answers to all the questions—that is the proof that God is not with him. It means that he is a false prophet using religion for himself. The great leaders of the people of God, like Moses, have always left room for doubt. You must leave room for the Lord, not for our certainties; we must be humble. Uncertainty is in every true discernment that is open to finding confirmation in spiritual consolation. [405]

In the above quote of the Holy Father, two types of theology are referred to: cataphatic and apophatic. The word cataphatic comes from the Greek word *cata* meaning to descend and *phanai* meaning to speak. Cataphatic theology, therefore, is an attempt to bring God down to the level of our intellects to speak about him in a humanly understandable manner. This is not necessarily wrong to do. It becomes disordered when an academic does so without humility. The word apophatic comes from the Greek word *apophasis* meaning denial. In apophatic theology, the theologian speaks about God by referring to what He is not. Both ways of theology can be distorted if one is stressed to the exclusion to the other as the Fourth Lateran Council in 1215 when explaining unity and perfection in God states,

> When, therefore, the Truth prays to the Father for those faithful to him saying I wish that *they may be one in us just as we are one*, this word one mean

---

for the faithful a union of love in grace, and for the divine persons a unity of identity in nature, as the Truth say elsewhere, *You must be perfect as your heavenly Father is perfect*, as if he were to say more plainly, *You must be perfect* in the perfection of grace, *just as your Father is perfect* in the perfection that is his by nature, each in his own way. For between creator and creature there can be noted no similarity so great that a greater dissimilarity cannot be seen between them.[406]

Pope Francis' predecessor, Pope Benedict XVI, as Cardinal Ratzinger, also warned against a theology that is excessively cataphatic. When this occurs, the Catholic faith becomes understood more as a problem to be solved and less as a mystery to be believed. In a 1985 interview with the Italian journalist Vittorio Messori, he asserted:

The only really effective apologia (defense) for Christianity comes down to two arguments, namely the *saints* the Church has produced and the *art* which has grown in her womb. Better witness is borne to the Lord by the splendor of holiness and art which have risen in the community of believers than by the clever excuses which apologetics has come up with to justify the dark side which, sadly, are so frequent in the Church's human history.

If the Church is to continue to transform and humanize the world, how can she dispense with beauty in her liturgies (and in all of her life) that beauty which is so closely linked with love and with the radiance of the Resurrection? No. Christians must not be too easily satisfied. They must make their Church into a place where beauty–– and

---

[406] Norman P. Tanner, *Decrees of the Ecumenical Councils*, Volume I (Washington, DC: Georgetown University Press, 1990), 232.

hence truth-- is at home. Without this the world will become the first circle of hell.[407]

Messori further relates that Ratzinger (Benedict XVI) spoke, "of a famous theologian, one of the leading figures of post-conciliar thought, who admitted without a qualm that he felt himself to be a 'barbarian.' He comments, 'A theologian who does not love, art, poetry, music and nature can be dangerous. Blindness and deafness towards the beautiful are not incidental: they necessarily are reflected in his theology.'"[408]

Why Ratzinger is so concerned that not only theologians but all people develop a capacity for recognizing and appreciating beauty is because beauty can lead us to God, above all moral beauty which is highly attractive as people who have encountered saints can attest. In his typical insightful manner, Ratzinger explains that the early Church Father Ignatius of Antioch (c. 35-107) identified moral goodness directly with Christ since in Greek the word *chrestos* means good while the word *christos* means *Christ*. Ratzinger adds that when Christians are persecuted, "the conspiracy of the *Christos* is a conspiracy of those who are *chrestos*, a conspiracy of goodness. Thus Tertullian... assert[s] that 'the word Christ comes from the word for goodness.'"[409]

In the thought of Ratzinger, theologians need to be open to aesthetic beauty and to moral beauty. When this occurs, their theology will reflect the beauty and goodness of Christ and help draw people to God. A possible example of a scholastic from the time we are studying who in many ways failed these requirements set forth by Ratzinger is Peter Abelard (1079-1142). Abelard was a French medieval scholastic theologian who systematized theology in his dialectical theological work *Sic et Non*. In *Sic et Non*,

---

[407] Joseph Ratzinger, *The Ratzinger Report: An Exclusive Interview on the State of the Church,* trans. Salvator Attansio and Graham Harrison (San Francisco: Ignatius Press, 1985) 129-130.

[408] Ratzinger, *The Ratzinger Report: An Exclusive Interview on the State of the Church,* 129-130.

[409] Joseph Cardinal Ratzinger, Heinz Schurmann, and Hans Urs von Balthasar, *Principles of Christian Morality*, trans. Graham Harrison (San Francisco: Ignatius Press, 1986), 60-61.

Abelard gathers together contradictory statements from Church Fathers and from Christian theology and then attempts to reconcile the apparent contradictions. He did much of his academic work as a master at the Cathedral School of Notre-Dame de Paris. While there he became excessively attracted to the beauty, both physical and intellectual, of a young woman named Heloise. In his own words he describes what he intended to do:

> Now having carefully considered all things that usually serve to attract a lover, I concluded that she was the best one to bring to my bed. I was sure it would be easy: I was famous myself at the time, young, and exceptionally good looking and could not image that any woman I thought worthy of my love would turn me down. But I thought that this particular girl would be even more likely to give in because of her knowledge and love of letters. Through the written messages we could send one another we could be together even when we were apart. We also could write some things to each other more boldly than we could ever speak them and so could always be carrying on some very pleasant dialogues. I was all on fire for the girl and needed a way I could get to know her on a private and daily basis to win her over. So I approached her uncle through some of his friends and arranged for him to take me as a lodger in his house, which was right next to the school. I would pay whatever he asked. ... I easily got what I wanted...On top of this, he begged me-actually begged-and it was beyond anything my love could have dared to hope-to take complete charge of the girl, to spend all the time I had free from school teaching her, night and day.... The simplicity of the man just staggered me, as if he had set a ravening wolf to watch over a lamb.[410]

---

[410] Peter Abelard and Heloise, *Abelard & Heloise: The Letters and Other Writings* ed. William Levitan (Hackett Publishing Co., 2007), 11.

After Abelard took up residence in Heloise's uncle Fulbert's home, the two became intensely in love with one another. Their love lead to a pregnancy after which Abelard married Heloise secretly. When their marriage became public, Heloise denied she was married to Abelard. Her uncle reacted by having men break into Abelard's room to castrate him. As Abelard relates, "They cut off the parts of my body with which I committed the wrong they complained of-and then they fled."[411] In disgrace, Abelard became a monk at the St. Denis monastery in Paris.[412]

Scholasticism and Art

We will end this chapter with a glance at a new style of art that was beginning during the age of the scholastics to replace the older more formal and stylized Byzantine style. The Florentine artist Cimabue (c. 1240-1302) was one the most important artists of the time who broke away from the iconographic Byzantine style, depicted below. Cimabue's example was further developed by his student Giotto di Bondone (c. 1266 –1337).[413]

---

[411] Abelard and Heloise, 18.
[412] Abelard and Heloise, ix, 13, 18,
[413] Georgio Vasari, *The Lives of the Artists*, trans, Julia Conaway Bondanella (Oxford: Oxford University Press, 2008), 12.

Art of St. Mark's Basilica (c. late 1000s-1100s AD) Venice

~ Italo-Byzantine Style ~

[414] Wolfgang Moroder. "Mosaic of the translation of the body of Saint Mark on San Alipio facade door of the Saint Mark's Basilica in Venice," photograph, http://commons.wikimedia.org/wiki/File%3AMosaico_traslazione_San_Marco _Venezia.JPG (accessed April 19, 2015).

[415] The Yorck Project: 10.000 Meisterwerke der Malerei. DVD-ROM, 2002. ISBN 3936122202. Distributed by DIRECTMEDIA Publishing GmbH, "10th-century gold and enamel Byzantine icon of St Michael, in the treasury," photograph, http://commons.wikimedia.org/wiki/File%3AMeister_der_Ikone_ des_Erzengels_Michael_001_adjusted.jpg (accessed April 19, 2015).

~ Cimabue's Art ~

[416] Sailko, "Cimabue's *Maestà, Santa Maria dei Servi*," photograph, https://commons.wikimedia.org/wiki/File%3ASanta_Maria_dei_Servi%2C_bo %2C_interno%2C_maest%C3%A0_di_cimabue_01.JPG (accessed August 8, 2015).

[417] http://www.wga.hu/cgi-bin/highlight.cgi?file=html/d/duccio/23castel. html&find=castelfiorentino, "Cimabue's Madonna di Castelfiorentino, 1280s," photograph, http://commons.wikimedia.org/wiki/File%3ACimabue_madonna_ castefliorentino.jpg (accessed April 20, 2015).

[418] Starlight modified by GunnarBach, "Cimabue's Fresco in the Lower Basilica of Assisi," photograph, http://commons.wikimedia.org/wiki/File%3A San_Francesco_Cimabue.jpg (accessed April 20, 2015).

Fr. Peter Samuel Kucer, MSA

~ Giotto di Bondone's Art ~

419

420

The Yorck Project: *10.000 Meisterwerke der Malerei.* DVD-ROM, 2002, "Bardi Chapel: the Mourning of St. Francis," http://commons.wikimedia.org/ wiki/File%3AGiotto_di_Bondone_060.jpg, DVDROM (accessed April 20, 2015).

Web Gallery of Art, "Giotto's Lamentation (The Mourning of Christ), Cappella degli Srovegni," http://commons.wikimedia.org/wiki/File%3AGiotto_-_Scrovegni_-_-36-_-_Lamentation_(The_Mourning_of_Christ)_adj.jpg (accessed April 20, 2015).

Quiz 13

1. Compare in at least three ways the monastic educational model with the scholastic educational model.

2. Explain how first medieval cathedral schools and then universities gained relative autonomy from the local bishop. In answering this question include the following: *scholasticus*, Gregory IX.

3. Distinguish between cataphatic and apophatic theology with respect to the monastic and scholastic educational models.

4. Why is Abelard **not** a model theologian? In answering this question include reference to the monastic and scholastic approach to education.

5. Describe the key distinguishing feature of the new art style that was developing during the scholastic age. Contrast it with the Byzantine style.

Chapter 14

Sickness Within and Without

Introduction

During the late medieval times, roughly from the 1300s through the 1400s, several elements within the Church and outside of the Church can be considered as illnesses. One example, which was entirely an illness in the literal sense, was the Black Plague that took millions of human lives including some of the best clergy and religious. Other examples that are less evident as illnesses are the Avignon Papacy, the Papal Schism, and the Hundred Years War.

Black Plague

The Black Plague, which began around 1346 was responsible for millions of deaths.[421] According to John Kelly in *The Great Mortality: An Intimate History of the Black Death, the Most Devastating Plague of All Time*, "Today a demographic disaster on the scale of the Black Plague would claim 1.9 billion lives."[422] In the Middle East, the plague claimed a third of the population. China lost 50 percent of its population due to the plague and wars. Various regions of Europe lost between 40 to 60 percent of its

---

[421] John Kelly, *The Great Mortality: An Intimate History of the Black Death, the Most Devastating Plague of All Time* (New York: HarperCollins Publishers, 2006), 8.
[422] Kelly, 12.

population to the plague.

The carrier of the plague virus were fleas carried by rats.[423] Poor sanitary conditions were a major factor in the spread of the Black Plague since they provided an ideal environment for rats to multiply. In describing the unsanitary conditions of medieval times, Kelly writes:

> [A] combination of people, rats, flies, waste, and garbage concentrated inside a few square miles of town walls...made the medieval city a human cesspool. By the early fourteenth century so much filth had collected inside urban Europe that French and Italian cities were naming streets after human waste. ... Other Parisian streets took their names from the animals slaughtered on them...One irate Londoner complained that the runoff from the local slaughterhouse had made his gardens "stinking and putrid," while another charged that the blood from slain animals flooded nearby streets and lanes, "making a foul corruption and abominable sight to all dwelling near." ... The medieval countryside, where 90 percent of the population lived, was an even more dangerous place than the medieval city. Thinly walled, peasant homes were highly permeable, and the rat-to-person ratio tended to be very high in rural areas. Urban rat colonies usually divided their attention among several homes on a street, but in the country, not uncommonly, a single peasant family would find itself the target of an entire rodent colony.[424]

Another major factor that contributed to the high rate of death during the time of the plague include a series of harsh winters and torrential rain in the early 1300s. The adverse weather conditions caused severe food shortages, an increase in food prices and

---

[423] Kelly, 11-12, 18.
[424] Kelly, 16-17.

famines. One significant famine (1315-1317) took place shortly before the first signs of plague symptoms were recorded. This meant before the plague began and rapidly spread many people had compromised immune systems making them more susceptible to disease, above all to the Black Plague.[425]

At the time of the plague, doctors did not have our knowledge of how viruses spread as the germ theory of the French chemist Loius Pastuer (1822-1895) well explains. One prominent explanation for the occurrence of the plague was proposed by the Paris Medical Faculty in 1348. According to their report, the plague was caused by the formation of three planets that caused pollution in the air which contained the plague.[426] A Franciscan friar from Franonia, Herman Gigas in his 1349 chronicle records, "some say that it [the Black Plague] was brought about by the corruption of the air." Immediately after this, he adds, "others that the Jews planned to wipe out all the Christians with poison and had poisoned the wells and springs everywhere."[427] In accordance with this false belief, many Jewish people were scapegoated and killed. According to one report, also from 1349, "all the Jews between Cologne and Austria were burnt."[428] This terrible action occurred despite Cologne's civic officials insisting that the Jewish people were innocent. Similarly, the Duke of Austria's efforts to protect the Jewish people from being scapegoated were repeatedly ignored.[429]

---

[425] Lucas, Henry S Lucas, "The Great European Famine of 1315, 1316, 1317," *Speculum* 5, no. 4 (October 1930): 346, 352, and 358.

[426] Rosemary Horrox, *The Black Death* (Manchester: Manchester University Press, 1994), 158-159.

[427] Horrox, 207.

[428] Horrox, 209-210.

[429] Horrox, 110.

~ Image of a Common Late Medieval Motif, the Dance of Death (c. 1400s) ~

430

Avignon Papacy

To what extent the Avignon Papacy was a manifestation of internal sickness within the Church is subject to debate. At Avignon, seven successive popes ruled from 1309-1376. Some scholars hold that far from being detrimental to the Church, the papal court at Avignon France was a necessity and in some way helpful to the Church. As Michael Jones in the *New Cambridge Medieval History* states, "In the thirteenth century (and earlier) Rome was a dangerous place because of the riots and tumults there, in which

---

[430] Unidentified photographer, "This image is the *Dance of Death* in the German printed edition, folio CCLXI recto from Hartman Schedel's Chronicle of the World (Nuremberg, 1493) thought to be created by Michael Wolgemut (b. 1434, Nürnberg, d. 1519, Nürnberg)." photograph, https://commons.wikimedia. org/wiki/File:Danse_macabre_by_Michael_Wolgemut.png (accessed August 6, 2015).

the Roman aristocracy took a leading part."[431] Besides the violent nature of Rome, another beneficial factor in the papacy residing in Avignon, argues Jones, was that Avignon "was more conveniently situated than central Italy for most countries with which the papacy was in frequent contact."[432] In this supposedly ideal location the second Avignon pope, John XXII (reigned 1316-1334) reformed Church administration by centralizing power and finances. When he died, he left the Avignon papacy in sound financial shape. His financial reforms were further adopted and developed by his successors.[433]

Despite some of the positive features of the Avignon Papacy, St. Catherine of Siena (1347-1380) of the Third Order Dominicans was convinced that the Pope needed to return to Rome. Rome is the site where the Apostles Peter and Paul bore witness to Christ by their martyrdoms. It is fitting, therefore, but not absolutely necessary, that Popes reside in Rome where Peter and Paul manifested heroic leadership. In accordance with this belief, St. Catherine of Siena begged in a letter to the seventh and last Avignon Pope, Gregory XI (reigned 1370-1378) that he return to Rome:

> I Caterina, servant and slave of the servants of Jesus Christ and your poor wretched unworthy daughter, am writing to you in his precious blood...
>
> ... vice and sin, the pride and filth that are rampant among the Christian people—especially among the prelates, pastors, and administrators of holy Church who have turned to eating and devouring souls, not converting them but devouring them! And it all comes from their selfish love for themselves, from which pride is born, and greed

---

[431] Michael Jones, *New Cambridge Medieval History: Volume 6, c. 1300-c. 1415* (Cambridge: Cambridge University Press, 2000), 653.

[432] Jones, 654.

[433] Johann Peter Kirsch, "Pope John XXII." The Catholic Encyclopedia. Vol. 8. New York: Robert Appleton Company, 1910. 7 Aug. 2015 <http://www.newadvent.org/cathen/08431a.htm>.

and avarice and spiritual and bodily impurity. They see the infernal wolves carrying off their charges and it seems they don't care. Their care has been absorbed in piling up worldly pleasures and enjoyment, approval and praise. And all this comes from their selfish love for themselves. For if they loved themselves for God instead of selfishly, they would be concerned only about God's honor and not their own, for their neighbors' good and not their own self-indulgence. Ah, my dear babbo, see that you attend to these things! Look for good virtuous men, and put them in charge of the little sheep. ...

...So come, come! Delay no longer, so you may soon set up camp against the unbelievers, and so you will not be frustrated in the endeavor by these rotten members who are rebelling against you! ...

Peace, peace, peace, my dear babbo, and no more war...Take courage, take courage, father! ...[434]

In 1377, Pope Gregory XI heeded St. Catherine of Siena's request and returned to Rome. The next year he died. During the papal conclave that followed his death, a Roman mob gathered outside. They violently demanded the conclave to elect a pope from Rome or at least from Italian lands. The mob chanted, "A Roman! A Roman! A Roman or at least an Italian...Or else we'll kill them all!"[435] Within this tense environment, the cardinals elected the Archbishop of Barri, Bartolomeo Prignano, who was neither from Rome nor from France but originally from Naples. Prignano took the name Urban VI (reigned 1378-1389). The same year Urban VI became Pope, the French Cardinals who had

[434] Catherine of Siena, "Catherine of Siena: Letter 74 to Pope Gregory XI, in Avignon," UC Davis, http://medieval.ucdavis.edu/20C/Catherine.html (accessed August 7, 2015).

[435] Jones, 675.

returned to France went into schism by electing a French anti-Pope, Clement VII, who ruled from Avignon.[436]

Papal Schism

The chart below chronologically shows the popes and antipopes during the Papal Schism.

Rome (Popes)	Avignon (Anti-Popes)	Pisa (Anti-Popes)
Urban VI (1378-1389)	Clement VII (1378-1394)	
Boniface IX (1389-1404)		Alexander V (1409-1410)
Innocent VII 1404-1406)	Benedict XIII (1394-1417)	
Gregory XII (1406-1415)		John XXIII (1410-1415)
Martin V (1417-1431)		

[437]

The Avignon papacy began when the French cardinals, out of dislike of Urban VI, elected the anti-pope Clement VII. The line of Pisan anti-popes occurred when an invalid Church council was held in Pisa in 1409. Participants of the Council of Pisa subscribed to the heresy of Conciliarism. According to Conciliarism, a Church council has greater power than a pope. Following this heresy, the Council of Pisa invalidly deposed the valid Roman Pope Gregory XII and then elected the anti-pope Alexander V. When Alexander V died another anti-Pope of Pisa was elected, John XXIII.[438]

The schism was finally resolved during the Ecumenical Council of Constance (1414-1418). At the council's request, the Roman

---

[436] Jones, 512-513, 675-676.

[437]"The List of Popes." The Catholic Encyclopedia. Vol. 12. New York: Robert Appleton Company, 1911. 8 Aug. 2015 http://www.newadvent.org/cathen/12272b.htm.

[438] Joseph Francis Kelly, *The Ecumenical Councils of the Catholic Church: A History* (Collegeville: The Liturgical Press, 2009), 107.

Pope Gregory XII (reigned 1406-1415) resigned. The anti-pope Benedict XIII of Avignon was excommunicated, and the Pisan anti-pope John XXIII resigned. Once this occurred, the Council of Constance then elected Martin V (reigned 1417-1431).[439]

The Papal Schism exacerbated tensions between countries that already were in conflict with one another, especially between France and England. The map below indicates which countries, prior to the Pisan anti-pope, supported the Avignon anti-pope and which supported the Roman pope. As is evident, England supported the Roman pope while France and Castile supported the Avignon anti-pope. The confusion that resulted from these divisions greatly decreased the respect leaders and their people gave to the papacy.

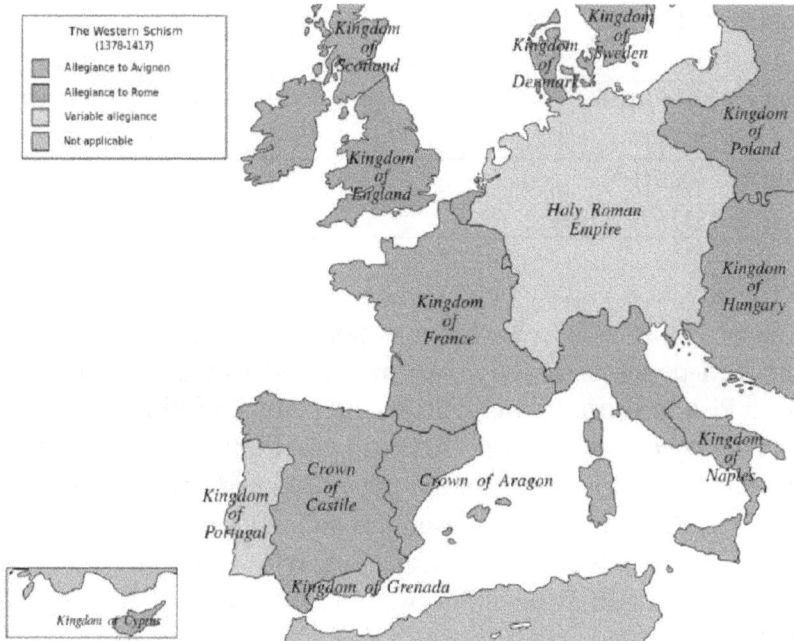

[439] Kelly, 108-111.
[440] Grand_schisme_1378-1417.png: @lankazame, derivative work: Mipmapped (talk), "Map showing support for Avignon (red) and Rome (blue) during the Western Schism; this breakdown is accurate until the Council of Pisa (1409), which created a third line of claimants," map, https://commons.wikimedia.org/wiki/File%3AWestern_schism_1378-1417.svg (accessed August 8, 2015).

Hundred Years War

At the same time the Avignon Papacy and the Papal Schism were occurring the so called Hundred Years War (1337-1453) between England (and allies), and France (and allies) was taking place. This war was made up by a series of successive small wars. In 1415, English forces led by King Henry V gained the upper hand and defeated the French at the 1415 Battle of Agincourt.[441] Inspired by St. Joan of Arc (1412-1431), French patriots regained control of their lands in 1453 at the Battle of Castillon.[442] As the French were fighting to gain back their lands from the English, St. Joan of Arc was captured by Burgundians and sold in 1430 to the English. [443] She was tried as a heretic by an ecclesiastical court controlled by the English which had her burned at the stake on May 30th, 1431. St. Joan was only nineteen years old when she died. As she was burning, she called on the name of Jesus.[444]

---

[441] Clifford J. Rogers, "Henry V's Military Strategy in 1415," in *The Hundred Years War: A Wider Focus* eds. L.J. Andrew Villalon and Donald J. Kagay (Boston: Brill, 2005), 399-429.

[442] L. J. Andrew Villalon and Donald J. Kagay, *The Hundred Years War: A Wider Focus*, Part 1 (Boston: Brill, 2005), xliii.

[443] Photographer unknown, "*Joan at the Coronation of Charles VII*, by Jean Auguste Dominique Ingres in 1854, is a famous painting that is often reproduced in books on Joan of Arc," photograph, https://commons.wikimedia.org/wiki/ File%3AIngres_coronation_charles_vii.jpg (accessed August 8, 2015).

[444] David Hugh Farmer, *Butler's Lives of the Saints*, New Full Edition, May (Collegeville: The Liturgical Press, 1996), 171-173.

Quiz 14

1. Why did the Black Plague claim so many lives? Provide at least three reasons that are referred to in chapter two.

2. Provide two medieval explanations, referred to in chapter two, for why the Black Plague occurred.

3. Why do some claim that the Avignon Papacy was helpful to the Church? Why did St. Catherine of Siena claim otherwise? What is your position?

4. Why did a line of anti-popes begin at Avignon?

5. Why did a line of anti-popes begin at Pisa?

6. What major European war was taking place during both the Avignon Papacy and the Papal Schism?

7. Who was the great patriotic French saint of the war referred to in number eleven? How and why was she killed?

Chapter 15

The Renaissance

Introduction

Before we begin studying the next phase in Church history, it may be helpful to situate ourselves in history according to the various eras into which historians often divide it. The following is one such division. Antiquity can be seen as beginning around 3000 BC and ending in 476 AD when the last Western Roman Emperor was deposed and the Western Roman Empire came to a definitive end. 476 AD to 1453 AD, then, can conveniently be understood as constituting the Middle Ages. The ending year 1453 AD is chosen since in this year the city of Constantinople, the Eastern capital of the Eastern Empire, fell to the Ottoman Empire. The Renaissance, or re-birth, is often seen as beginning in 1453, as intellectuals fled from the East to the West bringing their learning with them. The Renaissance can be understood as ending in 1650 with the death of Rene Descartes, a founder of modern philosophy.

Descartes's life and writings helped to give birth to the modern Enlightenment period, which can be considered as lasting from 1650, the year of his birth, and ending in 1789, which coincides with the first year of the French Revolution (1789-1799). The emotionally charged French Revolution gave rise to the Romantic era, with its emphasis on emotion and passion over reason and science. This era lasted from around 1789 and ended in the mid-

1900s. In the early 1900s, a new era coined the Modern era began.

Like the previous Enlightenment era, the Modern era was characterized by a fascination with exact science. During that same century, a new era dawned that is typically called the Post-Modern era. The Post-Modern era, influenced by deconstructionism and quantum physics, is skeptical of Modernism's exact claims. During this course, the divisions I have made will be flexibly used. Sometimes, certain notable people will be placed within a certain era that, according to the dates just given, do not correspond to the specific time the individual lived. This is because these eras are to aid our understanding of history. The people living during these eras were not conscious of our divisions that are to be flexibly understood by seeing a preceding era overlapping its successor.

1453: The Fall of Constantinople and the Beginning of the Renaissance (1453-1650)

As stated previously, in 1453 the capital city of the Eastern Empire, Constantinople, fell to the Ottoman Empire. Although the fall of the city dealt a devastating blow to the Greek Christians, many were not surprised that the city eventually fell. Prior to the fall, several actions were taken by Greek officials to strengthen their ability to resist the encroaching Ottoman Empire. In 1439, a Bull of Union was signed between Greek and Catholic Churches. Similarly, during the Ecumenical Council of Florence (1431-1449) other testimonies of union were signed between the Greek and Catholic Churches. These unions were affirmed by the Greek Emperor Constantine XI (1404-1453). Unfortunately, these unions did not last long for a variety of reasons, a principle one being the popular resistance in Greek lands to religious or political unions with the Catholic Church. In 1451, the Greek Emperor Constantine XI appealed to Western Europe (specifically Venice, Ferrara, Rome and Naples)[445] for help. The subsequent migration of intellectuals from the city to the west helped, along with other

---

[445] Marios Philippides and Walter K. Hanak, *The Siege and the Fall of Constantinople in 1453: Historiography, Topography, and Military Studies* (Farnham: Ashgate Publishing Limited, 2011), 361-362.

factors, to give birth to the Renaissance. During the siege of Constantinople in 1453, Emperor Constantine XI died in battle. His death almost dashed any hope among the Greeks that they would regain their beloved city from the Muslims invaders.

Pope Nicholas V (ruled from 1447-1455), who received Emperor Constantine XI's written plea for help, did try to help but without much success. In 1452, in the papal bull *Dum Diversas*, he authorized King Alphonso V of Portugal to go on crusade against the Ottoman Turks.[446] Similarly, in 1455, he issued another Bull affirming his previous permission to King Alphonso:

~ Pope Nicholas V ~

> We [therefore] weighing all and singular the premises with due meditation, and noting that since we had formerly by other letters of ours granted among other things free and ample faculty to the aforesaid King Alfonso -- to invade, search out, capture, vanquish, and subdue all Saracens and pagans whatsoever, and other enemies of Christ wheresoever placed.[447]

After Constantinople fell into Muslim hands, it became increasingly difficult for Europeans to travel to Asia for spices and other exotic goods desired by their countrymen. The Ottomans did permit travel through their lands but at a high price. These high fees incentivized Europeans to seek non-land based routes that would bring them to Asia. As a result, the 1500s, in addition to being considered the beginning of the Renaissance, is also called an Age of Discovery as Europeans sought out routes by sea rather than by land to reach the far East. For Christopher Columbus, this meant sailing west. In contrast, Bartolomeu Dias attempted to reach Asia by sailing east around Africa.

---

[446] Levi Maria Jordao, *Bullarium Patronatus Portugalliae Regum in Ecclesiis Africae* (Olisipone, 1863), 22.

[447] Nicholas V, "*Romanus Pontifex,* " January 8, 1455, Papal Encyclicals Online, http://www.nativeweb.org/pages/legal/indig-romanus-pontifex.html (accessed October 11, 2014).

Renaissance Writers

The Latin root on which the word Renaissance is based is *renasci*, meaning *re* – "again" plus *nasci* – "be born", and when put together means reborn. During this era, scholars revisited their cultural roots by studying ancient manuscripts. Notable writers from around this time include the great poet Dante Alighieri, the humanist Petrarch and his friend Boccaccio, the political philosopher Niccolò Machiavelli, the saintly statesman St. Thomas More, and the humanist and theologian Erasmus.

The Poet Dante Alighieri (1265-1321)

448

Although the Italian poet Dante preceded the Renaissance, at least by a common way of dating the Renaissance, he prepared for

---

[448] Sandro Botticelli [Public domain], via Wikimedia Commons, *Divina Commedia*, par. 9, http://www.hs-augsburg.de/~harsch/italica/Cronologia/ secolo14/ Dante/dan_d309.html (accessed October 12, 2014).

its rebirth. His most famous work *The Divine Comedy* is called a comedy since it contains the basic comedic form of happy beginning, sorrowful middle, and happy ending. In this case, the happy beginning refers to the original state of nature Adam and Eve enjoyed before the fall. The current state that we are experiencing on earth is the sorrowful state of the Fall. This "painful between state"[449] precedes the happy heavenly state to which we are all called. We may, though, either be detained in purgatory or miss the happy ending of our sad journey altogether in hell. Logically, *The Divine Comedy* is divided into a section on hell called, *Inferno*, a middle section called *Purgatorio* and an ending section, *Paradiso.* Dante's Italian composed work was so influential that some consider it as a key contributor in the development of Italian as a literary language. For this reason, he is sometimes referred to as "Father of the Italian language."[450] According to Elizabeth K. Haller, Dante has been granted this honorific title since his prose was so catching that it contributed "to the slow demise of Latin as a predominant literary tool."[451] During Dante's time, Latin was the dominant written language. Dante challenged Latin's dominance by transforming Italian into a competing literary language.[452]

Humanist Petrarch (1304-1374)

Like Dante, the Italian scholar Francesco Petrarch also preceded the dates we have assigned to the Renaissance. Similarly, he prepared the way for the European rebirth. For this reason, he is commonly known as the "Father of Humanism."[453] One way he

---

[449] Joseph Ratzinger, *Das Neue Volk Gottes* (Düsseldorf: Patmos, 1969), 167. " ...das bedeutet das schmerzliche „Zwischen", in dem die Kirche einstweilen noch steht."

[450] Elizabeth K. Haller, "Dante Alighieri," in *Icons of the Middle Ages: Rulers, Writers, Rebels, and Saints,* ed. Lister M. Matheson (Santa Barbara: Greenwood, 2012), 244.

[451] Haller, Ibid.

[452] Haller, Ibid.

[453] Nicholas Mann, "The Origins of Humanism," in *The Cambridge Companion to Renaissance Humanism*, ed Jill Kraye (Cambridge: Cambridge University Press, 1996), 8-9.

is humanism's father is found in his discovering, restoring, and promoting forgotten ancient manuscripts in monastic and cathedral libraries. For example, he restored Livy's *History of Rome* and made it accessible to other scholars.[454] He also discovered letters by Cicero. Along with Livy and Cicero, he promoted the writings of Seneca and Suetonius among other classical writers he made known.[455] Perhaps the best way to gain insight into Petrarch's love of ancient times is found within a description of his life in *Letter to Posterity*:

> I had a well-balanced mind rather than a keen one, one adapted to all kinds of good and wholesome study, but especially inclined to moral philosophy and poetry. In the course of time I neglected the latter and found pleasure in sacred literature, finding in it a hidden sweetness which I had previously taken lightly, and I came to regard the works of the poets as mere amenities. Though I was interested in many subjects, I devoted myself especially to study of antiquity, for I always disliked our own age-so much so, that had it not been for the love of those dear to me, I would have preferred to have been born in any other time than our own. In order to forget my own time, I have always tried to place myself mentally in another age; thus I delighted in history-though I was troubled by the conflicting statements, but when in doubt I accepted what appeared to me most probable, or else yielded to the authority of the writer.[456]

Petrarch's Friend Giovanni Boccaccio (1313-1375)

A friend and disciple of Petarch, Giovanni Boccaccio was an

---

[454] Mann, 9.

[455] Mann, 12.

[456] Petarch, "Letter to Posterity" in *Selections from the Canzionere and Other Works*, trans. Mark Musa (Oxford: Oxford University Press, 2008), 3.

influential poet and writer who, along with Dante and Petrarch, laid the groundwork for the flowering of the Renaissance.[457] He contributed to the development of the Italian language by following Dante's lead in composing his works in Italian. One specific contribution he made was his natural style of dialogue as particularly evident in his collection of short love stories entitled the *Decameron*.[458]

The Political "Scientist" Niccolò Machiavelli (1469-1527)

A Renaissance writer who was markedly different from Dante, Petrarch, and Boccaccio was Niccolò Machiavelli. Machiavelli is best known for his political thought in which he rejects rather than promotes the concepts of justice and virtue advanced by the two notable Greek thinkers Plato and Aristotle. According to his work, *The Prince*, dedicated to the Italian Florentine ruler Lorenzo di Medici, a wise ruler will choose to be immoral when convenient while maintaining an appearance of virtue. Machiavelli's defintion of politics as being an amoral realm is evident below:

~ Machiavelli ~

I say that every prince must desire to be considered merciful and not cruel. He must, however, take care not to misuse this mercifulness. ... A prince, therefore, must not mind incurring the charge of cruelty for the purpose of keeping his subjects united and confident; for, with a very few examples, he will be more merciful than those who, from excess of tenderness, allow disorders to arise, from whence spring murders and rapine; for these as a rule injure the whole community, while the executions carried out by the prince injure only one

---

[457] Mann, 10.

[458] Giovanni Boccaccio, *The Decameron*, trans. G.H. McWilliam (London: Penguin Books Ltd, 2995).

individual. And of all princes, it is impossible for a new prince to escape the name of cruel, new states being always full of dangers. ... Nevertheless, he must be cautious in believing and acting, and must not inspire fear of his own accord, and must proceed in a temperate manner with prudence and humanity, so that too much confidence does not render him incautious, and too much diffidence does not render him intolerant. From this arises the question whether it is better to be loved more than feared, or feared more than loved. The reply is, that one ought to be both feared and loved, but as it is difficult for the two to go together, it is much safer to be feared than loved, if one of the two has to be wanting. For it may be said of men in general that they are ungrateful, voluble, dissemblers, anxious to avoid danger, and covetous of gain; as long as you benefit them, they are entirely yours; they offer you their blood, their goods, their life, and their children, as I have before said, when the necessity is remote; but when it approaches, they revolt. And the prince who has relied solely on their words, without making other preparations, is ruined, for the friendship which is gained by purchase and not through grandeur and nobility of spirit is merited but is not secured, and at times is not to be had. And men have less scruple in offending one who makes himself loved than one who makes himself feared; for love is held by a chain of obligation which, men being selfish, is broken whenever it serves their purpose; but fear is maintained by a dread of punishment which never fails.[459]

---

[459] Machiavelli, *The Prince*, trans. Luigi Ricci (London: Penguin Books Ltd, 1952), 89-90.

The Saintly Statesman St. Thomas More (1478-1535)

460

St. Thomas More can be seen almost as a direct antithesis of the conniving political leaders that Machiavelli extols. Although St. Thomas More is well known for his writings, especially his political satire *Utopia*, his most important writing is represented by his life as a living scripture. Despite have the high political office of Lord Chancellor, St. Thomas More chose to obey God rather than the laws of England enacted by King Henry VIII. At

---

460 Hans Holbein the Younger [Public domain], via Wikimedia Commons, http://commons.wikimedia.org/wiki/File%3AHans_Holbein%2C_the_Younger_-_Sir_Thomas_More_-_Google_Art_Project.jpg (accessed November 12, 2014).

first, St. Thomas More was a dutiful, obedient subject of Henry VIII. This changed when Henry VIII insisted, without having been granted an annulment by the Pope, on divorcing his wife Catherine of Aragon to marry Anne Boleyn. The King then went one step further by declaring himself head of the Church of England thus beginning a schism. St. Thomas More heroically refused to recognize the King's invalid marriage and the King's claim to be head of the Church of England. Henry VIII responded by sentencing St. Thomas More to death. St. Thomas More's last words before he was executed are reputed to be, "I am the King's good servant but God's first." In recognition of St Thomas More's outstanding example and inspiration for all politicians, in 2000 St. John Paul II proclaimed him the patron saint of statesmen and politicians. St. Thomas More's life serves not only as a source of inspiration for Catholic politicians but also for "a political system which has its supreme goal the service of the human person."[461]

Erasmus the Humanist and Theologian (1466-1536)

At the same time that Henry the VIII was busy stirring up trouble in England against Catholics loyal to the pope there was another Catholic, Martin Luther, living in Germany who also was resisting papal authority. We will cover the former Augustinian friar and Catholic priest Martin Luther and the reasons why he choose to break from the Catholic Church in a later chapter. In this section, though, you will be introduced to another Catholic priest, Erasmus who although at times discouraged by papal corruption, nonetheless remained within the Catholic Church and was obedient to the pope. According to Erasmus, Luther and his supporters were being hypocritical since the vices that the Protestant reforms condemned in the Catholic Church were also present in their own communities.

---

[461] St. John Paul II, "Apostolic Letter Issued Motu Proprio Proclaiming Saint Thomas More Patron of Statesmen and Politicians" The Vatican, http://www.vatican.va/holy_father/john_paul_ii/motu_proprio/documents/hf _jp-ii_motu-proprio_20001031_thomas-more_en.html (accessed September 30, 2014), no. 1.

~ Erasmus to the Protestant Reformers ~

You declaim bitterly against the luxury of priests, the ambition of bishops, the tyranny of the Roman Pontiff, and the babbling of the sophists; against our prayers, fasts, and masses; and you are not content to retrench the abuses that may be in these things, but must needs abolish them entirely nothing, in short, that is generally received pleases you, but you must needs pluck up the wheat with the tares, or rather, the wheat instead of the tares. And what in the meantime do you offer us better or more worthy of the Gospel, to make us quit our ancient practices? Look around on this 'Evangelical' generation, and observe whether amongst them less indulgence is given to luxury, lust, or avarice, than amongst those whom you so detest. Show me any one person who by that Gospel has been reclaimed from drunkenness to sobriety, from fury and passion to meekness, from avarice to liberality, from reviling to well-speaking, from wantonness to modesty. I will show you a great many who have become worse through following it. . . . The solemn prayers of the Church are abolished, but now there are very many who never pray at all. ... I have never entered their conventicles, but I have some- times seen them returning from their sermons, the countenances of all of them displaying rage, and wonderful ferocity, as though they were animated by the evil spirit.[462]

---

[462] Erasmus, "Epistle to Vulturius Neocomus," in *The Reformers on the Reformation* (London: Burns & Oates, 1881), 13.

Influential "Renaissance" Artists

Cimabue (c. 1240–1302)

As mentioned in the previous chapter, Cimabue was a Florentine painter and maker of mosaics. He broke from the Italo-Byzantine style but not completely. According to the Italian historian Vasari (1511-1574)[463], Cimabue taught Giotto.

464

---

[463] Georgio Vasari, *The Lives of the Artists*, trans, Julia Conaway Bondanella (Oxford: Oxford University Press, 2008), 12.
[464] Cimabue [Public domain], via Wikimedia Commons, Uffizi Gallery, Florence, http://commons.wikimedia.org/wiki/File%3ACimabue_-_Maest%C3%Ao_di_Santa_Trinita_-_Google_Art_Project.jpg (accessed October 16, 2014).

Cimabue's *Maesta*

465

Cimabue's Fresco in Assisi's Lower Basilica

Giotto di Bondone (1266/7-1337)

Giotto also was a Florentine painter. He broke almost completely from the Italo-Byzantine style by painting according to nature, or as the eye sees its subjects. The two paintings on the next page naturally depict grief. In the first painting Christ's disciples and angels are in mourning, and in the second the followers of St. Francis of Assisi are mourning their master's passing from this world.

466

467

466 Giotto [Public domain], via Wikimedia Commons, The Mourning of Christ http://commons.wikimedia.org/wiki/File%3AGiotto_-_Scrovegni_-_-36-_-_Lamentation_(The_Mourning_of_Christ)_adj.jpg (accessed October 16, 2014).
467 Giotto [Public domain], via Wikimedia Commons, The Mourning of Francis, http://commons.wikimedia.org/wiki/File%3AGiotto_di_Bondone_060.jpg (accessed October 16, 2014).

Blessed Fra Angelico OP (1395-1455)

Blessed Fra Angelico was a Dominican of Florence's San Marco friary. There he painted the friary's walls, paying special attention to the cells. He was beatified in 1982 by Saint John Paul II. Below is a beautiful painting where the holiness of the Blessed Virgin shines forth. This painting is situated in the North Corridor of San Marco's friary.

468

Masaccio (1401-1428)

Masaccio was an Italian Renaissance artist, among others, who not only painted in a naturalistic style but also used linear perspective complete with a vanishing point. Can you identify the vanishing point in Masaccio's painting given below?

468 Fra Angelico, y carulmare [CC-BY-2.0 (http://creativecommons.org/licenses/by/2.0)], via Wikimedia Commons, San Marco, North Corridor, http://commons.wikimedia.org/wiki/File%3AANGELICO%2C_Fra_Annunciation%2C_1437-46_(2236990916).jpg (accessed October 16, 2014).

469

Michelangelo (1475-1564)

470

Brancacci Chapel, Florence, http://commons.wikimedia.org/wiki/File%3A
Masaccio7.jpg (accessed October 16, 2014).
470 Michelangelo Buonarroti [CC0], *Pieta*, via Wikimedia Commons,
ttp://commons.wikimedia.org/wiki/File%3AMichelangelo's_Piet%C3%A0_Saint
_Peter's_Basilica_Vatican_City.jpg (accessed October 13, 2014).

471

<hr />

471 Michelangelo Buonarroti [Public domain], via Wikimedia Commons, *Last Judgment*, http://upload.wikimedia.org/wikipedia/commons/b/be/ Michelangelo_Buonarroti_-_Last_Judgment_-_WGA15472.jpg (accessed, October 13, 2014).

472

Above are three of Michelangelo's best known works: the *Pieta* (in St. Peter's Basilica), the *Last Judgment* (in the Sistine Chapel), and the *David*, (in Florence). This Italian, Renaissance artist was multitalented as a painter, sculptor, and poet and even as an architect. He was responsible for designing St. Peter's Basilica.[473]

Raphael (1483-1520)

474

A contemporary of Michelangelo, Raphael was also a leading Renaissance painter and architect of his times. Above is one of his most famous works, *The School of Athens*, depicting Aristotle pointing straight ahead, in accordance with his moderate balance between the material world and the spiritual world, while Plato insists pointing straight up to the realm of ideas.

Below is a beautiful painting by Raphael of the Blessed Mother steading the baby Jesus as he inquisitively touches a cross.

Commons (accessed October 13, 2014).

473 Antonio Forcellino, *Michelangelo: A Tormented Life* (Cambridge: Polity Press, 2009), 272.

474 Raphael [Public domain], via Wikimedia Commons, http://commons.wikimedia.org/wiki/File%3ARaphael_School_of_Athens.jpg (accessed October 13, 2014).

475

475 Raphael [Public domain or Public domain], via Wikimedia Commons, http://commons.wikimedia.org/wiki/File%3ARaphael_-_Madonna_in_ the_Meadow_-_Google_Art_Project.jpg (accessed October 13, 2014).

Leonardo da Vinci (1452-1519)

Leonardo da Vinci was even more of polymath than either of the other two Renaissance masters. He not only was a painter, sculptor and architect but also was a philosopher, mathematician, engineer, map maker, anatomist, geologist, and writer.[476] Some of his most famous works include the moderately smiling *Mona Lisa*, *The Last Supper*, and *The Annunciation*. See below.

[477]

---

[476] Serge Bramly, *Leonardo: The Artist and the Man* (London: Penguin Books Ltd, 1998), 5, 13, 100, 390.

[477] Leonardo da Vinci [Public domain], via Wikimedia Commons, http://commons.wikimedia.org/wiki/File%3AMona_Lisa%2C_by_Leonardo_da _Vinci%2C_from_C2RMF_retouched.jpg (accessed October 14, 2014).

478

479

J. Sandro Botticelli (1445-1510) and Titian (1488-1576)

The Florentine artist Botticelli, whose patron was Lorenzo de Medici, represents a Renaissance artist who painted many scenes from Greek and Roman myths. See below for his famous painting

---

478 Leonardo da Vinci [Public domain], via Wikimedia Commons, http://commons.wikimedia. org/wiki/File%3A%C3%9Altima_Cena_-_Da_Vinci_5.jpg (accessed October 14, 2014).

479 Leonardo da Vinci [Public domain], via Wikimedia Commons, http://commons.wikimedia.org/wiki/File%3ALeonardo_Da_Vinci_-_Annunciazione.jpeg (accessed October 14, 2014).

of the *Birth of the Roman Goddess Venus*[480] (or Aphrodite in Greek). The other painting, *Primavera*, is also by Botticelli and is likewise centered on the goddess Venus. To the left of Venus in *Primavera* are her three daughters known as the Three Graces. During the Renaissance, the Three Graces represented different aspects of culture. To the far left is the god Mercury, symbol of reason, and to the right is the North Wind Zephyr who is attempting to capture Chloris. Chloris escapes by changing into Flora, goddess of spring.[481] Notice the modesty of Venus in *Birth of the Roman Goddess Venus*. In later paintings from the Renaissance modesty will be less evident, as most particularly evident in the painting *Venus of Urbino* by Titian (1488-1576).

482

---

[480] Aphrodite was the Greek Goddess of love. According to one version of a Greek myth, after Cronus, son of Gaia (earth goddess) and Uranus (sky god), cut off Uranus' genitals and cast them into the sea foam rose up and out of it Aphrodite was born. In accordance with her origins, her name means "foam-arisen". She arrived on land by floating on scallop shell. Robert Graves, *The Greek Myths* (London: Penguin Books, 1960), 49.

[481] William Kloss, *A History of European Art* (Chantilly: The Teaching Company, 2005), 108.

[482] Sandro Botticelli [Public domain], via Wikimedia Commons, *The Birth of Venus*, Uffizi Gallery, Florence, http://commons.wikimedia.org/wiki/File%3A La_nascita_di_Venere_(Botticelli).jpg (accessed October 16, 2014).

Bernini (1598-1680)

The Italian artist and architect Bernini is considered by some as Michelangelo's successor. Bernini designed the Piazza San Pietro in front of the St. Peter's Basilica. In accordance with the image of the Catholic Church being a holy mother, the placement of the pillars surrounding the Piazza resembles arms of a mother ready to embrace her children.[484] Another famous work by Bernini is his *Apollo and Daphne* sculpture. According to a myth described by Ovid in his *Metamorphis*, Daphne, not wanting to be captured by Apollo, has her wish granted and is changed into a tree. Bernini modeled the Apollo figure upon an ancient Roman statue, the *Apollo Belvedere*.[485] The *Apollo Belvedere* was rediscovered in Italy during the 15th century. Some art historians speculate that the Apollo Belvedere was in turn a Roman copy in marble of an even

---

[483] Sandro Botticelli [Public domain], via Wikimedia Commons, *Primavera*, Florence, Uffizi Gallery, http://commons.wikimedia.org/wiki/File%3ABotticelli-primavera.jpg (accessed October 16, 2014).

[484] William Kloss, *A History of European Art* (Chantilly: The Teaching Company, 2005), 199.

[485] Kloss, 197.

more ancient Greek bronze original.[486]

[487]

[486] "Apollo Belvedere" in *The Classical Tradition*, eds. Anthony Grafton, Glenn W. Most, and Salvatore Settis (Cambridge: Belknap Press, 2010), 55.

[487] By Diliff (Own work) [GFDL (http://www.gnu.org/copyleft/fdl.html), CC-BY-SA-3.0 (http://creativecommons.org/licenses/by-sa/3.0/) or CC-BY-SA-2.5-2.0-1.0 (http://creativecommons.org/licenses/by-sa/2.5-2.0-1.0)], via Wikimedia Commons, Piazza San Pietro, http://commons.wikimedia.org/wiki/File%3ASt_Peter's_Square%2C_Vatican_City_-_April_2007.jpg (accessed October 16, 2014).

488   489

Renaissance Popes

The time of the Renaissance papacy can be understood as beginning when the Western Papal Schism (1378-1418) ended. In review, during the time of the Western Papal Schism, two popes, and at one time three popes, claimed to be legitimate. The ecumenical Council of Constance (1414-1418) finally brought an end to the schism that had divided Catholic countries, and even recognized saints, over who was the valid pope. After two claimants to the papacy resigned, the third, the Avignon based anti-pope, was excommunicated. Once these events occurred the Council of Constance elected Martin V as the legitimate pope.[490]

---

[488] By Int3gr4te (Own work) [CC-BY-SA-3.0 (http://creativecommons.org/licenses/by-sa/3.0) or GFDL (http://www.gnu.org/copyleft/fdl.html)], via Wikimedia Commons, *Apollo and Daphne*, Galleria Borghese, Rome, http://commons.wikimedia.org/wiki/File%3AApolloAndDaphne.JPG (accessed October 16, 2014).

[489] After Leochares [Public domain], via Wikimedia Commons, *Apollo Belvedere*, http://commons.wikimedia.org/wiki/File%3ABelvedere_Apollo_Pio-Clementino_Inv1015.jpg (accessed October 16, 2014).

[490] James Hitchcock, *The History of the Catholic Church: From the Apostolic Age to the Third Millennium* (San Francisco: Ignatius Press, 2012), 216-217.

Both during the time of the Western Papal Schism and during the time of the Avignon Papacy (1309-1378), which had laid the groundwork for the schism, the city of Rome, the city of St Peter's and Paul's heroic martyrdom and witness to the faith, had been neglected. Aware of the need to build up the city of Rome, Martin V and subsequent Renaissance popes spent much time and financial resources in beautifying Rome. Under the great patron of the arts Pope Leo X (reigned 1513-1521), renovation of St. Peter's Basilica continued, Raphael decorated many papal rooms, and literatures, poetry and the antiquities were promoted. Pope Clement VII (1523-1534) also helped to build up the spiritual authority of the Church by refusing to grant Henry VIII's insufficiently grounded request for an annulment of his marriage to Catherine of Aragon, and by excommunicating him when Henry VIII insisted on divorcing his wife and marrying Anne Boleyn. Henry VIII responded in anger by issuing the 1534 Supremacy Act where he declared he was the head of the Church of England and not the Pope.

Despite the Renaissance popes' positive features of beautifying Rome, and remaining true to the teachings of the Church, as aided by the Holy Spirit, not even one of the Renaissance popes have been canonized or are in the process of being considered for canonization, and the lives of many of them were far from exemplary. Nepotism (promoting one's family members to high ecclesiastical offices) and the breaking of the vow of chastity by taking mistresses are but a couple of the papal vices prevalent during this time. In describing examples of Renaissance papal vice Eamon Duffy writes,

> Alexander VI (1492) flaunted a young and nubile mistress in the Vatican, was widely believed to have made a habit of poisoning his cardinals so as to get his hands on their property, and he ruthlessly aggrandized his illegitimate sons and daughters at the Church's expense. Julius II (1503-13), inspired patron of Raphael, Bramante, Michelangelo and Leonardo, was a very dubious Father of all the

Faithful, for he had fathered three daughters of his own while a cardinal, and he was a ferocious and enthusiastic warrior, dressing in silver papal armor and leading his own troops through the breaches blown in the city walls of towns who resisted his authority. Leo X (1513-21), son of Lorenzo the Magnificent of Florence, was made a cleric at seven and a cardinal at thirteen years old: as pope he ruled both Rome and Florence. He was the Pope whose Indulgence issued to fund the rebuilding of St. Peters led Luther to publish his Ninety-Five Theses. And so precipitated the Reformation. At his death, Leo left the church divided and the papacy close to bankruptcy.[491]

Renaissance Monarchs

One final way in this chapter that will help us to understand the Renaissance is by focusing our attention on a few of the notable monarchs of this age. We will begin with the tension between French and English monarchs before turning our attention to Spain.

Catholic England and Catholic France become Nation States

From around 1337-1453 England and France were engaged in a serious of wars that have been called the Hundred Years War even though these wars lasted longer than a hundred years.[492] This "war" can be understood as representing a gradual end of the feudal era, with its complicated and overlapping allegiances, and the beginning of the simpler, centralized nation state. In 1066, England fell under French feudal structure when the French

---

[491] Eamon Duffy, *Saints and Sinners: A History of the Pope* (Yale: Yale University Press, 1997), 133. Duffy is an Irish, Catholic historian and former member of the Pontifical Historical Commission.

[492] L. J. Andrew Villalon and Donald J. Kagay, *The Hundred Years War: A Wider Focus*, Part 1 (Boston: Brill, 2005), xxv.

Norman King, William the Conqueror invaded their lands. During the Battle of Hastings (1066) William the Conqueror decisively defeated the English. Consequently, the English people became a vassal to French overlords.[493]

As time went on, England began turning the tables of power so much that they became poised to become the overlords of the French. During the famous Battle of Agincourt (1415) in northern France, the English King Henry V defeated the French and began to rule most of Northern France. This infuriated the French so much that they fought back.[494] One renowned heroine and saint who led the French in battle against the English was St. Joan of Arc, whom we previously encountered. In review, in 1429 she persuaded Charles VII, whom many French people considered to be their French King, to fight the English King, Henry VI, who claimed to be the French King.[495] St. Joan was burned at the stake in 1431 after she was captured by the Burgundians and tried as a witch in an ecclesiastical court in favor of the English. Although St. Joan of Arc was tried by an ecclesiastical court, the court was controlled by the English crown and, hence, its outcome was politically determined.

St. Joan's vision of a free France, though, paid off and in the 1453 Battle of Castillon, France successfully regained its lands taken by the English.[496] France's numerous battles with England led the French people to want a centralized state ruled by the strong monarch who would secure them from English aggression. This meant, though, that French feudal lords with their numerous fiefdoms power needed to be weakened, and so they were under the French King Louis XI.[497]

[493] David D. Douglas, *William the Conqueror* (Berkeley: University of California Press, 1964), 181-211.

[494] Clifford J. Rogers, "Henry V's Military Strategy in 1415," in *The Hundred Years War: A Wider Focus* eds. L.J. Andrew Villalon and Donald J. Kagay (Boston: Brill, 2005), 399-429.

[495] L. J. Andrew Villalon and Donald J. Kagay, *The Hundred Years War: A Wider Focus*, Part 1 (Boston: Brill, 2005), xl-xli.

[496] Villalon and Kagay, xliii.

[497] Adrianna Bakos, *Images of Kingship in Early Modern France: Louis XI in Political Thought 1560-1789* (London: Routledge, 1997), 27-60.

Spain becomes a Catholic Nation State

After the Visigothic King of *Hispania*[498] (Spain) Reccared I converted from Arianism to Catholicism in 589, the local Third Council of Toledo (589) was held.[499] The council condemned Arianism and adopted Catholicism as the official religion of Hispania (Spain). Catholic rule of Spanish lands, though, was not to last long. In 712, Islamic forces defeated Catholic forces in the Battle of Guadalete.[500] Muslim rule lasted all the way up to 1492 when Queen Isabella I (1451-1504) and King Ferdinand II (1452-1516) retook Spain from the Muslims in what is known as the Spanish Reconquista. The year 1492 is chosen as the date when Catholics once again ruled over Spain since during that year the last Islamic stronghold of the Nasrid Kingdom of Granada fell to the Catholics.[501]

After the Battle of Granada (1491-1492), Queen Isabella and King Ferdinand intensified their efforts in building up a state that was bound together as a nation in part by Catholicism. They also built up national identity by instituting a monopoly on mints. Prior to their reign, Henry IV of the Kingdom of Castile (ruled from 1454-1474) had multiplied mints to around 150.[502] By drastically reducing the number of mints, Queen Isabella and King Ferdinand shrewdly unified the country economically.

---

[498] *Hispania* is the Roman name for what is now basically known as Spain.
[499] Michael Frassetto, *Encyclopedia of Barbarian Europe: Society in Transformation* (Santa Barbara:ABC-CLIO, 2003), 304.
[500] Clifford J. Rogers, *The Oxford Encyclopedia of Medieval Warfare and Military Technology Volume I* (Oxford: Oxford University Press, 2010), 226.
[501] Rogers, 215-216.
[502] Nancy Rubin Stuart, *Isabella of Castile: The First Renaissance Queen* (Lincoln: ASJA Press, 1991), 44, 98, 150.

Quiz 15

1. Place the following eras in proper order.

Renaissance, Antiquity, Modern Era, Romantic Era, Middle Ages, Post-Modern Era

2. In 1453 to whom did the capital city of the Eastern Empire (name this city by filling in the blank) 7. _____
fall to? 8. (fill in the blank) _____

3. After the above-mentioned city fell why did it become increasingly more difficult for European to travel to Asia to buy exotic goods to sell back home? How did the Europeans respond?

4. Match the following:

Dante Alighieri	Wrote the *Decameron.*
Petrarch	Wrote *The Divine Comedy.*
Machiavelli	Wrote "You declaim bitterly against the luxury of priests, the ambition of bishops, the tyranny of the Roman Pontiff...And what in the meantime do you offer us better or more worthy of the Gospel, to make us quit our ancient practices? Look around on this ' Evangelical ' generation, and observe whether amongst them less indulgence is given to luxury, lust, or avarice, than amongst those whom you so detest."

St. Thomas More	Considered by many to be the Father of Humanism. Discovered letters by Cicero.
Erasmus	Wrote in *The Prince*, "one ought to be both feared and loved, but as it is difficult for the two to go together, it is much safer to be feared than loved, if one of the two has to be wanting."
Boccaccio	Wrote *Utopia* and is the patron saint of politicians.

5. Why is *The Divine Comedy* called a comedy?

6. Compare the natural style of Giotto with the earlier Italo-Byantine style.

7. Who controlled and financed the ecclesiastical court that in 1431condemned St. Joan of Arc as a witch and burned her at the stake?

8. Describe two ways by which Queen Isabella I and King Ferdinand II built up Spain as a Catholic nation state.

Chapter 16

Protestant Reformation

Introduction

Corruption within the Catholic Church during the Renaissance led many to advocate reform. Some advocating reform, such as Erasmus, urged the Catholic Church leaders to study the more ideal early Christian era to re-form the Church according to that time while keeping legitimate development intact. Others, though, instead of advocating a reform proposed replacing the entire Renaissance ecclesial system which they deemed completely corrupt.[503] Those who tended in the direction of revolt were called Protestants, from the Latin verb *protestari* meaning to object. Martin Luther is often deemed as the first Protestant who lit the spark that has divided Christianity into Catholics and Protestants.

Martin Luther's revolt from the Catholic Church was prepared by two priests referred to as proto-protestants. These two priests were John Wycliffe, from England, and John Huss, from the Czech Kingdom. We will first briefly focus on Wycliffe and Huss before turning our attention to the following Protestant leaders: Martin Luther, Huldrych Zwingli, John Calvin, and Henry VIII.

---

[503] Steve Weidenkopf and Dr. Alan Schreck, *Epic A Journey Through Church History* (West Chester: Ascension Press, 2009), 71-73.

Proto-Protestants: John Wycliffe and John Huss

John Wycliffe (1330-1384)

504

Wcyliffe is considered a proto-protestant since he was a for-runner or first person who directly prepared for Martin Luther and the consequent divisions within Christianity that resulted. For this reason, he is sometimes referred to as the Morning Star of the Reformation.[505]

Wycliffe was ordained a priest on September 24, 1351.[506] Shortly after successfully completing a master's degree at Balliol College, he was assigned in 1361 as a parish priest in Fillingham, Lincolnshire. After ministering in several parishes, he once again returned to studying theology in 1363 at Oxford. In 1372, he received his doctorate degree in theology. During the time of Wycliffe's studies, the Archbishop of Canterbury, Simon Islip, appointed Wycliffe warden of the recently founded Canterbury College at Oxford.[507] Wycliffe became increasingly opposed to the

---

[504] By Manchester City Council. [Public domain], via Wikimedia Commons, http://commons.wikimedia.org/wiki/File%3ABrownManchesterMuralWyclif.jpg (accessed October 21, 2014).

[505] Religious Tract Society, *Life and times of John Wycliffe : The Morning Star of the Reformation* (London: Religious Tract Society, 1884).

[506] Stephen E. Lahey, *John Wycliffe: Great Medieval Thinkers* (Oxford: Oxford University Press, 2009), 5.

[507] Lahey, 5-6.

Church hierarchy of which he was a member. In an attempt to reduce the role of the priesthood that he deemed overly exalted, he translated the bible into English, advocated a form of Donatism that locates the validity of a sacrament in the holiness of the minister, denied that the bread and wine used in Catholic masses become the body and blood of Christ, and argued that the Church should give up all its property. His radical views inspired an anti-clerical movement called the Lollards.[508] Upon hearing of Wycliffe's teachings, Pope Gregory XI issued five bulls in 1377. In one he wrote:

> Recently, with great bitterness of hear we have learned from the report of many trustworthy person that John of Wiclyffe, rector of the church of Lutterworth, of the diocese of Lincoln, a professor of holy writ-would that he were not a master of error!-has burst forth in such execrable and abominable folly, that he does not fear to maintain dogmatically in said kingdom and publicly to preach, or rather to vomit forth from the poisonous confines of his own breast, some propositions and conclusions...which threaten to subvert and weaken the condition of the entire church.[509]

Shortly after his death, during the Council of Constance, Wycliffe was condemned as a heretic. This same council also denounced Wycliffe's Bohemian (or Czech) follower John Huss and had him burned at the stake,[510] an action for which St. John Paul II the Great later apologized.

---

[508] Lahey, ix, 23-24.
[509] Lahey, 18.
[510] Lahey, 29.

John Huss (1369-1415)

511

Along with Wycliffe, John Huss, a Catholic priest from the Kingdom of Bohemia, also known as the Czech Kingdom, may be considered the second proto-protestant. According to some historians, Huss was condemned at the Council of Constance not so much for what he taught, but rather for his refusal to condemn teaching associated with Wycliffe.[512] Others disagree. The council also asserted that Huss, along with Wycliffe, was condemned at the Council not simply because of his admiration of Wycliffe but also because of heretical teachings Huss espoused.[513] After carefully examining the condemnation of John Huss, the medieval historian Thomas A. Fudge concludes, "I believe that evidence shows conclusively that Jan Hus was a heretic. I am also convinced that a careful investigation of canon law and medieval criminal procedure demonstrates that, despite identifiable irregularities, the trial was legal. Even some of the most strident critics of the trial concede that the process co-

---

[511] By Janíček Zmilelý z Písku (Jena codex) [Public domain], via Wikimedia Commons, http://commons.wikimedia.org/wiki/File%3AJan_Hus_at_the_ Stake.jpg (accessed October 21, 2014).

[512] Thomas A. Fudge, *The Trial of Jan Hus: Medieval Trial and Criminal Procedure* (Oxford: Oxford University Press, 2013), 9.

[513] Fudge, 9.

nformed to current court practices."[514]

Pope St. John Paul II's omission of rehabilitating John Huss during the 1999 International Symposium on John Huss indicates that he concurred with Fudge.[515] Similarly, according to the documents of the Council of Constance, "This holy synod therefore pronounces the said John Huss on account of the aforesaid and many other matters, to have been a heretic and it judges him to be considered and condemned as a heretic."[516] After formally denouncing Huss and relinquishing him "to the judgment of the secular authority"[517] the council then lists 30 articles of John Huss that are heretical. A few of the condemned views of Huss are as follows; Jesus never appointed Peter head of the Catholic Church and therefore the papacy is not divinely instituted, the sins of priests and bishops affect the validity of sacraments, priests or bishops who are in mortal sin are no longer priests and bishops, and priests who are excommunicated may lawfully disobey this order by preaching.[518]

~ St. John Paul II Apologizes at an
International Symposium on John Huss~

Today, on the eve of the Great Jubilee, I feel the need to express deep regret for the cruel death inflicted on John Hus, and for the consequent wound of conflict and division which was thus imposed on the minds and hearts of the Bohemian people. It was during my first visit to Prague that I declared my hope that precisely in your land decisive steps could be taken on the path of reconciliation and true unity in Christ. The wounds of past centuries must be healed through a new attitude and completely renewed relationships. May

---

[514] Fudge, 347.
[515] Fudge, 345.
[516] Norman P. Tanner, *Decrees of the Ecumenical Councils*, Volume I (London: Sheed & Ward, 1990), 428.
[517] Tanner, 429.
[518] Tanner, 429-432.

our Lord Jesus Christ, "who is our peace... and has broken down the dividing wall of hostility" (Eph 2:14), guide the path of your people's history towards the rediscovered unity of all Christians, which we ardently hope for in the millennium that is about to begin.[519]

Martin Luther Sparks Protestantism

Martin Luther, formerly an Augustinian friar, and his wife
Katharina von Bora, formerly a Cistercian nun

[520]

---

[519] John Paul II, *Address of the Holy Father to an International Symposium on John Hus*, 17 December 1999,Vatican http://www.vatican.va/holy_father/john_paul_ii/speeches/1999/december/documents/hf_jp-ii_spe_17121999_jan-hus_en.html. (accessed October 21, 2014), 2.

[520] Workshop of Lucas Cranach the Elder [Public domain], via Wikimedia Commons, http://commons.wikimedia.org/wiki/File%3ALucas_Cranach_d.%C3%84._-_Doppelportr%C3%A4t_Martin_Luther_u._Katharina_Bora_(Hessisches_Landesmuseum).jpg (accessed October 21, 2014).

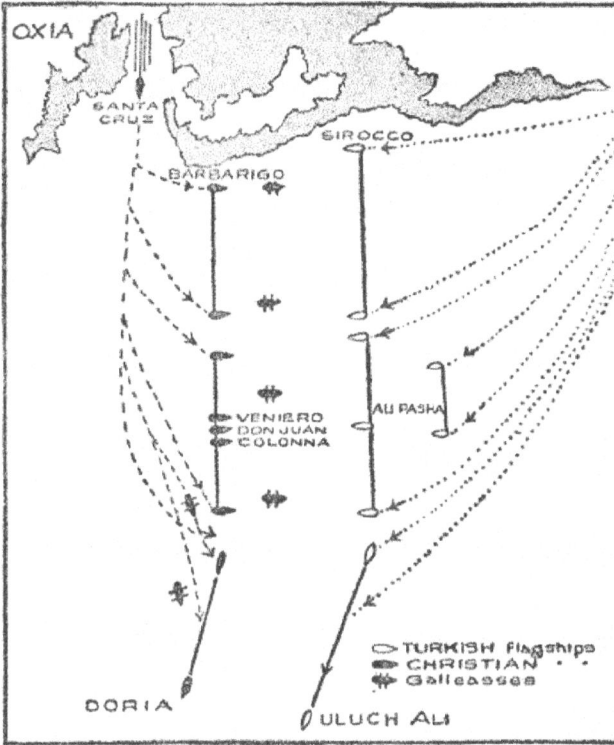

Why did Martin Luther's actions, and not those of Wycliffe & Huss, spark a revolt within the Catholic Church that led to the establishment of Protestantism? The answer lies in the proximate and immediate historical context in-to which Lu-ther had been born. These include, but are not limited to, the following six factors: the Western Schism, the Islamic threat, papal corruption, the appearance of selling indulgences, the invention of the printing press, and the marked desire of German political rulers for power and property. [521]

The Western Papal Schism (1378-1418)

For details on the Western Papal Schism, where at one point three men with considerable followers were all claiming to be pope, revisit the preceding chapter. This schism severely damaged the respect and credibility of the Church. If even the leaders at the top are breaking Church unity, why thought many, can we not do the same?

---

[521] By William Oliver Stevens and Allan Westcott [Public domain], via Wikimedia Commons, http://commons.wikimedia.org/wiki/File%3ALapanto_formation.png (accessed October 23, 2014).

The Islamic Threat

According to the great Catholic English historian Hilaire Belloc, another principle reason that Catholicism became divided into Catholics and Protestants during the 1500s was that the Holy Roman Emperor was devoting precious time and resources to resisting Islamic advances while paying less attention to maintain peace within in his empire. The German princes and other nobles, who wanted to wrest power away from the Emperor, took advantage of this situation by choosing to rebel, supporting Martin Luther and by promoting Protestantism.[522] Two examples of Islamic expansion in the 1500s by the Ottoman Empire are the Great Siege of Malta in 1565 involving the Knights Hospitaller on the island of Malta and the 1571 October 7 Battle of Lepanto near the western coast of Greece involving the Catholic Holy League. In both cases, despite overwhelming odds, the Ottoman Empire's aggression was repelled. Although these battles took place after the Protestant movement had already gained significant momentum, they still illustrate the continual pushing forward of the Ottoman Empire into Western lands. If the Islamic forces had been victorious during the latter battle, it is likely that they would have eventually been able to rule all Western Europe. As the director of the Prince Alwaleed Center for Muslim-Christian Understanding at Georgetown University John L. Esposito states, "From the fifteenth to the seventeenth century Ottoman forces seemed invincible to European Christians. Yet the Ottoman naval defeat at Lepanto in 1571 was a turning point, hailed as a victor of Christian Europe over the Muslim Turks."[523]

The pope at the time, the Dominican Saint Pius V, attributed the Catholic victory at the Battle of Lepanto to the praying of the

---

[522] Hilaire Belloc, *The Great Heresies*, http://www.ewtn.com/library/doctrine/heresy.htm (accessed October 22, 2014). "One of the reasons that the breakdown of Christendom at the Reformation took place was the fact that Mohammedan pressure against the German Emperor gave the German Princes and towns the opportunity to rebel and start Protestant Churches in their dominions."

[523] John L. Esposito, *The Islamic Threat: Myth or Reality?*, Third Edition (Oxford: Oxford University Press, 1999), 42.

rosary, specifically by the Roman confraternity who prayed in St Mary's basilica that the Catholic forces would prevail over the Ottoman. The date of October 7th, our current liturgical feast day of the Holy Rosary, was chosen because the battle was won on October 7, 1571.[524] A few years prior to this decisive victory, Saint Pius V in his 1569 Papal Bull *Consueverunt Romani* established the basic form of the rosary that so many of us pray.

~ St. Pius V on the Rosary ~

The Roman Pontiffs, and the other Holy Fathers, our predecessors, when they were pressed in upon by temporal or spiritual wars, or troubled by other trials, in order that they might more easily escape from these, and having achieved tranquility, might quietly and fervently be free to devote themselves to God, were wont to implore the divine assistance, through supplications or Litanies to call forth the support of the saints, and with David to lift up their eyes unto the Mountains, trusting with firm hope that thence would they receive aid.

....Dominic looked to that simple way of praying and beseeching God, accessible to all and wholly pious, which is called the Rosary, or Psalter of the Blessed Virgin Mary, in which the same most Blessed Virgin is venerated by the angelic greeting repeated one hundred and fifty times, that is, according to the number of the Davidic Psalter, and by the Lord's Prayer with each decade. ... This same method St. Dominic propagated, and it was, spread by the Friars of Blessed Dominic, namely, of the aforementioned Order, and accepted by not a few of the people. Christ's faithful, inflamed by these

---

[524] Nathan D. Mitchell, *The Mystery of the Rosary: Marian Devotion and the Reinvention of Catholicism* (New York: New York University Press, 2009), 22.

prayers, began immediately to be changed into new men. The darkness of heresy began to be dispelled, and the light of the Catholic Faith to be revealed. ...Following the example of our predecessors, seeing that the Church militant, which God has placed in our hands, in these our times is tossed this way and that by so many heresies, and is grievously troubled and afflicted by so many wars, and by the deprave morals of men, we also raise our eyes, weeping but full of hope, unto that same mountain, whence every aid comes forth, and we encourage and admonish each member of Christ's faithful to do likewise in the Lord.[525]

The Gutenberg Printing Press

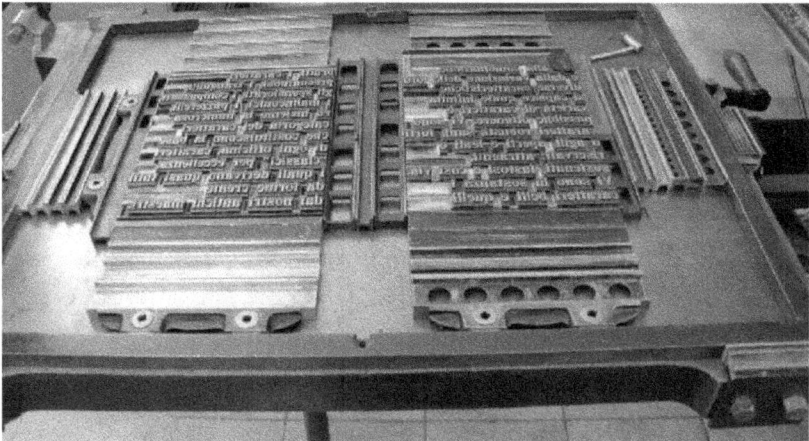

A third major factor that enabled the Protestant movement to

---

[525] Pope Pius V, *Consueverunt Romani*, September 17, 1569, http://www.ewtn.com/library/PAPALDOC/P5CONSUE.HTM (accessed October 23, 2014).

[526] By Kristian Bjornard from Baltimore, USA (Lock up on a metal Gutenberg-style press) [CC-BY-SA-2.0 (http://creativecommons.org/licenses/by-sa/2.0)], via Wikimedia Commons, http://commons.wikimedia.org/wiki/File%3ALock_up_on_a_metal_Gutenberg-style_press_-_Tipoteca_Museum_-_Cornuda%2C_Province_of_Treviso_-_Italy_-_June_2008.jpg (accessed October 24, 2014).

gain headway was the 1440s invention by the German Johannes Gutenberg of a printing press with metal movable type that could be quickly changed. Martin Luther and his followers used this technological advance to disseminate their views with a speed that was never before possible. The Protestants used the printing press significantly more than Catholics did. According to Cameron A. MacKenzie:

> [I]f Luther is compared to his Catholic counter-parts, the contrast is even more amazing. From 1518 to 1544 (less than two years before his death), Luther's German publications (not counting Bible translations) number 25,551 printings and reprintings. During the same period, the German works of *all* the Catholic publicists number only 514 printings. In other words, Luther alone outnumbered them by almost 5:1... Mark U. Edwards, a well-known historian of the Reformation, estimates that over the course of Luther's entire lifetime, over 3 million copies of Luther's German works appeared in print compared to only 600,000 for his Catholic opponents. And none of these statistics include Luther's German Bible, which was by far his most popular publication.[527]

Indulgences

In the early 1500s, the Dominican friar John Tetzel was sent to German lands by Pope Leo X to preach on indulgences. An indulgence "is a remission before God of the temporal punishment due to sins whose guilt has already been forgiven."[528] Money donated by the people for the indulgences was used by the Pope to

---

[527] Cameron A. MacKenzie, "Luther and Language: The Printing Press and the Bible," A Presentation at Cocordia Theological Seminary, March 24, 2004, http://www.ctsfw.net/media/pdfs/mackenzielutherandlanguage.pdf (accessed October 23, 2014).
[528] *Catechism of the Catholic Church*, 2nd ed., 1471.

reconstruct Rome's Basilica of St. Peters. No set fee was required to be granted an indulgence. People were only encouraged to donate according to their ability.[529] Unfortunately, Tetzel's preaching on indulgences was erroneously interpreted by Martin Luther as claiming, "so soon as the penny jingles into the money-box, the soul flies out [of purgatory]."[530] This phrase appears in Martin Luther's ninety-five theses that he tapped up on the door of the Castle Church in Wittenberg in 1517. In defending Tetzel's orthodox preaching of indulgences the early twentieth century German Catholic historian Ludwig Pastor well known for his *History of the Popes*, asserts:

> As regards indulgences for the living, Tetzel always taught pure doctrine. The assertion that he put forward indulgences as being not only a remission of the temporal punishment of sin, but as a remission of its guilt, is an unfounded as is that other accusation against him, that he sold the forgiveness of sins for money, without even any mention of contrition and confession, or that, for payment, be absolved from sins which might be committed in the future. His teaching was, in fact, very definite, and quite in harmony with the theology of the Church, as it was then and is now, *i.e*, that indulgences "apply only to the temporal punishment due to sins which have been already repented of and confessed."[531]

Some Corrupt Renaissance Popes

As briefly discussed in the last chapter, the lives of many

[529] Patrick Fr. O'Hare, *The Facts about Luther* (Rockford: Tan Books and Publishers, 1987), 60-61.

[530] Martin Luther, "Disputation of Doctor Martin Luther on the Power and Efficacy of Indulgences by Dr. Martin Luther (1517)", Project Wittenberg, http://www.iclnet.org/pub/resources/text/wittenberg/luther/web/ninetyfive.html (accessed October 24, 2014).

[531] Ludwig Pastor, *The History of the Popes from the Close of the Middle Ages* (St. Louis: B. Herder, 1908), 348.

Renaissance popes were not exemplary. Popes living at and around the time of Luther were guilty of nepotism, of poor financial management, and of breaking their vow of chastity. Perhaps, if all the Renaissance popes were instead saintly men the Protestant revolt would not have happened. However, it is important to recognize that the corrupt lives of some of the popes is only one factor among others that together helped to formally divide the Church.

Desire of German Princes and Nobles for Political Power, Money, and Property

The Protestant revolt was not only motivated for religious reasons but was also propelled by political motives. When this is recognized, then Martin Luther is not simply understood as a religious reformer but also as a German patriot who opposed the political power and influence held by both the Holy Roman Emperor and the Pope.[532]

Luther's local Lord Elector Frederick of Saxony also held Luther's patriotic views and served as Luther's protector when Luther was summoned to the 1521 Diet of Worms held in Worms, Germany. There Luther, backed by his Lord and other German nobles, defended his position before the Holy Roman Emperor Charles V who regarded Luther as a heretic.[533] Luther's position was especially attractive to the nobles since in his 1520 *Address to the German Nobility*, he demanded that payments by the nobles to Rome end.[534]

Although, publicly acknowledging that Luther was a heretic, Charles V was also keenly aware of the political dangers associated with opposing him as Wycliffe and Hus were in the recent past by

---

[532] Thomas F.X. Noble, *The Foundations of Western Civilization*, Lectures 25-48 (Chantilly: The Teaching Company, 2002), 334.

[533] Steve Weidenkopf and Dr. Alan Schreck, *Epic A Journey Through Church History* (West Chester: Ascension Press, 2009), 167. According to Weidenkopf Charles V stated at the Diet, "For it is certain that a single monk must err if he stands against the opinion of all Christendom. Otherwise Christendom itself would have erred for more than a thousand years. From now on I regard him as a notorious heretic..."

[534] Noble, 335.

Catholic leaders. To avoid civil war, Charles V then prudently, or at least he thought he was being prudent, did not stop Luther and the movement that Luther was promoting.[535]

Ninety-Five Theses

Contrary to popular belief, the 1517 posting of Ninety-Five Theses on the door of the Castle Church of Wittenberg was not necessarily an act of rebellion against the Catholic Church. Such a posting, possibly done by either Martin Luther or by one of his students,[536] was an ordinary act that professors at the University of Wittenberg, where Luther taught, did to formally engage people in a theological discussion.

When considered together with the other factors presented above, the posting of the ninety-five theses was only a symbolic tiny spark that lit the fire of the Protestant revolt against the Catholic Church. Below is a picture of the original Ninety-Five Theses. You can tell by the title on the right page, *Disputatio de Virtute Indulgen.*, that a main objection within the theses concerns the validity of indulgences.

---

[535] Noble, 340.

[536] As pointed out by Thomas A. Howard, professor of history at Gordon College and Mark A. Noll, professor of history at the University of Notre Dame, "The Ninety-five Theses...played virtually no role in early Protestant historical consciousness. At first, territories in the Holy Roman Empire that had sided with the Protestant cause commemorated annually either the date their individual princes adopted Protestantism or (and in some cases along with) the birth or death dates of Luther...In the sixteenth century, in fact, the only known written mention of the Wittenberg Castle church door as the site of the iconic posting (in fact, probably done by a student, not Luther himself) came in 1546 in a brief vita of the reformer by Philip Melanchthon and attached to the first collected edition of Luther's writings." Thomas A. Howard, and Mark A. Noll, "The Reformation at Five Hundred," *First Things* (November 2014), kindle edition.

537

A Few Details about Martin Luther and his Beliefs

Rejection of the Catholic Church

Luther's rejection of the Catholic Church is evident in his 1518 letter to his former teacher Dr. Jodocus Trutfetter and in his response to Henry VIII when countering Henry VIII's *Defense of the Seven Sacraments*, most likely written by St. Thomas More.

~ Luther to Trutfetter ~

To explain myself further, I simply believe that it is impossible to reform the Church unless the Canon Law, scholastic theology, philosophy and logic, as they are now taught, are thoroughly rooted out and other studies put in their stead. I am so fixed in this

---

537 By Wittenberg: Melchior Lotter d.J., 1522 (Martin Luther) [Public domain], via Wikimedia Commons, http://commons.wikimedia.org/wiki/File%3A95Thesen.jpg (accessed October 25, 2014).

opinion that I daily ask the Lord, as far as now may be, that the pure study of the Bible and the Fathers may be restored. You think I am no logician; perhaps I am not, but I know that I fear no one's logic when I defend this opinion....[538]

~ Luther to Henry VIII ~

Moreover, unless I am greatly mistaken, if this sacrament [Holy Orders] and this fiction ever fall to the ground, the papacy with its "characters" will scarcely survive. Then our joyous liberty will be restored to us; we shall realize that we are all equal by every right. Having cast off the yoke of tyranny, we shall know that he who is a Christian has Christ; and that he who has Christ has all things that are Christ's, and can do all things [Phil. 4:13]. Of this I will write more, 211 and more vigorously, as soon as I perceive that the above has displeased my friends the papists.[539]

Rejection of the Jewish People

In 1543, Martin Luther also wrote pointedly against the Jewish people in his *On the Jews and Their Lies*. See below for a notable excerpt from this work where he commands the German nobles to persecute the Jewish people:

I brief, dear princes and lords, those of you who have Jews under your rule-- if my counsel does not please you, find better advice, so that you and we all

---

[538] Ray Shelton, "Martin Luther and Scholastic Philosophy" http://www.fromdeathtolife.org/cphil/lsp1.html#note22 (accessed October 25, 2014). Shelton refers to the following resource. Preserved Smith (trans. and ed.), *Luther's Correspondence and other Contemporary Letters* Vol. I (1507-1521) (Philadelphia: The Lutheran Publication Society, 1913), 83-84.

[539] Abdel Ross Wentz *Luther's Works Volume 36 Word And Sacrament* (Philadelphia: Muhlenberg Press, 1959), 116.

can be rid of the unbearable, devilish burden of the Jews.... Do not grant them protection, safe-conduct, or communion with us.... Nor dare we make ourselves partners in their devilish ranting and raving by shielding and protecting them, by giving them food, drink, and shelter, or by other neighborly....

First to set fire to their synagogues or schools and to bury and cover with dirt whatever will not burn, so that no man will ever again see a stone or cinder of them....

Second, I advise that their houses also be razed and destroyed. ...

Third, I advise that all their prayer books and Talmudic writings, in which such idolatry, lies, cursing and blasphemy are taught, be taken from them....

Fourth, I advise that their rabbis be forbidden to teach henceforth on pain of loss of life and limb. ...

Fifth, I advise that safe-conduct on the highways be abolished completely for the Jews. ...

Sixth, I advise that usury be prohibited to them, and that all cash and treasure of silver and gold be taken from them and put aside for safekeeping. ...

Seventh, I commend putting a flail, an ax, a hoe, a spade, a distaff, or a spindle into the hands of young, strong Jews and Jewesses and letting them earn their bread in the sweat of their brow, as was imposed on the children of Adam (Gen 3[:19]}. ...[540]

Hitler in his *Mein Kampf* refers to Luther, along with Frederick the Great and Richard Wagner, as a one of history's great men.[541] Hitler's reference to Luther may raise the question as to what extent did Luther's anti-Semitism help to prepare for the much latter Nazi anti-Semitism? Were Luther's writings intentionally and explicitly followed by Hitler, Goering, and Himmler during World War II as William Shirer boldly argues in his popular book *The Rise and Fall of the Third Reich*?[542] Did Luther intend for something like the terrible WWII Holocaust (Shoah) of the Jewish people to occur? I do not subscribe to Shirer's "Luther to Hitler" thesis. Due to the complexity of history it cannot be reasonably demonstrated that a person's writings directly caused the decisions of another person who lived 400 years later from the first person. With that said we do influence future events, even ones hundreds of years ahead of us. To what extent this is the case, though, will always remain unclear.

Interestingly, the Nazis won a larger share of the vote in Protestant than in Catholic areas of Germany in elections from

---

[540] Martin Luther, *The Jews and their Lies*, Jewish Virtual Library, http://www.jewishvirtuallibrary.org/jsource/anti-semitism/Luther_on_Jews.html (accessed October 25, 2014)..

[541] Adolf Hitler, *Mein Kampf*, trans. James Murphy, Project Gutenberg, http://gutenberg.net.au/ebooks02/0200601.txt (accessed October 25, 2014), chap. viii. "To this group belong not only the genuinely great statesmen but all the great reformers as well. Beside Frederick the Great we have such men as Martin Luther and Richard Wagner."

[542] William L. Shirer, *The Rise and Fall of the Third Reich* (New York: RosettaBooks LLC, 1989), bk, 2, chap. 8. "It is difficult to understand the behavior of most German Protestants in the first Nazi years unless one is aware of two things: their history and the influence of Martin Luther. The great founder of Protestantism was both a passionate anti-Semite and a ferocious believer in absolute obedience to political authority. He wanted Germany rid of the Jews and when they were sent away he advised that they be deprived of "all their cash and jewels and silver and gold" and, furthermore, "that their synagogues or schools be set on fire, that their houses be broken up and destroyed... and they be put under a roof or stable like the gypsies... in misery and captivity as they incessantly lament and complain to God about us" – advise that Luther's advice was literally followed four centuries later by Hitler, Goering and Himmler." Also see Thomas A. Howard, and Mark A. Noll, "The Reformation at Five Hundred," *First Things* (November 2014), kindle edition.

1928 to November 1932.[543] In addition, capitalizing on many German people respect for Martin Luther, the Nazis, on November 9th 1938, the eve of Martin Luther's birthday, through November 10th, the day of Martin Luther's birthday, killed Jews, and vandalized Jewish shops. This event is infamously referred *Kristallnacht* to as Night of Broken Glass. See below for a photo taken shortly after this horrific event.

544

Dick Geary, *Hitler and Nazism*, Second Edition (London: Routledge 2000), 12, 23-24.

544 [Public domain], via Wikimedia Commons, http://commons.wikimedia. org/wiki/File%3ACleaning_the_street_after_Kristallnacht.jpg (accessed October 25, 2014).

Key Beliefs of Martin Luther

The beliefs that Martin Luther promoted are succinctly presented in the Lutheran confession of faith called the Augsburg Confession, written in 1530 at the Diet of Augsburg.[546] The following sampling of Lutheran beliefs comes from the Augsburg Confession's 28 articles.

> 1. The substance of the Eucharistic bread and wine is not changed, in the sense of transubstantiation, into the body and blood of Christ but rather both the reality of Christ and the reality of the bread are fully present. According to Lutheran theology what occurs is a consubstantiation by which Christ adheres in, with and under the bread and wine.[547]

---

545 By dalbera from Paris, France [CC-BY-2.0 (http://creativecommons.org/licenses/by/2.0)], via Wikimedia Commons, http://commons.wikimedia.org/wiki/File%3ALe_M%C3%A9morial_aux_juifs_assassin%C3%A9s_dEurope_(Berlin)_(2704805986).jpg (accessed October 25, 2014).

546 "The Augsburg Confession," Christian Classics Ethereal Library, http://www.ccel.org/ccel/schaff/creeds3.iii.ii.html (accessed October 25, 2014).

547 "The Augsburg Confession," article 10.

2. A Christian cannot merit anything. One is justified only by faith and not according to the Catholic sense of *fides caritate formata* or faith formed by charity. According to Catholic belief even an action as simple as donating money to the Church for an indulgence or for another charitable end can, with right intention, form one's faith.[548]

3. It is lawful for clergy, monks and nuns to marry.[549] Luther set the example by marrying Katharina von Bora, a former Cistercian nun.

5. In contrast with Catholic belief, for Lutherans the celebration of the mass does not have a sacrificial element. Instead, the mass only is centered on worship, praise, and thanksgiving.[550]

6. Every Christian is a confessor. Going to confession to a Lutheran pastor, which is encouraged, is essentially no different from going to confession to a member of the congregation.[551]

Huldrych Zwingli (1484-1531)

Zwingli, like Luther, was also formerly a Catholic priest.[552] At the same time that Luther was dissenting from Catholic teaching in German lands, Zwingli was resisting Church authority in his native land of Switzerland. His highly symbolic break occurred during Lent, in March of 1522. His actions that day are dubbed the Affair of the Sausages. This day can be considered as marking the beginning of Switzerland's Protestant movement. On that day,

---

[548] "The Augsburg Confession," articles 4-6.
[549] "The Augsburg Confession," second part, article 2, article 6.
[550] "The Augsburg Confession," second part, article 3.
[551] "The Augsburg Confession," second part, article 4.
[552] Johann Hottinger, *The Life and Times of Ulric Zwingli*, trans. Thomas Porter (Harrisburg: Theo. F. Scheffer, 1856), chapter 1, Project Gutenberg, http://www.gutenberg.org/files/31225/31225-h/31225-h.htm#div1_chap3 (accessed October 25, 2014).

some of Zwingli's followers with Zwingli's approval publicly ate sausages even though eating of any meat was forbidden by Catholic Lenten regulations.[553] Zwingli defended these rebellious actions in a sermon he published the following month called *Regarding the Choice and Freedom of Foods*.[554] According to him, eating sausages during Lent is permitted since faith and not good works save one. On this point and others, such as his approval of clerical marriages,[555] he agreed with Luther. He even went so far as to encourage the dissolution of monasteries and used the money obtained from the monasteries to build schools and help orphanages and poor houses.[556]

However, on another doctrinal position he disagreed significantly from Luther, and likewise from Catholicism. As noted above, Luther believed that the wine and bread used in a mass become the body and blood of Christ while retaining the reality of the wine and bread. Zwingli went one step further. He taught that the wine and bread used during a Eucharistic celebration only symbolize the body of Christ.[557]

John Calvin (1509-1564)

After Zwingli was killed in a battle between various Swiss regions, the Frenchman, and former Catholic, John Calvin, who had moved to Geneva, became the leader of the Protestant movement.[558] There, in 1536, Calvin published his *Institutes of the Christian Religion*. This work helped to institutionalize, in other

---

[553] G.R. Potter, *Zwingli* (Cambridge: Cambridge University Press, 1976), 74.

[554] Potter, 75, 76-77.

[555] Huldreich Zwingli, *Selected Works of Huldreich Zwingli* (Philadelphia: University of Pennsylvania, 1901), trans. Lawrence A. McClouth, Henry Preble, and George W. Gilmore, 73.

[556] Johann Hottinger, *The Life and Times of Ulric Zwingli*, trans. Thomas Porter (Harrisburg: Theo. F. Scheffer, 1856), chapter 3, Project Gutenberg, http://www.gutenberg.org/files/31225/31225-h/31225-h.htm#div1_chap3 (accessed October 25, 2014). "Out of the ordinary revenues of the government, aided by the property of the suppressed monasteries, schools were founded, an alms-house, a lazaretto for the plague-stricken, and an orphan-asylum."

[557] Hottinger, Ibid.

[558] Thomas F.X. Noble, *The Foundations of Western Civilization*, Lectures 25-48 (Chantilly: The Teaching Company, 2002), 342.

words, organize the Protestant movement that Martin Luther had inspired. Calvin's doctrinal teaching is often represented by the simple acronym T.U.L.I.P. This summary of Calvin's theology was not formulized by him but rather by the Calvinist Synod of Dort in 1619.[559] Nonetheless, T.U.L.I.P. is commonly accepted as accurately representing Calvinism. See below for an explanation of this acronym.

T stands for total depravity. This means, according to Calvinism, our human condition is totally deprived and not simply wounded by original and personal sin as Catholicism teaches.

U stands for unconditional election. According to Calvinism, God pre-ordains some people to be saved. Their salvation does not in any way depend on what they do in their lives.

L stands for limited atonement. This mean that Christ only died for his elect not for all mankind. In contrast, Catholicism holds, as clearly stated by the *Catechism of the Catholic Church*, "God predestines no one to go to hell."[560] Similarly, St. John Paul II asserted, "...salvation is offered to all..."[561]

I stands for irresistible grace. Those who are part of God's elect irresistibly follow grace. Since their cooperation with, or in a sense coercion by, grace is not in any way due to their efforts they cannot merit God's grace.

---

[559] Charles Partee, *The Theology of John Calvin* (Louisville: John Knox Press, 2008), 126.

[560] *Catechism of the Catholic Church*, 2nd ed., 1037.

[561] John Paul II, "Redemptoris Missio," no. 10, Vatican, http://www.vatican.va/holy_father/john_paul_ii/encyclicals/documents/hf_jp-ii_enc_07121990_redemptoris-missio_en.html (accessed October 26, 2014), "Since salvation is offered to all, it must be made concretely available to all."

P stands for persistence in grace. Once a person is elected he will automatically and persistently follow the promptings of God's saving grace.[562]

King Henry VIII (1491-1547)

While Luther, Zwingli, and Calvin were promoting Pro-testantism, Henry VIII was beginning a schism that would later develop into another version of Protestantism. Recall when we were discussing details concerning Luther, reference was made to Henry VIII's *Defense of the Seven Sacraments*. In this document, probably written by St. Thomas More, Henry VIII defended Orthodox, Catholic teaching against Protestant doctrine. Henry VIII dedicated this vigorous Catholic defense to the reigning Pope, Leo X (reigned 1513-1521).[563] In recognition of Henry the VIII's orthodoxy, Henry was awarded by the Church the title Defender of the Faith.[564] He lost this title, though, after he broke from the Church out of anger for not receiving a marriage annulment from the pope.

In the 1520s, Henry VIII requested that his marriage to Catherine of Aragon, daughter of King Ferdinand and Queen Isabella of Spain, be annulled.[565] One reason he wanted an annulment was because Catherine had not given birth to a son who could succeed his father. Henry VIII's argument was that his wife Catherine had previously been married for about five months to his deceased brother Arthur, who died of consumption in

---

[562] The summary of T.U.L.I.P. is worded by me. I used the following sources to explain its theology. Charles Partee, *The Theology of John Calvin* (Louisville: John Knox Press, 2008), 126-127; Thomas F.X. Noble, *The Foundations of Western Civilization*, Lectures 25-48 (Chantilly: The Teaching Company, 2002), 351.

[563] Preserved Smith and Charles M. Jacobs, *Luther's Correspondence and Other Contemporary Letters*, vol. 2 (Philadelphia: The Lutheran Publication Society, 1918), 33.

[564] James Hitchcock, *The History of the Catholic Church: From the Apostolic Age to the Third Millennium* (San Francisco: Ignatius Press, 2012), 262.

[565] David Loades, *The Six Wives of Henry VIII* (Gloucestershire: Amberley Publishing Plc, 2009), 45.

1502.[566] The Pope, though, refused to grant to Henry VIII an annulment. This refusal so enraged Henry VIII that in disobedience to the Pope he divorced Catherine of Aragon and married Anne Boleyn.

Then, in 1534 Henry VIII went one step further by declaring himself in the Supremacy Act head of the Catholic Church in England.[567] Upon doing so, he and his followers went into schism. Thomas Cromwell, who in 1532 was appointed Henry VIII's chief minister,[568] then instituted a nation-wide persecution of Catholics which included the removal and dismantling of Catholic statues/images (including from the shrine to St. Thomas Becket) and the dissolving of Catholic monasteries.[569] St. Thomas More and Bishop St. John Fisher are two notable saints who refused to sign the Supremacy Act and were martyred as a result.

Even though faithful Catholics were being persecuted throughout England, the church that Henry VIII had made himself the head of was not a form of Protestantism since it still held onto Catholic teaching. Not until Henry VIII's son Edward VI, whose mother was Jane Seymour, did the Church of England, under the direction of the Archbishop Thomas Cranmer (1489-1556) shift from being a schismatic Church to a Protestant Church complete with non-Catholic doctrine. For this reason, Pope Leo XIII in his encyclical *Apostolicae Curae* traced back the invalidity of Anglican ordinations to the time of Edward's reign.[570]

[566] Loades, 17.
[567] Alison Weir, *Henry VIII: The King and His Court* (New York: Random House Inc., 2001), 347.
[568] Weir, 313.
[569] Weir, 384-385.
[570] Leo XIII, "Apostolicae Curae" September 18, 1896, Papal Encyclicals Online, http://www.papalencyclicals.net/Leo13/l13curae.htm (accessed October 26, 2014), no. 3.

The Six Wives of Henry VIII

Catherine of Aragon	Anne Boleyn	Jane Seymour	Anne of Cleves	Catherine Howard	Catherine Parr
Validly Married to Henry VIII for 27 years	Married to Henry VIII for 3 years	Married to Henry VIII for 1 year	Married to Henry VIII for 6 months	Married to Henry VIII for 2 years	Married to Henry VIII for 5 years
Gives birth to a daughter Mary (reigns as Mary I 1553-1558)	Gives birth to a daughter Elizabeth (reigns as Elizabeth I 1558-1603)	Gives birth to a son Edward (reigns as Edward VI 1547-1553)			
Invalidly annulled	Executed	Died giving birth to Edward	Separated	Executed	Henry dies in 1547

571

---

571 This chart is in part based on the following chart. W. Cross, "Henry VIII's Wives," Mrs. Cross's Rockin' Classroom, http://mrscrossrockinclassroom. wordpress.com/2014/02/04/henry-viiis-wifes/ (accessed October 26, 2014).

Quiz 16

1. Why are John Wycliffe and John Huss referred to as proto-protestants?

2. List two non-Catholic teachings of John Wycliffe.

3. List two non-Catholic teachings of John Huss without repeating your answer given in 2.

4. Is the following phrase true or false? During a 1999 International Symposium on John Huss St. John Paul II apologized for Catholic Church officials' unjust treatment of Huss at the Council of Constance, and he also asserted that Huss was not a heretic but rather was a Catholic in good standing.

5. Describe four factors that helped to bring about the Protestant movement.

6. Fill in the blank. The event called the Affair of the Sausages directly involved the Swiss Protestant _____.

7. Define the Calvinist acronym T.U.L.I.P.

8. Fill in the blanks below.

The Six Wives of Henry VIII

Catherine of Aragon	Anne Boleyn	Jane Seymour	Anne of Cleves	Catherine Howard	Catherine Parr
Validly Married to Henry VIII for 27 years	Married to Henry VIII for 3 years	Married to Henry VIII for 1 year	Married to Henry VIII for 6 months	Married to Henry VIII for 2 years	Married to Henry VIII for 5 years
Gives birth to a daughter _____ _ (reigns as _____ 1553-1558)	Gives birth to a daughter _____ ___ (reigns as _____ 1558-1603)	Gives birth to a son _____ _ (reigns as _____ 1547-1553)			
Invalidly annulled	Executed	Died giving birth to Edward	Separated	Executed	Henry dies in 1547

Chapter 17

The Catholic Counter-Reformation and the "Wars of Religion"

Introduction

In the previous chapter, we focused on key players who prepared, inspired, and structured the Protestant movement. One of the factors, among others, which helped to strengthen the conviction of the Protestants was the corruption of members within the Catholic Church at the highest levels of office. Along with these bad examples of Catholicism, however, were exemplary representatives of Christian life. There were also, even prior to the formal beginning of Protestantism in Germany, Catholic renewal movements. We will begin with one such movement evident during the Fifth Lateran Council. Then, we will examine the Council of Trent before reflecting on the lives of a few renewal minded saints from this period. Finally, we will determine to what extent wars that occurred during this time of Catholic Counter Reformation and Protestant revolt are properly called "Wars of Religion."

The Fifth Lateran Council (1512-1517)

Before Martin Luther sparked the Protestant movement by reputedly posting his Ninety-Five Theses on the door of the All

Saint's Church in Wittenberg, Saxony, the Catholic Church had already held a five-year long reform minded council, Lateran V. A leader at Lateran V, Fr. Giles of Viterbo General of the Augustinians the religious family that Martin Luther once belonged to, asserted that "Religion reforms men; men do not reform religion."[572] In other words, if we wish to bring about genuine reform, it will not come up by changing the divinely instituted structures and divinely inspired teachings of the Church that give form to the Church as the mystical body of Christ, but rather by accepting the Church's structure and teaching while promoting individual conversions beginning with oneself.

The three goals of the council were "first, achieving a general peace between Christian rulers; second Church reform; and third, the defense of the faith and the rooting out of heresy."[573] Concerning the second goal the council condemned "simony when electing the Roman pontiff",[574] to reform the curia by "[checking] the evils from becoming to strong, [restoring] a great many things to their earlier observance of the sacred canons, [creating] with God's help an improvement in keeping with the established practice of the holy fathers."[575] Throughout the 12 sessions, the Council Fathers proposed practical ways to restore the Church to the holiness of its former days, a goal that many Protestants also held. The difference between the Protestants and the fathers of Lateran V was that unlike the Protestant leaders the fathers of the council desired to stay within the Catholic Church and renew her from within.

---

[572] James Hitchcock, *The History of the Catholic Church: From the Apostolic Age to the Third Millennium* (San Francisco: Ignatius Press, 2012), 248.

[573] Norman P. Tanner, *Decrees of the Ecumenical Councils*, Volume I (London: Sheed & Ward, 1990), 593.

[574] Tanner, Volume I, 600.

[575] Tanner, Volume I, 614.

The Council of Trent (1545-1563)

576

Unfortunately, despite the efforts of the Catholic reformers at Lateran V to implement a gradual reform, explains the Catholic historian James Hitchcock, "the sudden and explosive eruption of religious dissent immediately after Lateran V to a great extent destroyed the possibility of moderate, gradual reform."[577] The following council, the Council of Trent, took more decisive measures. These included the following. During the first part of the Council of Trent (1545-1548), Catholic teaching on the seven sacraments, justification, original sin, scripture and tradition were re-affirmed and clarified. In the second part (1551-1552), further teaching was issued on the sacraments in particular the Eucharist, penance (sacrament of reconciliation), and the last anointing (the anointing of the sick). Finally, in the last part (1562-1563) additional doctrinal aspects of the seven sacraments were clarified, reform in the Catholic Church was encouraged, and

[577] James Hitchcock, *The History of the Catholic Church: From the Apostolic Age to the Third Millennium* (San Francisco: Ignatius Press, 2012), 249.

penalties were specified for those guilty of serious sins.[578] For example, the Council of Trent specified the penalties attached to having a concubine by decreeing, "In order to meet this great evil with appropriate remedies, the holy council decrees that if, after being admonished on the matter even officially three times by the ordinary, they have not ejected their concubines and disassociated themselves with them, they are to be sentenced to excommunication and not absolved from it until they obey in deed the admonition given them."[579] Interestingly, during this final period of the Council, Protestants were invited to the council and assured safe passage. No Protestant, unfortunately, came.[580]

~ Protestants Invited to the Council of Trent ~

The same holy ecumenical and general council of Trent, lawfully assembled in the holy Spirit, with the same legates of the apostolic see as presidents, gives public pledge and safe-conduct in the same form of words as to the Germans, to each and all who are not in communion with us in matters of faith, from whatever kingdoms, nations, provinces, cities and places they come, in which there is public and uninhibited preaching or teaching or belief against the opinion of the holy Roman church.[581]

Shortly after the council ended, its teachings were succinctly formulated in the 1564 Tridentine Creed,[582] promulgated by Pope Pius IV, and in the 1566 Roman Catechism, promulgated by Pope

---

[578] Norman P. Tanner, *Decrees of the Ecumenical Councils*, Volume II (London: Sheed & Ward, 1990), 657-658.

[579] Tanner, Volume II, 758-759.

[580] Hitchcock, 287.

[581] Norman P. Tanner, *Decrees of the Ecumenical Councils*, Volume II (London: Sheed & Ward, 1990), 725.

[582] For the entire text see the following site. Pius IV, "The Profession of the Tridentine Faith, 1564" Christian Classics Ethereal Library, http://www.ccel.org/ccel/schaff/creeds1.vi.iv.html (accessed October 28, 2014).

Pius V.[583]

Saints of the Catholic Counter-Reformation

The Holy Spirit not only inspired the Catholic Church to come together in the two reform minded councils touched on above, but He also raised up a number of saints who were an essential component in the Catholic Reformation. I have chosen four such saints: St. Charles Borromeo, a leader during the Council of Trent, St. Ignatius of Loyola, a religious male founder and reformer, St. Teresa of Avila, a religious woman founder and reformer, and finally St. Philip Neri, known as the Apostle of Rome. We will begin with St. Charles Borromeo.

St. Charles Borromeo (1538-1584)

[584]

Following his uncle's election to the papacy as Pope Pius IV (1559-1565), St. Charles Borromeo, when only 21 years old and not yet ordained to the priesthood, was made a lay cardinal by the new

---

[583] Pius V, "Roman Catechism, 1566" Christian Classics Ethereal Library, http://www.ccel.org/ccel/schaff/creeds1.vi.iv.html (accessed October 28, 2014).

[584] Giovanni Ambrogio Figino [Public domain], via Wikimedia Commons, http://commons.wikimedia.org/wiki/File%3ACarlo_Borromeo.jpg (accessed October 29, 2014).

pope. Due to his great gifts as a leader and administrator, within a short space of time St. Charles was given a variety of important roles including administrator of the see of Milan, papal secretary, papal legate in Romagna, Bologna, and the March of Ancona, and cardinal-protector for a number of regions and religious communities. Despite his tremendous responsibilities, he was able to fulfill his duties without giving "the impression of being hurried."[585] In addition, "[h]e always found time to see to the affairs of his family and to seek recreation in music and physical exercise."[586]

In 1562, Pope Pius IV, St. Charles's uncle, reconvened the Council of Trent for its third and final stage. During this third stage of the Council of Trent, St. Charles's older brother died leaving St. Charles the head of the family. Instead of marrying, which some thought he would do, he asked his uncle Giulio to serve as head of the family and then sought ordination to the priesthood. In 1563, after being a lay cardinal for four years, St. Charles was finally ordained to the priesthood. After two months, he was then ordained a bishop. One way St. Charles helped to extend the fruits of the Council of Trent into the future was by helping to write Trent's Roman Catechism, and the various liturgical books associated with the Council.[587]

His great respect for and love of the priesthood, as testified by his sacrifice described above, spurred him to found seminaries that would form well-educated priests. According to St. Charles, one of the most effective ways for stemming the Protestant movement was by forming and educating quality candidates to the priesthood. He not only was concerned with formation prior to the priesthood but also with ongoing formation of priests. In order to meet this need, he set up retreats for priests and served as a model by daily confessing before his morning mass and by attending a retreat twice a year.[588]

Oddly, this great reformer who touched the hearts of so many

---

[585] Sarah Fawcett Thomas, *Butler's Lives of the Saints* (Collegeville: The Liturgical Press, 1997), 30.
[586] Thomas, 30-31.
[587] Thomas, 31.
[588] Thomas, 32.

and brought such needed reform suffered from a speech impediment. The Jesuit and friend of St. Charles, Achilee Gagliardi, once admitted:

> I have often wondered how it was that, without any natural eloquence or anything attractive in his manner, he was able to work such changes in the hearts of his listeners. He spoke but little, gravely, in a voice barely audible-but his words always had an effect.[589]

St. Ignatius of Loyola (1491-1556)

[590]

Unlike St. Charles Borromeo, the Spaniard St. Ignatius did not lead a holy life as a young man. Instead, "he was particularly reckless in gambling, in his dealings with women, in quarrelling, and with the sword." According to one documented 1515 court case, St.

---

[589] Thomas, 32.
[590] Peter Paul Rubens [Public domain], via Wikimedia Commons, http://commons.wikimedia.org/wiki/File%3ASt_Ignatius_of_Loyola_(1491-1556)_Founder_of_the_Jesuits.jpg (accessed October 29, 2014).

Ignatius, along with his blood brother while dressed in armor and armed with weapons, once even ambushed a group of clergymen.[591] The following year, St. Ignatius, eager for more action, but this time legal, joined the army of the viceroy of Navarre and served for about five years. His life as a soldier came to an abrupt halt when in 1521 he was seriously injured while defending Navarre's capital city, Pamplona. At Pamplona, a cannon ball smashed into his legs, fracturing one.[592]

Once his leg had been set twice, he recuperated for nine months, leading a relatively non-active life. During this time, he began reading a variety of books. He wanted to read chivalrous romance novels, but since he did not have ready access to these, he read instead on the life of Christ and the saints. For some reason, undoubtedly due to the working of the Holy Spirit within his heart, St. Ignatius compared and contrasted the happiness he experienced in reading the lives of the saints with the happiness he experienced when day dreaming about courtly exploits. He concluded that the former was significantly more fulfilling and attractive than the latter. When he was well enough to walk about and travel he went to the monastery of Montserrat and there made a general Confession. From that point on, St. Ignatius steadfastly remained true to his new way of life of seeking the greater glory of God and not his own glory.

St. Ignatius's spirit-led desire to serve the Lord and the Blessed Mother, and not an earthly lord and earthly lady, motivated him to be a missionary. Convinced that in order to be effective he needed to be educated he began formal studies at a number of universities, which culminated in a master's degree from a Parisian University. It was at Paris that he attracted six followers, including St. Francis Xavier and St. Peter Favre, who would become the first members of the Society of Jesus founded by Ignatius in 1540 with papal approval.[593]

Interestingly, even though at this time the Protestant move-

---

[591] Peter Doyle, *Butler's Lives of the Saints*, New Full Edition October (Collegeville: The Liturgical Press, 1997), 248.

[592] Doyle, 249.

[593] Doyle, 254.

ment was well under way, Ignatius's main concerns when founding the Jesuits were converting people from Islam and evangelizing pagan countries.[594] Even though these were his original intentions, his followers saw stemming the Protestant growth throughout Europe as an important calling of the Jesuit congregation.

St. Teresa of Avila (1515-1582)

595

Like St. Ignatius of Loyola, the Spaniard St. Teresa of Avila's life also coincided with the Council of Trent. When St. Teresa was only thirteen years old, her mother died prompting her father to send St. Teresa to a local Augustinian convent. After a period of illness and discernment, St. Teresa left the Augustinian convent and joined another local convent, the Carmelite Convent of The

---

Incarnation. According to St. Teresa, two benefits of her life as a nun were avoiding an early death when giving birth to a baby and not having to be submissive to a husband.[596] In her autobiography, St. Teresa admits that worldly reasons, such as the ones just mentioned, served as the principle reasons for her being a nun. A number of factors (including a prolonged period of illness, reading spiritual books, and occasional periods of practicing mental prayer) providentially coalesced together that greatly aided St. Teresa of Avila to be motivated not by what she could gain in the convent but what she could be and do for her spouse the Lord Jesus Christ. One particular incident that struck great fear in her heart and helped to say yes to the demands of the Lord was when she was mystically transported by Jesus into hell. In describing her experience in hell she writes:

> In that pestilential spot, where I was quite power-less to hope for comfort, it was impossible to sit or lie, for there was no room to do so. I had been put in this place which looked like a hole in the wall, and those very walls, so terrible to the sight, bore down upon me and completely stifled me... I never recall any time when I have been suffering trials or pains and when everything that we can suffer on earth has seemed to me of the slightest importance by comparison with this; so, in a way, I think we complain without reason. I repeat, then, that this vision was one of the most signal favors which the Lord has bestowed upon me. ... After I had seen this vision... I desired to find some way and means of doing penance for all my evil deeds and of becoming in some degree worthy to gain so great a blessing.[597]

The path she chose, as inspired by the Holy Spirit, to do

---

[596] Doyle, 95.

[597] Teresa of Avila, *The Life of Teresa of Jesus*, trans. E. Allison Peers (New York: Doubleday, 1991), 301-304.

penance and serve God was by observing the Carmelite rule according to its "primitive rigor."[598] Along with following the rule in a strict manner and encouraging other sisters to do so, St. Teresa also wished her community to do penance and pray for Protestants who were breaking away from the Catholic Church.[599] In 1562, her desire to found a Carmelite convent where sisters would pray and do penance out of love of God and in penance for sin was met when she received official permission to open the St. Joseph Carmelite convent in Avila.[600]

St. Philip Neri (1515-1595)

[601]

We will end this section with a reforming saint known for his humor, the Italian priest and friend of St. Ignatius of Loyola, St.

---

[598] Teresa of Avila, 301-304. 304.
[599] Doyle, 96.
[600] Doyle, 97.
[601] Giovanni Battista Tiepolo [Public domain or Public domain], via Wikimedia Commons, http://commons.wikimedia.org/wiki/File%3AGiovanni_ Battista_Tiepolo_025.jpg (accessed October 30, 2014).

Philip Neri.[602] A few examples of his humor are as follows. Once, when he was in a crowd of most likely very solemn looking people observing the relics of two martyrs being transferred from one location to another, "he cast his eyes upon one of the Swiss of the pope's guard, who was on duty there, and who had a splendid beard. Philip went up to him, took hold of his beard, and pulled it two or three times, and then caressed it in a most extraordinary manner; some of the spectators laughed; others were so lost in astonishment that they could not even laugh."[603]

Another time he shaved only one side of his face and then "went out with half a beard jumping and dancing, as if he had gained some victory." He also brought about laughter during the very trying times of the Protestant revolt and Catholic reformation by deliberately "reading in public, and then [by making] mistakes on purpose, especially when he saw that persons of education were standing near and listening; and afterwards he would ask his own people, 'What did such an one say?'"[604] In all of these examples, where St. Philip directed laughter safely at himself, he helped to alleviate the pain of so many who were suffering as their spiritual family of the One, Holy Catholic Church was breaking apart into Protestants in Continental Europe and schismatics in England.

Besides bringing about spontaneous laughter in his wake, he also belonged to an association of secular priests called San Girolamo. Here, along with his brother priests, he heard many hours of confession, preached and encouraged the forty hours of non-stop prayer before the Eucharist, called Forty Hours Devotion. As he collaborated in this fraternal society, the Holy Spirit inspired him to found a group of his own, the Congregation of the Oratory of St. Philp Neri, officially approved in 1575. The priests and laity at the oratory regularly met to read and discuss a spiritual book, followed by a period of prayer. Their meeting ended by going to a notable church or by listening to a concert. The Oratory drew people from a wide variety of backgrounds: aristo-

---

[602] Doyle, 145.

[603] Pietro Giacomo Bacci, *Saint Philip Neri, Apostle of Rome*, trans. St. Thomas of Canterbury (London: Thomas Richardson and Son, 1847), 305.

[604] Bacci, 304-305.

crats, artists, scholars, and craftsmen. No matter what station of life a member belonged to, St. Philip required all to not only pray but also to serve the poor in hospitals or in other ways. One high class Oratorian was the recently beatified, Blessed John Henry Cardinal Newman (1801-1890). This famous Anglican convert to Catholicism summed up St. Philip Neri's approach to reform by writing:

> He lived in an age as traitorous to the interests of Catholicism as any that preceded it, or can follow it. He lived at a time when pride mounted high, and the senses held rule; a time when kings and nobles never had more of state and homage, and never less of personal responsibility and peril; when medieval winter was receding, and the summer sun of civilization was bringing into leaf and flower a thousand forms of luxurious enjoyment; when a new world of thought and beauty had opened upon the human mind, in the discovery of the treasures of classic literature and art. He saw the great and the gifted, dazzled by the Enchantress, and drinking in the magic of her song; he saw the high and wise, the student and the artist, painting, and poetry and sculpture, and music, and architecture, drawn within her range, and circling round the abyss...he perceived that the mischief was to be met, not with argument, not with science, not with protests and warnings, not by the recluse or the preacher, but by means of the counter-fascination of purity and truth...he preferred to yield to the stream, and direct the current, which he could not stop, of science, literature, art, and fashion, and to sweeten and to sanctify what God had made very good and man had spoilt.[605]

---

[605] John Henry Newman, *The Idea of a University* (Notre Dame: University of Notre Dame Press, 1960), 178-179.

European "Wars of Religion"?

606

As the Protestant movement gained momentum and as Catholic leaders, some of whom were saints, reacted with a Catholic reformation, a series of wars broke out across Europe involving a number of countries including France, Spain, the Netherlands, England, Germany, and of course the Holy Roman Empire.[607] Is it fair to categorize these conflicts as primarily "wars of religion" as is commonly done?[608] William T. Cavanaugh in *The Myth of Religious Violence* proposes another explanation for these wars. He argues that religion was not the main motivating factor, instead gaining political power was, even at the cost of sacrificing one's religious loyalties.

---

[606] Unknown (French school) [Public domain], via Wikimedia Commons, http://commons.wikimedia.org/wiki/File%3AHenri_IV_%C3%A0_la_bataille_ d'Arques_21_septembre_1589.jpeg (accessed October 31, 2014).
[607] Mark Konnert, *Early Modern Europe: The Age of Religious War 1559-1715* (Ontario: Higher Education University of Toronto Press, 2008), 95-145.
[608] Konnert, Ibid.

A careful examination of history demonstrates that many of these wars, or at least phases within them, were primarily characterized by political leaders wanting to wrest power and land away from the Catholic Church. For example, princes in German lands profited greatly by adopting Lutheranism since it gave them justification to collectively fight against the Catholic Holy Roman Emperor while acquiring land that belonged to the Catholic Church.[609] Even the Holy Roman Emperors were not immune to competing with and wanting papal power and influence. This is evident in the claim that they were "blood relations of Roman and Byzantine emperors, the Old Testament patriarchs, and Christ himself."[610]

As the various rulers across Europe gained political power, often at the expense of the Holy Roman Emperor, they began fighting with each other. Many of these wars, therefore, were not so much wars of religion but rather were wars between nation states that were emerging out of a combination of de-centralized, localized feudalism and a wide reaching empire. That religion was often a minor issue, or one that came in play only when convenient for the rulers to justify their wars, is most particularly evident during the Thirty Years War (1618-1648) between the Catholic Holy Roman Empire and Lutheran Sweden. During this war, Catholic France chose to intervene on the side of Lutheran Sweden as a counter measure against the Holy Roman Empire whom King Louis XIII, as advised by his Chief Minister Cardinal Richelieu, viewed as a political competitor.[611] This sacrifice of religious loyalty for political interests was also due to the presence of two competing royal Catholic dynasties: the Bourbons, usually associated with France, and the Hapsburgs, usually associated with

---

[609] William T. Cavanaugh, *The Myth of Religious Violence* (Oxford: Oxford University Press, 2009), 166-167.

[610] Cavanaugh, 174.

[611] Cavanaugh, 149. "France under Cardinal Richelieu signed a treaty with Sweden in January 1631, in which France agreed to subsidize heavily the Swedish war effort. Cardinal Richelieu also made a pact with the Protestant principality of Hesse-Kassel. The French began sending troops to battle imperial forces in the winter of 1634-1635, and the latter half of the Thirty Years' War was largely a battle between Catholic France, on the one hand, and the Catholic Hapsburgs, on the other."

Spain and the Holy Roman Emperor.[612]

Cavanaugh also demonstrates that some of these conflicts, although having the appearance of being religiously motivated, were actually underneath really about a struggle for political power between the aristocracy and the monarchs. For example, in France both Charles VII (1403-1461) and Louis XI (1423-1483), wanted to centralize power by decreasing the power of the nobles who were accustomed to a more feudal, decentralized set up that was in part held together by allegiance not only to the king but also to the Holy Roman Emperor.[613] Simply put, a main driving force of so-called French religious wars was between the few (the aristocrats) against the one (the king).

Another important driving force was between the one (the king), the few (the aristocrats) against the many (the commoners). According to Cavanaugh, again in reference to the "French religious wars," during the conflict between the French Calvinist Huguenot minority against the French Catholic majority King Charles IX received a report in 1573 stating that, "the common people believed that the wars were rooted in a conspiracy of Protestant and Catholic nobles directed against the commoners."[614]

In conclusion, the series of wars that preceded, coincided and followed the beginning of the Protestant movement were not simply caused by differing religious beliefs. Instead, many times these wars were propelled by ambitious princes and kings who wanted to wrest away land and influence from the Catholic Church. Another important factor was that during this time there were two competing Catholic dynasties, the French based Bourbon dynasty and the Spanish/Austrian based Hapsburg dynasty. The French Bourbon dynasty even joined Protestant forces in order to defeat its opposing Catholic Hapsburg dynasty. The monarchical leaders of the dynasties sometimes went to war with the aristocrats who wanted to maintain their power. Finally, aristo-

---

[612] Cavanaugh, 11.

[613] Cavanaugh, 165. "The French wars of religion pitted the French Crown's determination to unite France under *un roi, une foi, une loi* against the nobility, who resisted such threats to their power and prestige."

[614] Cavanaugh, 144.

crats and monarchs, sometimes, under the cover of religion, also waged war with each other in order to further subject the commoner under their common authority.

Quiz 17

1. Who asserted the following? "Religion reforms men; men do not reform religion."

    a. Martin Luther
    b. John Calvin
    c. John Huss
    d. Fr. Giles of Viterbo

2. Explain the above quote with reference to leaders of the Protestant revolt and the Catholic Reformation.

3. List the three goals of Lateran Council V (1512-1517).

4. Name three specific ways by which the Council of Trent (1545-1563) helped to bring about a Catholic reformation.

5. True or False. (Circle one answer.) Protestants were officially invited to the Council of Trent.

      True   False

6. In four sentences describe key aspects of one of the following saints: St. Charles Borromeo, St. Ignatius of Loyola, St. Teresa of Avila, and St. Philip Neri.

7. Provide three reasons why the terminology "Wars of Religion" is

not quite accurate when applied to the series of European wars of the 1400s, 1500s, and 1600s.

Chapter 18

Explorers and Missionaries

Introduction

Kings and queens commissioned explorers and conquistadores to venture into unchartered territory. Since these explorers and conquistadores preceded missionary activity, we will first study notable Europeans sent out to discover and establish new trade routes before examining a few key saints who follow in their wake. The explorers, conquistadores, and people directly associated with their activity, whom we will discuss include: Marco Polo, Henry the Navigator, John II King of Portugal, Bartolomeu Dias, Vasco de Gama, Christopher Columbus, Ferdinand Magellan, John Cabot, Amerigo Vespucci, Hernando Cortes, and Francisco Pizarro Gonzalez.

Then, we will look at the saintly lives of the following missionaries: Bartolome de las Casas, St. Peter Claver, St. Francis Xavier, Matteo Ricci, St. Isaac Jogues, and St. Jean de Breubeuf. Finally, we will end this chapter with one of the greatest missionaries of all time, the Blessed Virgin Mary who appeared in Mexico during the 1500s. Before delving into the fascinating history of the age of exploration and missionary activity, I will briefly discount the popular belief that during the medieval and renaissance eras many thought that the earth was flat.

The Earth: Flat or Round?

Did many people of medieval and renaissance times really think that the earth is flat? Was Christopher Columbus one of the first to dispel this myth? The answer to both questions is no. The clear majority of both medieval and renaissance people took it for granted that the earth is round. However, many mistakenly believed that the round globe of the earth only had one very large land mass interpenetrated by water.

See below for an excerpt from the United States Conference of Bishops site written by the historian Jeffrey Burton Russell. Russell convincingly dismisses the myth that up until the late 1400s most Western people believed the earth was flat. Countering the claims of the anti-religious French academician Antoine-Jean Letronne (1787-1848) along with the persuasive story telling techniques of the American Washington Irving (1783-1859),[615] Russell argues, "With extraordinary few exceptions no educated person in the history of Western Civilization from the third century B.C. onward believed that the earth was flat."

> A round earth appears at least as early as the sixth century BC with Pythagoras, who was followed by Aristotle, Euclid, and Aristarchus, among others in observing that the earth was a sphere. Although there were a few dissenters--Leukippos and Demokritos for example--by the time of Eratosthenes (3 c. BC), followed by Crates (2 c. BC), Strabo (3 c. BC), and Ptolemy (first c. AD), the sphericity of the earth was accepted by all educated Greeks and Romans.

---

[615] Antoine-Jean Letronne in his 1834 book *On the Cosmographical Ideas of the Church Fathers* carefully crafted a false narrative that claimed the Church Fathers and the majority of medieval people thought the earth was flat. Washington Irving in his 1828 historical fiction *A History of the Life and Voyages of Christopher Columbus* (often more fiction than fact) invented a fictional account of Christopher Columbus arguing for the spherical nature of the earth.

Nor did this situation change with the advent of Christianity. A few--at least two and at most five--early Christian fathers denied the sphericity of earth by mistakenly taking passages such as Ps. 104:2-3 as geographical rather than metaphorical statements. On the other side tens of thousands of Christian theologians, poets, artists, and scientists took the spherical view throughout the early, medieval, and modern church. The point is that no educated person believed otherwise.[616]

Explorers

Marco Polo (1254-1324): Medieval Explorer

We will begin with the medieval, Venetian merchant Marco Polo. Since merchants had preceded Marco Polo in discovering a land based route to Asia, Marco Polo cannot properly be categorized as an explorer, as is popularly done.[617] With his father and uncle, he travelled to Asia on the routes commonly referred to as the Silk Routes. He detailed his Asian journeys in his book *The Travels of Marco Polo*[618] which served as an inspiration to explorers of the New World, in particular Christopher Columbus and Henry the Navigator.[619] On the next page is a picture from one of Marco Polo's first publications of his book *The Travels of Marco Polo*.

---

[616] Jeffrey Burton Russell, "The Myth of the Flat Earth" USCCB Library, http://veritas-ucsb.org/library/russell/FlatEarth.html (accessed November 2, 2014).

[617] Simon Guant, *Marco Polo's Le Devisement du Monde* (Cambridge: D.S. Brewer, 2013), 1-2.

[618] Marco Polo and Rustichello of Pisa, "The Travels of Marco Polo," http://www.gutenberg.org/cache/epub/12410/pg12410.html (accessed November 2, 2014).

[619] Guant, 1, 181.

620

Henry the Navigator (1394-1460)

Prince Henry of Portugal, more commonly known as Henry the Navigator, was the son of the King John I. With his wealth and influence as the son of a King Henry financed and supported Portuguese explorers. [621] Prince Henry's spirit of discovery was in part inspired by a book given to him by his brother John. Not surprisingly the book was Marco Polo's book, briefly touched upon in the previous section.[622] Inspiration to be a patron of explorers, though, is not enough. One also needs financial resources which Prince Henry had at his disposal after his father made him the grand master of the Order of Christ. The Order of Christ was well endowed military order of pontifical rite. Prince Henry used his position to pay for ships and to pay for the expeditions. Even with

---

[620]   [Public   domain],   via   Wikimedia   Commons, http://commons.wikimedia.org/wiki/File%3AMarco_Polo_traveling.JPG (accessed November 2, 2014).

[621] Peter Russell, *Prince Henry the Navigator* (New Haven: Yale University Press, 2001), 1-13.

[622] Ernle Bradford, *A Wind from the North: The Life of Henry the Navigator* (New York: Open Road Integrated Media Inc., 1960), 60.

the funds of the Templars, Prince Henry became deep in debt.[623] See below for the Atlantic navigation routes that Portuguese explorers, relying on their patron Prince Henry, took.

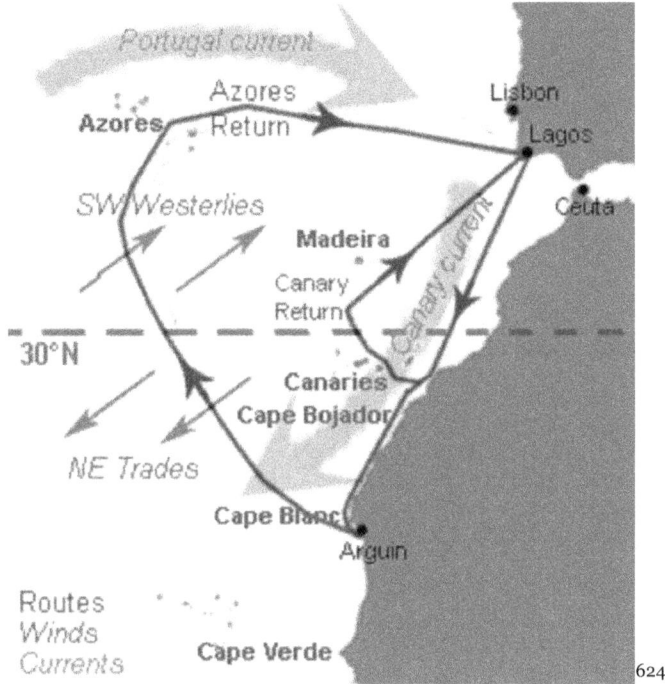

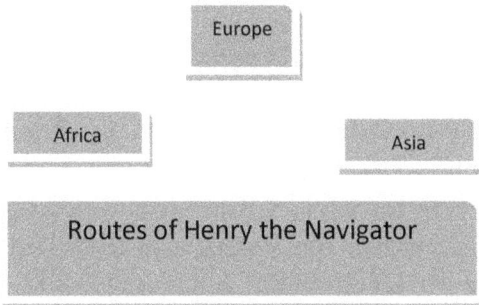

Routes of Henry the Navigator

624

---

[623] Bradford, 55.

[624] By Walrasiad (Own work) [CC-BY-SA-3.0 (http://creativecommons.org/licenses/by-sa/3.0)], via Wikimedia Commons, http://commons.wikimedia.org/wiki/File%3AHenrican_navigation_routes.gif (accessed November 2, 2014).

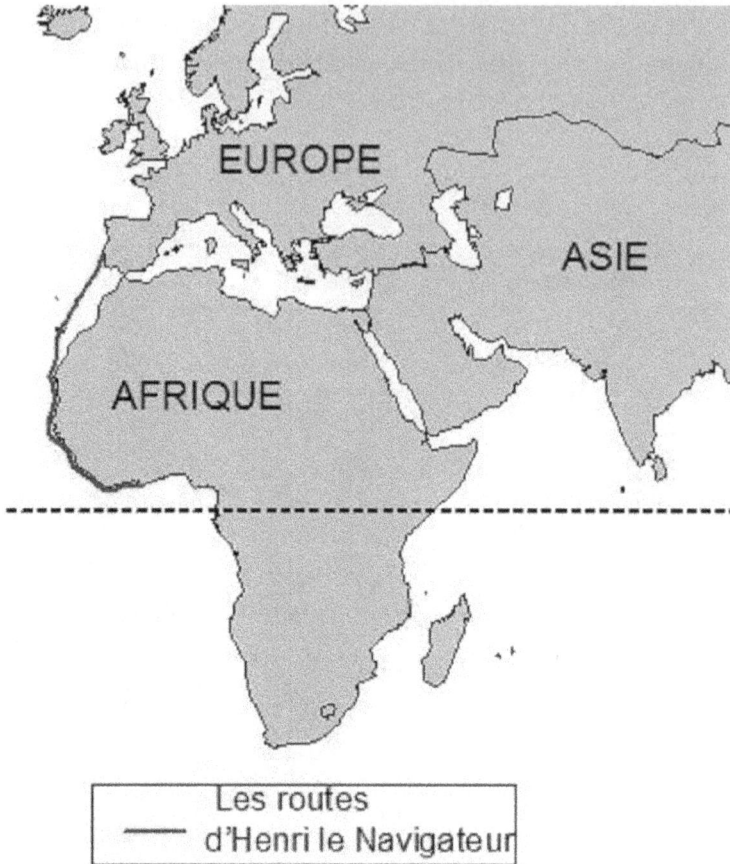

EUROPE

ASIE

AFRIQUE

Les routes
d'Henri le Navigateur

625

King John II of Portugal (1455-1495)

King John II followed the example set by Prince Henry by promoting and funding Portuguese Atlantic Ocean explorations. A main goal of his was for explorers to go around Africa to reach India. Once this occurred, the Portuguese then had a non-land based, alternative to reach India. Since 1453, when the Greek Orthodox city and surrounding land of Constantinople was captured by the Ottoman, Islamic Empire, it had become increasingly difficulty to journey by land to India to engage in trade. The

625 Except for the English titles the graphic is from the following Wikimedia Commons image. Les routes d'Henri le Navigateur Auteur G. Dulous Mars 2007, http://commons.wikimedia.org/wiki/File:Routes_d%27Henri_le_Navigateur.JPG#file (accessed November 2, 2014).

map below shows the Silk Routes that Marco Polo helped to establish. Notice that these routes are substantially land based. Once Eastern land boarding the Mediterranean Sea became controlled by the Ottoman Empire, trade with the Far East was difficult, and, consequently, there was a financial incentive to discover an alternative non-land based trade route to the Far East. As you saw in the map on the left, Portuguese explorers funded by Prince Henry only succeeded in going about half way down the coast of Africa. In February of 1488, a breakthrough was finally achieved when Bartolomeu Dias, backed by King John II, successfully rounded the southernmost tip of Africa, and landed at Mossel Bay (off the coast of modern day South Africa). See the map on the next page that illustrates this remarkable achievement.[626]

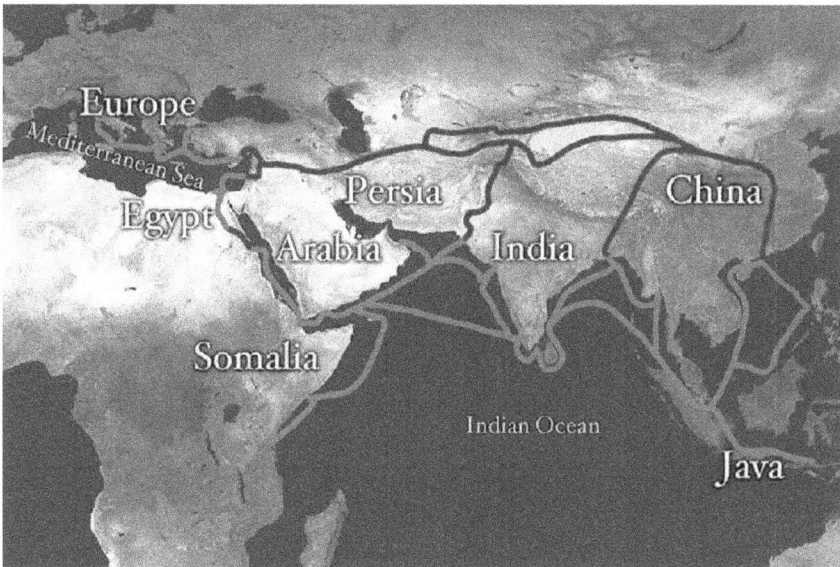

627

---

[626] A.R. Disney, *A History of Portugal and the Portuguese Empire: Volume Two, The Portuguese Empire* (Cambridge: Cambridge University Press, 2009), 38.

[627] By Whole_world_-_land_and_oceans_12000.jpg: NASA/Goddard Space Flight Center derivative work: Splette derivative work: Bongan NASA - Visible Earth, images combined and scaled down by HighInBC (20 megabyte upload limit) NASA Visible Earth [Public domain], via Wikimedia Commons,

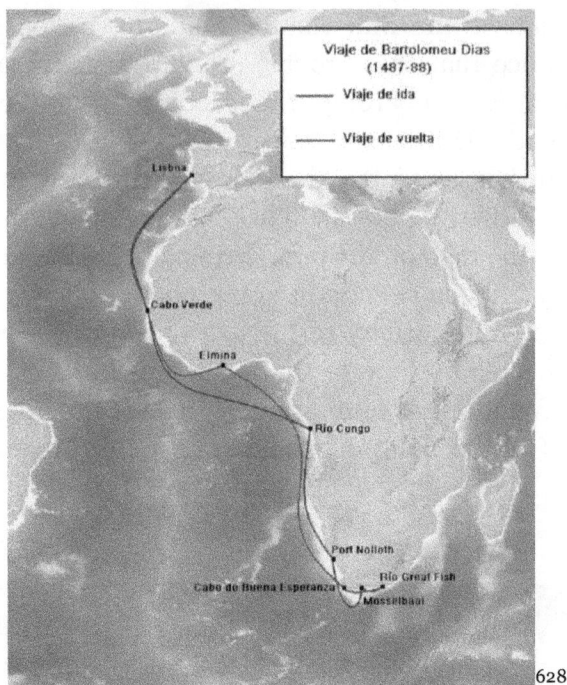

628

Bartolomeu Dias (1451-1500)

The Portuguese explorer Bartolomeu Dias is well known for his great accomplishment of sailing around the southernmost tip of Africa, shown above. His grueling 6,835 mile journey from Lisbon to Mossel Bay took around six months. During that time, he passed through the tropics twice and, as he rounded Africa's tip, came within the southern limits of the iceberg zone.[629] In 1500, as he captained one of thirteen ships under the command of Pedro Alvares Cabral, his ship was lost at sea.[630]

---

http://commons.wikimedia.org/wiki/File%3ASilk_route_copy.jpg (accessed November 3, 2014).

[628] [GFDL (http://www.gnu.org/copyleft/fdl.html), CC-BY-SA-3.0 (http://creativecommons.org/licenses/by-sa/3.0/) or CC-BY-2.5 (http://creativecommons.org/licenses/by/2.5)], via Wikimedia Commons, http://commons.wikimedia.org/wiki/File%3ABartolomeu_Dias_Voyage.PNG (accessed November 3, 2014).

[629] Disney, 38-39.

[630] James M. Anderson, *The History or Portugal* (Westport: Greenwood Press, 2000), 66.

Vasco de Gama (c. 1460-1524)

Following in the shoes of Bartolomeu Dias, or rather ocean routes soon to be trade routes, the Portuguese explorer Vasco da Gama became the first European to reach India, near Calcutta, by ship on May 18th, 1498.[631] This meant that the Portuguese finally had discovered a way to trade with the Far East other than by crossing land now controlled by the Islamic Ottoman Empire. Vasco da Gama's 1497-1499 breakthrough discovery of an ocean passage to India involved the longest distance of continuous sailing ever recorded in history at the time. To accomplish this feat, he sailed for over ten months to reach Calcutta and for about eleven months on his return to Lisbon.[632] See below for a graphic that illustrates the Portuguese trade routes that Vasco de Gama established.

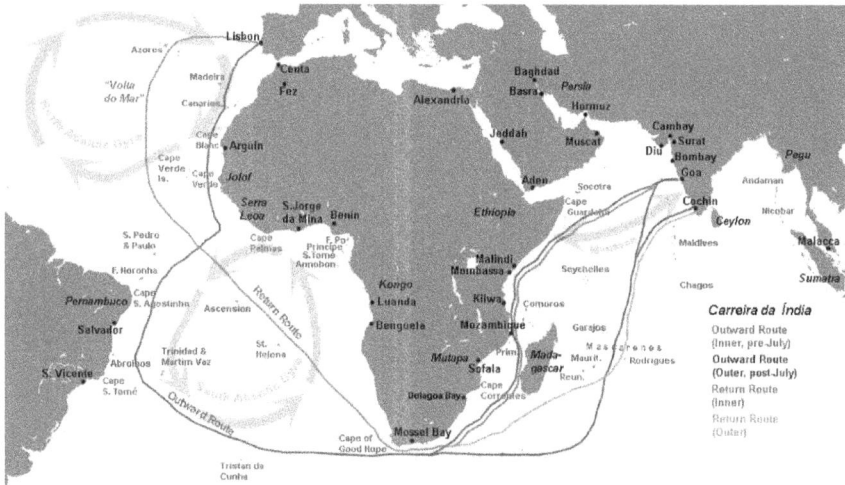

633

---

[631] Disney, 121.

[632] Disney, 122.

Christopher Columbus (c. 1450-1506)

Many know the little rhyme, "Columbus sailed the ocean blue in 1492." What is not as commonly known is why he did. Like the previously described Portuguese explorers, the Italian (more accurately Genoese) Christopher Columbus was an adventurer. After being turned down by King John II of Portugal, Columbus' desire to take risk, discover unchartered land, and find a Westward ocean trade route to India was finally fulfilled when Spanish monarchs Queen Isabella I and Ferdinand II agreed to sponsor him. As is evident in the map below, Columbus never landed on North America.[634] Instead, he landed in the Bahamas, Central America and South America. Convinced, or possibly more hoping, that he had successfully discovered a westward trade route to India Columbus called the inhabitants of these lands *Indios* (Indians in English).

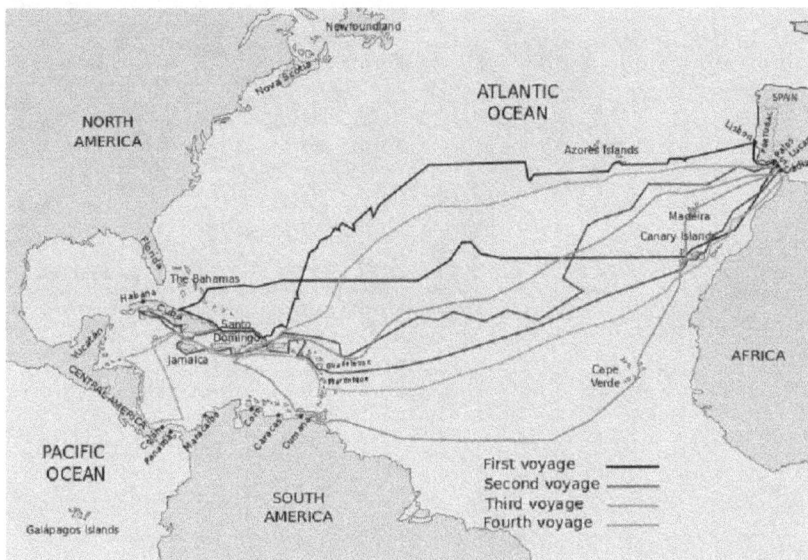

[635]

---

[634] Kirkpatrick Sale, *Christopher Columbus and the Conquest of Paradise*, Second Edition (London: Tauris Parke Paperbacks, 2006), 47-74.

[635] By Viajes_de_colon.svg: Phirosiberia derivative work: Phirosiberia (Viajes_de_colon.svg) [CC-BY-SA-3.0-2.5-2.0-1.0 (http://creativecommons.org/licenses/by-sa/3.0), CC-BY-SA-3.0-2.5-2.0-1.0 (http://creativecommons.org/licenses/by-sa/3.0) or GFDL (http://www.gnu.org/copyleft/fdl.html)], via

Ferdinand Magellan (c. 1480-1521)

Like Columbus, the Portuguese explorer Magellan, at the service of King Charles I of Spain, in 1521 also attempted to sail westward across the Atlantic Ocean with the hope of discovering a westward trade route to South East Asia, specifically to the "Spice Islands".[636] Unfortunately, he did not complete his goal. He died on route during a battle in the Philippines.[637] (The cross on the map below indicates where he died.) His expedition, continuing without him, successfully reached South East Asia and, upon returning to Portugal, became the first to circumnavigate the earth by ship. Although they were the first to accomplish this pheno-menal feat, there is no documented evidence that Magellan ever intended for his expedition to circumnavigate the world. He simply wanted to discover an Eastern route to South East Asia for the financial motive of establishing another trade route.[638]

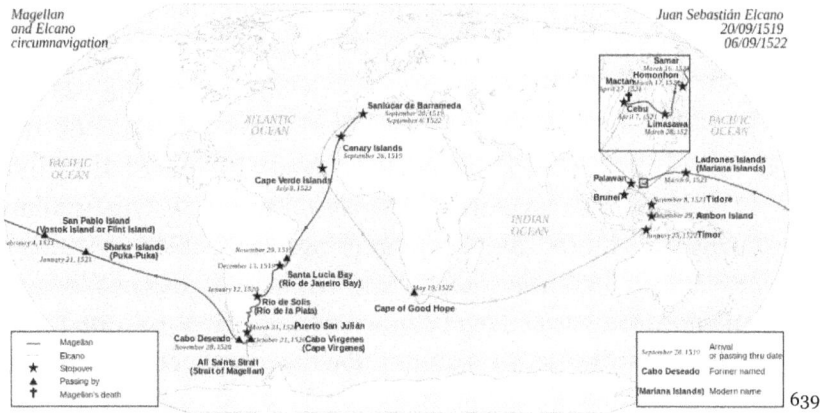

Wikimedia Commons, http://commons.wikimedia.org/wiki/File%3A Viajes_de_colon_en.svg (accessed November 4, 2014).

[636] Nancy Smiler Levinson, *Magellan: And the First Voyage around the World* (New York: Houghton Mifflin Co., 2001), 33-34, 36.

[637] Levinson, 87-96.

[638] Levinson, 33-34.

[639] y Magellan_Elcano_Circumnavigation-fr.svg: Sémhur derivative work: Uxbona (Magellan_Elcano_Circumnavigation-fr.svg) [CC-BY-SA-3.0-2.5-2.0-1.0 (http://creativecommons.org/licenses/by-sa/3.0) or GFDL (http://www.gnu.org/copyleft/fdl.html)], via Wikimedia Commons, http://commons.wikimedia.org/wiki/File%3AMagellan_Elcano_Circumnavigati on-en.svg (accessed November, 5, 2014).

John Cabot (c. 1450-c. 1499)

The Italian John Cabot, whose name was originally Zuan Chabotto before being anglicized, was commissioned by the English King Henry VII.[640] Once again, like Christopher Columbus, he also set sail westward with the hope of finding a westward passage to East Asia. Instead, he came into contact with a very large land mass now known as Canada and the United States of America. By so doing he became the first European, since the Vikings' ventures in the eleventh century, to land on the North American continent, while oddly enough, thinking he had landed on the mainland of Asia.[641]

Amerigo Vespucci (1454-1512)

The United States of America was just mentioned in the context of John Cabot's explorations. In the late 1400s, he, not Christopher Columbus, reached the North American continent, which of course includes what is now known as the USA. The closest Columbus came to the USA was by landing on the islands today known as the Bahamas. The last word America, of the United States of America, is the feminized version of the first name of yet another explorer, Amerigo Vespucci. This Italian (more properly Florentine) explorer was a well-known map maker.[642] In one of his maps, shown below, he outlines a continent, now known as America, which separates Europe from Asia and the Atlantic Ocean from the Pacific Ocean. In the map to your right, you will see the American continent to your left. Notice how thin he depicts it.

---

[640] Douglas Hunter, *The Race to the New World: Christopher Columbus, John Cabot and a Lost History of Discovery* (New York: Palgrave MacMillan, 2011), 12, 79

[641] Hunter, 174, 210.

[642] Frederick A. Ober, *Amerigo Vespucci* (New York: Harper and Brothers Publishers, 1907), 237-251, Project Gutenberg, http://www.gutenberg.org/files/19997/19997-h/19997-h.htm#XVI (accessed November 5, 2014).

~ Martin Waldseemüller (German Mapmaker) in 1507 ~

But now these parts have been more extensively explored and *another fourth part has been discovered by Americus Vespucius* (as will appear in what follows): *wherefore I do not see what is rightly to hinder us from calling it Amerige, or America—i.e., the land of Americus, after its discoverer, Americus, a man of sagacious mind*, since both Europe and Asia have got their names from women. Its situation and the manners and customs of its people will be clearly understood from the twice two voyages of Americus, which follow.[643]

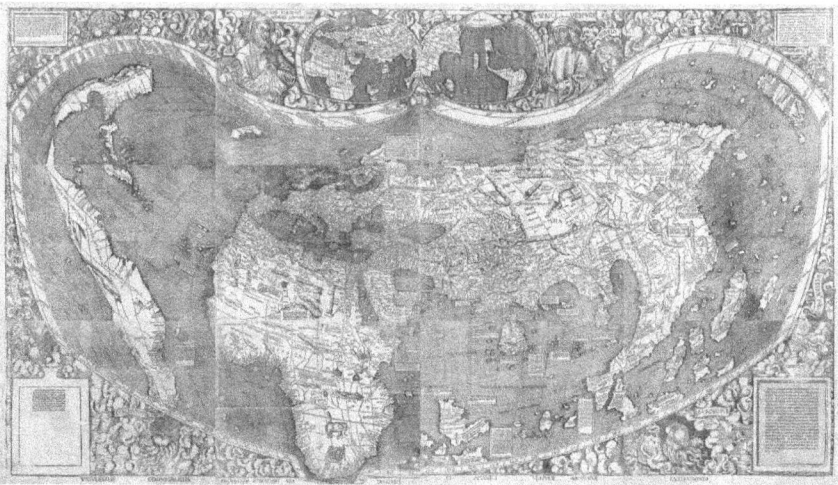

644

---

[643] Ober, Ibid. Europe is named after the princess Europa who was, according to Greek mythology, taken away by Zeus after he appeared as a white bull. Asia, in Greek mythology, is the name of a Titan Goddess.

[644] By Русский: Вальдзеемюллер, Мартин (1470-1521?)Français : Waldseemüller, Martin (1470-1521?)English: Waldseemüller, Martin (1470-1521?)中文：瓦尔德泽米勒，马丁 (1470-1521?)Português: Waldseemüller, Martin (1470-1521?)?)1521-1470(مارتن, والدسيمولر: العربية Español: Waldseemüller, Martin (1470-circa 1521) [Public domain], via Wikimedia Commons, http://commons.wikimedia.org/wiki/File%3AA_Map_of_the_Entire_World_Ac

Hernando Cortes (1485-1547) and Francisco Pizarro Gonzalez (c. 1471/6-1541)

We will end this section by very briefly touching upon two men known as conquistadores: Hernando Cortes and Francisco Pizarro Gonzalez. The Spanish man Cortes was responsible for beginning the Spanish colonization of North America in Mexico by conquering the Aztec Empire. Pizarro was responsible for beginning the Spanish colonization of South America in Peru by conquering the Incan Empire. After conquering the Incans, Pizarro founded, in 1535, the city of Lima.[645] He was buried in the Catholic Cathedral of Lima.

Missionaries

We have just completed an introduction to the major explorers and conquistadores of the 15th and 16th centuries. Shortly after these lands were discovered, they were later evangelized by Catholic missionaries. The missionaries traveled the newly formed trade routes in a similar manner that St. Paul and others used the well-constructed Roman roads to evangelize. Despite their at times heroic efforts, the work of these evangelists are often portrayed in a highly negative light. According to one such view, Catholic missionaries unjustly imposed a religion that was neither wanted nor compatible with the ancient cultures of Latin America and the Caribbean. Below is an excerpt from a speech given by Pope Benedict XVI in which he counters this critical view:

~ Pope Benedict XVI ~

Yet what did the acceptance of the Christian faith mean for the nations of Latin America and the Caribbean? For them, it meant knowing and welcoming Christ, the unknown God whom their

---

cording_to_the_Traditional_Method_of_Ptolemy_and_Corrected_with_Other _Lands_of_Amerigo_Vespucci_WDL369.jpg (accessed November 5, 2014).

[645] Fred Ramen, *Francisco Pizarro: The Exploration of Peru and the Conquest of the Inca* (New York: Rosen Publishing Group, 2004), 103.

ancestors were seeking, without realizing it, in their rich religious traditions. Christ is the Savior for whom they were silently longing. It also meant that they received, in the waters of Baptism, the divine life that made them children of God by adoption; moreover, they received the Holy Spirit who came to make their cultures fruitful, purifying them and developing the numerous seeds that the incarnate Word had planted in them, thereby guiding them along the paths of the Gospel. In effect, the proclamation of Jesus and of his Gospel did not at any point involve an alienation of the pre-Columbus cultures, nor was it the imposition of a foreign culture. Authentic cultures are not closed in upon themselves, nor are they set in stone at a particular point in history, but they are open, or better still, they are seeking an encounter with other cultures, hoping to reach universality through encounter and dialogue with other ways of life and with elements that can lead to a new synthesis, in which the diversity of expressions is always respected as well as the diversity of their particular cultural embodiment.

Ultimately, it is only the truth that can bring unity, and the proof of this is love. That is why Christ, being in truth the incarnate Logos, "love to the end", is not alien to any culture, nor to any person; on the contrary, the response that he seeks in the heart of cultures is what gives them their ultimate identity, uniting humanity and at the same time respecting the wealth of diversity, opening people everywhere to growth in genuine humanity, in authentic progress. The Word of God, in becoming flesh in Jesus Christ, also became history and culture.

The Utopia of going back to breathe life into the pre-Columbus religions, separating them from Christ and from the universal Church, would not be a step forward: indeed, it would be a step back. In reality, it would be a retreat towards a stage in history anchored in the past.

The wisdom of the indigenous peoples fortunately led them to form a synthesis between their cultures and the Christian faith which the missionaries were offering them. Hence the rich and profound popular religiosity, in which we see the soul of the Latin American peoples.[646]

Bartolome de las Casas O.P. (c. 1484-1566)

Although this Spanish born Dominican priest and Bishop of Chiapas Mexico has not been recognized a saint, he led an exemplary life that starkly contrasts with the injustices committed by some explorers and conquistadores. Bartolome de las Casas's desire to leave his home country for the New World of the Americas was in part inspired by an encounter he had as a young boy with Christopher Columbus on Palm Sunday of 1493. On that day, Columbus visited Bartolome's home city of Seville, Spain. Before a crowd of people, Columbus proudly displayed exotic items and creatures that he had brought back with him. Bartolome, only nine at the time, was part of the crowd.[647] After he was ordained a priest, Bartolome made preparations to go to Mexico where he hoped, according to Paul S. Vickery, "to acquire wealth and prestige"[648] similar to what Columbus had once displayed. In Mexico, though, Bartolome had a profound change of

---

[646] Benedict XVI, "Fifth General Conference of the Episcopate of Latin America and the Caribbean Pope Benedict, " Aparecida, 13 May, EWTN, http://www.ewtn.com/library/PAPALDOC/b16brazil11.htm (accessed December 16, 2014).

[647] Paul S. Vickery, *Bartolome de las Casas: Great Prophet of the Americas* (New Jersey: Paulist Press, 2006), 1.

[648] Vickery, 2.

heart and became a defender of the Indians and their representative to the Spanish monarchy. After his conversion, Bartolome argued that all people, regardless of their race, are born with inherent universal human rights and that slaves ought to be freed.[649]

St. Peter Claver, S.J. (1580-1654)

This Spanish born Jesuit saint did what he could to meet the needs of slaves in Cartagena, Columbia who suffered from tremendous injustice. It is reputed that over 300,000 slaves accepted his invitation to be baptized, and that he yearly heard thousands of their confessions.[650] St. Peter Claver, SJ, learned the basics of the African Angolan and relied on interpreters to best serve the slaves. In contrast, many of his brother priests chose to ignore the plight of the African slaves with the rationalization that their inability to communicate in African languages excused them from ministering to the slaves.[651]

~ St. Peter's Missionary Methodology of Mercy ~

Before visiting the, the zealous missioner implored the divine mercy by fervent prayers offered in presence of the Blessed Sacrament, by additional austerities, and by such works of piety as the ardor of his charity suggested. He then set off with a staff in his hand, of which the upper part formed a cross, a bronze crucifix upon his breast, and a kind of saddle bag upon his shoulder, one side of which contained stole, surplice, the holy oils, medals and rosaries: the other, tonics, scented water, biscuits

---

[649] Francis Augustus MacNutt, *Bartholomew de Las Casas: His Life, Apostolate, and Writings* (Cleveland: Arthur H. Clark Company, 1909), 105-106, Project Gutenberg, http://www.gutenberg.org/files/23466/23466-h/23466-h.html#toc22 (accessed November 6, 2014).
[650] Sarah Fawcett Thomas, *Butler's Lives of the Saints*, New Full Edition, September (Collegeville: The Liturgical Press, 2000), 78.
[651] Thomas, 77.

and delicacies for the sick. Although so heavily laden he walked on with such courage and agility, that his companion could scarcely keep pace with him. On his arrival he proceeded to the quarters of the sick, and began by washing their faces with scented water, to diminish the infection, giving them a little wine or brandy to strengthen them. He regaled them with biscuits and preserves, and then administered such sacraments as they were in a condition to receive. Never did he leave them till they were as much consoled as delighted with his goodness.[652]

St. Francis Xavier (1506-1552)

~ St. Francis Xavier in a letter to St. Ignatius of Loyola ~

The dangers to which I am exposed and the tasks I undertake for God are springs of spiritual joy, so much so that these islands are the places in all the world for a man to lose his sight by excess of weeping; but they are tears of joy. I do not remember ever to have tasted such interior delight, and these consolations take from me all sense of bodily hardships and of troubles from open enemies and not too trustworthy friends.[653]

St. Francis Xavier was a Jesuit Spanish born priest. His missionary work, though, was not directed to Spanish-speaking lands but rather to Asia. With the intent to follow trade routes established by the Portuguese explorers, in 1541 St. Francis embarked to sail around Africa. He finally reached Goa, India in 1542, 13 months later.[654] For five months, he served the people of Goa by

---

[652] A Father of St. Joseph Society, *The Life of St. Peter Claver: The Apostle of the Negroes* (Philadelphia: H.L. Kilner & Co., 1893), 59-60.

[653] Kathleen Jones, *Butler's Lives of the Saints*, New Full Edition, December (Collegeville: The Liturgical Press, 1999), 28-29.

[654] Jones, 25-26.

teaching basic Catholic doctrine, visiting prisons and hospitals, and defending the rights of native women trapped in concubinage to Portuguese men. After serving the people of Goa, he was told of a low class of people, the Paravas, who lived further down the coast of India. With Goa as his base, St Francis extended his missionary service to these neglected people. In 1545, St. Francis set sail once again to spread the good news to the people of Malacca, a city of Malaysia. Like his work in India, he expanded his missionary service to the people of modern day Indonesia. Then, in 1549, St. Francis was inspired to set sail to Japan. There, he quickly realized that dressing as a poor man worked well in India, but not Japan. By dressing as an educated man, he drew many more Japanese, including the Japanese Emperor, with whom he had an audience with. Once again, while serving the Japanese, St. Francis was moved by the Spirit to spread Christ's saving message to the Chinese. In 1552, he reached the island of Shang-chwan, near the coast of mainland China, became sick and, within a few months, died on the island.[655] His incorrupt body is currently enshrined in the Basilica of Bom Jesus Old Goa, India. On the next page is a picture of his tomb.

Servant of God Matteo Ricci (1552-1610)

This Italian Jesuit, unlike St. Francis Xavier, reached China to serve as a missionary. In China, he became one of the founding fathers of the Jesuit missions to China. Prior to being sent to China, Ricci spent four years in St. Francis Xavier's mission land, and former Portuguese Colony of Goa, India. In 1582, he set sail to the Portuguese administered region of Macau, China.[656] Shortly after arriving, Ricci began avidly learning the Chinese language, and studying Chinese literature. His mastery of the Chinese language and culture, even of dress, in conjunction with his impressive ability in astronomy and mapmaking, persuaded the Chinese Emperor to invite Ricci to an audience in the Forbidden

---

[655] Jones, 26-30.
[656] Michela Fontana, *Matteo Ricci: A Jesuit in the Ming Court* (Lanham: Rowman & Littlefield Publishers, 2011), 299.

City. Ricci graciously accepted the Emperor' offer and became

657

even more fascinated with Chinese culture.[658]

In reading and translating the Chinese philosophy of Confucius, Ricci was faced with the following question. To what extent is Confucius's teaching compatible with Catholicism? In his writings, Ricci argued that Confucianism and Catholicism are compatible with one another. In an effort to be as persuasive as possible in preaching and spreading the Gospel, he began to use

[657] Khariharan [Public domain or Public domain], via Wikimedia Commons, http://commons.wikimedia.org/wiki/File%3AMausol%C3%A9o_S%C3%A3o_Francisco_Xavier.jpg (accessed November 8, 2014).
[658] Fontana, 200-212.

Confucian concepts. When Dominican and Franciscan missionaries heard of Ricci's adoption of Confucian ideas, which included allowing Chinese Catholics to honor their dead, they became concerned. After Rome received several complaints, in 1645, about 35 years after Ricci had died, Pope Innocent X decreed that the "Chinese rites" promoted by Ricci were no longer permitted.[659] Below is a passage from Ricci's *The True Meaning of the Lord of Heaven* on Confucianism in relationship to Catholicism.

~ Mistaken Views about the Lord of Heaven ~

1. The Western scholar says: The work of creation is an enormous undertaking and it must have its own pivot; but this is established by the Lord of Heaven. If there were no first cause to serve as the source of phenomena, neither principle nor the Supreme Ultimate would be able to fill this role. I am sure that there initially must have been very profound reasons for the teachings concerning the Supreme Ultimate. I have read them, and I would not dare to cast aside these arguments in any casual manner. Perhaps I shall later be able to write another book in which I can discuss their important ideas.

101. The Chinese scholar says: From ancient times to the present the sovereigns and ministers of my country have known only that they should pay reverence to Heaven and Earth as if they were reverencing their fathers and mothers. They have therefore employed the ceremonial of state worship to sacrifice to them. If the Supreme Ultimate were the source of heaven and earth it would be the first ancestor of the world; and the first sages, emperors, and ministers of ancient times ought to have given

---

[659] Fontana, 291-294; "Father Matteo Ricci's Beatification Cause Reopened", Agenzia Fides, http://www.fides.org/en/news/ 25874?idnews=25874&lan= eng#.VF5r_-ktC1s (accessed November 8, 2014)

priority to the worship of it. But, in fact, this was not the case. It is obvious, then, that the explanation given of the Supreme Ultimate is incorrect. You have argued the matter exhaustively, Sir, and your views are the same as those of the sages and worthies of ancient times.

102. The Western scholar says: Despite what you say, the teaching that Heaven and Earth are the two things most honored is by no means easy to explain, since that which is most deserving of honor is unique and unparalleled. If we speak of "heaven" and "earth" we are talking about two things.

103. He who is called the Lord of Heaven in my humble country is He who is called Shang-ti (Sovereign on High) in Chinese. He is not, however, the same as the carved image of the Taoist Jade Emperor who is described as the Supreme Lord of the Black Pavilions of Heaven, for he was no more than a recluse on Wu-tang mountain. Since he was a man, how could he have been the Sovereign of heaven and earth?

104. Our Lord of Heaven is the Sovereign on High mentioned in the ancient [Chinese] canonical writings [as the following texts show]: Quoting Confucius, the Doctrine of the Mean says: "The ceremonies of sacrifices to Heaven and Earth are meant for the service of the Sovereign on High." Chu Hsi comments that the failure to mention Sovereign Earth [after Sovereign on High] was for the sake of brevity. In my humble opinion what Chung-ni [i.e. Confucius] intended to say was that what is single cannot be described dualistically. How could he have been seeking merely for brevity

of expression?[660]

St. Isaac Jogues (1607-1646) and St. Jean de Breubeuf (1593-1649)

We now turn our attention back to the West, specifically to North America. About thirty to forty years after Matteo Ricci's death, eight Jesuit missionaries were martyred in North America by some of the Indians they were attempting to evangelize. The two most well-known of this group are St. Isaac Jogues and St. Jean de Breubeuf.

St. Isaac Jogues was a Jesuit French priest who was sent to evangelize the Native Americans in North America. While ministering to the members of the Huron tribe, located in modern day Canada, he, and a few of his companions, were taken captive by a competing tribe, the Iroquois. In captivity, St. Isaac Jogues was severely beaten, tortured and his fingers were cruelly chopped off.[661] After being held as a slave by the Iroquois for a period of time, St. Isaac was rescued by Dutch settlers, who interestingly supplied the Iroquois with muskets and ammunition.[662] Upon returning to France, he sought and received a dispensation from Pope Urban VIII to celebrate mass even though he lacked fingers.[663] In 1644, after persistently asking permission to return to serve the Native Americans in North America, his desire was granted and he set sail back to New France (Canada) where he once had served in and where he had been viciously tortured.[664] In October of 1646, St. Isaac Jogues and St. Jean de la Lande were tomahawked and beheaded by a sub-group of the Iroquois known as the Mohawks who had invited the two to a meal.[665]

---

[660] Matteo Ricci, "The True Meaning of the Lord of Heaven," Christendom Awake, http://www.christendom-awake.org/pages/dlancash/chineseworks/tmlh.html (accessed November 8, 2014).

[661] Peter Doyle, *Butler's Lives of the Saints*, New Full Edition, October (Collegeville: The Liturgical Press, 1997), 129.

[662] Francis Talbot, *Saint Among Savages: The Life of St. Isaac Jogues* (San Francisco: Ignatius Press, 2002), 294.

[663] Talbot, 350.

[664] Talbot, 349.

[665] Doyle, 129.

St. Jean de Breubeuf was also a French Jesuit sent to New France (Canada) to evangelize the Native Americans. In 1649, he was captured by the Iroquois, beaten, tortured, and finally mortally wounded on the head with a blow by a tomahawk. Afterwards, the Iroquois ripped out his heart and drank his blood.[666]

~ Vow of St. Jean de Breubeuf ~

I vow in the presence of the Eternal Father and the Holy Spirit...never to shirk the grace of martyrdom if, in your mercy, you offer it someday to your unworthy servant...and when I am about to receive the stroke of death, I bend myself to accept it from your hand in the joy of my heart.[667]

Our Lady of Guadalupe

No account of the missionary work in the Americas would be complete without at least mentioning the fundamental role of Our Lady of Guadalupe. On four different occasions in 1531, St. Juan Diego (canonized in 2002) is believed to have seen and talked to an apparition of the Blessed Virgin Mary on hill called Tepeyac, currently located within Mexico City. The Basilica of Guadalupe in Mexico City houses St. Juan's cloak (*tilma*) upon which an image of the Blessed Virgin Mary was miraculously imprinted. The apparition led millions of Mexicans to convert to the Catholic faith. Even today, millions of pilgrims visit the Basilica of Guadalupe to catch a glimpse of the *tilma*.[668]

---

[666] Teresa Rodrigues, *Butler's Lives of the Saints*, New Full Edition, March (Collegeville: The Liturgical Press, 1999), 166.

[667] Rodrigues, 165.

[668] Carl Anderson, *Our Lady of Guadalupe: Mother of the Civilization of Love* (New York: Doubleday, 2009), 6-20.

669

Quiz 18

1. Is the following sentence true or false? Most medieval people thought the earth was flat.

    True
    False

---

669 By unknown (1531 presented by Juan Diego) (Nueva Basílica de Nuestra Señora de Guadalupe) [Public domain], via Wikimedia Commons, http://commons.wikimedia.org/wiki/File%3A1531_Nuestra_Se%C3%B1ora_de_ Guadalupe_anagoria.jpg (accessed November 11, 2014).

2. In a short paragraph, explain your answer given in question one. Include in your answer Antoine-Jean Letronne and Washington Irving.

3. Match the following

Marco Polo	(1455-1495) This man was the patron of Bartolomeu Dias.
King John II	(c. 1460-1524) This Portuguese explorer was the first European to reach India by sailing around the African continent.
Bartolomeu Dias	(c.1450-1506) Intending to find a Western trade route to India, this Italian explorer instead found the Bahamas, Central and South America.
Henry the Navigator	(c. 1450-1499) After being commissioned by the English King Henry VII, this Italian explorer ran into the mainland of North America.
Vasco de Gama	(c. 1480-1521) This Portuguese explorer attempted to sail westward across the Atlantic to the Spice Islands. He died en route before he could complete his goal.
Christopher Columbus	(c. 1471/6-1541) This Spanish man was responsible for beginning the Spanish colonization of South America in Peru by conquering the Incan Empire

Ferdinand Magellan	(1394-1460) This Prince of Portugal was a key patron of explorers of Atlantic routes.
John Cabot	(1451-1500) This Portuguese explorer successfully sailed around the southernmost tip of Africa. In 1500 he died at sea.
Amerigo Vespucci	(1485-1547) This Spanish man conquered and colonized Mexican lands.
Francisco Pizarro Gonzalez	(1254-1324) A Venetian merchant who helped to establish the Silk Routes and who recorded his journeys to the Far East.
Hernando Cortes	(1454-1512) The last word of the USA is named after this Italian Explorer and mapmaker.

4. Choose one of the following options.

a. In light of Pope Benedict XVI's speech at the Fifth General Conference of the Episcopate of Latin America and the Caribbean, explain why Catholic missionaries did not unjustly impose a religion that was neither wanted nor compatible with the ancient cultures of Latin America and the Caribbean.

b. Choose one of the following people and briefly describe key aspects/events of their life: Bartolome de las Casas, St. Peter Claver, St. Francis Xavier, Servant of God Matteo Ricci, St. Isaac Jogues and St. Jean de Breubeuf.

Chapter 19

The Enlightenment and Rejection of Papal Authority

Introduction

The previous chapter was on the Age of Discovery which was followed by missionary activity. Chapter nineteen will be on a following historical period, the Age of Enlightenment. This era roughly spans from the death of Rene Descartes in 1650 to the beginning of the French Revolution in 1789. We will not adhere strictly to these dates, which are a bit arbitrary. The dates are only to serve as an aid in recognizing noticeable movements within history. During the time of the Enlightenment, reason was emphasized, often excessively to the detriment of faith. Not surprisingly, this era was in turn followed by a Romantic era whose accent was on emotion and was also detrimental to the Catholic faith as particularly evident during the French Revolution (1789-1799).

In discussing the Age of Enlightenment we will first focus on some of the key scientists of the era: Rene Descartes, Francis Bacon, Nicolaus Copernicus, Galileo Galilei, and Isaac Newton. Then, you will be introduced to several Enlightenment ideas on human nature, on God, and on the Pope.

Enlightenment Scientists

Rene Descartes (1596-1650)

Descartes was a French born philosopher and mathematician who defined truth from the perspective of individual judgment without any reliance on external authority. This is represented in his well-known phrase "I think therefore I am".[670] See below for this saying of his in the context of searching for truth, rejecting external authority, and doubt:

> For a long time I had noticed that in matters of morality one must sometimes follow opinions that one knows to be quite uncertain, just as if they were indubitable, as has been said above, but because I then desire to devote myself exclusively to the search for the truth, I thought it necessary that I do exactly the opposite, and that I reject as absolutely false everything in which I could imagine the least doubt, in order to see whether after this process, something in my beliefs remained that was entirely indubitable. ...I noticed that, while I wanted thus to think that everything was false, it necessarily had to be the case that I, who was thinking this, was something. And noticing that this truth – *I think, therefore I am* – was so firm and so assured that all the most extravagant suppositions of the skeptics were incapable of shaking it, I judged that I could accept it without scruple as the first principle of the philosophy I was seeking.[671]

---

[670] Descartes, Discourse on the Method – written in French with "Cogito ergo sum" and 7 of Principles of Philosophy 1644 written in Latin.
[671] Rene Descartes, *Discourse on Method and Meditations on First Philosophy*, trans. Donald A Cress (Indianapolis: Hackett Publishing Company, 1998), 18.

Francis Bacon (1561-1626)

While the French man Descartes was grounding his approach to truth in the individual mind, the English empiricist Francis Bacon was searching for truth by examining the world perceived by his senses. His empirically-based methodology for ascertaining certainty has been called the Baconian method.[672] The modern scientific method is a further development of the Baconian method. With his Baconian inductive method (starting from the specific with the hope of discovering a general principle), Francis Bacon also distanced himself from seeking truth by relying on the authority of another.

~ The Empirically Based Baconian Method ~

Our method, though difficult to practice, is easy to formulate. It is to establish degrees of certainty, to preserve sensation by putting a kind of restraint on it. But to reject in general the work of the mind that follows sensation; and rather to open and construct a new and certain road for the mind from the actual perceptions of the senses.[673]

Nicolaus Copernicus (1473-1543)

The Polish mathematician and astronomer Nicolaus Copernicus unintentionally contributed to the Age of the Enlightenment's doubt of external authority and excessive reliance on empirically-based science. In his *On the Revolutions of the Celestial Spheres*, Copernicus provided convincing evidence that the earth is not at the center of the known universe (geocentric theory).[674] Instead, based on research, he argued that the sun is at the center of the known universe (heliocentric theory). This sun-centered

---

[672] Francis Bacon, *The New Organon*, eds. Lisa Jardine, and Michael Silverthorne (Cambridge: Cambridge University Press, 2000), xviii.
[673] Bacon, 28.
[674] Nicholas Copernicus, *On the Revolutions of the Heavenly Spheres*, trans. Charles Glenn Wallis (Amherst: Prometheus Books, 1995).

explanation was not a brand-new conception of the cosmos. As far back as the ancient Greeks, beginning with Greek astronomer Aristarchus (c. 310–c. 230 BC), this theory had been circulating.[675] Up until Copernicus's day, the dominant explanation for the order of the cosmos, though, was the one proposed by the Greco-Egyptian Ptolemy (c. 90-c. 168 AD). According to Ptolemy's account, the earth and not the sun is at the center of the universe. On your right is a depiction of Copernicus's view of the cosmos with the sun (*sol*) at the center. On the next page is a seventeenth century painting of the Ptolemaic, earth-centered, cosmic model. The diagram representing Copernicus's heliocentric model is a simplification since it does not represent Copernicus's epicycles (small circles) that he included in accounting for planetary motion. Later, the German scientist Johannes Kepler (1570-1630) eliminated the need for epicycles within the Copernican system by proposing elliptical orbits with the Sun at the focal point and center of planetary orbits.[676]

The Jesuit astronomer Guy Consolmagno points out that in proposing the earth at the center of the universe did not mean to Copernicus, Kepler, or, later Galileo, that the earth was the central, most important place of reality. Rather, the earth was seen more at the bottom of the universe, in the common-sense approach of identifying what is heavenly as above and what is earthly as below.

[675] Copernicus, 124, 130, 144.
[676] Guy Consolmagno, "Big Questions in Astronomy, Session 2," January 29, 2016 Re-Engaging Science in Seminary Formation," Tucson, Arizona, Redemptorist Retreat Center, January 28-February 1, 2016.

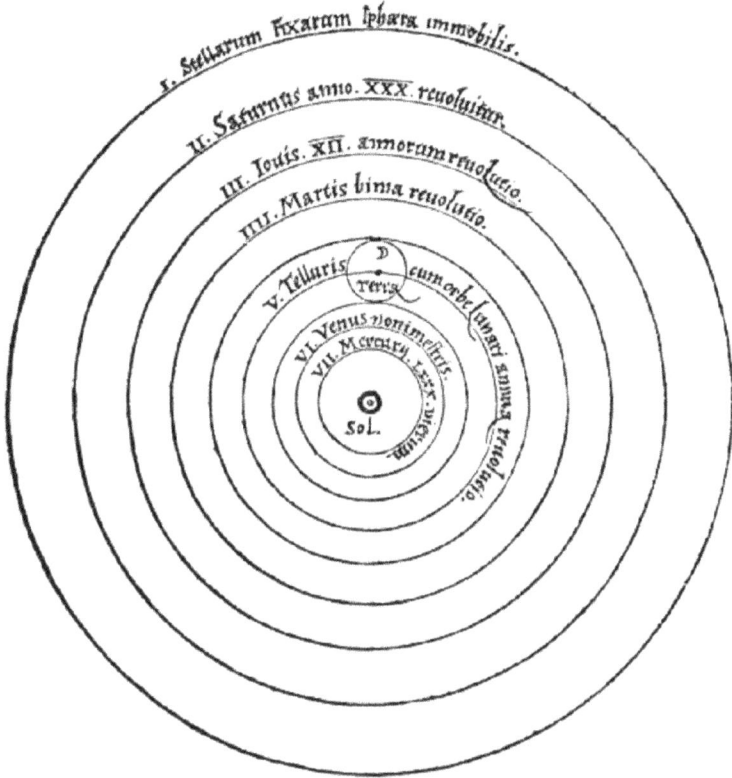

677

━━━━━━━━━━━━━━━━

677 y Nicolai Copernici Created in vector format by Scewing ([1]) [Public domain], via Wikimedia Commons, http://commons.wikimedia.org/wiki/File%3ACopernican_heliocentrism_theory_diagram.svg (accessed November 11, 2014).

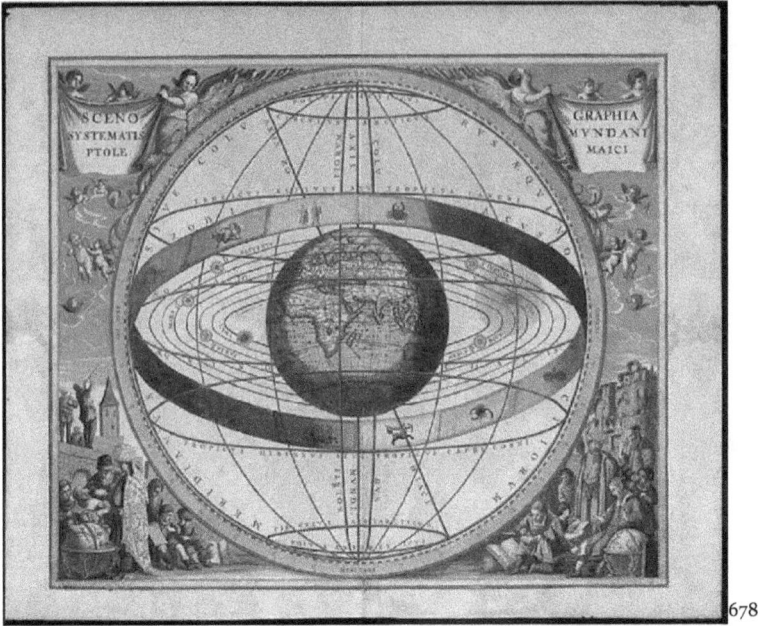

678

Unlike Galileo Galilei, Copernicus was not corrected by the Catholic Church for providing evidence that the sun and not the earth is at the center of the then-known cosmos. The reason is quite simple. Copernicus did not present his view as certain but rather as a possible explanation that needed further confirmation. Due to his diplomatic and careful approach in re-introducing the heliocentric theory, the prominent cardinal of Capua, Cardinal Nicholas Schönberg, even allowed an affirming letter of Copernicus to be published after the forward of Copernicus's 1543 book *On the Revolutions of the Celestial Spheres*. In the letter the Cardinal states:

~ Cardinal Schönberg's 1536 letter to Copernicus ~

Some years ago word reached me concerning your proficiency, of which everybody constantly spoke.

---

678 By Loon, J. van (Johannes), ca. 1611–1686. (http://nla.gov.au/nla.map-nk10241) [Public domain], via Wikimedia Commons, http://commons.wikimedia.org/wiki/File%3ACellarius_ptolemaic_system.jpg (accessed November 10, 2014).

At that time I began to have a very high regard for you, and also to congratulate our contemporaries among whom you enjoyed such great prestige. For I had learned that you had not merely mastered the discoveries of the ancient astronomers uncommonly well but had also formulated a new cosmology. In it you maintain that the earth moves; that the sun occupies the lowest, and thus the central, place in the universe; that the eighth heaven remain perpetually motionless and fixed; and that, together with the elements included in its sphere, the moon, situated between the heavens of Mars and Venus, revolves around the sun in the period of a year. I have also learned that you have written an exposition of this whole system of astronomy, and have computed the planetary motions and set them down in tables, to the greatest admiration of all. Therefore with the utmost earnestness I entreat you, most learned sir, unless I inconvenience you, to communicate this discovery of yours to scholars, and at the earliest possible moment to send me your writings on the sphere of the universe together with the tables and whatever else you have that is relevant to this subject. Moreover, I have instructed Theodoric of Reden to have everything copied in your quarters at my expense and dispatched to me. If you gratify my desire in this matter, you will see that you are dealing with a man who is zealous for your reputation and eager to do justice to so fine a talent. Farewell.[679]

Copernicus also displayed his diplomatic skills in his preface

---

[679] Nicholas Copernicus, *On the Revolutions*, trans. Edward Rosen (Baltimore: John Hopkins University Press, 2008), WebExibits, http://www.webexhibits.org/calendars/year-text-Copernicus.html (accessed November 11, 2014).

by dedicating his book to Pope Paul III. Why was diplomacy so critical in presenting this heliocentric explanation? The answer to this question becomes clearer when we remember that Copernicus was living during the same time as Martin Luther and the beginnings of the Protestant movement. It was imperative for the Catholic Church to be very careful in how the heliocentric theory was publicly presented so that Protestants would not be given additional reasons to criticize the Catholic Church. Even so, in 1616, well after Copernicus had died, the Catholic Church, for prudential reasons, placed Copernicus's *On the Revolutions of the Celestial Spheres* on her Index of forbidden books. Not until 1835 was this book removed from the Index.[680]

Galileo Galilei (1564-1642)

The Italian astronomer Galileo lacked Copernicus's diplomatic approach in promoting the heliocentric explanation of the cosmos. His lack of tact is particularly evident in his *Dialogue Concerning the Two Chief World Systems* in which the character *Simplicio* (simpleton) speaks words that Pope Urban VIII had said.[681] Needless to say, this mockery greatly angered Pope Urban VIII. Subsequently, Galileo was tried by the Inquisition, found suspect of heresy, forced to recant, and consigned to house arrest.[682]

The Church punished Galileo for the following reasons. Many Churchmen thought that it was not yet the opportune time for the heliocentric theory to be presented as a fact for a whole host of reasons including the following. More data was needed to confirm this theory. Protestants might accuse the Catholic Church of promoting an explanation that had not yet been sufficiently proven and that seemed to contradict Sacred Scripture. Many believed that the universe revolves around the earth and not the sun. Finally, before the Church could express openness to the heliocentric theory she needed to carefully deal with passages of

---

[680] Jack Repcheck, *Copernicus' Secret: How the Scientific Revolution Began* (New York: Simon & Schuster, 2007), 194.
[681] Galileo Galilei, *Dialogue Concerning the Two Chief World Systems*, trans. Stillman Drake (New York: The Modern Library,2001), xvi.
[682] Galilei, xiii-xxiii.

Sacred Scripture that phenomenologically describe the sun as revolving around the earth.

Isaac Newton (1642-1727)

The English mathematician and physicist Isaac Newton is the last key scientist of the Age of Enlightenment who will be briefly discussed. Some of his accomplishments include developing calculus, finding further evidence that the heliocentric theory is valid, and formulating laws of motion and of gravitation.[683] His three laws of motion, based on the simple principle that all material things move according to the same physical laws, overturned Aristotle's view that heavy bodies are naturally inclined downward, lighter bodies naturally move upwards, heavenly bodies naturally move in circles, and in order for something to be moved motion needs to be continually imparted to it.[684] Aristotle's conclusions seemed to be in accordance with common sense. After all, does not smoke rise and dirt, when dropped, fall? In contrast, according to Newton and as confirmed by modern science, every material object continues in either a state of rest or motion unless affected by force, the degree of change in motion of an object in motion is proportional to the force acting on it, and finally every action always entails an equal and opposite reaction. Once Newtonian physics replaced Aristotelian physics, theologians began to describe theological realities in a slightly different manner. For example, significantly prior to Newton's laws of motion the early Church Father St. Augustine, in accordance with the then common sense approach to physics, identified as Aristotelian, described love in terms of

---

[683] A. Rupert Hall, *Isaac Newton: Adventurer in Thought* (Cambridge: Cambridge University Press, 1992), 38, 76; Peter Guthrie Tait, *Treatise on Natural Philosophy*, Vol. 1 (Oxford: Clarendon Press, 1867), 179-184.

[684] Aristotle, *Physics*, trans. Robin Waterfield (Oxford: Oxford University Press, 2008), 35, 43, 57, 88-90; "The Physics of Aristotle versus the Physics of Galileo," Dept. Physics & Astronomy University of Tennessee, http://csep10.phys.utk.edu/astr161/lect/history/aristotle_dynamics.html (accessed January 15, 2016).

weight. In his *Confessions* he writes, "My weight is my love,"[685] meaning that if we love heavenly things we will naturally float upwards to heaven, but if we love earthly things we will sink like a rock downwards away from heaven.

~ St. Augustine's Pre-Newtonian Influenced Theology ~

A body gravitates to its proper place by its own weight. This weight does not necessarily drag it downward, but pulls it to the place proper to it: thus fire tends upward, a stone downward. Drawn by their weight, things seek their rightful places. ...Now my weight is my love, and wherever I am carried, it is this weight that carries me.[686]

Enlightenment Ideas and Movements

Human Nature is Pure

During the Age of the Enlightenment many became so confident in their enlightened state that they began looking down upon the previous era, by naming it the Dark Ages. Calling the previous era a dark one implied that the people living during this "dark" time were mentally shackled by superstitions, traditions and, hence, unenlightened. Another manifestation of Enlightenment era pride was the conviction that circumstances determine human vice. If, some claimed, the social environment abides by Enlightenment principles then crime, suffering and poverty will disappear from human societies. The Genevan born philosopher Jean-Jacques Rousseau (1712-1778) grounded this claim by denying original sin. According to Rousseau in his treatise *On Education*, "there is no original sin in the human heart." [687]

---

[685] Augustine, *Confessions*, trans. Maria Boulding (Hyde Park: New City Press, 1997), 280.

[686] Augustine, Ibid.

[687] Jean-Jacques Rousseau, *Emile*, trans. Barbara Foxley Project Gutenberg, "Emile" http://www.gutenberg.org/cache/epub/5427/pg5427.html (Accessed September 8, 2014).

~ Rousseau's Denial of Original Sin ~

Let us lay it down as an incontrovertible rule that the first impulses of nature are always right; there is no original sin in the human heart, the how and why of the entrance of every vice can be traced. The only natural passion is self-love or selfishness taken in a wider sense. This selfishness is good in itself and in relation to ourselves; and as the child has no necessary relations to other people he is naturally indifferent to them; his self-love only becomes good or bad by the use made of it and the relations established by its means. Until the time is ripe for the appearance of reason, that guide of selfishness, the main thing is that the child shall do nothing because you are watching him or listening to him; in a word, nothing because of other people, but only what nature asks of him; then he will never do wrong.[688]

Human Nature is Completely Corrupt

The modern ideology of political realism founded by Hans Joachim Morgenthau (1904-1980) which denies the existence of a moral law between nation states[689] is like the political, Enlightenment views of the English philosopher Thomas Hobbes (1588-1679).[690] Hobbes's approach to politics was even more pessimistically "realistic" since he denied the existence of morality, other than might makes right, unless a person was living within a political structure. As is evident, his political approach differs from Rousseau's understanding. According to Hobbes, when people are left to follow their natures, unhindered by a political state, they

---

[688] Rousseau, *Emile*, Ibid.
    [689] Hans Morgenthau and Kenneth Thompson, *Politics Among Nations*, 6th edition (New York: McGraw-Hill, 1985), 166.
    [690] Sometimes, political realism is overly confused with philosophical school of Pragmatism promoted by the Americans Charles Peirce and William James. According to pragmatism truth is defined by community practice.

will naturally wage war with one another. This is because, he contended, war defines human nature. Since Hobbes equates the state of nature with the state of war he describes all political arrangements as artificial. Only when men, through means of a social contract, begin to live within a political structure does morality apply. Outside of agreed upon political structures, he argued, there is no morality. In this natural state, life, claimed Hobbes, is "solitary, poor, nasty, brutish and short."[691]

This radically negative view of human nature directly contradicts the Catholic position of St. Thomas Aquinas who maintained that political communities are natural. According to St. Thomas Aquinas man is naturally a "civic and social animal."[692] Unjust, nasty, brutal elements that are present within political societies are not an indication that these elements are prior to political societies but rather are an indication of man's tendency to sin, since he is wounded, but not corrupted, by original sin.[693] Even though our attraction to good has been distorted by sin, the Catholic Church affirms that with the help of healing and sanctifying grace, our sinful, selfish, brutal tendencies can be diminished.[694]

God Does Not Care About Nature

The Enlightenment Deists also perceived nature in an obviously non-Catholic manner. According to the Deists, God leaves the world to its own devices. He does not, consequently maintained the Deists, intervene or miraculously suspend the natural laws of the universe.

---

[691] Thomas Hobbes, *The Leviathan* (St. Paul's Churchyard: Green Dragon, 1651), chapter xiii, Project Gutenberg, "Leviathan by Thomas Hobbes," http://www.gutenberg.org/files/3207/3207-h/3207-h.htm (Accessed June 15, 2014).

[692] Thomas Aquinas, *Summa Theologica*, trans. Fathers of the English Dominican Province (Allen: Christian Classics, 1981), I-II, q. 72 art. 4.

[693] Thomas Aquinas, *Sententia libri Politicorum Commentary on Aristotle's Politics*, trans. Ernest L. Fortin and Peter D. O'Neill (Spiazzi, 1951) Book 1, Lesson 1, Dominican House Priory, "*Sententia libri Politicorum Commentary on Aristotle's Politics*" http://dhspriory.org/thomas/Politics.htm (Accessed September 8, 2014); *Catechism of the Catholic Church*, 2nd ed., 405-406.

[694] *Catechism of the Catholic Church*, 2nd ed., 405-406.

Some of the Deists formed themselves into fraternities known as Freemasonry. Freemasonry has repeatedly been condemned by the Church: in 1738 by Pope Clement XII in *In Eminenti*,[695] in 1890 by Pope Leo XIII in *Ab Apostolici*,[696] in canon 2335 of the 1917 Code of Canon Law,[697] and indirectly in the 1983 Code of Canon Law. Shortly after the publication of the 1983 Code of Canon Law, Cardinal Joseph Ratzinger as head of the Congregation of the Doctrine of the Faithful clarified the code's implied reference to Freemasons by writing:

> It has been asked whether there has been any change in the Church's decision in regard to Masonic associations since the new Code of Canon Law does not mention them expressly, unlike the previous code. [T]he Church's negative judgment in regard to Masonic association remains unchanged since their principles have always been considered irreconcilable with the doctrine of the Church and therefore membership in them remains forbidden. The faithful who enroll in Masonic associations are in a state of grave sin and may not receive Holy Communion.[698]

Rejection of Papal Authority

Gallicanism

The anti-papal authority, Enlightenment movement known as Gallicanism was named after the ancient Roman province of Gaul that very roughly corresponds to modern day France. Supporters

---

[695] Pope Clement XII, "In Eminenti: On Freemasonry," Papal Encyclicals Online, http://www.papalencyclicals.net/Clem12/c12inemengl.htm (accessed November 12, 2014).

[696] Pope Leo XIII, "Ab Apostolici," EWTN, http://www.ewtn.com/library/ENCYC/L13MS1.HTM (accessed November 12, 2014).

[697] "1917 Codex Iuris Canonicis", JGray, http://www.jgray.org/codes/cic17lat.html (accessed November 12, 2014).

[698] Cardinal Joseph Ratzinger, "Declaration on Masonic Associations (Quaesitum est)" EWTN, http://www.ewtn.com/expert/answers/ freemasonry. htm (accessed November 12, 2014).

of Gallicanism claimed that papal authority does not overrule either French secular authority or the authority of French bishops. Gallicanism was officially formalized by Louis XIV in 1682 when four articles were published and distributed in his name. These anti-papal articles are listed below.

> 1. That the ecclesiastical power has no right over the temporalities of the kingdom.
> 2. That a General Council is superior to the Pope, as decided by the Council of Constance.
> 3. That the exercise of the Papal power should be controlled by canons and local customs.
> 4. That the judgment of the Pope is not infallible, except when confirmed by the Church.[699]

Febronianism

Another anti-papal, Enlightenment movement is Febronianism. It received its name from the pseudonym of a principle founder, the German Nicholas von Hontheim (1701-1790). Like Gallicanism, Febronianism held that a General Council is superior to the Pope and that papal authority does not extend into the territory of local bishops. Out of twenty-six German bishops, only 10 agreed to publish and disseminate a condemnation of Febronius issued by Rome. Not until Vatican Council I (1869-1870), when papal infallibility was defined, was Febronianism and Gallicanism substantially weakened.[700]

Josephenism

Josephenism was yet another anti-papal, Enlightenment movement. This movement received its name after the Holy Roman Emperor, Joseph II (1765-1790). In 1773, he decreed that he was responsible for determining the charitable and religious

---

[699] Julius Lloyd, *The Gallican Church: Sketches of Church History in France* (London: Society for Promoting Christian Knowledge, 1879), 126.

[700] Thomas Bokenkotter, *A Concise History of the Catholic Church* (New York: Doubleday, 2004), 276-277.

purposes of all church property.[701] In 1781, he suppressed contemplative monasteries which he believed were useless since they served no practical purpose.[702] Then, in 1782, he began establishing state-run seminaries and forbade the teaching of scholasticism at his general seminaries.[703] Finally, in 1782, he even claimed a quasi-papal gift in infallibility as is evident in his own words given below.

Joseph II can be understood as embodying the absolute monarch who received his power from a social contract that the Enlightenment political writer Thomas Hobbes advocated in his *Leviathan.* The few ways mentioned above by which Joseph II controlled the Church were part of his overall scheme to unify his state by centralizing power in himself as the one, absolute sovereign.[704]

~ Joseph II to Pope Pius VI ~

Without having to search the texts of Holy Scripture or of the Fathers, which in any case are always subject to interpretations and explanations, I have a voice inside me that tells me what, as legislator and protector of religion, it is proper for me to do and to leave undone; and it seems to me that this voice of mine – with the help of God's grace and the honest and equitable character that I feel I have – can never lead to error.[705]

---

[701] Derek Beales, *Joseph II, Against the World, 1780-1790* (Cambridge: Cambridge University Press, 2009), 279.

[702] Beales, 218.

[703] Beales, 79, 291-292.

[704] Beales, 1, 651.

[705] Beales, 78.

Quiz 19

1. Match the following.

Rene Descartes	Our method, though difficulty to practice, is easy to formulate. It is to establish degrees of certainty, to preserve sensation by putting a kind of restraint on it. But to reject in general the work of the mind that follows sensation; and rather to open and construct a new and certain road for the mind from the actual perceptions of the senses.[706]
Francis Bacon	Wrote *On the Revolutions of the Celestial Spheres,*
Nicholas Copernicus	"I think therefore I am." [707]
Galileo Galilei	Was placed under house arrest.
Isaac Newton	Proposed three laws of motion.

2. True or False?

As far back as the ancient Greeks, beginning with the Greek astronomer Aristarchus (c. 310- c. 230 BC), the geocentric theory was the only theory known for explaining the order of the cosmos. Copernicus and Galileo were first to propose that the earth actually revolves around the sun and not vice versa.

True
False

Francis Bacon, *The New Organon*, eds. Lisa Jardine, and Michael Silverthorne (Cambridge: Cambridge University Press, 2000), 28.
[707] Rene Descartes, *Discourse on Method and Meditations on First Philosophy*, trans. Donald A Cress (Indianapolis: Hackett Publishing Company, 1998), 18.

3. Write on one of the following options below.

Why was Copernicus not corrected by Catholic Church officials while Galileo was?

Provide three logical reasons why the Catholic Church punished Galileo while including the following: Protestants, and Sacred Scripture.

How did pre-Newtonian physics influence St. Augustine's theological description of love in his confessions?

4. Match the following.

Jean-Jacques Rousseau	This movement was named after a Holy Roman Emperor.
Thomas Hobbes	He held that the state of nature is a state of war.
Gallicanism	He believed that original sin does not exist.
Josephenism	This religious movement maintains that God does not intervene in the world.
Deism	This was a French movement that rejected the authority of the pope.

Fr. Peter Samuel Kucer, MSA

Chapter 20

The French Revolution

Introduction

The French Revolution and its horrors were prepared by Enlightenment philosophers, in particular by Jean-Jacque Rousseau. We will, therefore, first focus on how certain features of Rousseau's philosophy helped to lay the groundwork for this revolution. Then, we will turn our attention to the four phases of the French Revolution. Finally, the heroic witness to the Catholic faith during this repressive time by sixteen members of the French Carmel of Compiegne and by Catholic French peasants living in Vendee will be presented.

Jean-Jacques Rousseau (1712-1778): Philosopher of the French Revolution

Although Rousseau died in 1778, a little over ten years before the French Revolution began, his thought inspired the revolutionaries. According to the German philosopher Hannah Arendt, Rousseau's concept of a General Will was adopted by French revolutionaries who were intent on establishing a single political will, even at the cost of great bloodshed.[708] To see the connection with greater clarity, compare the two passages below, the first by

---

[708] Hannah Arendt, *On Revolution*, trans. (New York: Penguin Books Ltd., 2006), 66-69.

Rousseau and the second enshrined in the 1789 French Revolution's *Declaration of the Rights of Man and the Citizen:*

~ Rousseau's General Will ~

As soon as this multitude is so united in one body, it is impossible to offend against one of the members without attacking the body, and still more to offend against the body without the members resenting it. Duty and interest therefore equally oblige the two contracting parties to give each other help; and the same men should seek to combine, in their double capacity, all the advantages dependent upon that capacity.

... In order then that the social compact[709] may not be an empty formula, it tacitly includes the undertaking, which alone can give force to the rest, that whoever refuses to obey the general will shall be compelled to do so by the whole body. This means nothing less than that he will be forced to be free; for this is the condition which, by giving each citizen to his country, secures him against all personal dependence. In this lies the key to the working of the political machine; this alone legitimizes civil undertakings, which, without it, would be absurd, tyrannical, and liable to the most frightful abuses.[710]

---

[709] The historian Jonathan Steinberg points out that Rousseau's Social Contract, translated above as social compact, "was precisely what the founding Fathers [of the U.S.A] rejected, and the Constitution of 1787 was designed to prevent [such a] democracy, not encourage it." Jonathan Steinberg, *European History and European Lives: 1715 to 1914*, CDs and Course Guidebook (Chantilly: Great Courses, 2003), 37.

[710] Jean-Jacques Rousseau, "The Social Contract" (1762), Book 1, Section 7, Project Gutenberg, http://www.gutenberg.org/files/46333/46333-h/46333-h.htm (accessed November 15, 2014).

~ Article Six of the Declaration of the Rights of Man ~

Law is the expression of the general will.[711] Every citizen has a right to participate personally, or through his representative, in its foundation. It must be the same for all, whether it protects or punishes. All citizens, being equal in the eyes of the law, are equally eligible to all dignities and to all public positions and occupations, according to their abilities, and without distinction except that of their virtues and talents.[712]

The Four Phases of the French Revolution

The French revolution can be divided in four ways according to four different ruling bodies: The National Constituent Assembly (1789-1791), The Legislative Assembly (1791-1792), The National Convention (1792-1795), and The Directory (1795-1799).

The National Constituent Assembly (1789-1791)

Prior to the National Constituent Assembly, France was ruled by the Enlightenment minded, Bourbon, absolute monarch King Louis XVI (1754-1793). When the Americans were fighting a war of independence with Britain (1775-1783), King Louis XVI agreed to financially back the Americans, whose valiant struggle with the

---

[711] The *Catechism of the Catholic Church* defines law as, "a rule of conduct enacted by competent authority for the sake of the common good. The moral law presupposes the rational order, established among creatures for their good and to serve their final end, by the power, wisdom, and goodness of the Creator. All law finds its first and ultimate truth in the eternal law. Law is declared and established by reason as a participation in the providence of the living God, Creator and Redeemer of all. 'Such an ordinance of reason is what one calls law.'" "Catechism of the Catholic Church," vatican.va, http://www.vatican.va/archive/ccc_css/archive/catechism/p3s1c3a1.htm (accessed March 30, 2017).

[712] Article Six of the *Declaration of the Rights of Man*. Declaration of the Rights of Man – 1789, The Avalon Project, Yale Law School, http://avalon.law.yale.edu/18th_century/rightsof.asp (accessed November 15, 2014).

British King George III inspired some French to resist their own King, Louis XVI.[713] Aiding the Americans, came with a hefty price tag that increased the French government's debt.[714] In order to find ways to pay off the debt, and to address the dire situation of poor crops and rising food prices, King Louis XVI held an assembly called the Estates-General. Since 1614, the Estates-General had been defunct.[715]

The Estates-General was broken into three estates: clergy (First Estate), nobles (Second Estate), and commoners (Third Estate made up of lawyers, businessmen, and peasants). On June 15th of 1789, in a vote of 491 in favor to 89 in opposition, the members, including many clergy, voted to change the name from the Estates-General to the National Assembly, with the under-standing that it was a sovereign entity not beholden to the King. A few days later, on June 20th, 1789, the King and his counsel responded by locking out the assembly members. That same day, in outrage, assembly members, joined by "a majority of the clergy representatives" and three nobles held a meeting in a nearby tennis court.[716] There they took the "Tennis Court Oath," re-affirming that they were France's ruling body as the National Constituent Assembly of France.[717]

Shortly after taking this oath the finance minister of Louis XVI, Jacques Necker, was fired. This enraged many commoners since Jacques Necker had demonstrated his concern for the poor by supporting an initiative of increasing the Third Estate's representation in the Estates-General.[718] After he was fired, rioting and looting broke out in Paris culminating in the storming of the state prison at Bastille on July 14th, 1789. On "Bastille Day," currently celebrated nationwide in France, a mob attacked a fortress in Bastille that was holding seven people as prisoners: a

---

[713] Linda S. Frey and Marsha L. Frey, *The French Revolution* (Westport: Greenwood Press, 2004), 24.
[714] Frey, 24.
[715] Frey, 3.
[716] William Doyle, *Oxford History of the French Revolution*, Second Edition (Oxford: Oxford University, 2002), 105-106.
[717] Doyle, 105-106.
[718] Frey, 3.

nobleman, two severely mentally ill people, and four forgers.[719] After murdering both the governor of the Bastille and the city's chief magistrate, the mob grotesquely paraded their heads on pikes.[720]

The following month, in August of 1789, the National Constituent Assembly, issued The Declaration of the Rights of Man, affirming the equality of citizens and Rousseau's notion of a general will, as previously shown. In this declaration, freedom was defined from the perspective of freedom from political oppression, and freedom "to do anything that does not injure others".[721] Absent from this way of defining freedom was presenting freedom as for the good, in other words a good that is objectively true. As Catholics, we believe that only by orienting one's life towards God as the supreme good, and conforming one's life to Christ, as the embodiment of the good, will one experience fulfillment and hence deep inner freedom. As St. Augustine once wrote in relationship to Christ, "our heart is unquiet until it rest in you."[722]

The following year in July of 1790, the National Constituent Assembly turned against the Catholic way of life by prohibiting the taking of monastic vows and by enacting a civil constitution of the clergy. This constitution required clergy to be paid with public funds, and insisted that priests and bishops be elected by the people. In addition, all clerics were obliged to swear an oath of obedience to the constitution, a requirement that, as we shall see later, King Louis XVI was reluctant to enforce.[723] Other anti-Church legislation included the 1789 abolishment of the tithe (tax) that was given to the Church, some of which was used to pay clergy salaries, and the 1789 Assembly's approval and authorization of

---

[719] Simon Schama, *Citizens: A Chronicle of the French Revolution* (New York: Vintage Books, 1989), 392.

[720] Doyle, 112.

[721] "Declaration on the Rights of Man and the Citizen (August 1789)" art. 4, The History Guide: Lectures on Modern European Intellectual History, http://www.historyguide.org/intellect/declaration.html (accessed 11/16/2014).

[722] Augustine, *Confessions*, trans. Maria Boulding (Hyde Park: New City Press, 1997), 14.

[723] William Doyle, *The French Revolution: A Very Short Introduction* (Oxford: Oxford University Press, 2001), 46-47.

selling off Catholic Church land.[724]

The Legislative Assembly (1791-1792)

The governing body, the Legislative Assembly, which replaced the National Constituent Assembly was even more opposed to the Catholic Church. Under its rule, religious orders, specifically sisters dedicated to teaching and working in hospitals, were suppressed and their convents were sold by the government. According to some historical records, since the sisters were popular their suppression was not well received by most of the French population.[725] Clerical dress was also forbidden and Church funds, in addition to their property, were confiscated by the government.[726] Priests who did not swear an oath of allegiance to the constitution were hunted down and, if not killed, imprisoned. Their time in prison was fraught with danger. In a horrific event called the September Massacres, within the span of three days in September of 1792, 233 clerics were brutally murdered while in prison, and 115 other clerics, upon being discovered in a Carmelite monastery, were likewise killed.[727] Those clergy who had sworn an oath of allegiance would also soon be persecuted. A non-violent way that the Legislative Assembly repressed the Church was by officially removing the Church's traditional civic responsibility of keeping registers of births, marriages, and deaths.[728]

The history of why it was decided to have this anti-clerical governing body replace the preceding one merits a brief overview. In 1791, the National Assembly wrote France's first written constitution, presented it to King Louis XVI to sign, which he did.[729] According to the 1791 Constitution, France would no longer be ruled by a monarch with absolute power aided by assemblies

---

[724] Nigel Aston, *Religion and Revolution in France, 1780-1804* (London: MacMillan Press, 2000), 127, 133.

[725] Aston, 182.

[726] Aston, Ibid.

[727] Aston, Ibid.

[728] Aston, 183.

[729] Frey, 7.

that were only consultative in nature. Instead, French monarchs would be held accountable to a constitution that restricted his powers by distributing some of his power to a chamber assembly, the Legislative Assembly. The king, though, was able to veto by suspending legislation sent to him, a power that he exercised.[730] The three political parties that made up this legislative body were those who identified themselves as pro-royalists (Feuillants),[731] those who were opposed royal power but in a moderate manner (Girondins also known as Brissotins or Rolandins),[732] and those who wanted to suddenly, and radically overthrow the royalty who held power (Jacobins).[733]

Tension between those who wanted, or at least were willing to only gradually change the monarchical and aristocratic form of government, and those who wanted a radical break from their past of rule by one and by a few, specifically defined by those who owned property led to a quick disintegration of the Legislative Assembly. [734] The Jacobins, who were advocating sudden reform, emerged as the victors and, consequently, formed yet another ruling body, the National Convention.

~ Selections from the French Constitution of 1791 ~

The National Assembly, wishing to establish the French Constitution upon the principles it has just recognized and declared, abolishes irrevocably the institutions which were injurious to liberty and equality of rights.

Neither nobility, nor peerage, nor hereditary distinctions, nor distinctions of orders, nor feudal regime, nor patrimonial courts, nor any titles, denominations, or prerogatives derived therefrom, nor any order of knighthood, nor any corporations

---

[730] Frey, xviii, 6.
[731] Frey, 165.
[732] Frey, 163-164.
[733] Frey, 6.
[734] Frey, 165.

or decorations requiring proofs of nobility or implying distinctions of birth, nor any superiority other than that of public functionaries in the performance of their duties any longer exists.

....

The law no longer recognizes religious vows or any other obligation contrary to natural rights or the Constitution.

...

Chapter II

....

3. There is no authority in France superior to that of the law; the King reigns only thereby, and only in the name of the law may he exact obedience.[735]

The National Convention (1792-1795)

A principle reason why in 1792 yet another governing body with a different set of laws was formed was how representatives for the Legislative Assembly were chosen. According to the 1791 French constitution, electors, who were voted in by the general population, were required to be wealthy landowners. Once elected, the electors were then tasked with the responsibility of determining who would be the official representatives of the Legislative Assembly.[736] Effectively this meant that much of the population, which was poor, was excluded from voting for a representative who would best represent their interests. Naturally, this method of voting led to resentment and demands for more equal voting rights. Not surprisingly, the radical pro-democracy Jacobin party began advocating for sudden change, and that is what occurred.

After several disrupting factors coalesced, in 1792 the

---

[735] "French Constitution of 1791," World History Project, http:// worldhistoryproject.org/1791/9/3/french-constitution-of-1791 (accessed Nov. 17, 2014).
[736] "French Constitution of 1791," Ibid.

Legislative Assembly voted to suspend the King's rule. These factors included the following: a French declaration of war against the Holy Roman Emperor and his Austrian based monarchy, King Louis XVI's refusal to further penalize priests who had not taken an oath of obedience to the French constitution and King Louis XVI's refusal to penalize people seeking to leave France. After their vote, the Legislative Assembly then called for a new governing body to be formed, the National Convention, which was to be ruled by another constitution.[737] Once the National Convention was assembled their first act was to abolish the suspended monarchy. Those who were extremely opposed to monarchical rule also insisted that King Louis XVI be put on trial for crimes against his country.

A few of the factors that persuaded people to reject their king included the following: he had avoided receiving the sacraments from priests who had taken an oath of obedience to the constitution, and in June of 1791 he attempted to flee the country.[738] After his trial, in which he declared his innocence, a verdict was reached that passed by one vote. King Louis XVI was to be executed, and so he was on January 21, 1793.[739] Shortly after his execution, England, the Dutch Republic, Italian States and Spain joined the Holy Roman Emperor's war against France.[740] Then, a few months later, on October 16th, 1793 King Louis XVI's wife Queen Marie Antoinette was led to the guillotine and beheaded. Prior to her unjust beheading this royal woman who, undoubtedly was far from perfect, was slandered repeatedly and her reputation continues to be in our present times. She was accused of being a lesbian,[741] and of excessive spending while poor people were dying of hunger. While the latter accusation may be to certain extent true, there is no record that she ever said the cold hearted saying,

---

[737] William Doyle, *The French Revolution: A Very Short Introduction* (Oxford: Oxford University Press, 2001), 49-50.

[738] Doyle, *The French Revolution,* 47.

[739] Doyle, *The French Revolution,* 52.

[740] Doyle, *The French Revolution,* 52.

[741] Vincent Cronin, *Louis and Antoinette* (London: Harvill Press, 1996), 402, 404.

with reference to the poor, "Let them eat cake"[742] Below is a 1815 etching of the Queen moments before she was guillotined.

THE QUEEN OF LOUIS XVI KING OF FRANCE AT

THE GUILLOTINE OCT 16-1793

[743]

During this third phase when France was ruled by the National Convention, a time known as the Reign of Terror (1793-1794) was promoted by the lawyer Maximilien de Robespierre

---

[742] Cronin, 13.

[743] "Marie Antoinette, Queen of France, kneeling before the guillotine next to her confessor on the day of her execution, 16 October 1793. Line engraving with etching, 1815." http://wellcomeimages.org/indexplus/obf_images/66/ae/9b47e46a683b2c19cfc9c75fad65.jpg [CC-BY-4.0 (http://creativecommons.org/licenses/by/4.0), via Wikimedia Commons], http://commons.wikimedia.org/wiki/File%3AMarie_ Antoinette%2C_Queen_of_France%2C_kneeling_ before_the_guill_Wellcome_L0019312.jpg (accessed November 15, 2014).

(1758-1794).[744] Robespierre was the chief member of the National Convention's Committee of Public Safety. On May 7th, 1794 Robespierre and his Committee of Public Safety officially attempted to de-Christianize France by lending their support to the Deist cult of the Supreme Being.[745] The atheists wanted to go even further than Robespierre who insisted that public belief in a Supreme Being is important since, "it is the religious sentiment that imprints on souls the idea of the sanction given to moral precepts by a power superior to man's. Thus, I am totally unaware of any legislator who has ever been advised to nationalize atheism."[746] Of course, as Catholics we not only affirm that God is the ground of all being as existence itself, discoverable by natural reason, but also, as taught by revelation, that God is Triune, personal and intimately cares for us.

Despite the brutal persecution of the Catholic Church during the Reign of Terror research has confirmed that many lay people still practiced the Catholic faith. Some of the laity even began, to the extent they could, devoutly to follow Catholic rituals for funerals and marriages. Some even held "White Masses." In a white mass bread and wine was used in a type of dry mass that lacked consecration due to the absence of a priest.[747] Other laity reacted violently to their government's repression of Catholic priests. For example, in December of 1793, a mob of enraged peasants attacked a Jacobin club crying, "Long live the Catholic Religion, we want our priests, we want the Mass on Sundays and Holy Days."[748] Not all protests in support of the Catholic religion resorted to force. Respectful petitions, were sent to governmental officials. In one such petition sent to the mayor of a commune in Perche the petitioners stated, "We are French republicans, we accept the Constitution, we abhor royalism, but we will never renounce our holy religion and we will uphold it with all our power, a holy religion taught to us for more than 1700 years, and

---

[744] Amazon Peter McPhee R the revolutionary 22.
[745] Aston, 190.
[746] Aston, 271.
[747] Aston, 190.
[748] Aston, 189.

we are absolutely insistent that we will not take any other."[749]

Many women supported their Catholic faith in the face of oppression by hiding sacred images and objects that had once been in their parish churches, praying the rosary, even when ridiculed by being called priest-prostitutes, and by passing on the truths of the faith to their children.[750] In 1795, when the National Convention reluctantly permitted Catholics a limited right to publicly worship, "women rioted to get their churches reopened, pulling out priests from hiding to have them say Mass,... ringing bells to summon other women to join them in prayers and hymns."[751]

The number of people executed after a trial during the Reign of Terror has been carefully estimated at around 17,000. 30,000-40,000 more were executed without a trial.[752] In the last months of the Reign of Terror over thirty people were executed daily in Paris by guillotine.[753] Interestingly, this terrifying instrument used to efficiently sever a person's head was originally invented out of concern for a humane way of administering capital punishment.[754] Not all were murdered by guillotine. Other efficient ways of executing included mass drowning and placing many people before cannon fire.[755]

As described by John Marsh, the French Revolutionary Jean-Baptist Carrier, invented the following efficient method for murdering people:

> Carrier devised a system for mass drownings called 'noyades'. Boats were crammed full of prisoners and the hatches were closed. Then the boats were sunk. Once the captives had all drowned, the boats were refloated and taken back to the river bank,

---

[749] Aston, 190.

[750] Aston, 240.

[751] Aston, 241.

[752] Paul R. Hanson, *Contesting the French Revolution* (Oxford: Wiley-Blackwell, 2009), 173.

[753] Hanson, 173.

[754] Hanson, 174.

[755] Hanson, 175.

ready for the next batch. Anyone who tried to clamber had their hands hacked off. At Bourgneuf and Nantes special drownings were organized for children.[756]

Violence during the Reign of Terror was also directed against Church buildings and objects of worship. The French state went even so far as to sanction the destruction of Catholic signs: crosses, confessionals, altars, and statues. Precious metals confiscated from these violated Churches were then melted down and claimed by the state.[757] In one notable state sanctioned event of destroying religious art the "'Black Virgin' of Le Puy was blindfolded, put in a cart, and guillotined on the central square."[758] This intense time of violence concluded when in June of 1794 members of the National Convention, very likely out of fear that they would also be executed, turned on Robespierre and condemned him to death. Between July 27th and July 28th, on the orders of the Convention, Robespierre was guillotined along with twenty-one others.[759]

A few weeks before Robespierre was executed, on July 17, 1794, sixteen members of the Carmelite convent of Compiegne were guillotined for opposing the government's suppression of their convent.[760] Prior to their arrest these heroic women had been offering themselves daily to God for peace to be restored in France.[761] It is recorded that as they walked to their death they were praying the *Salve Regina*, and Psalm 117 *Laudate Dominum Omnes Gentes* (Praise the Lord all People).[762] On May of 1906, St. Pope Pius X beatified these sixteen Carmelites. Their story has been retold countless times in history books, novels, plays, films,

---

[756] John Marsh, *The Liberal Delusion: The Roots of Our Current Moral Crisis* (St. Edmunds: Arena Books, 2012), 134.
[757] Aston, 191.
[758] Aston, 193.
[759] Peter McPhee, *Robespierre, A Revolutionary Life* (Cornwall: Yale University Press, 2012), 220, 242.
[760] William Bush, *To Quell the Terror: The True Story of the Carmelite Martyrs of Compiegne* (Washington, DC: ICS Publications, 1999), xxii-xxiii.
[761] Bush, 6.
[762] Bush, 14-15.

and even in an opera.

The Directory (1795-1799)

A Directory of five men, whom collectively held executive power, was formed in order to prevent one man from consolidating and abusing power as Robespierre did. Although the Reign of Terror was brought to a conclusion after Robespierre was executed, acts of violence and mass killings did not cease. One notable example is the War in the Vendee which began in 1793 under the National Convention and did not conclude until well after the Directory had been in power. During this war, the government killed Catholic men, women and children without mercy. Approximately 200,000 people died during this civil strife centered in the predominantly Catholic population of Vendée[763] who insisted on openly practicing the faith.[764] According to the French General Westermann in his report to the Committee of Public Safety.

> There is no more Vendée. It died with its wives and its children by our free sabres. I have just buried it in the woods and the swamps of Savenay. According to the orders that you gave me, I crushed the children under the feet of the horses, massacred the women who at least will not give birth to any more brigands. I do not have a single prisoner to reproach me. I have exterminated them all. The roads are sown with corpses. At Savenay, brigands are arriving all the time claiming to surrender. We shoot them all. Mercy is not a revolutionary sentiment.[765]

---

[763] Hugh Gough, *The Terror in the French Revolution*, Second Edition (New York: Palgrave MacMillan, 2010), 2, 43.

[764] George James Hill, *The Story of the War in La Vend'ee: and the Little Chouannerie* (New York: D. & J. Sadlier & Co. 1885), vii-viii.

[765] It is debated among historians if this account was actually written by General Westermann. John Marsh, *The Liberal Delusion: The Roots of Our Current Moral Crisis* (St. Edmunds: Arena Books, 2012), 133-134.

As described by Georges James Hill, the "greatest glory" of those who fought against the their unjust government in Vendée "consisted in the fact, that the Catholic religion never ceased to be openly professed in La Vendée; nor did they consent to lay down their arms until liberty of worship was guaranteed to them, and their priests were recognized and protected by the laws."[766] Not until after Napoleon Bonaparte ended the French Revolution on November 9-10, 1799, in his *coup d'état* was Catholicism allowed to be practiced in all of France. For the sake of national unity, Napoleon permitted Catholicism once again to be freely practiced, and Catholicism was "pronounced 'the religion of the great majority of Frenchmen.'"[767] This decision of his may well have been based mainly on pragmatic reasons since he wanted to rally as many people as he could behind his cause. Napoleon's pragmatic approach to life is especially evident in a 1793 letter he wrote to his brother Lucien. In the letter Napoleon wrote, "Among so many conflicting ideas and so many different perspectives, the honest man is confused and distressed and the skeptic becomes wicked ... Since one must take sides, one might as well choose the side that is victorious, the side which devastates, loots, and burns. Considering the alternative, it is better to eat than to be eaten."[768]

Quiz 20

1. Who wrote the following phrase and what did the writer mean by it? "In order then that the social compact may not be an empty formula, it tacitly includes the undertaking, which alone can give force to the rest, that whoever refuses to obey the general will shall be compelled to do so by the whole body. This means nothing less than that he will be forced to be free..."

---

[766] George James Hill, *The Story of the War in La Vend'ee: and the Little Chouannerie* (New York: D. & J. Sadlier & Co. 1885), viii.

[767] Owen Connelly, *The Wars of the French Revolution and Napoleon, 1792-1815* (New York: Routledge, 2006), 104-105, 233.

[768] J. Christopher Herold, *Napoleon* (New Word City, 2015), Google Books, https://books.google.com/books (accessed March 8, 2016).

2. What French document adopted the essential idea from the above quotation? What was this essential idea?

3. Place three of the following French ruling bodies/people in their proper historical order:

Napoleon as Emperor of France, King Louis XVI as Absolute Monarch, The Directory, The Legislative Assembly, The National Convention. The National Constituent Assembly.

4. True or False?

On June 20th, 1789 assembly members held a meeting in a nearby tennis court in opposition to the King. Not a single member of the clergy, nor a member of the nobility joined them.

5. True or False?

On July 14th, 1789 French people stormed a state prison located at Bastille and freed hundreds of prisoners being held unjustly by the monarchy.

6. True or False?

According to reliable historical records Queen Marie Antoinette cold hearted said, with reference to the poor, "Let them eat cake."

7. List three different ways, besides killing, by which the French Government during the French Revolution persecuted the Catholic Church.

8. Describe either the Martyrs of Compiegne or the French Revolutionary Government's war against the Catholic people of Vendée.

Chapter 21

Empire and Nations

Introduction

In this chapter, we will begin with Napoleon Bonaparte who ended the French Revolution and then, after declaring himself Emperor, tried to turn France into a vast Empire with Europe under its control. He failed and instead spent his dying days in exile on the South Atlantic Island of Saint Helena. Around the time of his death, a surge of nationalistic enthusiasm spread across Europe. We will study this phenomenon in Germany, Italy and in post-Napoleonic France. Finally, we will end the chapter by becoming acquainted with the Catholic Austrian Empire's Prince Klemens Wenzel von Metternich. He served as the Foreign Minister of the Holy Roman Empire before it was dissolved in response to its defeat by Napoleon in 1806. After the Holy Roman Emperor's collapse, Metternich became the Chancellor of the Holy Roman Emperor's successor state, the Austrian-Hungarian Empire. As we will see, he was wary of nationalism and feared that if unchecked nationalistic ambitions could lead to war among competing nation states.

Napoleon's Empire and the Catholic Church

During the French Revolution, Napoleon served as an artillery officer.[769]   The above 1812 painting to the left by the French painter Jacques-Louis David realistically depicts Napoleon as Emperor. In contrast, the 1801 painting to the right, also by David, glorifies Napoleon by painting him, larger than the horse he is riding, crossing over the Alps into Spain.

[770]

---

[769] Paul Johnson, *Napoleon* (New York: Penguin Books, 2002), 8, 11.

[770] Jacques-Louis David [Public domain], via Wikimedia Commons, http://commons.wikimedia.org/wiki/File%3AJacques-Louis_David_-_The_Emperor_Napoleon_in_His_Study_at_the_Tuileries_-_Google_Art_Project.jpg (accessed November 22, 2014).

Notice the names on the bottom of the painting (Bonaparte, Hannibal and *Karlus Magnus*, or Charlemagne) that signify Napoleon as either being their equal, or even greater than these political leaders from the past. In anticipation of his greatness, Napoleon was rapidly promoted to brigadier (brigade general) and eventually to supreme Command.[772] Due to the French military's consistent success in battle, it became an institution that many French people identified with stability and hope for a future less marked by frequent political change.

---

[771] Jacques-Louis David [Public domain], via Wikimedia Commons, http://commons.wikimedia.org/wiki/File%3ADavid_-_Napoleon_crossing_ the_Alps_-_Malmaison1.jpg (accessed November 22, 2014).

[772] Paul Johnson, *Napoleon* (New York: Penguin Books, 2002), 20, 27-28.

Seizing on the admiration that France, as a whole, had for its military Napoleon successfully staged a coup d'état on November 9, 1799.[773] The following month he was named First Consul of France[774] and then on December 2, 1804, Napoleon crowned himself Emperor of the French.[775] Below is a painting by Jacques-Louis David of Napoleon crowning himself and his wife Josephine as Emperor and Empress with the Pope and bishops observing. This self-coronation took place in Paris's Notre Dame Cathedral.

776

Napoleon's popularity remained high as long as he was successful in battle. However, when in 1812 he invaded Russia, as punishment for Russia's refusal to obey his Continental System,[777] his popularity quickly plummeted. Even though he technically defeated the Russians in battle, in a certain sense he lost since so many French soldiers whom he led into battle died during the

---

[773] Gregory Fremont-Barnes, *Napoleon Bonaparte* (Oxford: Osprey Publishing, 2010), 13.

[774] Fremont-Barnes, Ibid.

[775] David Nicholls, *Napoleon: A Biographical Companion* (Santa Barbara: ABC-CLIO, 1999), 67-68.

[776] Jacques-Louis David [Public domain], via Wikimedia Commons , "Coronation of Emperor Napoleon I and Coronation of the Empress Josephine in the Notre-Dame de Paris, December 2, 1804", http://commons.wikimedia.org/wiki/File%3AJacques-Louis_David%2C_The_Coronation_of_Napoleon_edit.jpg (accessed November 23, 2014).

[777] Nicholls, 66.

harsh Russian winter. Capitalizing on France's weakened state Russia, along with Prussia, Austria and England, in turn successfully invaded France and defeated France's military led by Napoleon.[778]

King Louis XVIII (1755-1824), the brother of King Louis XVI, who had been in exile for twenty three years after his brother was decapitated during the French Revolution, was then called from his hiding in England to France to serve as the French King.[779] From May of 1814 until his death he ruled as King.[780] There was, though, a brief period of time during this reign when King Louis XVIII lost his power to Napoleon who in 1814 escaped from the Mediterranean island of Elba, returned to France, raised an army, and ruled for about one hundred days until he was finally defeated by troops loyal to King Louis XVIII on June 18th, 1815, during the Battle of Waterloo.[781] After the battle, Napoleon was once again exiled but to a different island of Saint Helena,[782] where he died after receiving the Last Rites (Sacrament of Anointing of the Sick) from Father Ange Vignali.[783] We have some certainty, therefore, that he passed from this world into the next at peace with the Catholic Church and God.

During the time he was Emperor, though, his relationship with the Catholic Church was often not consistently a peaceful one. Even though in 1801, in a concordat with Pope Pius VII, he restored the Catholic Church to the "religion of the great majority of the French citizens", and allowed seminaries, monasteries and convents to be re-established and recognized the legitimacy of clerics who had not sworn allegiance to the French Constitution, he tried on numerous occasions to control the Church.[784] In

---

[778] Rory Muir, *Britain and the Defeat of Napoleon*, 1807-1815 (New Haven: Yale University Press, 1996), 220-231, 240, 247, 282-283, 299.

[779] George F. Nafziger, *Historical Dictionary of the Napoleonic Era* (Lanham: Scarecrow Press, 2002), 176.

[780] Nafziger, 176.

[781] Nafziger, 1, 55, 75, 249, 301.

[782] Nafziger, xxvii, 52, 56, 90.

[783] John Stevens Cabot Abbott, *The History of Napoleon Bonaparte*, Volume 2 (New York: Harper and Brothers Publishers, 1904), 647

[784] Owen Connelly, *The Wars of the French Revolution and Napoleon, 1792-1815* (New York: Routledge, 2006), 104-105, 233; "Napoleon's concordat (1801):

retaliation to Pope Pius VII's refusal to support the Continental System with its embargoes against British trade, Napoleon forcefully annexed the Papal States.[785] Pius VII responded by excommunicating Napoleon.[786] Napoleon, then, in turn imprisoned the pope.[787] Napoleon also exhibited his willful disobedience to Church authority by insisting on divorcing his validly married wife Josephine so as to marry Marie-Louise of Austria.[788]

Nationalism and Anti-Catholicism

As mentioned in a previous chapter, during the Hundred Years War (1337-1453) between England and France the feudal era, with its complex social space[789] and its many overlapping allegiances, was gradually replaced by a less complex, highly centralized nation state, given definition by common customs, language, borders etc. In the 1880s, centralization and the consequent nationalistic fervor increased. This was expressed by centralizing political power and, in some countries, the continued practice of economic mercantilism, where trade was centrally controlled for the benefit of the nation in competition with other nations.[790] Napoleon's Continental System with its embargo of British goods and his insistence that other European countries, including the Papal States, follow suit is a concrete example of mercantilism in practice. (Soon, though, this economic form would be replaced by economic liberalism where international trade is directed primarily by companies and not by competing nation states.) Napoleon, in accordance with mercantilism, wanted to eliminate England as a competitor to better establish France as the

---

text", Concordat Watch, http://www.concordatwatch.eu/kb-1496.834 (accessed November 23, 2014).

[785] Nicholls, 51; Robert Asprey, *The Reign of Napoleon Bonaparte* (New York: Basic Books, 2001), 98, 170.

[786] Asprey, 175.

[787] Nicholls, Ibid.

[788] Nicholls, 288.

[789] This terminology comes from John Milbank. Milbank, *Theology and Social Theory* (Oxford: Blackwell Publishing, 1990), 408.

[790] Allen C. Guelzo, *The History of the United States*, 2nd Edition (Chantilly: The Teaching Company, 2003), 112.

dominant nation state that oversaw a vast European empire. He failed to accomplish this dream. His failure was followed by even greater centralization of power and a rise of Nationalism across Europe. In their desire for ever greater control, nationalists at times wanted to control even the Catholic Church whom they perceived as a threat to national identity and security. We will focus our attention on three examples of such anti-Catholic nationalism: German, Italian and French.

German Nationalism

Otto von Bismarck (1815-1898) was a politician from Prussia who became Chancellor of the German Empire. He unified German states into a German Empire with a specific national identity. One way he attempted to bring about a greater sense of national identity was by repressing the Catholic Church during his *Kulturkampf*, begun in 1871.[791] The First Vatican Council I's (1869-1870) definition of papal infallibility had been one influential factor that increased his desire to clamp down on the supposed threat he thought Catholics posed to German national unity. During his struggle against Catholic culture discriminatory laws were enacted and enforced in the German state of Prussia. Religious orders were expelled,[792] Catholic clergy were prohibited to speak on political matters from the pulpit,[793] many Catholic bishops were imprisoned or expelled from Prussia, and many parish priests also were imprisoned or exiled. In June of 1875, the Frankfurter newspaper reported that 241 clergy had been either imprisoned or fined, 1,000 rectories were now empty.[794] Shortly

---

[791] John Vidmar, *The Catholic Church Through the Ages: A History* (Mahwah: Paulist Press, 2004), 316..

[792] "Anti-Jesuit Law (July 4, 1872)" http://germanhistorydocs.ghi-dc.org/sub_document.cfm?document_id=1837 (accessed November 24, 2014).

[793] "Imperial Law Concerning the Supplement to the Penal Code for the German Reich from December 10, 1871, § 130 of the Penal Code for the German Reich is supplemented by the following § 130 a." "Pulpit Law (December 10, 1871)," http://germanhistorydocs.ghi-dc.org/sub_document.cfm?document_id=669 (accessed November 24, 2014).

[794] Jonathan Steinberg, *Bismarck: A Life* (Oxford: Oxford University Press, 2011), 317.

afterward, in 1876, all the bishops of Prussia were either in prison or in exile.[795]

Other anti-Catholic measures included the ending of state subsidies to the Catholic Church,[796] the closure of some Catholic seminaries and the tight state regulations of others,[797] and the subjection of clergy appointments to state veto.[798] Bismarck's persecution of the Catholic Church wound down around the turn of the century for two primary reasons. First, Catholics banded together to form the Center Party to resist anti-Catholic measures in non-violent, parliamentary ways.[799] Second, Pope Leo XIII persuaded Bismarck to lessen his aggressive anti-Catholic stance.[800] See below for Bismarck's 1871 Pulpit Law directed against Catholic clergy.

> Any cleric or other minister of religion shall be punished with imprisonment or incarceration for up to two years if he, while exercising his occupation or having his occupation exercised, makes state affairs the subject of announcements or discussion in public before a crowd, or in a church, or before any number of people in some other place designated for religious gatherings in such a way that endangers the public peace.[801]

---

[795] Steinberg, Ibid.

[796] Bob Whitfield, *Germany, 1848-1914* (Oxford: Heinemann Educational Publishers, 2000), 53.

[797] "School Inspection Law of March 11, 1872," http://germanhistorydocs.ghi-dc.org/sub_document.cfm?document_id=670 (accessed November 24, 2014).

[798] Whitfield, Ibid.

[799] "Program of the Catholic Center Party's Reichstag Caucus (late March 1871)," http://germanhistorydocs.ghi-dc.org/sub_document.cfm?document_id=683 (accessed November 24, 2014); "Elections to the German Reichstag (1871-1890): A Statistical Overview," http://germanhistorydocs.ghi-dc.org/sub_document.cfm?document_id=1850, (accessed November 24, 2014); Bob Whitfield, *Germany, 1848-1914* (Oxford: Heinemann Educational Publishers, 2000), 54-55.

[800] "Bismarck's Conception of a modus vivendi with Rome (December 19, 1882)," http://germanhistorydocs.ghi-dc.org/sub_document.cfm?document_id=1839 (accessed November 24, 2014).

[801] "Imperial Law Concerning the Supplement to the Penal Code for the German Reich from December 10, 1871, § 130 of the Penal Code for the German

Italian Nationalism

In 1796, the lands we now know as Italy were divided into the following states: Papal States, Kingdom of Sardinia, Republic of Venice, Republic of Genoa, Grand Duchy of Tuscany, and the Kingdom of Sicily. See the map below.

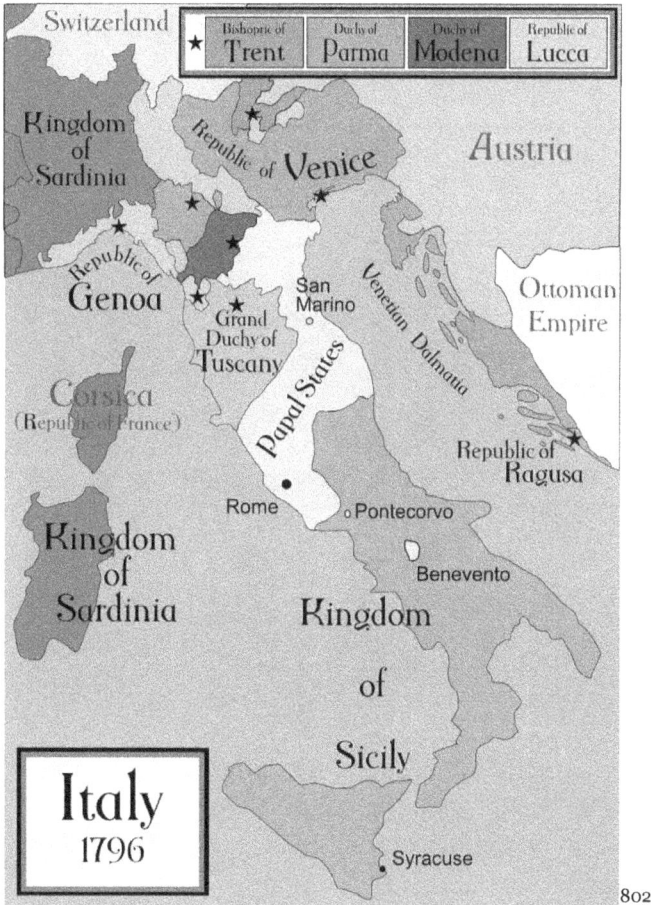

Reich is supplemented by the following § 130 a." "Pulpit Law (December 10, 1871)," http://germanhistorydocs.ghi-dc.org/sub_document.cfm?document_id=669 (accessed November 24, 2014).

802 Capmo (Own work) [GFDL (http://www.gnu.org/copyleft/fdl.html) or CC-BY-SA-3.0 (http://creativecommons.org/licenses/by-sa/3.0/)], via Wikimedia Commons, http://commons.wikimedia.org/wiki/File%3A Italy_1796.png (accessed November 25, 2014).

During the year of 1796, the above arrangement of states was changed when the French Revolutionary army under the command of Napoleon Bonaparte invaded their lands.[803] In 1805, Napoleon was crowned in Milan the King of Italy.[804] In 1809, Napoleon annexed to France the Papal States.[805] In 1814, Napoleon's land grabbing came to an end when he was defeated by a coalition of European powers and banished to the Island of Elba. In 1814, the Congress of Vienna re-established the states according to their 1796 status.[806] See below.

In the years following, a desire among many Italians for a unified Italy began steadily increasing. Key leaders of this nationalistic movement included, Giuseppe Mazzini (1805-1872),

---

[803] Christopher Duggan, *A Concise History of Italy* Second Edition (Cambridge: Cambridge University Press, 2014), xxi, 89.

[804] Duggan, xxi.

[805] "Documents upon the Annexations of 1809-1810," http://www.napoleon-series.org/research/government/diplomatic/c_annexations.html (accessed November 25, 2014).

[806] Duggan, xxi.

[807] The International Commission and Association on Nobility [Public domain], via Wikimedia Commons, http://commons.wikimedia.org/wiki/File%3AMap_congress_of_vienna.jpg (accessed November 25, 2014).

Count of Cavour (1810-1861), Giuseppe Garibaldi (1807-1882), and King Victor Emanuel II (1820 –1878). Giuseppe Mazzini put his literary skills and political activism at the service of promoting the union of Italian lands.[808] The Count of Cavour aided the Italian unification efforts with his political leadership skills as Prime Minister of the Kingdom of Piedmont-Sardinia.[809] King Victor Emanuel II also helped Italian lands unite by giving the unification movement royal support. He, consequently, became the first king of a united Italy. Finally, General Giuseppe Garibaldi backed the unifiers with military power, thus greatly enabling them to be successful.[810]

In 1861, after a number of battles, a unified Kingdom of Italy was announced and Rome was declared its capital.[811] There was one problem. The French Garrison, protecting the Pope, was preventing the Italians from taking Rome.[812] In 1870, however, this garrison was called backed when France went to war with Prussia.[813] After a brief, light skirmish, on September 20, 1870 Rome was captured and the Kingdom of Italy annexed what remained of the Papal States.[814] The popes from September 20th 1870 to February 11, 1929 then became self-imposed prisoners of the Vatican. This 59 year imprisoned state of the papacy ended when the Vatican City State was created upon the signing of the Lateran Treaty on February 11, 1929.[815] This treaty was signed in the Lateran Palace by Benito Mussolini, Prime Minister and Head of Government, for King Victor Emmanuel III and by Pietro

---

[808] George Holmes, *The Oxford Illustrated History of Italy* (Oxford: Oxford University Press, 1997), 188-190, 224

[809] Holmes, 199, 367

[810] Holmes, 189, 194, 196, 201-203.

[811] Derek Beales, and Eugenio F. Biagini, *The Risorgimento and the Unification of Italy*, Second Edition (New York: Routledge, 2002), 61-62, 63, 76, 113, 117.

[812] Beales and Biagini, 155.

[813] Beales and Biagini, Ibid.

[814] Beales and Biagini, 155-156.

[815] Beales and Biagini, 3, 118; "Inter Sanctam Sedem et Italiae Regnum Conventiones Initae Die 11 Februarii 1929," Vatican http://www.vatican.va/roman_curia/secretariat_state/archivio/ documents/rc_seg-st_19290211_patti-lateranensi_it.html (accessed November 26, 2014).

Cardinal Gasparri, the Vatican Cardinal Secretary of State, for Pope Pius XI.[816]

French Nationalism

Anti-Catholic nationalism returned to France with a vengeance right at the time Italy was unified. If you recall, a French garrison left Rome in 1870 to fight in France's war with Prussia (1870-1871). This war concluded with France and its leader Emperor Napoleon III, nephew of Napoleon I, being defeated by Prussia.[817] Emperor Napoleon III's Second French Empire 1852-1870[818] was replaced by France's Third Republic. This democratic form of government lasted up until 1940 when the Nazis, during World War II, defeated France.

During France's Third Republic several anti-Catholic measures were enacted. In 1879, priests were prohibited from being on administrative committees of hospitals, and lay women began replacing nuns in many hospitals. Also in 1879, under the French Minister of Education Jules Ferry, a bill on Freedom of Education was proposed. Article seven of this bill was directed against religious, especially the Jesuits. It stated, "No person belonging to an unauthorized religious community is allowed to govern a public or private educational establishment of whatsoever order or to give instruction therein."[819] Although the much-debated article seven was rejected, anti-Catholic sentiment did not end. More anti-Catholic legislation was proposed and passed including, a law permitting divorce, a law ending military chaplaincies, the gradual removal of the Sisters of Mercy from

---

[816] "Inter Sanctam Sedem et Italiae Regnum Conventiones Initae Die 11 Februarii 1929," Vatican http://www.vatican.va/roman_curia/secretariat_state/archivio/documents/rc_seg-st_19290211_patti-lateranensi_it.html (accessed November 26, 2014).

[817] David Baguley, *Napoleon III and his Regime: An Extravaganza* (Baton Rouge: Louisiana State University Press, 2000), xxi, 90.

[818] Baguley, xvi-xvii.

[819] Milorad N. Vuckovic, "The Suppression of Religious Houses in France 1880, and the Attitude of Representative British Press," Canadian Catholic Historical Association, Report, 28 (1961), 9-23, http://www.cchahistory.ca/journal/CCHA1961/Vuvkovic.htm (accessed November 26, 2014).

hospital work, prohibiting Catholic universities from granting degrees, and requiring clergy to serve in the military.[820]

French anti-Catholic fervor increased when the former Catholic seminarian and Mason Emile Combes was elected as Prime Minister in 1902.[821] His cabinet, not surprisingly, was almost entirely composed of Masons.[822] Under his political leadership, from 1902 to 1903, all parochial schools, around 12,000, were closed, fifty-four male religious congregations were dissolved, and eighty-one female congregations were prohibited. This was followed by a law that forbade the remaining congergations in France from teaching in any manner.[823] In 1905, the *Law on the Separation of the Church and the State*[824] was passed. This law mandated the confiscation of all Church property.[825] In 1906, St. Pope Pius X responded to the French law of 1905 with its strict separation of Church and state by asserting:

> 3. That the State must be separated from the Church is a thesis absolutely false, a most per-

---

[820] J.P.T. Bury, *France, 1814-1840* (London: Routledge, 2003), 367; Milorad N. Vuckovic, "The Suppression of Religious Houses in France 1880, and the Attitude of Representative British Press," Canadian Catholic Historical Association, Report, 28 (1961), 9-23, http://www.cchahistory.ca/journal/CCHA1961/Vuvkovic.htm (accessed November 26, 2014).

[821] Francis A. Cunningham, The War Upon Religion: Being an Account of the Rise and Progress of Anti-christianism in Europe (Boston: The Pilot Publishing Company, 1911), 327-330, 350, Project Gutenberg, http://www.gutenberg.org/files/38391/38391-h/38391-h.htm (accessed November 26, 2014).

[822] Maurice Larkin, *Religion, Politics and Preferment in France Since 1890: La Belle Epoque and its Legacy* (Cambridge: Cambridge University Press, 1995), 370.

[823] Bury, 158.

[824] "Loi du 9 décembre 1905 concernant la séparation des Eglises et de l'Etat." Legifrance, http://www.legifrance.gouv.fr/affichTexte.do?cidTexte=JORFTEXT000000508749&fastPos=1&fastReqId=1194187241&categorieLien=cid&oldAction=rechTexte (accessed November 26, 2014).

[825] Article 9, 1, 1 "Loi du 9 décembre 1905 concernant la séparation des Eglises et de l'Etat." Legifrance, http://www.legifrance.gouv.fr/affichTexte.do?cidTexte=JORFTEXT000000508749&fastPos=1&fastReqId=1194187241&categorieLien=cid&oldAction=rechTexte (accessed November 26, 2014).

1° Les édifices affectés au culte lors de la promulgation de la loi du 9 décembre 1905 et les meubles les garnissant deviendront la propriété des communes sur le territoire desquelles ils sont situés.. http://www.legifrance.gouv.fr/affichTexte.do?cidTexte=JORFTEXT000000508749&fastPos=1&fastReqId=1194187241&categorieLien=cid&oldAction=rechTexte

nicious error. Based, as it is, on the principle that the State must not recognize any religious cult, it is in the first place guilty of a great injustice to God; for the Creator of man is also the Founder of human societies, and preserves their existence as He preserves our own. We owe Him, therefore, not only a private cult, but a public and social worship to honor Him. Besides, this thesis is an obvious negation of the supernatural order. It limits the action of the State to the pursuit of public prosperity during this life only, which is but the proximate object of political societies; and it occupies itself in no fashion (on the plea that this is foreign to it) with their ultimate object which is man's eternal happiness after this short life shall have run its course. But as the present order of things is temporary and subordinated to the conquest of man's supreme and absolute welfare, it follows that the civil power must not only place no obstacle in the way of this conquest, but must aid us in effecting it. The same thesis also upsets the order providentially established by God in the world, which demands a harmonious agreement between the two societies. Both of them, the civil and the religious society, although each exercises in its own sphere its authority over them. It follows necessarily that there are many things belonging to them in common in which both societies must have relations with one another. Remove the agreement between Church and State, and the result will be that from these common matters will spring the seeds of disputes which will become acute on both sides; it will become more difficult to see where the truth lies, and great confusion is certain to arise. Finally, this thesis inflicts great injury on society itself, for it cannot either prosper or last long when due place is not left for religion, which is the supreme rule and the sovereign mistress in all questions touching the rights and the duties of men. Hence the Roman Pontiffs have never ceased, as circumstances required, to refute and condemn the doctrine of the separation of Church and State. ...

4. And if it is true that any Christian State does something eminently disastrous and reprehensible in separating itself from the Church, how much more deplorable is it that France, of all nations in the world, would have entered on this policy; France which has been during the course of centuries the object of such great and special predilection on the part of the Apostolic See whose fortunes and glories have ever been closely bound up with the practice of Christian virtue and respect for religion. Leo XIII had truly good reason to say: "France cannot forget that Providence has united its destiny with the Holy See by ties too strong and too old that she should ever wish to break them. And it is this union that has been the source of her real greatness and her purest glories.... To disturb this traditional union would be to deprive the nation of part of her moral force and great influence in the world."[826]

---

[826] http://www.vatican.va/holy_father/pius_x/encyclicals/documents/hf_p-x_enc_11021906_vehementer-nos_en.html accessed 01/03/2013.

Metternich and the Concert of Europe

The Catholic Austrian Empire's Prince Klemens Wenzel von Metternich (1773-1859) distrusted the various expressions of European nationalism. This is in part is explained by his former position as an ambassador[827] of the Holy Roman Empire that was dissolved after it was defeated by Napoleon in 1806.

As Foreign Minister of the Holy Roman Empire, Metternich had grown accustomed to the Holy Roman Empire's role of balancing competing power interests. As Chancellor of the Holy Roman Emperor's successor state,[828] the Austrian Empire, Metternich worked towards restoring the traditional balance of power by checking nationalistic ambitions. He believed that if nationalistic aspirations were not moderated then wars between competing nations were more likely to occur.

As chair of the Congress of Vienna (1814-1815) Metternich took practical pro-Monarchy steps restore a harmonious "Concert of Europe". To ensure peace, he established boundaries, opposed both German and Italian unification efforts,[829] and moderated Russian ambitions by including the Russian Empire in the Congress.[830] See next page for the national European boundaries established by the Congress of Vienna in 1815.

---

[827] Clemens Wenzel Lothar Metternich, *Memoirs of Prince Metternich 1773-1835*, Volume One (New York: Charles Scribner's Sons, 1881), 26.

[828] Metternich, 526.

[829] Bela Menczer, *Catholic Political Thought 1789-1848* (Notre Dame: University of Notre Dame Press, 1962), 139, https://archive.org/stream/catholicpolitica00menc#page/n11/mode/2up, The Internet Archive (accessed November 28, 2014).

[830] Menczer, Ibid.

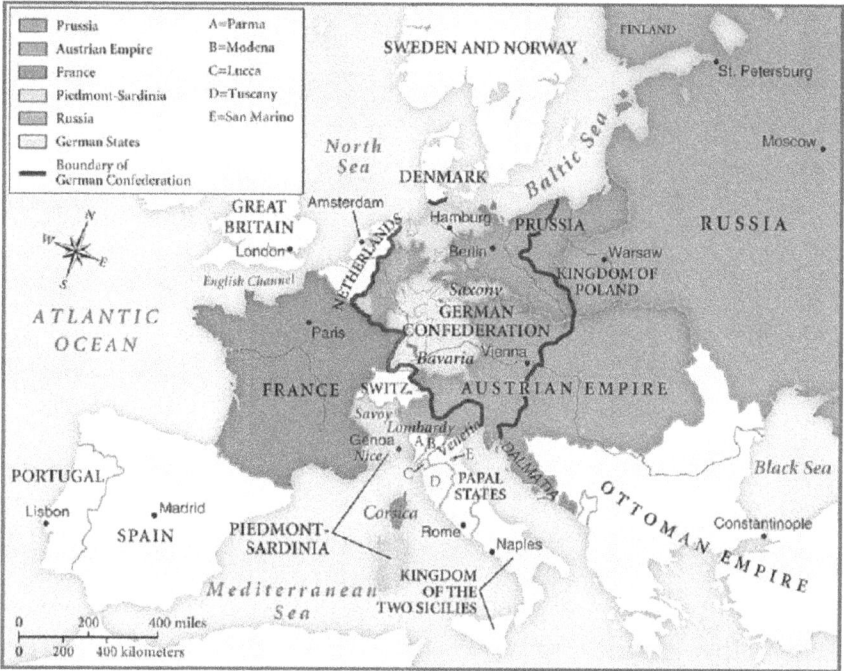

Prussia   A=Parma
Austrian Empire   B=Modena
France   C=Lucca
Piedmont-Sardinia   D=Tuscany
Russia   E=San Marino
German States
Boundary of German Confederation

831

The principle actors of the Congress of Vienna at first were the Austrian Empire, Prussia, Great Britain and the Russian Empire. By signing a treaty on November 20, 1815, they were formed into a Quadruple Alliance. Later, France was allowed into this alliance. Gradually, the common goal of peace that the Great Powers originally intended became overshadowed by the ever growing rivalries among themselves. This tension led to a rupture and two rival camps were formed: The Triple Alliance of the German Empire (under Prussian Leadership in 1871), the Austro-Hungarian Empire (formed in 1867), and Italy vs. the Entente Powers of Britain, France and the Russian Empire. See below.

---

831 The International Commission and Association on Nobility [Public domain], via Wikimedia Commons, http://commons.wikimedia.org/wiki/File%3AMap_congress_of_vienna.jpg (accessed November 28, 2014).

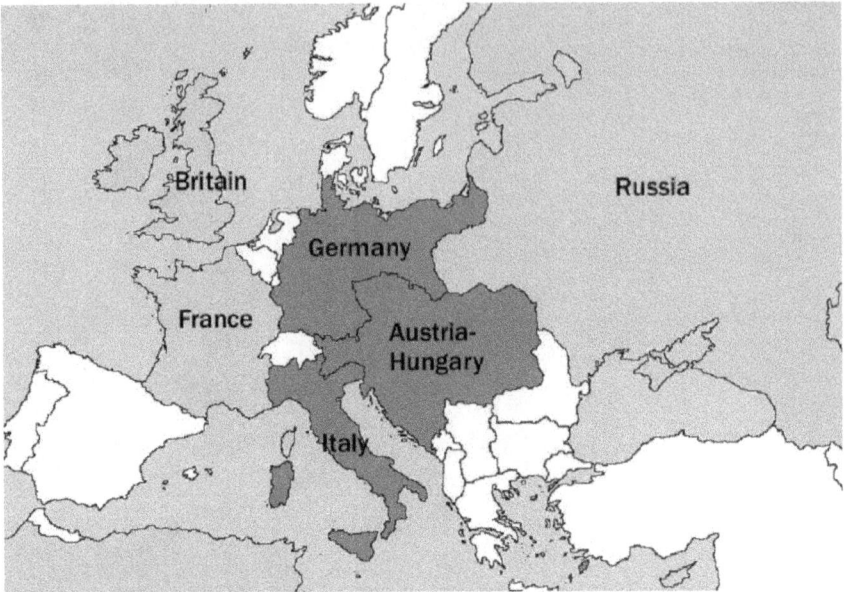

832

During this tension war broke out, World War I (1914-1918). This war brought a decisive end to four empires: Austro-Hungarian, German, Ottoman, and Russian.

Below is an excerpt from Metternich's *My Political Profession of Faith* that well demonstrates his belief that monarchies when united help to bring about political stability.

~ Metternich's *My Political Profession of Faith* ~

[L]et all the great Monarchs come closer together and prove to the world that if they are united, it can only be beneficial, for union between them will assure the political peace of Europe; that they are only firmly united in order to maintain public order at a time when it is menaced on all sides; that the principles they profess are as paternal and as much intended for the protection of good citizens, as they

---

832 Nydas at en.wikipedia (Transferred from en.wikipedia) [Public domain], via Wikimedia Commons, http://commons.wikimedia.org/wiki/File%3ATriple_ Alliance.png (accessed November 28, 2014).

are repressive for dissident factions. Governments of lesser Powers will see in such a projected union the anchor of their salvation and will hasten to associate themselves with it. Peoples will regain confidence and courage, and the deepest and most salutary pacification which the world has ever witnessed in all its long history could be established...[833]

Quiz 21

1. What is a possible explanation for the French people placing their hope for political stability in General Napoleon Bonaparte?

2. Why in 1812 did Napoleon lose much political support?

3. After Napoleon was defeated who became head of France? In answering this question name the new ruler's brother.

4. Name one specific way where Napoleon tried to control the Catholic Church.

5. Contrast nationalism with feudalism with respect to centralization.

6. List two specific ways by which Chancellor Otto von Bismarck repressed the Catholic Church during the *Kulturkampf*
7. State two reasons why Bismarck ended his repression of the Catholic Church.

---

[833] Menczer, 155.

8. Briefly describe how the Papal States were taken by the Kingdom of Italy.

9. What is the name of the 1929 treaty that created the Vatican City State?

10. List two specific ways by which the Catholic Church was repressed during France's Third Republic.

11. In 1906 how did St. Pope Pius X respond to the French law of 1905 with its strict separation of Church and state?

12. What was Metternich's view on monarchies?

Chapter 22

World Wars and the Church

Introduction

Metternich's plan for peace across Europe by maintaining a system of traditionally based checks and balances failed and the world was caught up by a succession of wars. A few of them, including of course the two World Wars, are as follows: World War I (1914-1918), during which the apparitions at Fatima occurred, the Mexican Cristero War (1926-1929), the Spanish Civil War (1936-1939) and World War II (1939-1945). World War I radically transformed political boundaries by ending four empires: Austro-Hungarian, German, Ottoman, and Russian. World War II also greatly altered the political world. During the Mexican and Spanish wars, as will be seen, Catholics were specifically targeted.

After World War II, the United States became established as one of the two dominant world superpowers, the other being the Soviet Union. These two superpowers subtly fought with each in what is known as the Cold War. Throughout these wars, including the Cold War, the Catholic Church fulfilled her mission as an agent of peace and reconciliation. During World War I, Pope Benedict XV (1914-1922) promoted peace, specifically in his 1914 encyclical *Ad Beatissimi Apostolorum*. Similarly, both Pius XI (1922-1939) and Venerable Pius XII (1939-1958) promoted peace before, and during World War II. Pope St. John XXIII (1958-1963) fulfilled the very meaning of the Latin based word pontiff (*pontifex*) by serving as a successful bridge builder during the Cold War. Pope

St. John Paul II (1978-2005) also greatly helped to bring an end to the Cold War and strongly spoke out against the atrocities of war.

World War I, Pope Benedict XV and the Message of Fatima

World War I Breaks Out

In 1908, the Austro-Hungarian Empire annexed the former Ottoman territory of Bosnia and Herzegovina.[834] The Russian Empire, and the Kingdom of Serbia became deeply resentful of this annexation.[835] Tension between the two military alliances of the Entente Powers (France, UK, and Russia) and the Triple Alliance (Germany, Austria-Hungary, Italy), later called the Central Powers when other countries joined, reached a peak on June 28th, 1914. On that day, the Austrian Archduke and heir to the throne of the Austro-Hungarian Empire, Franz Ferdinand was assassinated in Sarajevo by a Serbian nationalist.[836] The Austro-Hungarian Empire responded by issuing an ultimatum to the Kingdom of Serbia, with which the Kingdom of Serbia refused to comply.[837] To make matters worse, the German Emperor Wilhelm II, crowned in 1888, aggressively approached foreign policy in his "New Course."[838] According to Wilhelm, "For ever and ever there will be only one true Emperor in the world and that is the German Kaiser."[839] A month later on July 28th, 1914, the Austro-Hungarian Empire declared war against Serbia leading to a war involving the German Empire, and the Austro-Hungarian Empire, against Britain, France and the Empire of Russia.[840] Between 1914 and 1915, the German Empire and Austro-Hungarian Empire were joined first by the Ottoman Empire, followed by Bulgaria.[841]

---

[834] Margaret MacMillan, *The War that Ended Peace: The Road to 1914* (New York: Random House, 2013), xxviii.

[835] MacMillan, Ibid.

[836] MacMillan, xxvii, 30, 232, 257

[837] MacMillan, 570-571.

[838] MacMillan, 81.

[839] MacMillan, Ibid.

[840] MacMillan, 577-580.

[841] MacMillan, 637.

During this terrible world war, tens of millions of combatants and civilians were killed. It ended on November 11, 1918, Armistice Day.[842] After the war, the four imperial powers (the German Empire, the Russian Empire, the Austro-Hungarian Empire and the Ottoman Empire) were dismantled and replaced by nation states.

In the midst of World War I, the Ottoman Empire began actively persecuting Christians living in modern day Turkey. At first, under the 1915 Tehcir law, or Law of Deportation, thousands of Armenians and others considered as non-desirable who were living in modern day Turkey were deported. During this time, estimates the International Association of Genocide Scholars, one million Armenian Christians were murdered in modern day Turkey. This genocide had been prepared in advance by decades of contempt shown to the Armenian Christians living in the Ottoman Empire. William Ramsay's first hand description of the discrimination Armenian Christians experienced in the 1890s gives us insight into this pre-World War I time:

> Turkish rule...meant unutterable contempt...The Armenians (and Greeks) were dogs and pigs...to be spat upon, if their shadow darkened a Turk, to be outraged, to be the mats on which he wiped the mud from his feet. Conceive the inevitable result of centuries of slavery; of subjection to insult and scorn, centuries in which nothing belonged to the Armenian, neither his property, his house, his life, his person, nor his family, was sacred or safe from violence – capricious, unprovoked violence – to resist which by violence meant death.[843]

---

[842] MacMillan, 638.

[843] Peter Balakian, *The Burning Tigris: The Armenian Genocide and America's Response* (New York: HarperCollins, 2003), 43, 397, 404.

Pope Benedict XV: Faith and Peace

Throughout the war, and all its atrocities committed by both sides, Pope Benedict XV (1914-1922) promoted peace. In his 1914 encyclical *Ad Beatissimi Apostolorum*, issued on November 1st Feast of All Saints, he asserted that only when people remember, in faith, that the goods of this world are passing and only the goods of heaven can make us happy will nations be able to attain peace. See below for the context of his message of peace attained in faith:

> 17. Now, the whole secret of this divine philosophy is, that what are called the goods of this mortal life have indeed the appearance of good, but not the reality; and, therefore, that it is not in the enjoyment of them that man can be happy. In the divine plan, so far are riches and glory and pleasure from bringing happiness to man that if he really wishes to be happy, he must rather for God's sake renounce them all: "Blessed are ye poor . . . Blessed are ye that weep now; . . . Blessed shall you be when men shall hate you and when they shall separate you, and shall reproach you and cast out your name as evil" (Luke vi. 20-22). That is to say, that it is through the sorrows and sufferings and miseries of this life, patiently borne with, as it is right that they should be, that we shall enter into possession of those true and imperishable goods which "God hath prepared for them that love Him" (I. Cor. ii. 9). This most important teaching of our Faith is overlooked by many, and by not a few it has been completely forgotten.
>
> 18. Hence it is necessary, Venerable Brethren, to revive it once more in the minds of all, for in no other way can individuals and nations attain to peace. Let us, then, bid those who are undergoing

distress of whatever kind, not to cast their eyes down to the earth in which we are as pilgrims, but to raise them to Heaven to which we are going: "For we have not here a lasting city, but we seek one that is to come" (Heb. xiii. 14). In the midst of the adversities whereby God tests their perseverance in His service, let them often think of the reward that is prepared for them if victorious in the trial: "For that which is at present momentary and light of our tribulation worketh for us above measure exceedingly an eternal weight of glory" (II Cor. iv. 17). We must strive by every possible means to revive amongst men faith in the supernatural truths, and at the same time the esteem, the desire and the hope of eternal goods. Your chief endeavors, Venerable Brethren, that of the Clergy, and of all good Catholics, in their various societies, should be to promote God's glory and the true welfare of mankind. In proportion to the growth of this faith amongst men will be the decrease of that feverish striving after the empty goods of the world, and little by little, as brotherly love increases, social unrest and strife will cease.[844]

Our Lady of Fatima: Faith and Peace

The Blessed Mother, in her appearances at Fatima, Portugal, similarly affirmed that genuine peace will only be likely to occur when human beings remember that they were created not to be fulfilled by earthly goods and earthly pleasures but for heavenly goods that transcend this world. The details of the Fatima apparitions include the following. On the thirteenth day of six

---

[844] Benedict XV, "Ad Beatissimi Apostolorum Encyclical of Pope Benedict XV Appealing for Peace to our Venerable Brethren the Patriarchs, Primates, Archbishops, Bishops, and other Local Ordinaries in Peace and Communion with the Apostolic See," The Vatican, http://www.vatican.va/holy_father/ benedict_xv/encyclicals/documents/hf_ben-xv_enc_01111914_ad-beatissimi- apostolorum_en.html (accessed November 30, 2014).

consecutive months in 1917, beginning on May 13th, it is believed the Blessed Mother revealed herself to three children: Lúcia dos Santos and her cousins Jacinta and Francisco Marto. The picture below, printed on October 29th, 1917, in the Portuguese Newspaper *Ilustração Portuguesa*, captures tens of thousands of people looking in awe during the October 13th, 1917, miracle of the sun, when the sun appeared to descend.

[845]

In another Portuguese newspaper, *O Século* (dated October 17, 1917), Avelino de Almeida, in describing the miracle of the sun,

---

[845] Anonymous [Public domain or Public domain], via Wikimedia Commons, http://commons.wikimedia.org/wiki/File%3ANewspaper_fatima.jpg (accessed December 1, 2014).

reported, "Before the astonished eyes of the crowd, whose attitude carries us back to biblical times and who, full of terror, heads uncovered, gaze into the blue of the sky, the sun has trembled, and the sun has made some brusque movements, unprecedented and outside of all cosmic laws-the sun has 'danced,' according to the typical expression of the peasants..."[846]

In one vision, containing the "Second Secret," Mary warned Lúcia dos Santos of another World War with the words, "if people do not cease offending God, a worse one will break out during the Pontificate of Pius XI." See below.

~ Mary's Fatima Prophecy of World War II ~

You have seen hell where the souls of poor sinners go. [] To save them, God wishes to establish in the world devotion to my Immaculate Heart. If they do what I will tell you, many souls will be saved and there will be peace. The war is going to end. But if they do not stop offending God, another and worse one will begin in the reign of Pius XI. When you see a night illuminated by an unknown light, know that it is the great sign that God gives to you that he is going to punish the world for its crimes, by means of war, of hunger, and of persecution of the Church and of the Holy Father. To prevent this, I come to ask for the consecration of Russia to my Immaculate Heart, and the Communion of reparation on the first Saturdays. If they listen to my requests, Russia will be converted, and there will be peace. If not she will scatter her errors throughout the world, provoking wars and persecutions of the Church. The good will be martyrized; the Holy Father will have much to suffer; various nations will be annihilated. In the end, my Immaculate Heart will triumph. The Holy Father will consecrate

---

[846] William T. Walsh, *Our Lady of Fatima* (New York: Doubleday, 1954), 147.

Russia to me, and she shall be converted, and a certain period of peace will be granted to the world.[847]

On January 25th, 1938, shortly before the outbreak of World War II, the "great sign" promised to Lucia appeared in the form of an enormous Aurora Borealis across the sky of the northern hemisphere.[848]

Wars between the World Wars

Before we examine World War II, we will look at two wars that took place after World War I and before World War II, the Mexican Cristero War (1926-1929), and the Spanish Civil War (1936-1939). In both conflicts, Catholics were targeted by their governments.

The Mexican Cristero War (1926-1929)

The Mexican Revolution that began in 1910 is the context in which the Cristero War occurred. In 1910 Mexico was ruled by President Porfirio Diaz.[849] As a former military general, Diaz ruled in a highly centralized and autocratic manner that caused people to protest, especially the rural poor. Many of the poor, including the native Mexican Americans, living in rural areas became enraged when Diaz privatized indigenous lands, required landowners to possess formal legal titles, and invited in a French foreign mining company, all in order to rapidly industrialize and modernize Mexico.[850] In order to ensure that he would win in the Presidential elections of 1910 Diaz restricted free speech, was accused of rigging votes in his favor, and had his opponent Francisco I. Madero arrested and put in jail.[851]

---

[847] Walsh, 81-82.
[848] Walsh, 200-201, 209.
[849] Marshall C. Eakin, *The History of Latin America: Collision of Cultures* (New York: Palgrave Macmillan, 2007), 223.
[850] Eakin, 223, 224-26.
[851] Eakin, 289.

After escaping from jail, Madero, with the help of General Pancho Villa and other notable revolutionaries, led a revolt that overthrew Diaz. In 1911, new elections were held. During these elections, Madero won over the rural poor vote by promising agrarian reforms. Their votes enabled him to win the election and to become Mexico's president. A few years later, in 1913 General Victoriano Huerta, whom Madero had appointed commander of the army, led a revolt that overthrew Madero and, in the process, Madero was killed.[852]

Huerta's presidency only lasted about a year from 1913 to 1914. In 1914, leadership of the country again changed when Venustiano Carranza, who was a Madero supporter and a supporter of agrarian reforms, overthrew Huerta, and became Mexico's new president. At first the prominent leader of Mexico's rural poor revolution, Emiliano Zapata supported Carranza. Later, though, Zapata turned on Carranza, fought Carranza's forces and was killed in 1919. In turn, Carranza was assassinated in 1920.[853] During Carranza's presidency the 1917 anti-Catholic Mexican Constitution was signed into law.[854] According to article three, all Mexican education is to be secular and non-religious. This meant that Catholic schools were prohibited from functioning. In addition, monasteries were also prohibited.[855] These anti-religious

---

[852] Eakin, 289-290.

[853] Eakin, 290.

[854] Eakin, 287, 290-291,

[855] "1917 Constitution of Mexico," Latin American Studies, http://www.latinamericanstudies.org/mexico/1917-Constitution.htm (accessed December 3, 2014). Anti-clerical articles from the Mexican Constitution 1917 "Article 3.(1) The education imparted by the Federal State shall be designed to develop harmoniously all the faculties of the human being and shall foster in him at the same time a love of country and a consciousness of international solidarity, in independence and justice. I. Freedom of religious beliefs being guaranteed by Article 24, the standard which shall guide such education shall be maintained entirely apart from any religious doctrine and, based on the results of scientific progress, shall strive against ignorance and its effects, servitudes, fanaticism, and prejudices. Moreover: a. It shall be democratic, considering democracy not only as a legal structure and a political regimen, but as a system of life founded on a constant IV. Religious corporations, ministers of religion, stock companies which exclusively or predominantly engage in educational activities, and associations or companies devoted to propagation of any religious creed shall not in any way participate in institutions giving elementary, secondary and normal education and education for laborers or field workers.... Article 24.

aspects of the constitution enraged many, but other parts of the constitution won over significant support especially among the poor. For example, the constitution protected workers by insisting on an eight-hour work day, by forbidding child labor, by protecting female workers, by establishing a minimum wage, by mandating the institution of boards of arbitration, by mandating holidays, and by requiring termination compensation be given to workers.[856]

Everyone is free to embrace the religion of his choice and to practice all ceremonies, devotions, or observances of his respective faith, either in places of public worship or at home, provided they do not constitute an offense punishable by law. Every religious act of public worship must be performed strictly inside places of public worship, which shall at all times be under governmental supervision. ...Article 27. Ownership of the lands and waters within the boundaries of the national territory is vested originally in the Nation, which has had, and has, the right to transmit title thereof to private persons, thereby constituting private property. II. Religious institutions known as churches, regardless of creed, may in no case acquire, hold, or administer real property or hold mortgages thereon; such property held at present either directly or through an intermediary shall revert to the Nation, any person whosoever being authorized to denounce any property... Article 130. (58) The federal powers shall exercise the supervision required by law in matters relating to religious worship and outward ecclesiastical forms. To practice the ministry of any denomination in the United Mexican States it is necessary to be a Mexican by birth. Ministers of denominations may never, in a public or private meeting constituting an assembly, or in acts of worship or religious propaganda, criticize the fundamental laws of the country or the authorities of the Government, specifically or generally. They shall not have an active or passive vote nor the right to form associations for religious purposes. Permission to dedicate new places of worship open to the public must be obtained from the Secretariat of Government, with previous consent of the government of the State. There must be in every church building a representative who is responsible to the authorities for compliance with the laws on religious worship in such building, and for the objects pertaining to the worship. ...Trials for violation of the above provisions shall never be heard before a jury."

[856] "1917 Constitution of Mexico," Latin American Studies, http://www.latinamericanstudies.org/mexico/1917-Constitution.htm (accessed December 3, 2014). "Article 123.(50) A. Workers, day laborers, domestic servants, artisans (obreros, jornaleros, empleados domésticos, artesanos) and in a general way to all labor contracts: I. The maximum duration of work for one day shall be eight hours. II.(51) The maximum duration of night work shall be seven hours. The following are prohibited: unhealthful or dangerous work by women and by minors under sixteen years of age; industrial nightwork by either of these classes; work by women in commercial establishments after ten o'clock at night and work (of any kind) by persons under sixteen after ten o'clock at night. III. The use of labor of minors under fourteen years of age is prohibited. Persons above that age and less than sixteen shall have a maximum work day of six hours. IV.For every six days of work a worker must have at least one day of

President Carranza was succeeded briefly by the interim president Felipe Adolfo de la Huerta Marcor. After Huerta Marcor's brief six-month stint[857], President Álvaro Obregon Salido, a military commander who turned on Carranza, became president and ruled until 1924.[858] Obregon, who was assassinated during the Cristero war in 1928[859], was in turn succeeded by a staunchly anti-Catholic President Plutarco Calles (ruled from 1924 to 1928). As president, Calles strongly enforced the anti-Catholic articles of Mexico's constitution.[860] According to Calles, the Catholic Church was an oppressive institution that stood in the way of progress, redistribution of wealth, social justice, labor rights and democracy. Along with the 1917 constitution, Calles used this anti-Catholic rhetoric to justify his seizure of Church property, the expulsion of foreign priests, and the closing down of religious schools, convents and monasteries.

Not surprisingly, it was during Calles's presidency, in 1926, that the two-year Cristero War broke out.[861] During this war, when Catholics banded together to fight their government, tens of

---

rest. V. During the three months prior to childbirth, women shall not perform physical labor that requires excessive material effort. In the month following childbirth they shall necessarily enjoy the benefit of rest and shall receive their full wages and retain their employment and the rights acquired under their labor contract. During the nursing period they shall have two special rest periods each day, of a half hour each, for nursing their infants. VI. The minimum wage to be received by a worker shall be general or according to occupation. The former shall govern in one or more economic zones; the latter shall be applicable to specified branches of industry or commerce or to special occupations, trades, or labor. The general minimum wage must be sufficient to satisfy the normal material, social, and cultural needs of the head of a family and to provide for the compulsory education of his children. The occupational minimum wage shall be fixed by also taking into consideration the conditions of different industrial and commercial activities Farm workers shall be entitled to a minimum wage adequate to their needs. The minimum wage is to be fixed by regional committees, composed of representatives of the workers, employers, and the Government, and will be subject to approval by a national committee, organized in the same manner as the regional committees. VII. Equal wages shall be paid for equal work, regardless of sex or nationality. VIII. The minimum wage shall be exempt from attachment, compensation, or deduction."

[857] Michael S. Werner, *Concise Encyclopedia of Mexico* (Chicago: Fitzroy Dearborn Publishers, 2001), 164.

[858] Eakin, 287, 291.

[859] Eakin, 293.

[860] Eakin, 292.

[861] Eakin, 292-293.

thousands of people were killed, including the well-known Jesuit priest Blessed Miguel Pro. Blessed Miguel Pro was executed by the government on November 23rd, 1927 on false charges of having attempted to assassinate the former president Obregon. Below is a picture of him before a firing squad. Before being killed he cried out, "Long Live Christ the King" (*Viva Christo Rey!*):[862]

[863]

The end of the Cristero war in 1929 did not bring an end to Catholic persecution by the Mexican government. One notable example, was the horrific abuse that Catholics suffered under the governor of the state of Tabasco, Tomas Garrido Canabal who ruled from 1922-1926 and from 1931-1934. Canabal was a member of the Marxist oriented Radical Socialist Party of Tabasco (PRST). Under his leadership all Tabasco priests were required to marry,

---

[862] Sarah Fawcett Thomas, *Butler's Lives of the Saints*, New Full Edition, November (Collegeville: The Liturgical Press, 1997), 195.
[863] Grentidez (Scanning of an old photograph) [Public domain], via Wikimedia Commons, http://commons.wikimedia.org/wiki/File%3AMiguel_Pro's_execution_(1927).jpg (accessed December 3, 2014).

many priests and Catholic faithful were killed, and churches were destroyed. He is also known for naming his son Lenin, a bull God, a donkey Christ, a cow the Virgin of Guadalupe, an ox and a hog Pope, and a nephew Lucifer.[864] It was during Canabal's second term that Pope Pius XI, in his 1932 encyclical *Acerba Animi*, condemned Catholic persecution in Mexico. See below for an excerpt.

~ Pope Pius XI on Persecution of the Church in Mexico ~

10. An effort has been made to strike the Church in a still more vital spot; namely, in the existence of the clergy and the Catholic hierarchy, by trying to eliminate it gradually from the Republic. Thus the Mexican Constitution, as We have several times deplored, while proclaiming liberty of thought and conscience, prescribes with the most evident contradiction that each State of the Federal Republic must determine the number of priests to whom the exercise of the sacred ministry is allowed, not only in public churches, but even within private dwellings. This enormity is further aggravated by the way in which the law is applied. The Constitution lays down that the number of priests must be determined, but ordains that this determination must correspond to the religious needs of the faithful and of the locality. It does not prescribe that the Ecclesiastical Hierarchy is to be ignored in this matter, and this point was explicitly recognized in the declarations of the modus vivendi. Now in the State of Michoacan one priest was assigned for every 33,000 of the faithful, in the State of Chiapas one for every 60,000, while in the State of Vera Cruz only one priest was assigned to

---

[864] Donald J. Mabry, "Garrido Canabal, Tomás," Historical Text Archive, http://historicaltextarchive.com/sections.php?action=read&artid=339 (accessed December 3, 2014).

exercise the sacred ministry for every 100,000 of the inhabitants. Everyone can see whether it is possible with such restrictions to administer the Sacraments to so many people, scattered for the most part over a vast territory. Indeed, the persecutors, as though sorry for having been too liberal and indulgent, have imposed further limitations. Some Governors closed seminaries, confiscated canonries, and determined the sacred buildings and the territory to which the ministry of the approved priest would be restricted.[865]

Not until 1992, did the Mexican Government finally amend its constitution regarding religious freedom. According to the current amended constitution, Catholic clerics and religious have legal status, may vote, religious and clerics may also own property, and students may be instructed in religion in private schools.[866]

The Spanish Civil War (1936-1939)

The Spanish Civil War is best understood in its historical context. In 1923, General Miguel Primo de Rivera seized power, named himself head of the government while allowing King Alfonso III to remain as the relatively symbolic head of state.[867] There was hope that this reform minded General would end political corruption. However, after losing much public confidence, the support of the military, and the support of key industrialist leaders in 1930, Rivera resigned.[868] King Alfonso III then requested that another General, Damaso Berenguer lead the

---

[865] Pope Pius XI, "Acerba Animi Encyclical of Pope Pius XI on Persecution of the Church in Mexico to Our Venerable Brothers of Mexico, the Archbishops, Bishops, and Ordinaries in Peace and Communion with the Apostolic See.," The Vatican, http://www.vatican.va/holy_father/pius_xi/encyclicals/documents/hf_p-xi_enc_29091932_acerba-animi_en.html (accessed December 3, 2014).

[866] Werner, 94.

[867] Paul Preston, *The Spanish Civil War: Reaction, Revolution and Revenge*, Revised and Expanded (New York: Harper Collins Publishers, 2006), 34-37.

[868] Andrew Forrest, *The Spanish Civil War* (New York: Routledge, 2000), 6; Preston, 35-36.

country as head of government.[869] After Berengeur's government foundered, King Alphonso III left Spain in order to avoid being removed forcefully.[870] That same year, in April of 1931 after a new set of elections, a provisional anti-monarchical government was drawn up, headed by Alcala Zamora.[871] Near the end of 1931, the radical leftist and socialist friendly Manuel Azana Diaz[872] became the First Prime Minister of the Second Spanish Republic, and Alcala Zamora was elected President.[873] Azana's political views led him, and others, to falsely define the Catholic Church as an oppressive institution. For this reason, according to Spain's 1931 constitution, article 26, Spain's clerical budget was to end in two years' time, religious orders "whose activities constitute a danger to the security of the state"[874] were banned, and the property of Catholic religious orders were "subject to nationalization."[875]

The Second Republic's intent to radically restructure Spain, including its religious affiliation to Catholicism, caused an uprising led by General Francisco Franco. In 1936, General Franco led his rebel Nationalist forces in a war against Spain's Second Republic. The socialist Republicans were supported by the Soviet Union.[876] The Nationalists, on the other hand, received support from both Nazi Germany and from Fascist Italy.[877] On the first of April 1939, the Nationalists decisively defeated the Republicans.[878] Franco then ruled Spain for thirty-six years, from 1939 until 1975, the year of his death. During this horrific civil war, the Catholic

---

[869] Preston, 6.

[870] Preston, 36-37.

[871] Julian Casanova, *The Spanish Republic and Civil War* (Cambridge: Cambridge University Press, 2010), vii-viii.

[872] Francis Lannon, *The Spanish Civil War, 1936-1939* (Oxford: Osprey Publishing, 2002), 20.

[873] Casanova, viii, 34.

[874] Stanley G. Payne, *Spain's First Democracy: The Second Republic, 1931-1936* (Madison: The University of Wisconsin Press, 1993), 82; "Constitución de la República Española de 1931" Wikisource http://es.wikisource.org/wiki/Constituci%C3%B3n_de_la_Rep%C3%BAblica_Espa%C3%B1ola_de_1931:_04 (accessed December 4, 2014).

[875] Payne, 81-82.

[876] Casanova, x, 231, 251-252.

[877] Casanova, xi, 214, 315.

[878] Casanova, xii.

Church repeatedly faced the Republican's destructive rage.[879] Although the Nationalists were friendly towards the Catholic Church and protected the Church from the Republicans, they also were responsible for unjustifiable violent acts. In 2007, Pope Benedict XVI recognized 498 Spanish Catholic martyrs of this terrible civil war by beatifying them. These martyrs account only for a fraction of Catholics who were savagely killed by the Republicans.[880] According to careful research done by Antonio Montero, during Spain's "Red Terror" at least 6,832 clergy and religious were murdered by the Republican forces.[881] In the diocese of Barbastro, the Republican forces killed eighty eight percent of the diocesan clergy.[882]

~ Cardinal José Martins on the Catholic Martyrs of Spain ~

We cannot be content with only celebrating the memory of Martyrs, admiring their example as we trudge wearily on in our own lives. What message do the Martyrs offer to each one of us present here?[883]

World War II

During the same year that Spain's civil war ended the world became enmeshed in World War II (1939-1945). A cause, among others, of World War II was the 1919 Treaty of Versailles that Germany was required to sign at the end of World War I. It was

---

[879] Casanova, 3.

[880] "Mass For The Beatification of 498 Martyrs Who Died During the Religious Persecution of The Spanish Civil War," The Vatican, http://www.vatican.va/roman_curia/congregations/csaints/documents/rc_con_csaints_doc_20071028_martiri-spagnoli_en.html (accessed December 4, 2014).

[881] Julio de la Cueva, "Religious Persecution, Anticlerical Tradition and Revolution: On Atrocities against the Clergy during the Spanish Civil War," *Journal of Contemporary History* Vol. 33 (July 1998), 355; Julius Ruiz, *The 'Red Terror' and the Spanish Civil War* (Cambridge: Cambridge University Press, 2014), 1.

[882] Julio de la Cueva, 355; Ruiz, 1.

[883] "Mass For The Beatification of 498 Martyrs Who Died During the Religious Persecution of The Spanish Civil War," Ibid.

not, of course, the intention of those who had made the treaty to bring about another world war. On the contrary, a peace keeping league called the League of Nations, which the United Nations (founded in 1945 to prevent World War III) is a further development of, was written into the Treaty of Versailles. As demanded by the US President Woodrow Wilson and reflected in the treaty, "a general association of nations must be formed under specific covenants for the purpose of affording mutual guarantees of political independence and territorial integrity to great and small states alike."[884] The primary difficulty that the League of Nations faced was how to enforce peace even if member states submit their disputes to the League of Nations as the arbitrator. In addition, if the League of Nations did have the military power to enforce its decisions would such a concentration of power in a supra-national body be prudent? As Lord Acton warned, "Power tends to corrupt, and absolute power corrupts absolutely."[885]

War Guilt Clause

Despite President Wilson's good intentions, there was a section in the treaty that instead of increasing stability in Europe helped to further destabilize Europe, in particular Germany, due to its excessive demands. According to article 231 of the Versailles treaty, known as the War Guilt clause, "The Allied and Associated Governments affirm and Germany accepts the responsibility of Germany and her allies for causing all the loss and damage to which the Allied and Associated Governments and their nationals have been subjected as a consequence of the war imposed upon

---

[884] Woodrow Wilson, "President Woodrow Wilson's Fourteen Points 8 January, 1918," Yale Law School, Lilian Goldman Law Library, http://avalon.law.yale.edu/20th_century/wilson14.asp accessed 12/28/2013.

[885] John Dalberg-Acton, *Letter to Bishop Mandell Creighton, April 5, 1887*, Online Library of Liberty, "Lord Acton writes to Bishop Creighton that the same moral standards should be applied to all men, political and religious leaders included, especially since "Power tends to corrupt and absolute power corrupts absolutely" (1887)," Liberty Fund (accessed May 15, 2014).

them by the aggression of Germany and her allies."[886] By signing the treaty, Germany agreed to disarm, admitted it was responsible for causing World War I, promised to pay a significant amount of money in reparation for having caused the war, and gave over territory to the victors. To meet the required payments Germany began borrowing. This, in part, caused German inflation in the 1920s to rapidly spiral out of control.[887] As vividly described by Eric D. Weitz:

> By the end of November 1923, a single U.S. dollar bought 4.2 trillion marks...Germans carried suitcases and pushed wheelbarrows full of money-to buy a loaf of bread or a pair of shoes. They swarmed over the countryside and railroad yards like biblical gleaners or latter-day thieves, gathering potatoes that had been left behind in the field or coal that had fallen off train cars, or they dismantled fences and took the wood for heating.[888]

When the stock market crashed in 1929 Germany's reparation payments were finally suspended. They resumed in 1953. Not until October 3rd, 2010 did Germany finally pay back its reparation payments.[889] The rapid inflation that people in Germany had experienced caused many of them to want strong leaders who would bring an end to what they perceived as unjust demands imposed upon their country. The political group that more and more Germans began looking towards with hope was, unfortunately, the National Socialist Party, otherwise known as

---

[886] "The Versailles Treaty, article 231" A Multimedia History of World War One, http://www.firstworldwar.com/source/versailles231-247.htm (accessed December 6, 2014)..

[887] Eric D. Weitz, *Weimar Germany: Promise and Tragedy*, New and Expanded Edition (New Jersey: Princeton University Press, 2007), 38, 91, 1010, 102.

[888] Weitz, 102.

[889] David Crossland, "Legacy of Versailles: Germany Closes Book on World War I With Final Reparations Payment," Speigal Online International, September 28th, 2010, http://www.spiegel.de/international/germany/legacy-of-versailles-germany-closes-book-on-world-war-i-with-final-reparations-payment-a-720156.html (accessed December 6, 2014).

the Nazis.

Appeasement Policy

Another possible major factor for creating an environment conducive towards a world war was not another set of harsh measures but precisely the opposite, represented in a policy called appeasement. According to the policy of appeasement, which would supposedly avoid another world war, countries were willing to make concessions to a dictatorial power even if this meant recognizing the illegitimate taking of territory. The British Prime Minister Neville Chamberlain (1937-1940) was a principle proponent of this policy and acted according to this policy when dealing with Nazi Germany in the late 1930s. When in October of 1938 Adolf Hitler insisted that Germany take the Sudetenland (German name for areas in Czechoslovakia with a German majority) Chamberlain appeased Hitler by agreeing to his demands.[890] Supported by the French Government, Chamberlain told the Czech president to give into Hitler's demands for there to be peace. In promising peace, Chamberlain stated:

> The settlement of the Czechoslovakian problem, which has now been achieved is, in my view, only the prelude to a larger settlement in which all Europe may find peace. (The crowd cheers). This morning I had another talk with the German Chancellor, Herr Hitler, and here is the paper which bears his name upon it as well as mine. (Waves paper to the crowd which responds with loud cheers.) Some of you, perhaps, have already heard what it contains but I would just like to read it to you.[891]

---

[890] Antony Beevor, *The Second World War* (New York: Bay Back Books, 2012), 8-9.
[891] *Neville Chamberlain-Peace in Our Times*, https://www.youtube.com/watch?v=FO725Hbzfls (accessed December 6, 2014).

In hindsight, it does not appear that the policy of appeasement was an effective way of ensuring peace, but, rather, further embolden dictators, such as Hitler, to be even more insistent in their demands while building up their military to take what they want when it is not given to them. On May 10th, 1940, Neville Chamberlain resigned and was replaced by Winston Churchill who served as Britain's Prime Minister from 1940 to 1945 and from 1951 to 1955.[892] During Chamberlain's term as prime minister, Churchill had been very vocal in warning about the dangers associated with the policy of appeasement. He, instead, urged Britain to rearm and prepare for war, not for war's sake but for greater peace and justice in the future.

On September 1st, 1939, Germany invaded Poland and France declared war on Germany.[893] World War II had begun. The two opposing military alliances were the Allies and the Axis Powers (Germany, Japan and Italy). Not all the countries involved in World War II had aligned themselves when war officially broke out. For example, Italy did not join the Axis Powers until 1937, and the USA did not join the Allies until Hawaii's Pearl Harbor was bombed by the Japanese on December 7, 1941.[894]

Several months earlier in June of 1941, Germany, under Hitler's leadership, invaded the USSR.[895] This proved to be an error on the part of Germany since by invading the USSR it overstretched itself similarly as Napoleon had done when he invaded Russia in 1812. Around a year later, in 1942, the Axis Power's advance was halted by the Allies. The war, though, still dragged on even after D-Day of June 6th, 1944 when the Allies successfully landed on the beaches of Normandy France.[896] Finally, on May 8th, 1945, Germany unconditionally surrendered, and on August 15th, 1945, Japan surrender after being bombed with nuclear weapons by the USA.[897]

---

[892] Robert C. Self, *Neville Chamberlain: A Biography* (Burlington: Ashgate Publishing Company, 2006), 430.
[893] Beevor, 1, 22, 23.
[894] Beevor, 256.
[895] Beevor, 269.
[896] Beevor, 571-573.
[897] Beevor, 760, 775.

In 1985, Pope St. John Paul II strongly condemned the dropping of nuclear weapons on Hiroshima and Nagasaki.

~ Pope St. John Paul II to the People of Japan ~

To speak of Hiroshima and of Nagasaki is to become vividly aware of the immense pain and horror and death that human beings are capable of inflicting upon one another. But it is also to be conscious of the fact that such a tragic destiny is not inevitable. It can and must be avoided. Our world needs to regain confidence in its capacity to choose moral good over evil...The Catholic Church is irrevocably committed to the challenge of promoting genuine peace between peoples and nations, against war and death. The Church sees this challenge as a duty before God, the Lord of Life, and as inexorable service of love towards every man, woman and child on this earth...Hiroshima is a living witness to what can happen but need not and should never happen. When I visited Hiroshima in 1981 I wished to emphasize that "one must affirm and reaffirm, again and again, that the waging of war is not inevitable or unchangeable".[898]

Pius XI and Pius XII in Relationship to World War II

Now that we have covered the essential facts of World War II we will take a careful glance at how two popes approached World War II. Shortly before the Second World War, Pius XI (1922-1939) in his 1937 German written encyclical, *Mit Brenneder Sorge,* denounced Nazi anti-Semitism. This document was read from the pulpit in Germany's Catholic Churches. He followed this in 1938

---

[898] John Paul II, "Radio Message of Pope John Paul II to the People of Japan, Tuesday, August 6, 1985," The Vatican, http://www.vatican.va/holy_father/john_paul_ii/speeches/1985/august/documents/hf_jp-ii_spe_19850806_radiomessaggio-giappone_en.html (accessed December 6, 2014).

by arguing that anti-Semitism has no place in the Catholic Church since "Spiritually we are Semites."[899] Despite the popular perception that Pius XII (1939-1958) at worst was a virulent anti-Semite and at best ignored the plight of the Jewish people during World War II, the historical facts prove that these two ways of seeing Pius XII are inaccurate. Listed, below are but a few ways to dispel the myth that Pius XII was an anti-Semite.

A. Pius XII acted diplomatically in order to Save More Lives

On May 13th, 1940, Pius XI, in audience with Italy's Ambassador Dino Alfieri, asserted:

> The Italians are certainly well aware of the terrible things taking place in Poland. We might have an obligation to utter fiery words against such things; yet all that is holding us back from doing so is the knowledge that if we should speak, we would simply worsen the predicament of these unfortunate people.[900]

In the October 2014 international conference in Rome on Pope Pius XII, Dr. Limore Yagin of the University of Paris argued that Pius XII, as evident above, chose not to directly denounce Nazi action so that the pope could more effectively save lives behind the scenes.[901] According to the papers of a former CIA director, Allan Dulles, Pius XII was warned by the US not to outwardly condemn

---

[899] Benedict XVI, "Meeting with Representatives of the Jewish Community Address of his Holiness Benedict XVI, September 12, 2008" The Vatican, http://www.vatican.va/holy_father/benedict_xvi/speeches/2008/september/do cuments/hf_ben-xvi_spe_20080912_parigi-juive_en.html (accessed December 6, 2014)..

[900] Emilia Paola Pacelli, "Pius XII: The Martyrdom of Silence," EWTN Library, http://www.ewtn.com/library/ISSUES/PIUS12M.HTM (accessed December 6, 2014). Dr. Pacelli the following source. Audience with Italian Ambassador Dino Alfieri, 13 May 1940, in *Actes et Documents du Saint Siège relatifs à la Seconde Guerre mondiale*, Libreria Editrice Vaticana, Vatican City, vol. 1, 1970, pp. 454-455.

[901] Inside the Vatican Staff, "Pope Pius XII and the Vatican Archives," *Inside the Vatican* (November 2014), 44.

Hitler. The fear was that if Pius XII did so Hitler would retaliate in terrible ways.[902] Despite being cautioned and his own caution, in his 1942 Christmas message, Pius XII publicly denounced ethnic cleansing, which included the Nazi's systematic murder of the Jewish people:

> Should they ... rather... vow not to rest until in all peoples and all nations of the earth a vast legion shall be formed of those handfuls of men who, bent on bringing back society to its center of gravity, which is the law of God, aspire to the service of the human person and of his common life ennobled in God. ... Mankind owes that vow to the hundreds of thousands of persons who, without any fault on their part, sometimes only because of their nationality or race, have been consigned to death or to a slow decline.[903]

B. The New York Times Repeatedly Praises Pius XII

On Christmas Day, 1941, the New York Times, stated, "The voice of Pius XII is a lonely voice in the silence and darkness enveloping Europe this Christmas."[904]

C. The Conversion of the Chief Rabbi of Rome

From 1939 to 1945 Israel Zolli served as Rome's Chief Rabbi. After the war, he converted to Catholicism taking the name Eugenio out of gratitude to Pope Pius XII.[905]

---

[902] Inside the Vatican Staff, 45.

[903] Pius XII, "The Internal Order of States and People: Christmas Message of 1942," EWTN Library, http://www.ewtn.com/library/PAPALDOC/ P12CH42.HTM (accessed December 6, 2014).

[904] Philip Jenkins, *The New Anti-Catholicism: The Last Acceptable Prejudice* (Oxford: Oxford University Press, 2003), 193.

[905] Eugenio Zolli, *Before the Dawn: Autobiographical Reflections by Eugenio Zolli* (San Francisco: Ignatius Press, 2008), 11, 14, 18.

D. Israel's Foreign Minister Praises Pope Pius XII

In 1958, after the death of Pope Pius XII, Golda Meir, as Israel's Foreign Minister,[906] wrote:

> We share in the grief of humanity. When fearful martyrdom came to our people, the voice of the Pope was raised for its victims. The life of our times was enriched by a voice speaking out about great moral truths above the tumult of daily conflict. We mourn a great servant of peace.[907]

E. Nazi Newspaper Denounces Pius XII

The day after Cardinal Eugenio Pacelli was elected Pope and assumed the name Pope Pius XII, the Nazi Berlin newspaper, *Morganpost* stated:

> The election of Cardinal Pacelli is not accepted with favor in Germany because he was always opposed to Nazism and practically determined the policies of the Vatican under his predecessor.[908]

F. A Former Russian KGB Agent Admits to Character Assassination

According to the former KGB agent Ion Mihai Pacepa:

> In my other life, when I was at the center of Moscow's foreign-intelligence wars, I myself was caught up in a deliberate Kremlin effort to smear the Vatican, by portraying Pope Pius XII as a

---

[906] Golda Meir was Israel's 4th Prime Minister from 1969-1974.
[907] Margherita Marchione, "Pope Pius XII and the Jews," http://www.catholiceducation.org/en/culture/history/pope-pius-xii-and-the-jews.html (accessed December 5, 2014).
[908] David G. Dalin, *The Myth of Hitler's Pope: Pope Pius XII and his Secret War against Nazi Germany* (Washington: Regnery Publishing, 2005), 64.

coldhearted Nazi sympathizer...In February 1960, Nikita Khrushchev approved a super-secret plan for destroying the Vatican's moral authority in Western Europe... Pope Pius XII, was selected as the KGB's main target, its incarnation of evil, because he had departed this world in 1958. "Dead men cannot defend themselves" was the KGB's latest slogan. ...Because Pius XII had served as the papal nuncio in Munich and Berlin when the Nazis were beginning their bid for power, the KGB wanted to depict him as an anti-Semite who had encouraged Hitler's Holocaust. The hitch was that the operation was not to give the least hint of Soviet bloc involvement. The whole dirty job had to be carried out by Western hands....[909]

G. Pius XII is slandered in the play *The Deputy*.

As described by *Inside the Vatican*:

In order for the character assassination to be done by Western hands the Soviets promoted and funded a play written by the West German Rolf Hochhuth under the direction of a Communist producer Erwin Piscator. In the play, Pius XII is portrayed as supporting Hitler's goal to murder all the Jewish people. This play was first shown in 1963 and greatly helped in spreading a misconception of Pius XII in relationship to the Nazis.[910]

H. The 1989 book *Hitler's Pope* is published.

In this book, John Cornwell continued the character assassin-

---

[909] Ion Mihai Pacepa, "Moscow's Assault on the Vatican, January 25, 2007," The National Review, http://www.nationalreview.com/articles/219739/moscows-assault-vatican/ion-mihai-pacepa (accessed December 6, 2014).

[910] "Inside the Vatican Staff," 45; Pacepa, Ibid.

nation campaign by portraying Pius XII as an anti-Semite.

The Cold War

Shortly after World War II ended, there began another type of war called the Cold War that lasted to 1991 when Soviet Union collapsed. During the Cold War, the United States and its allies and the USSR and its allies were in a constant state of tension. The great friction between these two countries led to a fast-paced arms race between these two superpowers. The constant fear during the Cold War was that some event, or series of events, would trigger a nuclear world war that would practically end human civilization.

Pope St. John XXIII Prepares the Way for the End of the Cold War

John XXIII prepared the way for the end of the Cold War by reaching out to the Soviet Union's leader Nikita Khrushchev. As recounted by Archbishop Capovilla, personal secretary of John XXIII, the Pope's ongoing dialogue with Khrushchev began in 1961:

> It all began on 25 November 1961...Angelo Roncalli had been Pope for three years and was celebrating his 80th birthday. While the Holy Father was having lunch, he received a telephone call. It was Cardinal Amleto Giovanni Cicognani, Secretary of State, who asked if he could visit the Pope in his private apartment to deliver a very urgent message to him. I informed the Pope who told me to let him in. I met him and showed him to the dining room. The Secretary of State was carrying a message from the Soviet ambassador to Italy, Semen Kozyrev. The message said: "On behalf of Khrushchev, I have been entrusted with the task of communicating to His Holiness, Pope John XXIII, on the occasion of his 80th birthday, my congratulations and sincerest wishes for good health and success in the

continuation of the noble aspiration of contributing to the strengthening and consolidation of peace on earth and the solution of international problems through candid pronouncements. [911]

Those who doubted that dialogue with a committed Communist leader would bring about anything positive were proven wrong when in 1963 Khrushchev "of his own initiative, and out of his liking for John XXIII, freed Archbishop Slipyi."[912] Slipyi had been imprisoned in Siberia by the Soviets. John XXIII again proved the doubters wrong when he acted as the prime bridge builder between the US and the USSR during the Cuban Missile Crisis of 1962. President Kennedy capitalized on Khrushchev's appreciation of John XXIII by requesting that the Pope serve as an unofficial mediator between the two superpowers. John XXIII graciously agreed and wrote a message of peace that was delivered to the US and USSR embassies. Both Khrushchev and President Kennedy responded back to John XXIII's plea for peace by assuring him they also wanted peace and not war. Soon after, the Cuban Missile crisis was resolved.[913]

Pope St. John Paul II Helps to Conclusively End the Cold War

As well argued by the self-identified "agnostic liberal"[914] and British historian Timothy Garton Ash, without John Paul II's role in encouraging, as a Polish Pope, Poland's 1980s Solidarity movement, there would have not been a substantial reason for the Soviets to change their policy in Eastern Europe. Without this reason, the likelihood that the Soviet Union would relatively peacefully break up in 1991 would have been highly unlikely. It is

---

[911] Renzo Allegri, "An Unusual Alliance," Messenger of St. Anthony http://www.saintanthonyofpadua.net/messaggero/pagina_stampa.asp?R=&ID= 193 (accessed November 28, 2014).

[912] Allegri, Ibid.

[913] Allegri, Ibid.

[914] Timothy Garton Ash, "The First World Leader" The Guardian, http://www.theguardian.com/world/2005/apr/04/catholicism.religion13?INTC MP=SRCH (accessed December 5, 2014).

reasonable to conclude, therefore, that John Paul II was the key person in bringing about the dissolution of the Soviet Union through diplomatic, peaceful means.

~ The British Historian Timothy Garton Ash
on John Paul II's Decisive Role ~

No one can prove conclusively that he was a primary cause of the end of communism. However, the major figures on all sides - not just Lech Walesa, the Polish Solidarity leader, but also Solidarity's arch-opponent, General Wojciech Jaruzelski; not just the former American president George Bush Senior but also the former Soviet president Mikhail Gorbachev - now agree that he was. I would argue the historical case in three steps: without the Polish Pope, no Solidarity revolution in Poland in 1980; without Solidarity, no dramatic change in Soviet policy towards eastern Europe under Gorbachev; without that change, no velvet revolutions in 1989.[915]

Quiz 22

1. What was the 1915 Tehcir law and whom did it target?

2. According to Benedict XV in his 1914 encyclical *Ad Beatissimi Apostolorum,* what is the necessary pre-condition for there to be genuine peace on earth?

3. Is it reasonable to believe in the apparitions of Fatima? Give two documented reasons in your answer.

4. Choose one of the following people and write a paragraph on

---

[915] Ash, Ibid.

their lives in relationship to the Catholic Church: Tomas Garrido Canabal, and Blessed Miguel Pro.

5. Name or describe the two opposing sides during the Spanish Civil War (1936-1939). You may also choose to briefly state how, according to Cardinal José Martins, we are to learn from the Catholic Martyrs of Spain.

6. Name the two main reasons, according to the lecture, that set the stage for World War II.

7. True or False?

Pope St. John Paul II never condemned the dropping of nuclear weapons on Japan. He only cautioned that it need not have happened not that it should not have happened.

8. Defend Pius XII against his slanderers in three concrete ways. You may also choose to explain either how John XXIII helped to prepare the way for the dissolution of the Soviet Union or how John Paul II played a critical role in bringing the Soviet Union to an end.

Chapter 23

Vatican II and the Papacy

Introduction

[Image of John XXIII][916]

We will begin this chapter with Pope St. John XXIII who was elected in 1958 as a stop-gap pope who, some hoped, would basically keep the status quo until another pope was elected. He surprised many when in 1962 he called the Second Vatican Council. After examining Vatican Council II, we will then focus our attention on the most recent post-Vatican II popes: Blessed Pope Paul VI, Pope St. John Paul II, and Pope Benedict XVI.

The native Italian Angelo Giuseppe Roncalli (1881-1963) was

---

[916] Unknown author via Wikimedia Commons, http://commons.wikimedia. org/wiki/File%3APope_John_XXIII_-_1959.jpg (accessed December 12, 2014).

born into a relatively poor farming family in the Lombardy town of Sotto il Monte.[917] At age eleven, he entered Bergamo's minor seminary.[918] In 1904, he was ordained to the priesthood, after having a month earlier obtained a doctorate.[919] One of his earliest assignments was serving as the secretary to the bishops of Bergamo.[920] After being a priest for only a few years, he was then assigned as a seminary teacher of Church History and then later of Apologetics.[921] In 1925, he was asked to serve in the Vatican's diplomatic corps and was appointed as the Apostolic Visitor to Bulgaria, a predominantly Orthodox Christian country.[922] That same year he was consecrated a bishop. His assignment to Bulgaria ended in 1934 when he was given a new assignment as the Apostolic Delegate to the Islamic based country of Turkey and to the Orthodox Christian country of Greece.[923] Near the end of World War II, Roncalli received yet another diplomatic assignment as Papal Nuncio to France.[924] As France's nuncio he helped to secretly save thousands of Jewish lives, at risk of being sent to Nazi concentration camps.[925] His last assignment, before being elected to the papacy, was as the Patriarch of Venice, which entailed receiving the title of Cardinal in 1953.[926] In 1958, Roncalli was elected pope on November 4 and assumed the name John XXIII. As pope, he became well known as someone who cares for people in practical ways. He visited prisoners, the sick, invited people to eat with him etc.[927] On January 25th, 1959, only three months into his papacy, he announced an ecumenical council would be held, Vatican Council II.[928] Once necessary preparations

---

[917] Gerard Mannion, *Pope John XXIII, A Now You Know Media Study Guide* (Rockville: Now You Know Media, Inc., 2014), 4.

[918] Mannion, 6.

[919] Mannion, 15.

[920] Mannion, 16.

[921] Mannion, 18.

[922] Mannion, 34-35.

[923] Mannion, 37-38.

[924] Mannion, 46.

[925] Mannion, 44-45.

[926] Mannion, 55.

[927] Mannion, 68.

[928] Mannion, 70-71.

were made, the council finally opened on October 11, 1962.[929] His prior ministry of working in the non-Catholic lands of Bulgaria, Turkey and Greece helped him greatly in opening the Church to the world.[930]

Vatican Council II 1962-1965

931

According to the historian Fr. John O'Malley SJ, Vatican Council II was "quite possibly the biggest meeting in the history of the world."[932] A meeting in this context refers to an ordered event where issues are discussed. 2,200 bishops, 500 theologians, Protestant and Orthodox observers, and media representatives all attended this largest meeting in history.[933] When it comes to Church history, the size of Vatican II was not its primary distinctive quality. Vatican Council II distinguished itself in its style

---

[929] Mannion, 79.

[930] Mannion, Ibid.

[931] Manhal, "Vatican Letter," Flickr Creative Commons, https://flic.kr/ p/e7xgqE (accessed December 13, 2014)."In this panoramic view, bishops of the world line the nave of St. Peter's Basilica during the opening session of the Second Vatican Council Oct. 11, 1962. This year marks the 50th anniversary of the start of the council, one of the monumental events in modern religious history. (CNS photo) See VATICAN-LETTER Jan. 27, 2012."

[932] John W. O'Malley, *What Happened at Vatican II*, Kindle Edition (Cambridge: The Belknap Press of Harvard University Press, 2008), locations 379-392.

[933] John W. O'Malley, *Vatican II, A Now You Know Media Study Guide* (Rockville: Now You Know Media, Inc., 2010), 8; John W. O'Malley, *What Happened at Vatican II*, Kindle Edition (Cambridge: The Belknap Press of Harvard University Press, 2008), locations 102, 4075.

from all other Ecumenical Church Councils, beginning with the first Ecumenical Council of Nicaea (325). Unlike all the previous councils, Vatican Council II did not issue a single canon that condemned behavior.[934] See below for an example from the Council of Constance (1414-1418) and compare it with a passage from the Vatican II constitution *Decree on Ecumenism*.

~ The Council of Constance's Condemnation of John Hus ~

> It is very clearly established from the depositions of these witnesses that the said John has taught many evil, scandalous and seditious things, and dangerous heresies, and has publicly preached them during many years. This most holy synod of Constance, invoking Christ's name and having God alone before its eyes, therefore pronounces, decrees and defines by this definitive sentence, which is here written down, that the said John Hus was and is a true manifest heretic and has taught and publicly preached, to the great offence of the divine Majesty, to the scandal of the universal church and to the detriment of the catholic faith, errors and heresies that have long ago been condemned by God's church and many things that are scandalous, offensive to the ears of the devout, rash and seditious, and that he has even despised the keys of the church and ecclesiastical censures... [T]his holy synod of Constance therefore declares and decrees that the same John Hus is to be deposed and degraded from the order of the priesthood and from the other orders held by him...[935]

~ Vatican II's Reference to "Our Separated Brethren"

---

[934] John W. O'Malley, *Vatican II, A Now You Know Media Study Guide*, 8.
[935] Norman P. Tanner, *Decrees of the Ecumenical Councils*, Volume I Nicaea I to Lateran V (Washington: Georgetown University Press, 1990), 428-429.

[T]he separated Churches and communities as such, though we believe they suffer from the defects already mentioned, have been by no means deprived of significance and importance in the mystery of salvation. For the Spirit of Christ has not refrained from using them as means of salvation which derive their efficacy from the very fullness of grace and truth entrusted to the Catholic Church.

Nevertheless, our separated brethren, whether considered as individuals or as communities and Churches, are not blessed with that unity which Jesus Christ wished to bestow on all those to whom he has given new birth into one body, and whom he has quickened to newness of life-that unity which the Holy Scriptures and the ancient Tradition of the Church proclaim.[936]

Despite it conciliatory style, there were hotly debated issues at the council. The five most debated issues, as identified by O'Malley, were the following: the liturgy, Scripture in relationship to Tradition, the Catholic Church in relationship to non-Christian religions, religious liberty, and collegiality.[937] A number of sub-themes were also interwoven throughout these debates. These included, the relationship of the center to the periphery, change in relationship to stability, Western culture in relationship to non-Western cultures, and styles of leadership.[938] When these documents are read these debated issues and the sub-themes become concretely evident.

Vatican Council II issued 16 documents that are arranged in

---

[936] Second Vatican Council, Decree on Ecumenism *Unitatis Redintegratio*,no. 3 (21 November 1964), in Vatican Council II: The Conciliar and Post Conciliar Documents, ed. Austin Flannery (Boston: Daughters of St. Paul, 1980), 456.
[937] O'Malley, *Vatican II, A Now You Know Media Study Guide*, 12-13; O'Malley, *What Happened at Vatican II*, locations 168-220.
[938] O'Malley, *Vatican II, A Now You Know Media Study Guide*, 8; O'Malley, *What Happened at Vatican II*, locations 216-225.

the following hierarchical order with the first having the most weight: four constitutions, nine decrees, and three declarations.

The four constitutions are *Dei Verbum* (Dogmatic Constitution on Divine Revelation), *Lumen Gentium* (Dogmatic Constitution on the Church), *Gaudium et Spes* (Pastoral Constitution on the Church in the Modern World), and *Sacrosanctum Concilium* (Constitution on the Sacred Liturgy).

The nine decrees are *Christus Dominus* (On the Pastoral Office of Bishops), *Apostolicam Actuositatem* (On the Apostolate of the Laity), *Ad Gentes* (Decree on the Church's Missionary Activity), *Optatam Totius* (Decree on the Training of Priests), *Orientalium Ecclesiarum* (Decree on the Catholic Oriental Churches), *Perfectae Caritatis* (Decree on the Renewal of Religious Life), *Presbyterorum Ordinis* (Decree on the Life and Ministry of Priests), *Unitatis Redintegratio* (Decree on Ecumenism), and *Inter Mirifica* (On the Mass Media).

The three declarations are *Dignitatis Humanae* (Declaration on Religious Liberty), *Gravissimum Educationis* (Declaration on Christian Education), and *Nostra Aetate* (Declaration on the Church's Relations with Non-Christian Religions).

Debated Issue One: The Liturgy

The Constitution on the Sacred Liturgy is the fruit of much debate. One common misconception that people have about this

---

939 Manhal, "Vatican II Opening Session," Flickr Creative Commons, https://flic.kr/p/e7rDDF (accessed December 13, 2014).

constitution concerns the use of Latin. According to a popular account, after heated debate most of the Council Fathers eliminated Latin from the liturgy. Actually, the Council Fathers voted to retain Latin as the official language of the Western Roman Rite while permitting some vernacular to be used. See below for a key excerpt. An influential council father during this debate was the Melkite Patriarch, Maximos IV Saigh. Saigh argued that Latin is not the universal language of the Church, especially of Eastern Churches. Furthermore, he boldly stated in French and not in Latin as the other bishops were doing, "Christ after all spoke the language of his contemporaries."[940] In tension with Saigh's argument some held that Latin well serves as the symbol of the Catholic Church's universality. Others, though, disagreed with the contention that many at the time perceived the Church's use of Latin in non-Western cultures as a remaining sign of past Western Imperialism. Obviously, there were other debates besides the use of Latin such as the role of the laity in the liturgy, active vs. passive participation, etc. Since we do not have space to go into the council documents in depth, if you wish to do so, please see the resources on Vatican Council II given in the cited sources.

> 36. (1) The use of the Latin language, with due respect to particular law, is to be preserved in the Latin rites (2) But since the use of the vernacular, whether in the Mass, the administration of the sacraments, or in the other parts of the liturgy, may frequently be of great advantage to the people, a wider use may be made of it, especially in readings, directives and in some prayers and chants...[941]

> 54. A suitable place may be allotted to the vernacular in Masses which are celebrated with the

---

[940] O'Malley, *What Happened at Vatican II*, Kindle Edition, locations 2674-2686.

[941] Second Vatican Council, The Constitution on the Sacred Liturgy, *Sacrosanctum Concilium* no. 36 (4 December 1963), in Vatican Council II: The Conciliar and Post Conciliar Documents, ed. Austin Flannery (Boston: Daughters of St. Paul, 1980), 13.

people, especially in the readings and "the common prayer," and also, as local conditions may warrant, in those parts which pertain to the people, according to the rules laid down in Article 36 of this Constitution.[942]

Debated Issue Two: Scripture in Relationship to Tradition

The Constitution on Divine Revelation represents the culmination of the discussions the Council Fathers had on Scripture, and, in part, Scripture's relationship to Tradition. The meaning of the two-source teaching, of Scripture and Tradition stemming from the Council of Trent, was debated. To what extent, they argued, does Tradition contain truths not found in Sacred Scripture?[943] They finally settled on stating in *Dei Verbum* (Dogmatic Constitution on Divine Revelation):

> 9. Sacred Tradition and sacred Scripture, then, are bound closely together, and communicate one with the other. For both of them, flowing out from the same divine well-spring, come together in some fashion to form one thing, and move towards the same goal...Hence, both Sacred Scripture and Tradition must be accepted and honored with equal feelings of devotion and reverence.

> 10. Sacred Tradition and sacred Scripture make up a single deposit of the word of God, which is entrusted to the Church. ... [T]he task of giving an authentic interpretation of the word of God, whether in its written form or in the form of Tradition, has been entrusted to the living teaching

---

942 Second Vatican Council, The Constitution on the Sacred Liturgy, *Sacrosanctum Concilium* no. 54 (4 December 1963), in Vatican Council II: The Conciliar and Post Conciliar Documents, ed. Austin Flannery (Boston: Daughters of St. Paul, 1980), 18.

943 O'Malley, 12.

office of the Church alone. ... [S]acred Tradition and sacred Scripture and the Magisterium of the Church are so connected and associated that one of them cannot stand without the others. Working together, each in its own way under the action of the one Holy Spirit, all contribute effectively to the salvation of souls.[944]

Debated Issue Three: The Catholic Church and non-Christian Religions

In accordance with Vatican Council II's overall conciliatory style, the Declaration on the Church's Relations with non-Christian religions (*Nostra Aetate*), does not condemn errors within non-Christian religions, in particular, Hinduism, Buddhism, Judaism and Islam. *Nostra Aetate* carefully states:

The Catholic Church rejects nothing of what is true and holy in these religions. She has a high regard for the manner of life and conduct, the precepts and doctrines which, although differing in many ways from her own teaching, nevertheless often reflect a ray of that truth which enlightens all men. Yet she proclaims and is in duty bound to proclaim without fail, Christ is the way, the truth and the life (Jn. 1:6).[945]

[944] Second Vatican Council, Dogmatic Constitution on Divine Revelation, *Dei Verbum* no. 10 (18 November 1965), in Vatican Council II: The Conciliar and Post Conciliar Documents, ed. Austin Flannery (Boston: Daughters of St. Paul, 1980), 755-756.
[945] Second Vatican Council, Declaration on the Relation of the Church to Non-Christian Religions, *Nostra Aetate,* no. 2 (28 October 1965), in Vatican Council II: The Conciliar and Post Conciliar Documents, ed. Austin Flannery (Boston: Daughters of St. Paul, 1980), 739.

Debated Issue Four: Religious Liberty and the Separation of Church and State

Up until Vatican Council II, Catholics commonly held that the Church ought to be supported by the state and be the official religion of the state. After the French Revolution at the end of the eighteenth century, Catholics associated democracy and freedom with violent persecution of the Catholic Church.[946] In many people's minds the political system that was most fitting for the Catholic Church was the pre-French Revolution, markedly hierarchical political order of a monarch supported by nobility. Full political rights, it was held, was not to be granted to non-Catholic religions in countries that are predominantly Catholic, since "error has no rights" and the Church and State ought to be mutually intertwined.[947] However, during Vatican Council II the Council Fathers in the *Declaration on Religious Liberty* acknowledged that non-Catholic religions do have rights and that the Catholic Church and the state may be legitimately separated in a moderate manner. The declaration states, "The Vatican Council declares that the human person has a right to religious freedom. ... This right of the human person to religious freedom must be given such recognition in the constitutional order of society as will make it a civil right."[948] Earlier, in 1963, Pope St. John XXIII in his encyclical *Pacem in Terris* affirmed the legitimate freedom to choose one's religion by declaring,

> Also among man's rights is that of being able to worship God in accordance with the right dictates of his own conscience, and to profess his religion both in private and in public. According to the clear

---

[946] O'Malley, *What Happened at Vatican II*, Kindle Edition, locations 137, 201, 236, 239, 241, 242, 252, 776, 815, 4200; O'Malley, *Vatican II, A Now You Know Media Study Guide*, 15, 48.

[947] O'Malley, *What Happened at Vatican II*, location 4200.

[948] Second Vatican Council, Declaration on Religious Liberty, *Dignitatis Humanae*, no. 2 (7 December 1965), in Vatican Council II: The Conciliar and Post Conciliar Documents, ed. Austin Flannery (Boston: Daughters of St. Paul, 1980), 800.

teaching of Lactantius, "this is the very condition of our birth, that we render to the God who made us that just homage which is His due; that we acknowledge Him alone as God, and follow Him. It is from this ligature of piety, which binds us and joins us to God, that religion derives its name".'"[949]

Debated Issue Five: Collegiality

The *Decree on the Pastoral Office of Bishops* recognized that bishops have authority by virtue of their office. This means that their authority as bishops is not simply delegated to them by the pope. In the words of the Council, "The bishops, by virtue of their sacramental consecration and their hierarchical communion with the head of the college and its other members, are constituted members of the episcopal body."[950] *Lumen Gentium* even more pointedly asserts that bishops are not "to be regarded as vicars of the Roman Pontiff; for they exercise the power which they possess in their own right and are called in the truest sense of the term prelates of the people whom they govern."[951] As well described by O'Malley, it is incorrect to perceive the bishops' relationship to the pope as equivalent to a regional managers' relationship to their Corporate Executive Officers.[952] Instead, bishops as shepherds "together with their head, the Supreme Pontiff, and never apart from him"[953] participate individually and corporately in apostolic

---

[949] John XXIII, "Pacem in Terris," April 11, 1963 The Vatican, http://www.vatican.va/holy_father/john_xxiii/encyclicals/documents/hf_j-xxiii_enc_11041963_pacem_en.html (accessed December 11, 2014).

[950] Second Vatican Council, Decree on the Pastoral Office of Bishops in the Church, *Christus Dominus,* no. 4 (28 October 1965), in Vatican Council II: The Conciliar and Post Conciliar Documents, ed. Austin Flannery (Boston: Daughters of St. Paul, 1980), 565-566.

[951] Second Vatican Council, Dogmatic Constitution on the Church, *Lumen Gentium,* no. 27 (21 November 1964), in Vatican Council II: The Conciliar and Post Conciliar Documents, ed. Austin Flannery (Boston: Daughters of St. Paul, 1980), 283.

[952] O'Malley, *What Happened at Vatican II*, Kindle Edition, locations 6059-6069.

[953] Second Vatican Council, Decree on the Pastoral Office of Bishops in the Church, *Christus Dominus* (28 October 1965), in Vatican Council II: The

succession and in the one priesthood of Jesus Christ.

Sub-Themes

As explained by O'Malley, Vatican Council II's debates and discussion were interwoven with several sub-themes. One subtheme concerned the relationship between the center (the Pope as assisted by the curia) and everyone else (bishops, priests, deacons, sisters, laity, all people etc.).[954] Another subtheme that was discussed throughout the council was Western culture in relationship to non-Western cultures.[955] Two questions that the Council Fathers faced were as follows. May Catholic worship, the training of seminarians, and the expression of theology be legitimately influenced by a non-Western context and if so to what extent? In addition, what aspects in doctrine must remain stable and what aspects may be legitimately changed? Blessed Pope Paul VI, the Pope who succeeded Pope St. John XXIII, clamped down on excessively innovative expressions of Eucharistic doctrine by asserting in his 1965 encyclical *Mysterium Fidei*:

~ Paul VI on Eucharistic Doctrine ~

10. For We can see that some of those who are dealing with this Most Holy Mystery in speech and writing are disseminating opinions on Masses celebrated in private or on the dogma of transubstantiation that are disturbing the minds of the faithful and causing them no small measure of confusion about matters of faith, just as if it were all right for someone to take doctrine that has already been defined by the Church and consign it to oblivion or else interpret it in such a way as to weaken the genuine meaning of the words or the

---

Conciliar and Post Conciliar Documents, ed. Austin Flannery (Boston: Daughters of St. Paul, 1980), 566.

[954] O'Malley, *What Happened at Vatican II*, Kindle Edition, location 216-225.

[955] O'Malley, *Vatican II, A Now You Know Media Study Guide*, 9.

recognized force of the concepts involved.

11. To give an example of what We are talking about, it is not permissible to extol the so-called "community" Mass in such a way as to detract from Masses that are celebrated privately; or to concentrate on the notion of sacramental sign as if the symbolism—which no one will deny is certainly present in the Most Blessed Eucharist—fully expressed and exhausted the manner of Christ's presence in this Sacrament; or to discuss the mystery of transubstantiation without mentioning what the Council of Trent had to say about the marvelous conversion of the whole substance of the bread into the Body and the whole substance of the wine into the Blood of Christ, as if they involve nothing more than "transignification," or "transfinalization" as they call it; or, finally, to propose and act upon the opinion that Christ Our Lord is no longer present in the consecrated Hosts that remain after the celebration of the sacrifice of the Mass has been completed.[956]

The Post-Vatican II Papacy

Blessed Pope Paul VI (1963-1978)

After John XXIII died, Pope Paul VI took over leading the Council and the Church universal. By selling the Papal tiara, the crown worn by popes, and giving the money to the poor,[957] Paul VI confirmed a servant style of leadership in accordance with the ancient papal title, "A servant of the servants of God" used by Pope St. Gregory the Great (590-604). One way he served the people of God was by overseeing the revision of the liturgy. This culminated

[956] http://www.vatican.va/holy_father/paul_vi/encyclicals/documents/hf_p-vi_enc_06081964_ecclesiam_en.html accessed 01/04/2014.

[957] Eamon Duffy, *Saints and Sinners: A History of the Pope* (Yale: Yale University Press, 1997), 275.

in 1969 when he approved a new "ordinary" of the Roman Rite Mass.[958]

He was also at the service of unity with non-Catholics. His deep concern for unity led him to meet the Ecumenical Orthodox Patriarch Athenagoras in Jerusalem in 1964. In 1965, these leaders signed a Catholic-Orthodox Joint declaration that lifted the excommunications of 1054.[959] This gesture, though, did not end the schism between the Catholic Church and the Orthodox churches. Another example of his service of unity with non-Catholics was his outreach, in continuation with the John XXIII's spirit, to the leaders of the Soviet Union. In 1966, he graciously received at the Vatican the Soviet Foreign Minister Andrei Gromyko and then in 1967 the Soviet President Nikolai Podgorny.[960] The following year in 1968 Paul VI issued the encyclical *Humanae Vitae* that many interpreted at the time and even now as having caused a deep division in the Catholic Church. Paul VI, though, issued this encyclical not for the goal of short-term unity but for deep, lasting unity founded on truth. As is well known, the truth he defended in this encyclical was that of babies and bonding,[961] or the unitive and procreative dimensions of marriage, are never to be deliberately separated. As Pope Paul VI states:

> Though it is true that sometimes it is lawful to tolerate a lesser moral evil in order to avoid a greater evil or in order to promote a greater good," it is never lawful, even for the gravest reasons, to do evil that good may come of it —in other words, to intend directly something which of its very nature

[958] Paul VI, "Apostolic Constitution Issued by his Holiness Pope Paul VI Missale Romanum on New Roman Missal" April 3, 1969, The Vatican, http://www.vatican.va/holy_father/paul_vi/apost_constitutions/documents/hf_p-vi_apc_19690403_missale-romanum_en.html. (accessed December 12, 2014).

[959] Duffy, 278.

[960] Frank J. Coppa, *Politics and the Papacy in the Modern World* (Westport: Greenwood Publishing Group, 2008), 159.

[961] Janet E. Smith, "The Moral Use of NFP," October 27, 2014, Janet E. Smith's Sexual Common Sense, http://janetesmith.org/ (accessed December 12, 2014).

contradicts the moral order, and which must therefore be judged unworthy of man, even though the intention is to protect or promote the welfare of an individual, of a family or of society in general. Consequently, it is a serious error to think that a whole married life of otherwise normal relations can justify sexual intercourse which is deliberately contraceptive and so intrinsically wrong.[962]

Servant of God John Paul I (August 26 1978 - September 28 1978)

John Paul I succeeded Pope Paul VI but only was pope for thirty-three days after his papal inauguration until he died on September 28th, 1978. In his first radio message of October 17, 1978, John Paul II gave homage to John Paul I by saying:

> But what can we say of John Paul I? It seems to us that only yesterday he emerged from this assembly of ours to put on the papal robes—not a light weight. But what warmth of charity, nay, what "an abundant outpouring of love"— which came forth from him in the few days of his ministry and which in his last Sunday address before the Angelus he desired should come upon the world. This is also confirmed by his wise instructions to the faithful who were present at his public audiences on faith, hope and love.[963]

Pope St. John Paul II (1978-2005)

At only 58 years old Karol Wojtyla became the first non-

[962] Paul VI, *Humanae Vitae* July 25, The Vatican, 1968 http://www.vatican.va/holy_father/paul_vi/encyclicals/documents/hf_p-vi_enc_25071968_humanae-vitae_en.html (accessed December 12, 2014).

[963] John Paul II, "First Radio Message "Urbi Et Orbi" Address of his Holiness John Paul II," Tuesday, 17 October 1978, The Vatican, http://www.vatican.va/holy_father/john_paul_ii/speeches/1978/documents/hf_jp-ii_spe_19781017_primo-radiomessaggio_en.html (accessed December 12, 2014).

Italian pope for over 455 years since 1522.[964] A sampling of events from his fascinating life as Pope include the following. After traveling to the Soviet ruled Poland in 1979 he helped to bring about the Polish Solidarity movement which led to the breakup of the Soviet Union in 1991.[965] In 1980, he approved a pastoral provision that permitted former Anglican priests to become Catholic priests.[966] The following year on the feast day of Our Lady of Fatima, May 13th, the Turk Mehmet Ali Agca attempted to assassinate John Paul II. John Paul II credited the Blessed Mother for saving his life on her feast day.[967] Out of other worldly compassion for the man who tried to kill him, John Paul II visited Mehmet Ali Agca in prison and the two talked privately.[968] In 1995, another attempt on John Paul II's life was made, this time by the radical Islamic terrorist organization, Al-Qaeda. Al-Qaeda had planned to kill John Paul II by situating a suicide bomber, dressed as a priest, close to the Holy Father when he was celebrating World Youth Day in the Philippines on January 15th, 1995.[969] Despite the numerous assassination attempts on his life, John Paul II continued to be an agent of mercy and reconciliation as is evident in his support of Vatican and Lutheran representatives signing a Joint Declaration on the Doctrine of Justification on October 31st, 1999,[970] in his 2000 visit to Israel, where he prayed at the Western Wall and visited the Yad Vashem Holocaust memorial museum,[971] and in 2001 when he prayed at the Umayyad Mosque

---

[964] Duffy, 282.

[965] George Weigel, *Witness to Hope: The Biography of Pope John Paul II* (New York: Cliff Street Books, 1999), 399-411.

[966] Sacred Congregation for the Doctrine of the Faith, "Declaration," March 31, 1981, The Vatican, http://www.vatican.va/roman_curia/congregations/ cfaith/documents/rc_con_cfaith_doc_19810401_chiesa-episcopaliana_en.html (accessed December 12, 2014).

[967] George Weigel, *Witness to Hope: The Biography of Pope John Paul II* (New York: Cliff Street Books, 1999), 411-413, 440.

[968] Weigel, *Witness to Hope*, 474.

[969] Weigel, *Witness to Hope*, 750-751.

[970] John Paul II, "Angelus," October 31, 1999, The Vatican, http://www.vatican.va/holy_father/john_paul_ii/angelus/1999/documents/hf_ jp-ii_ang_31101999_en.html (accessed December 12, 2014).

[971] John Paul II, "Jubilee Pilgrimage of his Holiness John Paul II to the Holy Land (March 20-26, 2000) Speech of John Paul II Visit to the Yad Vashem Museum," The Vatican, http://www.vatican.va/holy_father/john_paul_ii/

in Damascus, Syria.[972]

Benedict XVI (2005-2013)

John Paul II's successor, Benedict XVI, continued the path of reconciliation and communion but was often misunderstood. His concern for communion was made explicitly evident as far back in 1972 when he founded the theological journal *Communio* along with Hans Urs von Balthasar.[973] Aware of the then Cardinal Ratzinger's ability to unite people in truth, John Paul II appointed him prefect of the Congregation of the Doctrine of the Faith, a position he held until 2005. In 2005, he was elected Pope and assumed the name Benedict XVI. In 2006, during a September 12 lecture at Germany's University of Regensburg, Benedict XVI caused some Muslims to become exceedingly angry when he referred to a 1391 conversation that the Byzantine Emperor Manuel II Paleologus had with a Persian. In their dialogue, the Emperor commented, "Show me just what Mohammed brought that was new, and there you will find things only evil and inhuman, such as his command to spread by the sword the faith he preached."[974] A few years later, in 2007, during a visit in Brazil, Benedict XVI once again was the subject of controversy when he described the native population at the time of the Spanish Conquest of the Americas as silently longing for the Christian faith.[975]

---

travels/documents/hf_jp-ii_spe_20000323_yad-vashem-mausoleum_en.html (accessed December 12, 2014).

[972] John Paul II, "Meeting with the Muslim Leaders Omayyad Great Mosque, Damascus Address of the Holy Father," Sunday, 6 May 2001, The Vatican, http://www.vatican.va/holy_father/john_paul_ii/speeches/2001/documents/hf_jp-ii_spe_20010506_omayyadi_en.html (accessed December 12, 2014).

[973] Gianni Valente, "It Seemed the End of the Line. And Instead...," *30 Days* no. 8 (2006), 30Days, http://www.30giorni.it/articoli_id_11124_l3.htm?id= 11124 (accessed December 12, 2014).

[974] Benedict XVI, "Papal Address at University of Regensburg," Zenit, http://www.zenit.org/en/articles/papal-address-at-university-of-regensburg (accessed December 12, 2014).

[975] Benedict XVI, Aparecida: 13 May, Fifth General Conference of the Episcopate of Latin America and the Caribbean," May 13, 2007, EWTN, https://www.ewtn.com/library/PAPALDOC/b16brazil11.htm (accessed December 12, 2014).

~ Benedict XVI and Silently Longing for Christ ~

Yet what did the acceptance of the Christian faith mean for the nations of Latin America and the Caribbean? For them, it meant knowing and welcoming Christ, the unknown God whom their ancestors were seeking, without realizing it, in their rich religious traditions. Christ is the Savior for whom they were silently longing. It also meant that they received, in the waters of Baptism, the divine life that made them children of God by adoption; moreover, they received the Holy Spirit who came to make their cultures fruitful, purifying them and developing the numerous seeds that the incarnate Word had planted in them, thereby guiding them along the paths of the Gospel. In effect, the proclamation of Jesus and of his Gospel did not at any point involve an alienation of the pre-Columbus cultures, nor was it the imposition of a foreign culture. Authentic cultures are not closed in upon themselves, nor are they set in stone at a particular point in history, but they are open, or better still, they are seeking an encounter with other cultures, hoping to reach universality through encounter and dialogue with other ways of life and with elements that can lead to a new synthesis, in which the diversity of expressions is always respected as well as the diversity of their particular cultural embodiment.[976]

Benedict XVI's ability to go to the core of issues received great appreciation when he publicly corrected the founder of the Legionaries of Christ, Father Marcial Maciel Degollado. Under Benedict XVI's leadership in 2006, the Vatican stated, "since 1998,

---

[976] Benedict XVI, Aparecida, Ibid.

the Congregation for the Doctrine of the Faith has received accusations, which were already made public in part, against Father Marcial Maciel Degollado, founder of the Congregation of the Legionaries of Christ, for offenses reserved to the exclusive competency of the dicastery."[977] This was followed by the Vatican issuing another statement which ordered Fr. Maciel to live "a reserved life of prayer and penance, renouncing all public ministry."[978] Finally, in 2010, after "more than 1,000 Legionaries were interviewed, and hundreds of written testimonies were sifted through"[979], the Holy See stated that, "The very serious and objectively immoral behavior of Father Maciel, as incontrovertible evidence has confirmed, sometimes resulted in actual crimes, and manifests a life devoid of scruples and of genuine religious sentiment."[980] In this statement, Pope Benedict XVI assured Fr. Maciel's victims, "...they will not be left on their own: The Church is firmly resolved to accompany them and help them on the path of purification that awaits them. It will also mean dealing sincerely with all of those who, within and outside the Legion, were victims of sexual abuse and of the power system devised by the foun-der."[981] Possibly due to a combination of factors including the stress of the office, and the repeated misinterpretations of his actions and words, Benedict XVI resigned the papacy in 2013. Cardinal Jorge Mario Bergoglio of Argentina succeeded him as Pope Francis and took to heart the ancient concept of the Pope as a servant leader.

[977] "Vatican Communiqué on Legionary Founder, Zenit, http://www.zenit.org/en/articles/vatican-communique-on-legionary-founder (accessed December 12, 2014).

[978] "Vatican Communiqué on Legionary Founder, Zenit, http://www.zenit.org/article-16067?l=english (accessed October 12, 2012).

[979] "Vatican Statement at Conclusion of Visit to Legionaries of Christ," Zenit, http://www.zenit.org/article-29109?l=english (accessed October 29, 2012).

[980] "Vatican Statement at Conclusion of Visit to Legionaries of Christ," Ibid.

[981] "Vatican Statement at Conclusion of Visit to Legionaries of Christ," Ibid.

Pope Francis (2013-)

~ Pope Francis on the Pope as a Servant Leader ~

[T]he Church is Christ's – she is His bride- and all bishops in communion with the Successor of Peter, have the task and the duty of guarding her and serving her, not as masters but as servants. The Pope, in this context, is not the supreme lord but rather the supreme servant – the "servant of the servants of God"; the guarantor of the obedience and the conformity of the Church to the will of God, to the Gospel of Christ, and to the Tradition of the Church, putting aside every personal whim, despite being – by the will of Christ himself – the "supreme Pastor and Teacher of all the faithful" (Can. 749) and despite enjoying "supreme, full, immediate, and universal ordinary power in the Church" (cf. Cann. 331-334).[982]

Reflecting on our most recent popes, in light of God's providence, it has been remarked that John Paul II clearly taught the Church what to believe; Benedict XVI complemented this papal style by explaining why we believe what the Church teaches; Pope Francis, in continuity with his predecessors, then mandated that the Church practice what she believes.[983]

Quiz 23

1. How did Vatican Council II's style differ, with respect to condemning canons, from all other Ecumenical Councils?

---

[982] Pope Francis, "Pope Francis Speech at the Conclusion of the Synod," News VA, Official Vatican Network, http://www.news.va/en/news/pope-francis-speech-at-the-conclusion-of-the-synod (accessed December 14, 2014).

[983] James Mallon, *Divine Renovation* (Toronto: Novalis Publishing, 2014), locations 553-555.

2. Listed below are the four constitutions of Vatican II. First (2), do these four documents have the most amount of authority among the sixteen documents issued by Vatican II? Second (3-6), briefly state what these constitutions focused on.

Dei Verbum

Lumen Gentium

Gaudium et Spes

Sacrosanctum Concilium

3. Listed are five key issues that were debated at the Council: The Liturgy, Scripture in Relationship to Tradition, The Catholic Church and non-Christian Religions, Religious Liberty and the Separation of Church and State, and Collegiality. Chose two of these debated issues and then provide specific elements for each issue chosen.

4. Blessed Pope Paul VI in his encyclical letter *Humanae Vitae* names two dimensions of the marital act that may not be separated. Names these two dimensions either in the words of the encyclical or in the similar terms that Janet Smith uses.

5. Name one specific act of reconciliation that St. John Paul II did.

6. Name one specific act of Benedict XVI that was misinterpreted, misconstrued, and vigorously rejected.

Chapter 24

The Catholic Church in the USA

Introduction

In this concluding chapter, you will be introduced to the history of the Catholic Church in the United States of America. We will begin with the Spanish and French who were first responsible for bringing Catholicism to the New World. This will be followed by a section on Catholicism during the American British Colonial and the post-Revolutionary eras, with a focus on Maryland. Finally, the development of Catholicism during and after the birth of the US will be presented.

Spanish and French Colonies

On April 2, 1513, the Spanish became the first Europeans to set foot on what is today Florida.[984] The head of the expedition was the Catholic Juan Ponce de Leon. He was responsible for giving the name Florida to this land. He did so because when he landed in Florida,

---

[984] Loker, Aleck. *La Florida: Spanish Exploration & Settlement of North America, 1500 to 1600* (Williamsburg: Solitude Press, 2010), 23.

Catholics were celebrating Easter, which, among other titles, the Spanish call *Pascua Florida* (Festival of Flowers) since the opening of flowers well represents the rising of Christ.[985]

Shortly afterwards, another Spanish expedition arrived in 1559. Under the command of Don Tristan de Luna y Arellano,[986] the first Catholic Mass was celebrated on August 15th, the Assumption of the Blessed Virgin Mary, in Pensacola, Florida by Dominican Friars at St. Michael the Archangel's Church, now the Basilica of St. Michael the Archangel.[987]

In 1565, the Spanish founded the first permanent European and Catholic settlement of the New World. The Spanish later also established settlements in the Western side of the New World in lands now known as Texas, New Mexico, and California.[988] The Spanish Franciscan, Saint Junipero Serra O.F.M. was responsible for founding twenty-one Californian missions including at the following sites, now modern cities: Los Angeles, San Francisco, San Diego, and Santa Clara.

The map below shows the extent of New Spain in 1795.

---

[985] Loker, 23.

[986] Loker, 172, 174.

[987] "History of St. Michael," Basilica of St. Michael the Archangel, http://www.stmichael.ptdiocese.org/our_history.php (December 16, 2014).

[988] 61, 167, 238, 269.

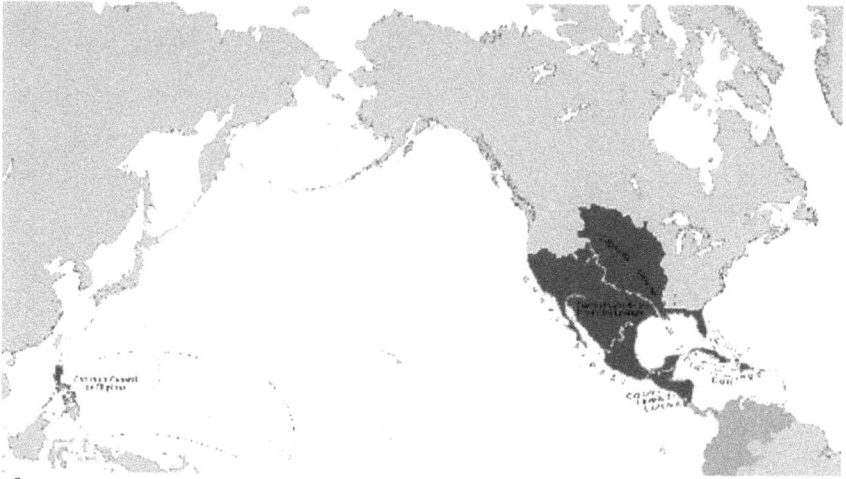

989

The following century, in 1699, the French Catholics established the colony of Louisiana (*La Louisiane Française*) which is not to be confused with US state called Louisiana.[990] This French territory was named after the reigning French King Louis XIV.[991]

At one point French Louisiana extended roughly from the Great Lakes to the Gulf of Mexico and from the Rocky Mountains to the Appalachian Mountains. In 1803, Emperor Napoleon Bonaparte sold French Louisiana to the United States.[992] Below in blue is the extent of French Louisiana circa 1750.

---

[989] Trasamundo, "File:Nueva España 1795.png," Creative Commons Attribution-Share Alike, http://commons.wikimedia.org/wiki/File:Nueva_ Espa%C3%B1a_1795.png#file (accessed December 14, 2014).

[990] Bradley G. Bond, *The French Colonial Louisiana and the Atlantic World* (Louisiana: Louisiana State University Press, 2005), 111.

[991] Bond, 245.

[992] Bond, 11, 145, 246.

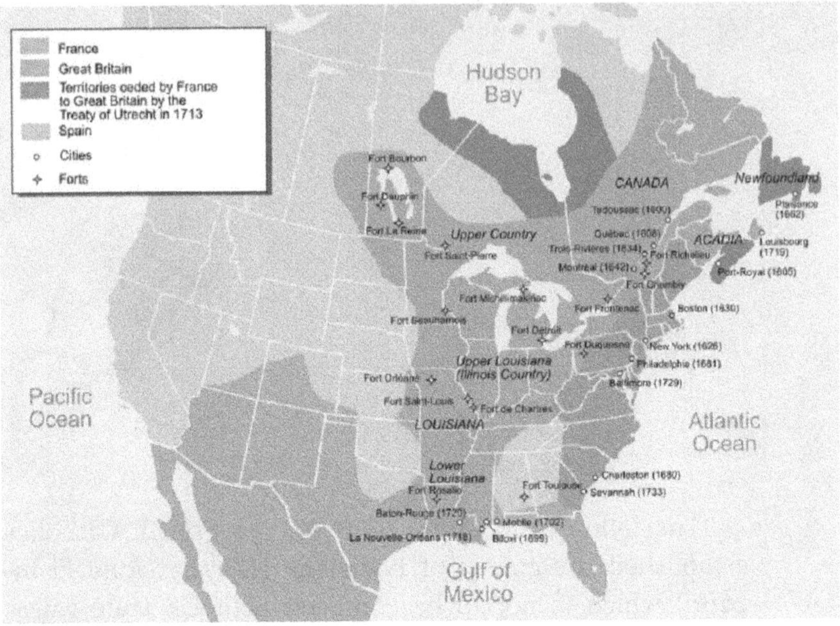

993

American British Colonialism and the Post-Revolutionary Era

Profit Based Protestant Colonies

We now turn our attention to the British and mainly Protestant regions of the New World that are depicted above spanning the east coast from Acadia, French Louisiana, or New France, to the Spanish controlled Florida. After the failed attempt, under Queen Elizabeth, to establish in the late 1500s a colony off the coast of the modern state of Carolina, on an island formerly dubbed the Roanoke Island, the British finally established a colony in

---

993 Pinpin, "File:Nouvelle-France map-en.svg," Creative Commons Attribution-Share   Alike,
http://commons.wikimedia.org/wiki/File:Nouvelle-France_map-en.svg
(accessed December 14, 2014).

early 1600s named Jamestown in modern day Virginia. The purpose of this settlement was not religiously oriented, as would later settlements be north in modern day New England. Instead, Jamestown was founded for imperial and financial reasons by a corporation that had obtained a charter from the English King James I, hence the name Jamestown. One seldom referred to purpose of this settlement was for it to serve as a base from which the Protestant British Empire could raid ships of Catholic Spain known for carrying gold. Under the previous Protestant monarch, Queen Elizabeth I, piracy against Catholic Spain had become sanctioned. The 1588 invasion of England by the Spanish Armada, which failed, was in part caused by the English piracy of Spanish ships.[994]

Religiously Based Protestant Colonies

Unlike the southern colony of Jamestown, the northern colonies were founded not primarily out of hope for profit and expansion of the British Empire but rather out of desire to live a form of Calvinistic Protestantism now known as Puritanism. The Puritans had fled England, which they deemed as overly Catholic with its high liturgies and retention of the office of bishop. To leave England discreetly, in the 1600s a group of Puritans founded the Massachusetts Bay Company complete with a corporate board of directors. After arriving in Massachusetts, they then converted their company into a province, their board of directors into a legislative body, and the corporate head, John Winthrop, into their governor.[995] Another group of

---

[994] Allen C. Guelzo, Gary W. Gallagher, and Patrick N. Allit, *The History of the United States*, 2nd Edition, Lectures 1-36 (Chantilly: The Teaching Company, 2003), 36-39.

[995] Allen C. Guelzo, Gary W. Gallagher, and Patrick N. Allit, *The History of the United States*, 2nd Edition, Lectures 1-36 (Chantilly: The

puritanical Protestants, named in the eighteenth century as the Pilgrims, fled England in the Mayflower ship and sought refuge near the Massachusetts Bay. They named their Protestant colony, the Plymouth Colony.[996]

Religiously Based Colony of Maryland

Not only Puritans but also English Catholics left England to avoid persecution. Between 1634 and 1776, Catholics from England set up Catholic friendly settlements in the colonies Maryland and Pennsylvania.[997] The Catholic convert George Calvert played a key role in establishing a Catholic settlement in Maryland. In 1619, George Calvert was appointed by Charles I of England as one of two Secretaries of State.[998] Charles I predecessor, King James I, granted George Calvert a twenty-three-hundred-acre estate in County Longford, Ireland, the Manor of Baltimore.[999] In 1625, George Calvert resigned his service to the King and around the same time converted

---

Teaching Company, 2003), 46. See https://www.mtholyoke.edu/acad/intrel/winthrop.htm

[996] James Deetz, and Patricia Scott Deetz, *The Times of their Lives: Life, Love, and Death in Plymouth Colony* (New York: Anchor Books, 2000), xv, 301.

[997] Patrick W. Carey, *Catholics in America: A History* (Westport: Praeger Publishers, 2004), 10.

[998] William Hand Browne, *George Calvert and Cecilius Calvert: Barons Baltimore of Baltimore* (New York: Dodd, Mead, and Company, 1890), 6.

[999] Robert J. Brugger, *Maryland: A Middle Temperament, 1634–1980* (Baltimore: Johns Hopkins Press, 1988), 4.

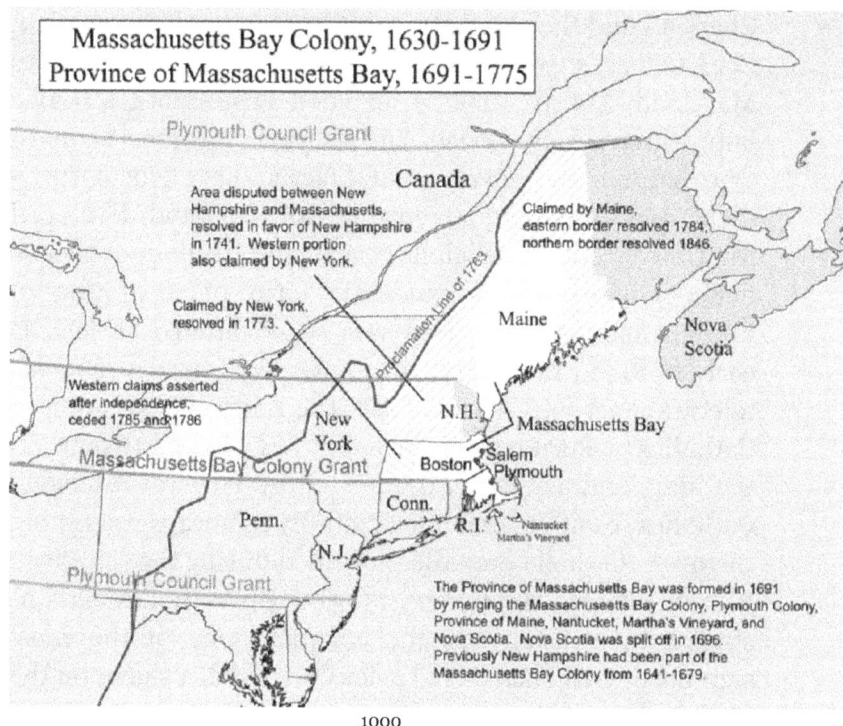

Massachusetts Bay Colony, 1630-1691
Province of Massachusetts Bay, 1691-1775

Plymouth Council Grant

Canada

Area disputed between New
Hampshire and Massachusetts,
resolved in favor of New Hampshire
in 1741. Western portion
also claimed by New York.

Claimed by Maine,
eastern border resolved 1784,
northern border resolved 1846.

Claimed by New York,
resolved in 1773.

Maine

Nova
Scotia

Western claims asserted
after independence,
ceded 1785 and 1786

New
York

N.H.

Massachusetts Bay

Massachusetts Bay Colony Grant

Boston   Salem
Plymouth

Penn.

Conn.

R.I.   Nantucket
Martha's Vineyard

N.J.

Plymouth Council Grant

The Province of Massachusetts Bay was formed in 1691
by merging the Massachusetts Bay Colony, Plymouth Colony,
Province of Maine, Nantucket, Martha's Vineyard, and
Nova Scotia. Nova Scotia was split off in 1696.
Previously New Hampshire had been part of the
Massachusetts Bay Colony from 1641-1679.

1000

from Anglicanism to Catholicism. In 1629, after having already set up a settlement of Avalon in Newfoundland (off the coast of modern day Canada), George Calvert arrived in Jamestown.[1001] The Puritans there insisted that he leave which he did.[1002] Finally, in 1632, George Calvert, as Lord Baltimore, was granted by King Charles I a royal charter to settle in the colony of Maryland. He died, though, before the charter was sealed. His son Cecil Calvert continued his father's mission by obtaining, in 1633, a charter from King

---

[1000] Kmusser, "File:Masscolony.png," This file is licensed under the Creative Commons Attribution-Share Alike 3.0 Unported license, Wikimedia Commons, http://commons.wikimedia.org/wiki/File:Masscolony.png (accessed December 15, 2014).

[1001] Browne, 16-27.

[1002] Browne, 27.

Charles I and then by setting sail to Maryland. [1003] In 1634, Cecil Calvert's two ships, the Ark and the Dove, landed in Maryland. The passengers included Protestants, Catholic laity, three Jesuit Priests and Calvert's brother Leonard who became the governor of Maryland.[1004] Not surprisingly, due to its religious mix, out of Maryland developed the US concepts of religious liberty, the freedom to choose one's religion, and a moderate form of separation of Church and State.[1005] This was demonstrated in law as early as 1649 when Maryland's Assembly issued a religious toleration act for Christians.[1006] The religious toleration of Catholics by Puritans only lasted by law up until 1654 when the Maryland assembly, dominated by Puritans, excluded Catholics from "general toleration" by politically restricting them.[1007] Catholic prejudice subsided during the American War of Independence (1775-1783) when Catholics demonstrated their loyalty to the colonies. One of the most significant Catholics was Charles Carroll III, a signer on the Declaration of Independence. According to Carroll, he signed the Declaration to support, "not only our independence of England but the toleration of all sects, professing the Christian religion..."[1008] When in 1778 France allied itself with the Americans against the British, the association of Catholicism with France also helped to reduce prejudice against Catholics.

The Acceptance of Catholicism in the United States

Charles Carroll III's cousin, John Carroll, also played a central role in the acceptance of Catholicism in the US. In

---

[1003] Carey, 10; Browne, 31-32.
[1004] Carey, 10.
[1005] Carey, 11.
[1006] Carey, 12-13.
[1007] Carey, 13.
[1008] Carey, 15.

1789, he was elected as the first US bishop of a diocese, Baltimore, that later in 1808 would be recognized by Rome as an archdiocese.[1009] Under his leadership, the Catholic Church became more established in the United States by the founding of Georgetown, the erection of three seminaries and a number of colleges and academies for the laity, and the expansion and founding of various religious orders.[1010] Near the turn of the 18th century, and the latter portion of John Carroll's episcopacy, anti-Catholic sentiment began to increase as immigrants from Ireland began steadily coming to the US.

US Anti-Catholicism

Fear of Catholics was expressed in 1834 in a terrifying manner when an unruly mob set fire to an Ursuline convent in Charlestown, Massachusetts.[1011] The mob was encouraged by the US nativist movement, which held that Catholics were destroying the US with their immorality.[1012] During the 1830s, Maria Monk, capitalizing on anti-Catholic hysteria, published her popular virulently anti-Catholic book *Awful Disclosures of the Hotel Dieu Nunnery in Montreal*. In her book, she depicts nuns as sex-slaves of the clergy, who had their infants baptized and then killed.[1013] People who were deeply suspicious of the Catholic Church not only included the US nativist movement and novelists like Maria Monk but also were highly influential office holders specifically the second and third president of the US: John Adams and Thomas

---

[1009] Carey, 17-21.

[1010] Carey, 22.

[1011] Katie Oxx, *The Nativist Movement in America: Religious Conflict in the Nineteenth Century* (New York: Routledge, 2013), 2.

[1012] Oxx, 2.

[1013] Philip Jenkins, *Pedophiles and Priests: Anatomy of a Contemporary Crisis* (Oxford: Oxford University Press, 1996), 26.

Jefferson. John Adams, second president of the US (1797-1801) even questioned in a May 19th, 1821 letter to Thomas Jefferson, "can a free government possibly exist with the Roman Catholic religion?"[1014] The third US president, Thomas Jefferson, similarly stated, "History I believe, furnishes no example of a priest-ridden people maintaining a free civil government."[1015] Jefferson also asserted in his March 17th, 1814 letter to Horatio G. Spafford that, "In every country and in every age, the priest has been hostile to liberty. He is always in alliance with the despot, abetting his abuses in return for protection to his own."[1016]

Another war, the American Civil War (1861-1865) would once again help to convince Protestant US citizens that Catholics were not a threat to national unity. Protestants witnessed Catholic sisters and priests heroically tending to the wounded and dying and Catholic men fighting for either the North or the South. As Sean Fabun explains, the US bishops were instrumental during the Civil war in quenching anti-Catholic sentiment by carefully not taking sides:

> [T]he hierarchy of the Church in America saw the turmoil as an opportunity to promote acceptance for Catholicism by undermining the prejudices against it, thereby establishing it as a genuinely American faith. The bishops' plan to execute this change relied mostly on example: in the North they flew the US flag at cathedrals,

[1014] James A. Haught, *2000 Years of Disbelief* (Amherst: Prometheus Books, 1996), 83.
[1015] Thomas Jefferson, "To Alexander von Humboldt, December 6, 1813," American History from Revolution to Reconstruction and Beyond, http://www.let.rug.nl/usa/presidents/thomas-jefferson/letters-of-thomas-jefferson/jefl224.php (accessed December 16, 2014).
[1016] Haught, 92.

and in the South they altered prayers to reflect their Confederate allegiance. Further, the bishops knew that a large Catholic element in the armies – one that carried itself with dignity and performed well- would do much to help Catholics gain a place in America, and they urged all enlisted Catholics to fight with courage and honor, so as to reflect well upon their faith.[1017]

In the 1920s, anti-Catholicism once again was promoted, with the Klu Klux Klan (KKK) along with the Scottish Rite Masons leading the way.[1018] Catholics, respectful of the democratic process, fought back and successfully won a key court case, Pierce v. Society of Sisters (1925). In this case the US Supreme Court ruled that Oregon's Compulsory Education Act that prohibited Catholic schools, was unconstitutional. This victory did not deter anti-Catholics from obtaining high offices. The Alabama State Senator, Hugo Black was able to gain votes by speaking at KKK gatherings where he repeatedly condemned Catholicism.[1019] In 1937, he was appointed an Associate Justice of the US Supreme Court, an office he held until 1971.[1020]

Yet another war, World War II (1939-1945), where Catholics fought side by side with Protestants and other believers and non-believers, once again greatly helped to decrease anti-Catholic sentiment. The Cold War that followed World War II with its pronounced anti-

---

[1017] Sean Fabun "Catholic Chaplains in the Civil War" *The Catholic Historical Review* October, vol. XCIX, No. 4 (2013): 700-701.

[1018] Carey, 81.

[1019] Roger K. Newman, *Hugo Black: A Biography* (New York: Pantheon Books, 1997), 91-100, 104.

[1020] Newman, 265, 515.

Communism in the US, spearheaded by the Wisconsin Republican Senator Joseph McCarthy, also helped to displace anti-Catholicism. Verification that Catholics had been accepted nationwide with little suspicion took place during the 1960s presidential election when the Catholic John F. Kennedy emerged as the winner. Less than forty years earlier, in 1928, the Catholic presidential Democratic candidate Al Smith lost to the Republican Herbert Hoover in part due to the Republicans use of anti-Catholicism as a way to take votes away from Smith. At that time many voters feared that if Al Smith won he would be beholden to the Pope. In order to alleviate a similar fear, John F. Kennedy told his countrymen:

> I am not the Catholic candidate for President. I am the Democratic Party's candidate for President who also happens to be a Catholic. I do not speak for my Church on public matters – and the Church does not speak for me. ...Whatever issue may come before me as President--on birth control, divorce, censorship, gambling or any other subject--I will make my decision in accordance with these views, in accordance with what my conscience tells me to be the national interest, and without regard to outside religious pressures or dictates. And no power or threat of punishment could cause me to decide otherwise...[1021]

[1021] John F. Kennedy, "John F. Kennedy to the Greater Houston Ministerial Association, September 12, 1960," John F. Kennedy, Presidential Library and Museum, http://www.jfklibrary.org/Asset-Viewer/ ALL6YEBJMEKYGMCntnSCvg.aspx (accessed December 16, 2014).

Do you find the above excerpt from John F. Kennedy's speech problematic? Why or why not?

Catholic Sanctity amidst US Anti-Catholicism

Since sanctity is one the most persuasive factors in convincing people of the goodness of Catholicism we will end this chapter and this book by looking at three US saints: the first US citizen saint, the first US native born saint, and the first US man to be canonized. Keep in mind that all three of the saints lived in a time when anti-Catholic sentiment was prevalent in the US as briefly described in the previous section.

Saint Francis Xavier Cabrini (1850-1917)

The first US citizen, but not native-born, to be canonized was Saint Francis Xavier Cabrini (1850-1917). Saint Francis Cabrini was born to an Italian farming family at Sant' Angelo, Lodigiano.[1022] Desiring in her twenties to join a religious congregation she applied to two: The Daughters of the Sacred Heart and the Canossian Sisters. Due to her poor health, both congregations rejected her application. Not deterred, she followed an inspiration to found her own religious community of Catholic mission-aries, something unusual at the time since at that time men had been Catholic missionaries not women.

In 1880, her rule of life for her Missionaries of the Sacred Heart community was accepted. Then, in 1887 after she travelled to Rome for papal approval, her institute was approved at the highest, ecclesial level. Since the US was still considered a missionary country, her first mission was to the United States, with special attention to be given to

---

[1022] Kathleen Jones, *Butler's Lives of the Saints*, New Full Edition, December (Collegeville: The Liturgical Press, 1999), 168.

Italian immigrants. In 1889, she and six of her sisters arrived by ship in New York. Strangely, the New York Archbishop, who wanted priests and not women religious, told St. Francis Cabrini to return to Italy since he had no need for her. She responded by informing him that she had approval from the pope and, therefore, intended to stay, which she did.

In New York, Saint Francis Cabrini and her sisters set about surviving by finding shelter and begging for money. Eventually, they were able to meet not only their own needs but also of many poor Italian immigrants by feeding their hungry, teaching their children and caring for their sick. Saint Francis Cabrini used her ability to raise funds and win over people's trust by establishing orphanages and even a hospital, the Columbus Hospital.[1023] After her missionary work was fairly well established in the United States Pope Leo XIII requested that she "hurry all over the earth if possible, in order to take the holy name of Jesus everywhere."[1024] Heeding the Holy Father's request, Saint Cabrini began evangelizing Central America and then South America. On December 22nd, 1917 this great female, missionary saint died in the hospital she had founded, the Columbus Hospital, while wrapping up presents for children.[1025]

[1023] Jones, 168-170.

[1024] Jones, 170.

[1025] Missionary Sisters of the Sacred Heart of Jesus, "Mother Cabrini's Life Story: Founding the Institute" Missionary Sisters of the Sacred Heart of Jesus: Stella Maris Province http://www.mothercabrini.org/legacy/life4.asp (accessed December 16, 2014); Jones, 171.

Saint Elizabeth Ann Bayley Seton (1774-1821)

The first native-born US citizen to be canonized was Saint Elizabeth Ann Bayley Seton (1774-1821). Saint Elizabeth Ann Seton was born into a prominent, New York, Protestant family and raised according to her mother's Episcopalian religion. When twenty, she married a shipping merchant, William Magee Seton and with him had five children. Tragedy struck the Seton family when William's shipping business went bankrupt. The bankruptcy was followed by yet another tragedy when William contracted tuberculosis, travelled with his wife to Italy for respite and there died. While in Italy, grieving over her beloved husband's death, St. Elizabeth was drawn to the Catholic Church. Upon returning to the US she requested instruction in the faith and was received into the Catholic Church in 1805. After her conversion, many of her friends, and acquaintances stopped supporting her. She was able to make ends meet by teaching. In the midst of these trying times she followed a call deep within her heart to found a religious community. In 1809, the previously mentioned Archbishop of Baltimore John Carroll, approved her request to take religious vows and begin a new religious community, the Sisters of St. Joseph. Her community began specializing in teaching, and caring for orphans.[1026]

[1026] Paul Burns, *Butler's Lives of the Saints*, New Full Edition, January (Collegeville: The Liturgical Press, 1998), 36-38.

Saint John Neumann (1811-1860)[1027]

The first US man to be canonized was St. John Neumann CSsR. (1811-1860). In his native country of Bohemia, St. John Neumann felt called to the priesthood and entered in the Czech Budweis seminary. Four years later, after completing nearly all the requirements to be ordained a priest, the bishop of St. John Neumann's diocese cancelled priestly ordinations for that year since he thought his diocese did not need any more priests. Not unduly discouraged, St. John Neumann then travelled to the US, to New York and that same year was accepted by the New York bishop and ordained to the priesthood. After ministering for four years in the New York diocese St. John Neumann felt called to the religious life and applied to the Redemptorist order. He was accepted, and in 1842 he took his vows. His superiors quickly noticed his extraordinary Christian leadership abilities and appointed him vicar of all US Redemptorists. In 1852, he was once again asked to lead in yet another position, that of bishop of Philadelphia.[1028]

[1027] Unknown author, Public Domain via Wikimedia Commons, "File: Neumann.png," http://commons.wikimedia.org/wiki/File%3ANeumann.png (accessed December 16,2014).
[1028] Burns, 40-41.

~ St. John Neumann's Humble Obedience ~

Letter to the Holy See

> I am indeed prepared either to remain in
> the same condition in which I am present,
> or if God so inspires His Holiness to give the
> whole administration of the diocese to the
> Most Reverend James Wood, I am equally
> prepared to re-sign from the episcopate and
> to go where I may more securely prepare
> myself for death and for the account which
> must be rendered to the Divine Justice. I
> desire nothing but to fulfill the wish of the
> Holy Father whatever it may be.[1029]

Quiz 24

1. Why did Juan Ponce de Leon name the American Southern peninsula Florida? (In your answer provide the Spanish origin of the name.)
2. Where was the first Catholic Mass celebrated, and by whom, in land that is now part of the United States of America?

3. What and where did Junipero Serra found?

4. Name and locate, in modern day USA, the territory that French Catholics established in 1699.

[1029] Blessed John Neumann, *Liturgy of the Hours*, vol. 1 (New York: Catholic Book Publishing Co., 1975), 1694.

5. What was a key distinguishing difference, regarding motivation, between the Protestant founders of colonies in modern day Virginia and Protestant and Catholic founders of colonies in modern day Maryland and New England?

6. Who was Charles Carroll III? (Include his religious affiliation and why he signed a key document in 1776. Name this document as well.)

7. Who was John Carroll? (In your answer, name what he was elected to.)

8. Write a short paragraph on either one of three saints (Saint Francis Cabrini, Saint Elizabeth Ann Bayley Seton) and St. John Neumann **or** explain why you think, from a Catholic perspective, the following excerpt from John F. Kennedy is problematic or is not problematic.

~ John F. Kennedy ~

I am not the Catholic candidate for President. I am the Democratic Party's candidate for President who also happens to be a Catholic. I do not speak for my Church on public matters – and the Church does not speak for me. ...Whatever issue may come before me as President--on birth control, divorce, censorship, gambling or any other subject--I will make my decision in accordance with these views, in accordance with what my conscience tells me to be the national interest, and without regard to outside religious pressures or dictates. And no power or threat of punishment could cause me to decide otherwise...[1030]

[1030] John F. Kennedy, "John F. Kennedy to the Greater Houston Ministerial Association, September 12, 1960," John F. Kennedy, Presidential Library and Museum, http://www.jfklibrary.org/Asset-Viewer/ALL6YEBJMEKYGMCntn SCvg.aspx (accessed December 16, 2014).

Fr. Peter Samuel Kucer, MSA

INDEX

Charlemagne, 129, 190-196, 207, 399
Charles Borromeo, 319, 321
Charles Carroll III, 476, 477
Charles Martel, 143, 159, 160, 190, 195
Childeric, 130, 156
Chinese rites, 353
Christopher Dawson, 165
Cimabue, 237, 264
Clotild, 130, 156, 158
Clovis, 130, 156, 158, 159, 161
Cold War, 417, 418, 442, 443, 479
Columbus, 255, 333-335, 342-344, 347, 348
Combes, 409
Concert of Europe, 412
Conciliarism, 249
Concordat of Worms, 203
Congress of Vienna, 406, 412, 413
Constantine, 52, 66, 77, 91, 101-107, 111, 119, 122, 131, 169, 177, 179, 190, 195, 218, 254, 255
Constantinople, 112-114, 119, 126, 167, 169, 173, 177, 179, 180-187, 190, 212, 220, 253-255, 338
Constantinople I, 112
Continental System, 400, 402
Copernicus, 361, 363, 364, 366, 367, 368
Council of Clermont, 212, 215
Council of Constance, 249, 250, 279, 289-291, 450
Council of Nicaea, 110-112, 179, 450
Cristero War, 417, 424, 427, 428
Crusades, 211, 215, 218, 220-223, 227
Cyril, 113, 166, 167

D
Dante, 256, 257, 259
Dark Ages, 227, 370
Decius, 90, 91, 132
Defender of the Faith, 310
Deists, 372, 373
Descartes, 253, 361-363
Didache, 80
Diocletian, 91, 101-104, 112, 162
Dionysius Exiguus, 38, 193
Docetism, 109, 110

I

J

O

Obregon, 427, 428
Oswald Spengler, 3
Ottoman Empire, 119, 173, 177, 184, 218, 253, 254, 294, 339, 341, 418, 419
Our Lady of Guadalupe, 356

P

Pachomius, 132-134
Pancho Villa, 425
papal infallibility, 374, 403
Papal Schism, 243, 249-251, 279, 280, 293
Papal States, 402, 405-407
Parens Scientiarum, 231
Paul VI, 184, 185, 447, 459-462
Pelagianism, 113
Pepin, 160, 189, 190
Perpetua and Felicity, 91
Peter Abelard, 235
Peter Claver, 333, 349
Peter Damian, 205, 206
Peter Favre, 322
Peter J. Kreeft, 49
Petrarch, 256-259
Pharisees, 31, 41, 42
Philip IV, 217
Philip Neri, 319, 325, 327
Pierce v. Society of Sisters, 479
Pilgrims, 474
Pius V, 294, 295, 319
Pius VII, 401, 402
Pius X, 224, 391, 409, 410
Pius XI, 408, 417, 423, 429, 437, 438
Pius XII, 36, 417, 437-442
Plato, 2, 196, 259, 272
Pliny the Younger, 26, 28, 90
Plymouth Colony, 474
Pompey, 24, 25
Pope Joan story, 199
Porfirio Diaz, 424
prisoners of the Vatican, 407
Puritans, 473-476

St. Paul the Hermit, 132, 133
St. Thomas More, 256, 261, 262, 301, 310, 311
Stoic, 1, 2
Stoicism, 2
Sudetenland, 435
Suetonius, 26, 27, 87, 88, 258

T
T.U.L.I.P., 309
Tacitus, 26, 87, 89
Tehcir law, 419
Teresa of Avila, 319, 323, 324
Tertullian, 52, 56, 59, 86, 87, 192, 235
Tetrarchy, 102
Tetzel, 297, 298
The Divine Comedy, 257
The Shepherd of Hermas, 32
Theodosius I, 119, 173, 174
Thomas Hobbes, 371, 375
Titian, 275, 276
Trajan, 28, 29, 90
Treaty of Versailles, 432, 433
Trent, 19, 315, 317-320, 323, 455, 460
Trinity, 16, 51, 113, 114, 139, 148, 176, 204
Triple Alliance, 413, 418
Triumvirate, 24, 25

U
Umayyad Mosque, 463
United Nations, 433
universities, 227-229, 231, 232, 322, 409
Urban II, 200, 211, 212, 214-216, 218
Urban VIII, 355, 368

V
Vandals, 125, 129, 161, 175
Varro, 77-79
Vasco de Gama, 333, 341
Vatican Council I, 374, 403